Northumberland Dreaming

Northumberland Dreaming

Mary Rhees Mercker

HAMPTON ROADS
PUBLISHING COMPANY, INC.
for the evolving human spirit

Cover design by Grace Pedalino
Photos by Mary Rhees Mercker

For information write:
Hampton Roads Publishing Company, Inc.
134 Burgess Lane
Charlottesville VA 22902

Or call: (804)296-2772
FAX: (804)296-5096
e-mail: hrpc@hrpub.com
Web site: http://www.hrpub.com

If you are unable to order this book from your local
bookseller, you may order directly from the publisher.
Quantity discounts for organizations are available.
Call 1-800-766-8009, toll-free.

Library of Congress Cataloging-in-Publication Data Number
98-072214

ISBN 1-57174-086-4

10 9 8 7 6 5 4 3 2 1

Printed on acid-free paper in the United States of America

Contents

Maps

Publisher's Preface

Northumberland Dreaming by Mary Rhees Mercker is the sixth in our River Lethe series of books about remembered past lives, and follows the recent publications of *Under the Inquisition* by Linda Tarazi, Ph.D., and *Dear Companion* by Kelly Joyce Neff. At first we considered calling these books historical fiction, but then we realized the need for a new genre of books within the category of visionary fiction by those who have begun adding their testimonies about life in other times.

* * *

Few people today have any idea what it meant to be a knight in the middle ages, even in England, let alone on the continent. No doubt, to most the very idea of knighthood seems utterly irrelevant. Our images of knights tend to be slightly comic. We think of men in armor impaling each other on lances or chopping each other to pieces with broadswords or whatever. We think of The Round Table and the musical Camelot, and perhaps we consign the entire period to mythology.

But Mary Mercker here reminds us that there was a time when chivalry was responsible for such order as existed in a very dangerous world. *Northumberland Dreaming* portrays a frontier society—northern England, near the Scottish border—which was primitive and poor, not only by our standards, but even by the standards of its day, the 1100s.

John Forster reminds us that knights were men who held society together in many ways, more like farmers or plantation owners in colonial America than like modern frivolous stereotypes. He reminds us that the men who fought the crusades did so for a mixture of motives, among them piety, duty, and escape from boredom.

And he reminds us that nonetheless the major issues of life, then as now, were matters of family, friendship, love, strife, duty, and property. From his earliest days as a lonely page, through the long years when he was a squire, on to the crusade that got him his knighthood and nearly cost him his life, back home on a long return that provided him a sweet if forbidden love, and then through the long years remaining, John is a living, breathing human to whom we can relate.

John Forster was a good man—who was not without his temptations. He was an effective man, like his fellow knights a critical link in his local society—who was not without his frustrations. He was a solid citizen with his feet firmly on the ground—who more than once had visions and other experiences we would term paranormal.

When I first read this manuscript, I saw no way we could ever publish it. But, with the author's permission, I held onto it year after year. It gave so fascinating a picture of a different time and place, I couldn't bear to let it go. It's a great pleasure now to see it make its way into print. The addition of photos taken by Ms. Mercker of what remains of the sites that were important to Sir John (and there are more remains than one would have thought) gives this memoir an added appeal, we think. I have no doubt that *Northumberland Dreaming* will find its way into the hearts of many, many readers for a long time to come.

Frank DeMarco, Chairman
Hampton Roads Publishing Co.

Gossip

Family, Friends, and Foes in Northumberland

John Forster, Crusader, of Glororum Manor, Bamburgh, Northumberland. Knighted at Messina, Sicily, by King Richard the Lion-heart, in 1190. John's knightly spirit adventured through myriad dangers to flesh and soul, returning in the twentieth century to tell how he found the Grail of Immortality in the hearts of those whom he most loved. *b. 1159, d. 1220*

William Forster, John's father who was knighted in Wales by English King Henry II. Crippled in battle by the rashness of his temper, William vowed to make his son a stronger knight. *d. 1176*

Mary, William's courageous wife. Daughter of Sir Rhys of Colin's Wood, Cornhill, and Gwenlyn. Both Mary and her mother were wise women, versed in healing. *d. 1193*

Henry the Grey, Sir Rhys' eldest son, and Mary's half brother. Henry inherited Colin's Wood at Cornhill and became patriarch of the Northumbrian Greys. *d. 1209*

Kenneth, Mary's red-haired, happy-go-lucky younger brother. Castle knight at Alnwick, he later married Eadra de Mill, widow of Berwick-on-Tweed, and became a miller. *d. 1214*

Maud, John's younger sister. Married Stephen de Essh, of the manor of Hutton, south of Durham. Stephen was knighted with John at Messina, during the Third Crusade, and died in the Holy Land. Hutton was later called Hutton Henry, after Maud and Stephen's son and grandson.

Mary Rose, their daughter, John's god-child. Remained unmarried.

Stephen, the eldest son, died young.

Henry, or Hutton Henry, the youngest son, married Helewise fitz Alan. Though he died young, their son Henry cared for the estate throughout a long lifetime.

Henry the Squire, Sir William's companion-in-arms in the Welsh Marches, went as unwilling guardian to John when he was sent to Alnwick for schooling.

Adela, Mistress of Pages at Alnwick, held a soft spot in her heart for her charges, especially John.

David, John's childhood friend and ally at Alnwick, was later made knight to King William of Scotland. David married the lovely Glenda, bringing tragedy to both their lives.

Baldwin, bully among the pages at Alnwick.

Duncan, Baldwin's ally, who later became John's fast friend and tourney companion. With David, he was knighted by King William. Duncan married Aethelfritha, descendent of the old British royal house, and a distant relative of King William's. Their children were Margaret, William, Malcolm, and David.

Sir Malwin, a poor castle knight of Alnwick, aided in his wooing of the haughty Lady Blanche by circumstance and two quick-thinking pages.

Lady Agnes Morton, whom John served as lady's page while at Alnwick, and her boorish husband, the powerful Sir Brian Morton.

Sir Bran, a household knight at Alnwick, whom John later served as squire.

William de Vesci, baron who held the castle at Alnwick, first in fief to Scotland, then England. His son, Eustace de Vesci, was one of the great barons in revolt against King John at Runnymeade.

Kate, John's first love, daughter of Andrew the ploughman. Married Alan, the smith's son.

Herleve de Guagy, John's arrogant, ill-starred wife. Her madness brought tragedy to John, his family, and all of Glororum.

Randolph, their eldest son, usually called Randall by his father. Spoiled by his mother and the despair of his father. Randall married Margaret, daughter of Duncan and Aethelfritha. Randolph was knighted "for friendship," but their son, Sir Alfred, was a strong and respected knight.

William, the second son, spurned and abused by his mother, redeemed by his grandmother Mary, and by Maud and her steward, Sir John de Hawthorne. Remained unmarried, but became a knight in the Fourth Crusade and visited Jerusalem to pray for his family. William commissioned the effigy of his father in Bamburgh church.

Henry, the sunny-natured youngest son, was raised by his old uncle, Henry the Grey of Cornhill, and became his heir. Married Jane of the Waterford.

Tippie, christened Agnes, John and Herleve's youngest daughter, and the apple of her father's eye. Married Raynaud de Ros; their children were John, Maurice, and Maud.

Sir Randolph de Guagy of Ellingham, Herleve's father, was eager to pawn her off to maintain his lifestyle. Given to drink and bluster and little else, he had been a widower since his wife Agnes had died in childbirth with son Hugh. Herleve, age four, was at that time sent to France to be raised by relatives.

Hugh de Guagy, a weak and vacillating man, aided his sister in her mischief and was later banned from Glororum.

Father Cedric, clerk and chaplain at Glororum, lived a long and productive life, ministering to the estate and teaching the young.

Sir Bors, knight and steward of Glororum, Sir William's strong right arm. Tough and scarred, disdainful of "John the Child," Bors at last came to be John's stalwart ally.

Sir Giles, household knight of Glororum, a "Holy Mary" knight from Yorkshire, rode the marches to keep the peace and was master of Glororum's squires.

Sir Raynaud de Ros, youngest son of an important Northumbrian family, came to Glororum as household knight after Sir Giles died. A mischief maker and favorite with the women, Ray had no heart for any save Tippie, John's young daughter.

Robin, christened Robert, Kenneth's son by a villein woman, who was raised at Glororum and Hutton. Mary Rose's staunch, life-long friend. Robin was devoted to John, and became steward at Glororum after Sir Bors died.

Allie, a waif bound for slavery, saved by Sir John on one of his marches. She became his ward and head of the stables; then later, his greatest comfort in life. Their son, Baby John, died when two months old.

Blaine and Carrie of the Nether Lea proved to be Allie's parents; her brothers were Matthew, Mark, Luke and John.

Alyse, lady of France who, with Robin, saved John from death and became his lover. Her husband, Arnaud, had gone to the Holy Land on Crusade with King Philip of France. Denis, her cousin, an infuential member of Philip's court, saved the lady's bacon.

Philip, John and Alyse's red-haired son.

Nichola, matrimonial prospect for John, bargained for by Randall.

Chatta, the frontiersman who settled at Chatton was John's lifelong friend, dying in John's arms. The son who kept the inn after him was Simon.

Ben-Ami, a merchant Sir John befriended, whose amity brought many benefits to Glororum. His daughter, Devorah, also became Allie's friend.

Hugh Puisset, Bishop of Durham, Prince Palatinate in the North of England. An energetic builder and canny businessman, he was kin to Stephen de Essh and friend of Glororum.

Bertram, Prior at Durham after Hugh died, was responsible for the day-to-day operations at both school and cathedral. The new Palatinate was Bishop Philip of Poitou in France, an absentee landlord.

Alfric, one of Hugh's best masons, and his wife, Jene. They built Hutton manor house, finished building Glororum, and were building Bamburgh church when Alfric was killed.

Edwin the Monk, came to Glororum and Bamburgh from Durham. Of an old Northumbrian family, Edwin was priest, clerk, and doctor.

Robert de Ros of Yorkshire, one of the great Northern barons involved in the rebellion against King John, was elder brother to Raynaud de Ros.

Peter de Brus, lord of Danby and Skelton, another of the great Northern barons. Sir John rode in his entourage at Runnymede.

Nicolaa de la Haye, widow and castellan of Lincoln Castle, outfoxed the rebel army in 1217 and ended the barons' rebellion.

Philip of Oldcote, King John's emmissary to Bamburgh.

Walter, warder at Bamburgh Castle, was replaced after his death by Gilbert (Gib). Gib's son, Gilbert, was squire to Sir Raynaud during the rebellion.

Annie, Glororum's canny seeress, daughter of widowed Ruth, who was ale vender and midwife in the Glororum vill.

Andrew, John's childhood friend at Glororum, son of freeholder, Peter. Peter was in charge of the stables at Glororum throughout his long life. Andrew married Margaret, daughter of an innkeeper at Alnwick. Their only child, Ralph, died young. Andrew was knighted during the Crusade and died in the Holy Land.

Cross, daughter of Thomas the villein, who went to live with the widowed Margaret and old Peter.

Carl, freeman and sergeant (man-at-arms) at Glororum, married Nicolette, Herleve's long-suffering handmaid. Carl was knighted and died on Crusade. Their son, Carl Carlson, also became squire and household knight at Glororum. Their daughter, Elaine, became handmaid to Tippie.

Old Will, sergeant of Glororum, took over care of the hunting lodge in the Forster west forest. His son, Will, went on Crusade and was knighted. After the war, young Will bought a farm at Elsdon from the widow, Elna, and married her daughter, Brenda. Old Will's second son, James, took up land at Ellingham. Japeth, the youngest son, remained on the west forest holding. Japeth's son, Richard, became squire to John when he was in hiding in Scotland.

Crinan, raised at Cornhill, became squire at Glororum, and was knighted on Crusade.

Richard, Glororum's long-suffering reeve, in charge of the farm labor. His son, Thomas, became a squire of Glororum.

Rafe, man-at-arms at Glororum, died during the pestilence of 1187.

Julian, man-at-arms at Glororum, fretted at home during the war.

Blaise, sergeant at Glororum who undertook the thankless job of beadle, or under-steward, at Ellingham.

Dirk, unrepentant outlaw from Glororum who followed John into the twentieth century.

William of Lucker, John's neighbor.

Odo, sergeant; Mark, squire; and Alan, household knight; left from Hutton with Stephen on Crusade.

Gilbert Thorson of Bamburgh who became a yeoman knight at Glororum.

St. Oswald, early King of Northumbria, along with the monk, St. Aidan, brought Christianity to Northern England in the Seventh Century.

St. Cuthbert, or St. Cuddy, legendary patron saint of Northumbria, lent his name to numerous places in Northern England.

**ENGLAND AND WALES
C. 1200**

Prologue
Northumberland Dreaming

It's hard to say when the homesickness for some far, green land first began its haunting. It was part of me as long as I can remember. Conscious memory had nothing to do with this longing for the hills of home; it was more a state of almost-dreaming. I was restless in the city that my mother had so ardently embraced; hills and woods meant everything to her changeling child. I could find the smallest patch of undeveloped hillside, overgrown with Missouri's spoils of hawthorn, mayhaw, persimmon, and walnut, and there hide by the hour. The soul was eased but my mind deliciously half-afraid that, as mother had warned, a tramp might come by and snatch me from the rosy-blooming tree where I sat dreaming.

With the deepest feeling of contentment pervading me, the tree became my castle, and the woods my domain. By simply breathing its aroma, I became one with that kingdom, knowing myself as part of an ageless whole. Ensconced above the ragged parcel like a prince, I would forget awhile that life had cast me as pauper. This land was not truly mine; it was a substitute for the green hills and forests of home, wherever that might be. Never mind. A child's optimism knows that some dreams can only be found in tomorrow.

Once there had been two boys who exchanged clothes as a joke, then found themselves cruelly meshed in each other's lives. In the end, all came right; their lives claimed them for who they were.

As a child, my sympathies were entirely with Twain's prince. It was only after many years' existence on the outskirts of pauperdom that I understood the bewilderment—even impatience—of poor Tom Canty who found himself in Edward's kingly shoes, surrounded by regal ritual and incomprehensible privilege. But from the perspective of childhood's leafy perch, I felt more at one with the prince's frustration; a wider awareness forced to dwell in the rags of an unsuitable life. That wasn't the worst. The worst, beyond being misunderstood by everyone in the family, was being laughed at. Like Edward, the fact that I was born to give orders seemed perfectly reasonable to me. It was a source of great merriment to everyone else. Laughter soon turned to anger at my incorrigible innate pride. Punishment is a great master; one soon learns to keep the mouth shut. But jibes and taunts then worm inside and eat the wings from heart's innocence.

The absolute worst was when my stepbrothers called me "scullery maid," laughing while I scrubbed the kitchen as they went out to skate or play ball. Dim images haunted my mind, angry images that lay far from Missouri's surrogate domain. Fleeting pictures recalled most demeaning servitude, severed from land and freedom and the fresh smell of the wind. Eventually, this became a prophecy for my life. I was a girl, after all, in an era when girls still had little to say about their own destinies. The Great War had not yet come along to untie women's apron strings.

Never mind that my thoughts always regarded Self as a boy, a princeling born to war, to build, and to administer. My favorite toys were soldiers and I envied my brother's castle that held so many. Ill-hidden disappointment dismayed well-meaning adults who brought dolls as presents. Mother would mention what a famous brand it was, and how prettily it was dressed, and how, in her poor childhood, she would have loved such a doll, and why wasn't I grateful? I was thankful for their kindness, but nonplussed at their poor taste. In the end, they left me alone with toys of war—guns and lead soldiers—and with football and pocketknife.

And books. The curiosity about my unknown heritage was not left untaught. Hidden in those books were stories of chivalry and honor, stories of the Grail and Arthur. Lancelot and Gawain enthralled my eager mind by the hour, speaking of forbearance and courage and the knight's-measure of an honest heart. Robin Hood and Richard the Lion-Hearted taught strategy and the art of ancient warfare. A man's sword, I learned, is raised in defence of God, the helpless, and the welfare of home, no matter how humble that domain might be. Soul fulfilled, I learned of ancient kings who rode across the green English countryside, from places like Wessex, and Mercia, and Northumbria. Northumbria! The very name gave me a feeling of longing and pride, my homeland to defend.

Maturity brings a different perspective, one that often loses sight of the child's clear view of who it is. Even so, as a high school girl primping her hair in the mirror, I was at times startled by the face of a lad who stared out at me, a storybook pageboy. I often wore my hair rolled under, to do honor to the shy loneliness I saw in his face. It really didn't confuse me to see myself as a boy, for mother would often glance up startled as I came into the room, and tell me how—for an instant—I looked just like my father. He had died when I was about a year old, and I never met a person who had touched his quiet humanity that wasn't better off for it. I was happy that at moments I could unwittingly capture something of his too-short life. That a lad might be growing up inside me and occasionally peeping out was beyond any of our wildest imaginings.

I married and had children that I loved dearly. But I couldn't stop learning; searching for meanings in a life I didn't always understand. The rushes of homesickness for a green land to build upon, a land to call my own, never went away. Neither did the face in the mirror. When the oldest boys were still babies and I was young and often hungry, the face that sometimes peered out at me became a youthful squire. Again, he appeared to have a strength that I never felt in myself. At one point, so obvious was he, I had a neighbor take my picture up close, in front of the house wall. There was only a hint of that squire there. The same face, only different; the strength faded into a sort of sullenness. Few of us in the Fifties had even a clue that we might have lived before, been someone else in a land far away. And few of us would have expected that someone to surface as obviously as did my squire, a knight still in training.

It wasn't until the Sixties that a friend set me to reading and learning about Dr. J.B. Rhine's work in parapsychology. We discussed Edgar Cayce, and the possibility that individuals were not expected to perfect themselves in just one lifetime. About this time, a sister of my father also got in touch with me. I hadn't seen Aunt Ferne since I was a toddler. Grief over my father's death had dug trenches between family where none should have been.

It was Aunt Ferne who told me at last of my father's family, the Fosters and the Rheeses. Her mother had been a Foster; my father was Foster Rhees. The Rheeses she honored as being sturdy, kind, and caring; the sort of people who had nourished this country with their sweat. The Fosters were soldiers, judges, builders. Her mother's uncle, John R.P. Foster, had been a decorated colonel in the Civil War. Suddenly, I remembered the old humpback trunk my mother had covered in pink fabric. Before I was born, my grandparents had given it to her for me. It was a Civil War trunk. They told her: keep it for Foster's girl. I had it for awhile. My half brother, in a fit of frenzy, kicked it to pieces. It was only an old wooden trunk, my mother had said, and valueless.

Ferne gave me an understanding of deeper values. With the Rheeses and particularly with the Fosters, I began moving closer to the homeland of my dreams. Just before coming down, irretrievably, with Alzheimer's disease, Ferne gave me a bound copy of the Foster family tree. It had been researched and printed by my grandmother's brother, Frank Foster, the last male in the line. I read Frank's little book with relish, then put it in the desk and forgot about it.

My innate restlessness channeled into finding questions, finding answers. I had all but forgotten the dreams of childhood. Harsh reality overlaid them like a black bulk, sucking away at their wisdom. In the Seventies, I studied for a ministry in a New Age religious organization, the Church of Universal Philosophy. We delved into many religions, and we studied counseling and parapsychology. In two years, I earned ordination and a deeper understanding of the great wheel of lives that turns beneath the web of present circumstance. With meditation and dreams, I began to slip back to a more innocent awareness. Old lives began to unroll like a string of interconnected movies. But they all centered around one life; a life that began to crack and emerge from its centuries-old shell.

At age thirty-seven, the face in the mirror confronted me again. This time the appearance was unmistakable, for now I was ready. I had progressed enough to meet the person whose life had always walked through mine; whose dreams were made real in my heart. The face was mine but it wasn't; it was undeniably male. "Hello, Sir John," I said, as if I'd known who he was all along. He spoke back, a somewhat different voice in my head. Although I could understand his English, his speech was more deliberate than mine and his wording echoed in archaic forms. He told me that it was quite a different world now from when he had lived before. For days, he kept up a running conversation, as if some frozen spell of silent centuries had finally thawed. He was relieved to speak again. Yet I never had the slightest doubt that this Sir John was an intrinsic, though long-forgotten, part of myself.

(It shouldn't be a barrier to think that we might change gender through lifetimes. After all, men and women think alike in their hearts, in their agonies and loves and aspirations. Sexuality is only a blanket we wear over our soul, aligning it with the body we receive.)

The people John most loved, almost 800 years ago, were the same ones I found in my life again. My childhood trust —that time would bring fulfillment for my dreams—had not been betrayed.

Only one other person ever caught a glimpse of my ghostly knight. When I hesitantly admitted John's existence to my dear friend, I was not disbelieved. But Jaeger had been invested as a Knight of Malta, and he was singularly unimpressed by both robe and ritual. He snorted at the pomposity and puffery of knighthood that so distorted its ideals in later centuries. Suddenly, John quite literally exploded to the surface. He was angry. Sternly but not unkindly he spoke as if to a child, "Ye make mock of all I gave my life for. Knighthood was my honour, and I earned it with blood. From the time when I was sent from home as a child of five, I struggled to earn that honour." Unspoken, but hanging in the air between us were the words, "You should be ashamed of yourself."

My tough and flippant Jaeger ducked his head in contrition like any wench. Both of us admitted to the feeling that it was not the first time for this conversation. We had retreated into a past that still lay largely unexplored. But John was not quite through. "Ye were still the best hostler I ever knew," he chuckled. And with those clues, we began to piece together our ancient lives.

Always, I struggled with the deep-seated emotions I picked up from John. They triggered visions, or "seeing." If you are a seer, you can understand. If not, all I can tell you is that one sees a scene quite clearly, obviously in the mind, but not part of any conscious process. These clear, dreamlike images are completely spontaneous, leaving plain imagination gasping in the dust. The face that followed me in the mirror was more real than those illusions, yet less so than the everyday mug I usually confronted. John had grown up playing hide-and-seek with me, trying to encourage me when most needed. For centuries, his mouth had been stopped. Now, even his visions became my own. Like reflections in a dark mirror descrying those of yet another mirror, John's dreams tantalized me with strange and shadowed scenes.

What I didn't understand at first was why I had so quickly and unhesitatingly called the man in the mirror "Sir John." Who was this John? Go get your family tree, he told me. I remembered then a theory that past lives come forth from our own antecedents. Far memory—recollection of past life—may be genetically coded. In the end, after I rummaged up Frank Foster's precious book, my finger went unerringly to the entry: "Sir John Forster accompanied Richard I to Palestine, where he received the honor of knighthood for his valor. He was one of those who compelled John to sign the Magna Charta in 1215. He died 1220 and was succeeded by his son." I had him at last. Now there were two lives to deal with: the one I was still in, and the amazing one that had been.

An enormous amount of research lay yet to be done. One of my first encounters was with English English, and its often incomprehensible pronunciations. The "r" had been dropped from Forster in America; it wasn't pronounced anyway. Alnwick was "Annick;" Bamburgh, "Bamboro."

Old knight and twentieth century seer were connected primarily by scenes that swept the heart with despair or anger or heartfelt love. With each vision, the mind filled in details that colored the situation. It was a knowing beyond learning, a memory beyond time. Whenever possible, I sought a book to find details, to check the old knight's anecdotes against what history had written. Doors opened on a past that held greater clarity. Too often I found history wrong; some author had inserted his ideas into a blank spot in the records. I came to trust John more. He was myself, of course, but older and stronger and wiser. He was versed in a world that lay largely forgotten. He introduced me to people who made a difference in his life, just as they do in mine now. Though much of their essence still reposes unchanged, later lives have wrought changes in personality. We have all widened in ways that will eventually matter, but we have often left something nobler behind.

Even more amazing were the casual contacts, people in my study groups who would come out of meditation with some story connected to John's. They were there. These instances, as I was able to verify them, gave me a tremendous sense of interconnectedness. Time, loss, alienation...all are artificial barriers set up so that our minds can get on with the business of learning. Yet, at the point that those illusions are sundered, growth distends the mind in a wild ride of unimaginable spaciousness. Where, indeed, is thy sting, O Death?

John was an honest knight, more sensitive than many, even for those spiritual (and superstitious) times. Yet he sheltered such confident power that I embarked on a search for what he stood for, in the context of his own time and place. I had the pictures and feelings, but not necessarily continuity or reason. Above all, I knew John's life to be rooted within his entrusted land, even while his arms reached for Heaven. For this reason, I went to Northumbria to find him, just as he had gone on Crusade. These quests are part of our common soul. Step by step, over the years, I have retraced parts of his journey, and found the challenges in both lives resonating curiously with one another, like a panpipe playing with an echo.

Eventually, after his Crusade, Sir John came home, to the fresh wind from the sea, to the scent of mown fields and heather, and the sound of the burn chuckling like children's laughter. It was first his children that John greeted upon his return, then the adult family and the priest, then those who had tilled the land faithfully while he was gone. But his homecoming was not yet complete. Only alone in the early morning could it be truly fulfilled. He walked out in a light leather jerkin, with the wind from the sea at his back, to make peace with the land for his absence. It greeted him silently, but pleased at his presence, as always. On the field berm, spiders were busy weaving a matrix for jewels cut from dew, and a hare trod quickly through the hedge. A riot of uncut weeds lay everywhere along the berm, blooming the last of summer away—widow's lace, columbine, wild rose—all in a happy tangle. John stood at last on the cultivated field, golden in the damp morning sunshine. Plucking heads of wheat, just a few days before harvest, he tasted again the sweetness that rose from the Northumbrian soil. That moment held a communion so deep that not even time could erase it. With the indescribable taste of northland wheat, John knew he was at last home; his body part of the soil, and his soul at one with the field and trees and air.

Nearly eight hundred years later, the same inexplicable communion overtook me as I sampled the wheat of his fields. The master to whom its care was entrusted, more bound to that land than any other man could be, was anchored there; his roots entwined with every stalk of wheat, every blade of grass that would ever grow. I was his inheritance. The land was home. Never had bread so fed a soul as bread from that Northumbrian wheat. Never had taste of grain so fulfilled a soul. I, too, was home at last.

We are still finding the stories of our lives, John and I, though at 61 the patterns are less adept at hiding away. In the hope that these ancient pathways may guide feet yet to come, I have set down what I ken of the life and times of that doughty knight and his often-rowdy descendants. Though I may read history to help me understand, his patience often wears thin when my mind runs off on some tangent. No, he'll tell me, that wasn't important; it was like this. And I'll get a vision so clear, it bowls me over, like the stench of the slaughterhouse and tannery waking me from a sound sleep. At times, John simply takes over the computer, while I marvel at the stories he spins.

Even so, some names and minor details had to be reinvented; they were lost in the compost heap of time. But the earnest passions that have filled our lives have grown and blossomed and set seed in the sunshine of truth. We did the best we could.

Chapter 1

John the Child

My first clear memory of Northumberland life was being sent from home as a lad of five. It was just before Michaelmas in 1164, and, willy-nilly, I was off to Alnwick, to begin schooling as a page. Mother would not weep, nor I. My fears were tempered by a sense of excitement, of the unknown, a bent that often got me into trouble later in life. She, poor woman, had no temper for her sorrow, save a strong will. She bit back tears saying, "I will not betray my blood, nor must you. You will learn to be an honest knight; strong, and with a noble heart. You will have an arm to give our Lord; a succor for the helpless. Your heart which turns so readily in pity (I had just buried a cat the village boys had tormented to death) will learn strength." I could not do less than remember her words. Between us lay the unspoken promise—that I would become a better knight than my father. We had no mention or thought of disloyalty. It was simply there, a unity of hope. My father was too often crabbed in mind as he was in body.

As a young householder, father had gone to Wales at the behest of the English King, Henry II. Why, my mother said privately, she never knew. Her own kin were related to some of the knights he fought against. What affair was the king's quarrel to a country knight from Northumbria? Yet even as a child I understood the system, a way of life we took in with our mother's milk. All life was part of a divine chain; as children look to their parents, so the knights looked to the sovereign who granted them lands and support. The king himself looked to God and the Church for the right to anchor the chain of existence of every person within the realm. We knights, in turn, were responsible for every class of person below us, the villeins and cottars who worked the land and mills the King had assigned to our family and heirs. Because of the court of honor we were obliged to hold for our area, even the local freemen were our responsibility. Grave matters, or those pertaining to landed rights or taxes, were usually reserved for the king's court or the shire court. But everyday quarrels that stood amongst our country folk (some were always willing to harvest their neighbor's plowing, unbeknownst; or tap another man's herd for meat) needed firm settlement at once, not at some future meeting of a higher court.

Grants of land, loosely based on virgates, or thirty-acre measures, were held by men who owed knight-service to some overlord as payment. With these grants, a man might sustain himself and his family while maintaining a militia on call by earl or king. Indeed, we knights were then known more often by the French *miles*, than by the British word, "cniht." From the time of the Conqueror, when all of England and much of Scotland was divided up, families like my own had served as the *miles agrarios*, the country knights who were the backbone of law and order throughout the land.

When these knights squabbled, they were judged by the traveling judges of the royal court, or in the shire courts under the king's appointed shire reeve, which now you call sheriff. If his job was different in my time, the same call of money and power reached the sheriff's ears then as now. A poor knight was oft times better served out of the shire courts, unless he had the ear of the king. In my days, the kings were the English Henry II, and his quarreling sons Richard and John. Only John bided much time in England, to the detriment of the land. But that is ahead of my story.

I was born one pleasant night at the end of June 1159, the 29th, to be sure. It was dawn when I made my appearance. My grandmother always said that I had a good sign; Venus had married the Sun of my birth, and silver-girt Jupiter had just slipped over the horizon. Gwenlyn, my mother's mother, was both Scots and Welsh, and she had the eye for the greater world. The churchmen decried her knowing, but for healing arts and wisdom she had no equal; and she was pious as she was wise. My birthing-room lay in the manor we called Old Hall; it was also called Glororum, the place where glory dwells. Glororum was old in the time of my great-great grandfather, Richard, when my family first settled at this spot, half a league from towering Bamburgh castle.

Richard was the younger brother of Maud (Mathilda), King William's wife. He left his homeland in Flanders as a stripling to follow William, and became a knight after that bloody day at Hastings. King William, faced with the stubborn resistance of Northumbria, even after the rest of England had granted him the crown, marched north in 1069. Richard was by his side on that bloody harrying of the North. William laid cruel waste to all the land between York and Durham; the peasants starved there for years after. When the northmen capitulated, William marched on to Bamburgh, to the old British stronghold by the North sea.

(Most say Bamburgh got its name from the ancient queen, Bebba. Folk who have lived here for generations declare that her spirit still walks in warning, whenever the fortress faces grave danger. Others argue that the castle's name came from the great logs or beams—bams—which formed the old stronghold.)

King William was quick to see the advantage of the rock of Bamburgh. A small corps of men-at-arms was left at the cold and inhospitable castle, under command of a warder. Standing high on its cliff, jutting into the sea, Bamburgh castle was a fortress but little fit for regular habitation. There needs must stand a fief, a land grant to support the king's interests in this windy northern stronghold. As blood-kin of the king's wife, young Richard was given a settlement of

Brooding Bamburgh Castle

twenty virgates. Two virgates were under haphazard cultivation, and the rest was forest and waste—most fitting, since
the Forster clan had held charge of the royal forests of
Flanders. This new trust established what was then called a
berewick, or adjunct property to Bamburgh.

Ancient Northumbria had once led all the country in
accepting Christ, and long before Hastings, monks from Iona
had settled at Holy Island, just north of Bamburgh, and had
begun to spread the faith. Later, French Benedictines came
to set their priories across the north. Our virgates had once been
priory land. Even before the war between William and
Harold, when Northumbria rebelled against the misrule of
Earl Tostig, Harold's brother, Glororum had been burned and
abandoned. Only the old church had escaped, and the lands
were in pitiable shape, with most of its villeins dead or flown.

Since there was still a missionary priest from Holy Island
at Bamburgh village, William must have thought that
Church enough. When he took the vacant priory lands to
reward his young brother-in-law, displaced plowmen from

Durham were sent north to work the property. Villeins hate to move from their place, but it was either off to Glororum or starve. A new vill was built, and the land finally began to come 'round. The priors' fine church was rebuilt as Old Hall. I was the fourth generation of Richard's heirs to be born there.

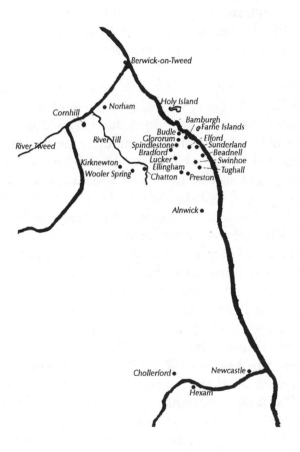

Bamburgh, Alnwick, and Environs

We thus held our property at the behest of the English crown, and owed knight-service to the English kings, though the bulk of Northumbria at that time lay in the hands of the kings of Scotland. Northumbrians had long been an independent people. A Northumbrian king had once ruled all Britain by his might of arms. Our people themselves were a sturdy mix of Briton, Anglo-Saxon, and Scot, with but little Norman admixture. Viking blood showed often; our knights, like Lancelot, were the tallest in the realm. I received not this heritage of height, despite being well-grown as a young lad.

Though the Forsters had first come to England with Norman Duke William, we regarded ourselves as Northumbrians, nothing else. We valued our heritage as a people apart, we of this far north land; but even then we could not disregard the power of politics. My father William was called to knight service in '58; he rode away a squire and returned a knight. Only his father's death had kept him from being called the year before, when he had just been new-married. Men then were not knighted as a matter of course, but need must earn it in battle. War was the means by which a knight became invested after long training and proving himself worthy by service. I too would receive knighthood that way. But I never had William's temper, which flared like a pine knot in the heat of an instant. It was that temper which had crippled him.

He was called again to Wales in 1163. I was but four, and never kenned all that happened, except that there in the mists of a Welsh morning, he had been sore wounded. Taunted, William chose single combat with a crafty Welsh warrior. It had been better settled in the melee of battle. Later, I was to understand how words can make the hot blood course through a young man's veins, and a fight—in any war—is the only antidote. It is an antidote that sickens and kills and destroys. My father rode away, fair in his height and horse, singing. He returned upon a palfrey, bent by his fall, trampled and broken in wind, in body, and spirit. When he was called again in '65, he was glad to pay the scutage, or knight-fee, for another man to take up his arms. He was done with it.

My mother had taken the burden of the estate whilst he was gone and the villeins respected her stewardship. North country women were strong and, in the main, treated with great regard in our days. When they brought William home—broken, more dead than alive—she had then this burden as well. His body mended, twisted; his mind too often showed forth the same state. In time, he was able to go forth and mind the affairs of the forge and mill and fields, but our people's respect did not always follow him as readily as it should. Henry had rewarded him well, but there was not gold enough to buy his strength, nor wine enough to make him sing again.

Scattered glimpses are all I retain of that last summer before going to Alnwick. There was mother cropping the flat golden hair which hung in my eyes. There was the farm, where I ran the fields and wood lots and hedge rows, usually accompanied by Andrew or by one of the housecarls. Andrew was the only son of my father's hostler, Peter. Three years older than I, he was already beginning the responsibilities of manhood. Whenever Peter could spare him, Andrew would be by my side and my mother never worried. He taught me all that he was learning about the horses and their training, which is an art lost to many. In turn, I showed him the Hall, how it had been built of rough stones by men who lay so far back in time as to be beyond our ken. The form of buildings and field walls, the lay of the fields themselves—of ditches and earthworks and all the cunning of the builder's hands—gave me great wonder. I would dream of the men who had gone before: monks and knights, brave men on great horses. I could already recite most of the Forestrius ancestry, which had begun in old Flanders. My mother's people were from the Welsh marches. Forced out by William's barons, they came north to Scotland, where they had stayed as loyal vassals and men-at-arms to the Scots kings.

My great-grandfather Sir Hugo Forster, whose name was still revered in my day, had strengthened the earthworks of Old Hall, which faced the sea. Magnus of Norway came to invade, and Hugo's was the arm that turned him.

(Romans, too, it was said, men who might have glimpsed Christ, worked and built here. Annie, the girl who was seeress of the farm in my youth, had seen them marching, and I among them, a great dog by my side. My father had snorted rudely when I spoke of it at table, but mother had a faraway look in her eye that I knew well. The Welsh are fey, and keen in understanding things unseen. I took after her in that. In my mind I could see them all, spinning out their days on these green rolling hills, all blown away in the sweet wind from the sea.)

Though the hall was old when I was born, grandfather Reginald had begun a tower for the west end. That was in the days of English King Stephen, when men took upon themselves to build what battlements and towers were needed, without royal license. War and uncertainty wracked the land in the quarrels between that weak king and the headstrong woman, Maud, who was supposed to have inherited the throne. My father made shift to finish Reginald's work, but never got beyond the second level; his heart lay not with building. We made do, though often in winter the tower rooms were cold and drafty. In the days of my childhood, the Northumbrian weather was mild with little snow. Later, cold weather made great fires necessary in every room, and the open wind holes had to be closed with drapes or shutters. The call then began for glass, which we had seen on Crusade in Italy and the Holy Land. Our ways began to change.

When it was chill, mother would bring my younger sister and me down to the old chamber, which lay at the east end of the hall, and have pallets made for us. The round-ended chamber seemed like the warm heart of the house. Here the family ate their meals, apart from the great table in the hall where priests, travelers, housecarls, and our men-at-arms had their supper. In the chamber, we always had clean straw upon the floor, and the dogs were banished to the hall. On cold evenings, servants would bring braziers of hot coals from the fireplace in the kitchen. I remember the last evening before I left, looking through the great arch into the hall, watching our people sup and make laughter in their ease. The smell of the cool straw and the bread and meat mingled with the sweet odor of my father's good corn ale. The night air was beginning to cool, and the braziers were brought. In the hall, the lights danced along the walls as wind came through the windows above and made the flames lick upward. Were it not for the trouble of my leaving, my mother would have looked almost happy. The crops were in, there was no sickness about, and my father, deep in his ale, seemed more content than he had in a long time. It was a picture I carried in my heart always, a small spot of solace for the misery to come.

It was not until I was a father myself that I saw William's motive in sending me away so young. I thought then that my presence angered him, for he was ever gruff with me. Now I understand that he was trying to prepare me for manhood. A knight must carry an armor that is not often visible. Perhaps five was too young, but he desperately wanted me to succeed where he felt that he had failed.

I took little for the journey. There was a new linen shirt, warm hosen and cloak, and my old leather jerkin which was still serviceable. Old, too, was the oaken sword with which I had practiced many a battle, and the little wattle shield that had often turned my playmates' staves. My father laid his hand upon my head in blessing, before clapping on a tough leather cap. Mother knelt and held me a moment. She smelt, as always, of herbs and comfort, warm as milk. Yet all she said to me was, "Be strong, and remember your blood. I will pray for you." I trow she did, every day. She died when I was sore ailing in France; her loving prayers, I know, saved my life then and brought me home.

I was sent to Alnwick in the company of old Henry; he had been a squire to my father but he was now so bent by age as to be unfit for either work or war. I'm sure that tending a brat filled his cup with bitterness, though my father truly had his welfare at heart. His warrior's pride could not see the man who had so faithfully ridden by his side reduced to lying in the doorway of some hovel from sun to sun, useless and waiting for death. But I was a trial to Henry, and he to me.

Still, the old man's craft took us safely to Alnwick. Armed, he stayed close by my side, for a knight's son was prey for ransom. Two men-at-arms with lance and axe went before, and two behind. Every burn we crossed, every patch of forest we need must pass through, Henry sent two in first to reconnoiter. I was impatient; I ran the fields and woods without fear at home, but Henry saw an enemy shadow behind every tree. I learned later that the caution which helps men grow old is the one thing which remains frozen in their mind in the ice of old age. And I noted his craft, and respected his unswerving sense of responsibility to a task which must have seemed odious. Even at five, I could watch and learn.

Alnwick Castle through the mists of morning

Alnwick castle lay inland perhaps six leagues from Old Hall, which itself was half a league from Bamburgh. Alnwick nestled far from the stormy winds which sent the grey North Sea flying against Queen Bebba's great castle rooted on its rocky cliff. Unlike Bamburgh, which in our days was naught but a fortress, holding little cheer save in times of grave danger, Alnwick was a place where people went bustling to and fro daily. Behind its golden stones were priests and minstrels and artisans, and even then the countryfolk held their fairs beneath the walls. It was also the place where the sons of neighboring knights came to learn their trade as warriors. My mother's brother, Kenneth, was there then, a knight in the service of the king of Scotland.

Alnwick in 1164 did not belong to the house of Percy, but was held by William de Vesci, vassal of Malcolm the Maid. Malcolm had become duke of Northumbria after his father, Earl Henry, died in 1152, and then had inherited the Scots throne when his grandfather, David I, died in 1153. King Malcolm was but 23 when he, too, passed from this earth. His brother, William the Lion, then became king of the Scots and reigned over most of the north country: Northumbria, Cumbria, and Scotland. That stalwart lion later became the symbol of Northumberland. Only scattered parcels, largely near the coast like our own, were held in fief from the English king. Though English Henry chose to quarrel with William over property and money, 'twas but his Plantagenet fervor that spoke. There was no bad blood between the Scots king and his neighbors. Indeed, there was kinship among us and no clear boundary to divide us. Peace—as peace was found in those days—prevailed with Northumbria. Only a few roving bands of thieves and slavers trod the border paths, and the knights rode the marches to prevent them.

Men still speak of the days when law and order along the Border finally broke down, so fearsome were those days after the death of King Alexander III in 1286. He was the last of William's lineage, the staunch Canmore Kings. War with England again came to the Border, with reivers and outlaws in full measure. Men would be forced to build strong towers to protect themselves, towers with desperate stories that stand even unto your times.

Yet in my life I had no ken of this history to come, which, written down, cast a shadow across our earlier, more halcyon time.

Sons of knights were sent for training to another household, usually to one wherein the father's own knight service lay, or where, as in my case, there was kin. Our world was ordered; from highest to lowest, each man had his obligations to those set above him. At the same time, he was required to give succor to those placed beneath him. Even the king had to intercede for us all before God. We thus saw that each person within the realm was cared for. Englishmen, both north and south, were often quarrelsome, and would brook no tyranny for long. Nor would any Northman worth his salt bear the burden of slavery on his demesne. To the south, where other bloodlines were accustomed to such, it often happened that villeins were mistreated and slaves were entered on the manor-rolls. Northumbria was a prouder place. Our villeins were treated like family, as they were among our neighbors. Men of the South called us poor rustics, and perhaps we were. But they never said it to our faces, for respect of our arms.

I was no sooner delivered to the graces of the Alnwick Mistress of Pages, Adela, than my man Henry was off to the stables to look up old cronies. For the first time since leaving home, my courage began to falter as I looked up into Adela's stern face. I felt truly alone for the first time in my life. I do remember answering her questions politely, and being shown to a cot in a long dormitory room, far bigger than our squires had at home. A cot itself was a luxury—a pallet was all I had at home—but I would then, and often after, have traded Alnwick's splendor for my own humbler place.

It was common in those times to have a woman of good blood, usually a widow, in charge of the pages. In training for knighthood, a page was most often between seven and fourteen years of age. After giving decent service, he would then become a squire. As he neared maturity, his lessons grew harder. His taskmaster was usually some tough and grizzled old knight who had managed to survive many battles. Both Mistress of Pages and Master of Squires were most often childless, and spent their parental love upon their charges. But we were hard, resourceful youngsters, often vain, sometimes cruel. Our overseers need must be canny, stern, and resourceful to meet the calamities we too often presented. Adela was certainly all these things. It took me many years to realize that beneath her hard, implacable exterior, her heart was filled with all our pains, all our joys. How little we understood the little machinations Adela constantly wove to keep our lives as safe and as bearable as possible.

She seemed to me, at the time, an old woman; certainly older than my mother. But I realized later that she was only about thirty-five; not much older than I when I finally achieved knighthood. Her husband, whom they said she had truly loved—a thing beyond my ken then—had been killed in a melee, in a tournament. William of Scotland was a distant relative of her husband; he took her into his care and she found her life among the children who came to the royal court to be trained. With grim resolve, she undertook to make us the best possible knight candidates, in memory of the man she herself had lost.

Adela's first move with me, as a pawn in her game of pages, was to assign a workplace. To my dismay, it was in the great, greasy kitchen that fed the whole of Alnwick castle. I was a knight's son, not a villein or servant, but the pride of her charges was subject to the skillful forge of Adela's will. I am sure she had much reason to put this scrap of young rooster in such an odious place. For one, I was far younger than the other pages, and needs must be kept out of their way as much as possible. Men-children of seven and eight thrive in their own small wars; to win handily requires the most helpless victim. While she never held the intent to shelter me completely from harm, she knew there was a limit to which a page must be tormented or he would be broken in spirit, like a maltreated colt.

There was misery enough in the dormitory and at training sessions. The other pages called me White Hands, like the poor knight of the ballads who was forced to work in the kitchen. Because of my size and age, they also called me John the Child. But the worst was when they called me the Scullery Maid. Indeed, my task was the cleaning of ewers and wooden trenchers, and the great cauldrons wherein food was cooked. They would hold their noses as I walked by, complaining of the odious smell, though they too smelled bad—of horse and dirt and urine.

Adela was also wise in the ways of our country knights; how food was seldom scarce for a boy running among the kitchens of his own demesne, but strictly rationed by protocol in the training halls of the great castles. We were always hungry, but a lively lad who knew the kitchen and its cooks might often find stray morsels. Since I was the youngest and smallest of the lot, I'm sure our Mistress wished for my growth not to be held back for want of proper food. And it was warm, except for the cold water in the stone trough wherein my hands spent too much time. Unbeknownst to me, also, in my struggles with the cauldrons, I was building muscles in my arms that I would need when my battle training began in earnest.

None of these things did I ken at the time. I was young enough that, betimes, I would go behind the building to weep in frustration, all unseen. My heart was heavy with sorrow to be cast from a warm and loving home into this basest of servitude, not even able to call my soul my own. Yet there were bright spots in my misery. Chiefest among them was my uncle, Sir Kenneth. As younger son, he held no fief of his own, and lived as knight-at-arms, first to Malcolm, and then to William. His prospects of marriage were dismal, unless perchance a widow with some property might find his arms and manner appealing. So far that had not happened. He was witty and loved to sing romantic ballads; the ladies all found him charming. But he was a toy for their amusement. Good-heartedly, he took what spoils were offered and bore no malice to any man. Yet in a fight—several times I saw him tourney—he was tough and implacable. I adored him.

It was not often I saw Kenneth; his duties kept him on marches to the north where the forest was thickest, and outlaws, men without friend or family to succor them, found refuge. These men were often depraved criminals, and lived by preying on the villeins of the estates. When pressed, they trod to the highlands, where they took children as slaves to work the great manors in the south. Especially in the valleys whose cheeses were already famous, labor was scarce and stewards of the great estates, whose owners were in France, were not overly nice as to the source of that labor.

Nor was it meet that a knight interest himself too greatly in the affairs of a page. Yet I can remember Kenneth, sitting in the great hall with his head thrown back in song and the firelight glinting off his ruddy hair. Half-asleep, I would sing his brave and bawdy songs along to myself, to be repeated over the cauldrons next day. I ached to grow quickly, to become as doughty a knight as Kenneth. On the rare times when he came to watch the pages sword-play with our oaken staves, I fought with a frenzy. The other pages dreaded to see his red head among the loungers and spectators. When we were through, he would unarm me himself, and take me to the hall for ale. There he would carefully tell me what I had done wrong. Old Sebastian, who was master-at-arms for the pages, never resented the knight's occasional interference with his charge. Kenneth had a way of charming the boots off everyone. My mother said it was the Celt, the Cymry, in him.

Even old Henry behaved around Sir Kenneth. Far from looking after me as his charge, Henry spent most of his time in the stable and deep in his cups. I learned to look out for myself. But each time Kenneth went to see him, Henry would look in on me, meek as a lamb, for a day or two. It was no surprise, then, that the first Christmas after I went to Alnwick, Kenneth himself rode me home, and Henry minded not a tittle.

With the old man going before as scout and advance guard—he was proud to do so for Kenneth—my uncle and I rode at leisure, singing under our breath, for to make too much noise would have been unseemly and have made a mockery of Henry's caution. My mother welcomed us all, even Henry, though I am sure she knew his faults as well as any. Kenneth she was careful not too make too much over, for my father was unholy jealous of the younger knight. She was guarded also in her greetings to me, as if to acknowledge that it was meet for us now to grow apart. Later, though, she came to the pallet where I slept, and brushed the hair from my eyes. I knew she wept for her man-child, and my heart ached for her. We were pawns to our times and destinies, just as today.

William, my father, was glad to see me too, though he needs must be read through his usual grumpiness. He had made ready for me a new jerkin of boiled leather, hard as armor. It was a little large, but he had had it padded well with sheep's leather, tanned with the wool. I was pleased, because my old jerkin was becoming too small, but more because my father had taken such care in my behalf.

We had no snow that Christmas. After hearing mass, the villeins and men-at-arms held a shooting contest, three arrows at a peeled willow wand. Old Rafe won, as usual, and took home the prize of a great gray goose. His grandchildren watched greedily as my mother presented it. Like their fathers and grandfather, they were strong tall lads, and always hungry. It was beginning to drizzle as we went in to feast, but with fresh straw on the floors and all the braziers burning brightly, Old Hall was festive. After we had supped, there was a contest of minstrels, for two wandering singers had graced our table that day. Kenneth, I thought, bested them all, but it would not have been seemly had my mother presented him the prize. Instead, it went to a dark- haired young Briton with piercing blue eyes, who sang of his lost family and lands of long ago. He then made us all merry again with his ballad of Peter the Monk, who was defrocked and tried to become a knight. Mother gave him a new wallet for his journey, and even the other troubadour received a new set of points—thongs to hold up his hose.

Kenneth rode off in the grey of dawn next morning, for my father had made his unwelcome plain. Even at Christmas, my uncle told me with a wink, a knight had his patrol to fulfill. He was off to Berwick Town, and would see me betimes back at Alnwick. I was uncommonly sad to see him go, but I comforted myself with singing Kenneth's songs whenever my father was not near to hear. I made shift, too, to visit with Andrew, and we ran the fields and woodlots. It was not as before. There was a subtle difference; I was growing into a master, and he into my man, a difference I had never realized before.

I rode back to Alnwick with Henry and two men-at-arms. Besides the new jerkin, mother had made me a new linen shirt and warm woolen hose and a serviceable woolen cloak with a hood. In my saddlebag was a honey cake which I would hide from the other pages, and cherish for days. There would be other Christmases at home, all formed alike and running together in their traditions. Never again, though, would I know such a keen sense of being apart; growing alone toward God and my own destiny as a knight.

Chapter 2

Becoming A Man

Christmas of 1164 marked the ending of childhood. I was not yet a man nor even fully a man-in-training, but I was no longer a child. The cold, grey days that began 1165 matched my mood. Not cold enough to snow, nor yet brave enough to rain, the clouds hung over Northumberland like misery from the grave. I settled into the kitchen, loathing the work, but grudgingly glad for the warmth and for the extra morsels of bread I was able to steal. Even lessons among the other pages seemed dismal, not worth the attempt to excel at anything. Truly, I was often lost in the mind, out running the hills in the sunshine among the cattle and sheep. Bland answers, or none, earned me the title of Sir Knothead, but the other pages left me alone when within hearing of elders. It was not until night fell and we were left to the cold darkness of the dorter—our dormitory—that the trials began.

Whatever I valued, I slept with, or it would disappear. My head or feet would be soundly thumped if I slept unwarily. Cold water would be poured on my hands, to make me wet my cot. If this proved fruitless, the water would simply be emptied in my bed. I was taunted; John the Child, who smelled of the kitchen, a hopeless dunce who would never live beyond another year. The older pages relished the details of just how ignominiously I would die, my wretchedness being assisted from this earth by the might of their own small hands. There was no part of my body or blood or heritage that was not attacked and sullied. I soon found that to fight back, with either word or fists, brought me to be blood sport. I could only cower silently in my bed and hope their bedevilment turned to someone else. Too often, it was my one friend, David; he, too, had learned the trick of icy silence while murder lurked in every corner of his head. Often, there were brawls among the older boys; then the men-at-arms, who slept outside our door, would burst in, much annoyed, and break heads without discrimination. After that happened there would follow a night of blessed sleep, unlike our usual wary unrest.

Leader among the older pages was an overgrown lout named Baldwin. As often happens among lads of greater bulk, he used his size to intimidate the rest of us and take whatever he wished. Try as I might, I could not believe that he could make a true knight, for he had the manner of an outlaw. Yet the mark of an outlaw in those days was being turned out of family, and his family at Durham, while abandoning him to the relative hardships of school at Alnwick, often sent him gifts of food—even wine—and of clothes. He was hard on his clothes, for he had no thought of the hands which had to provide them. Many of his better castoffs he would offer to those who would assist him in some mischief. Most of the pages would rather die than be so beholden, but one sharp-faced Scots lad named Duncan shadowed Baldwin as a jackal does a lion.

Nothing perhaps better tells of our times than the roster of pages during my time at Alnwick. There were nearly always a dozen or more, though through some wandering of Fate one would leave or die, and another would come. Usually we lost one lad a year to death, often through foolishness. Those of us with any wit at all learned the first great lesson of knighthood here. A man walks always with death. We did not ignore him, as people do now only to find him by surprise. The wise knight consulted his death before every decision.

Like Baldwin, whose family held much land from English Henry both in Normandy and at Durham, there were some lads of nearly pure Norman blood. There were others like Duncan, who were sons of Scots thanes, courtiers of William, the Scots' king. Also among the north people were some Welsh, the Cymry, who had been driven from their homeland and come north to find new endowment. With what resource they were able to salvage, and the strength of their arms, they had made new homes for their families among the Scots.

My mother's father, Rhys, was one of these. With nothing more than fierceness of arms, he had acquired property and goods as a soldier under Henry of Scotland. Henry had granted him the land of a thane who had been killed at Hastings. The abandoned settlement, Colin's Wood, had been naught but a palisade surrounding a log house such as the Norse are wont to build. Rhys built it into a fine manor; he was a man of great energy. His eldest son, my uncle Henry, still held the family estate, which was near Cornhill, on the edge of the great forest. The Welsh had age-old blood ties with even more ancient settlers, northern Celts whose roots had twined into Scots soil like the hoary oaks of the forest.

Others, like my father's family, had already been in Northumbria for several generations, and were sons of Norman knights by Anglo-Saxon or perhaps Danish mothers. Indeed, my parents met while my father was serving as squire at Alnwick, and my mother was traveling with the Scots court, learning the graces of a lady. Despite the hardships of her life, my lady mother always took pains to teach my sister Maud and myself the ways of gentlefolk. Some of the pages had many hard raps under Adela because their manners were only fit for the swine lot. At least, I was spared this.

Sharp division rose between us as pages, due to our blood; it was a division we often heard at home. The Normans with holdings still in France regarded the rest of us as beasts of burden. Whether Anglo-Saxon, Scot, or Welsh, we existed only to pour wealth into Norman coffers.

Most of us were mixed in allegiance as in blood. The court of the Scots king, William, was as grand as any place in France, and he was content to let the English king worry at his Angevin claims on the Continent, as a hound worries a bone. Later, ideas would come to change till men believed that only Norman ways were the herald of civilization. I return to tell you this was not true. We of the North inherited the earth; our blood was the red of Welsh soil and English heather, our eyes blue as the great North Sea from whence came both Norse and Saxon. Our heads became greyed and hard like the stones of Scotland. We spoke words of Saxon and Celt and Pict, as well as those of France and the Latin church. Yet we felt always the freedom of our own Northumbrian hills and forests, and our land supported us and became blood and bone to our bodies and the meat of our souls.

There was a great lot to be learned as a page, even without benefit of books. We each had work to perform for at least half a day; this brought us strength, humility, and discipline. We were taught prayers by our chaplain, a monk from Durham. Father Anselm told us stories of our faith and of the Holy Land, where he had made pilgrimage. He taught us to read and write, to sign our names in Latin at the very least. I would have liked to learn more, but already I suffered enough ridicule. Later, when I was older, I used to go to him secretly and practice writing Johannes Forestrius and copy out prayers, such as the Pater Noster. I began to spell out words enough to read adequately, though never was there time enough to become artful at it. Nor did it behoove a man to be too versed in such things, except he were to become a monk. But late in life, this skill was a comfort to me, when I was fortunate to own a Book of Hours to give direction to my prayers.

Adela schooled us in manners and courtesy, in how to treat the ladies. One of the chief duties of pages as they matured was as errand boys for the women of the court. It was hoped that by those attentions we would come to treat our future wives gently and with respect. Often the lads learned far more than was intended.

Garth was our fighting-master, and he goaded us upon one another unmercifully. We fought with stave swords and reed lances, with old flint knives cast off by the peasants because they lacked sharpness, and with fist and foot and tooth, mainly when Garth wasn't looking. We were not allowed upon horseback yet, but we needs must groom and care for our own horse. And we were taught to hunt a little, enough so that when one of us would take small game, we were allowed to dress and field-cook it. Such privilege, spurred by hunger, gave us skill in provisioning ourselves.

The thing always left for last was the lesson I enjoyed most. Of nights, when all else was done, we might sing or play the lute. Lute had I none, but I learned to sing all the ballads from my mother's brother, Kenneth, and from every minstrel who came to stay in that great household at Alnwick. Indeed, Adela used to say she knew when I was truly sick, for I could not then sit up late for the singing. Later, I came to make ballads for myself, having the instinct of the Welsh for the weaving of words. It was not then a highly regarded knightly skill, as it would come to be later, but Kenneth possessed it, and none dared call him other than a worthy knight. It was a skill that helped me pass many lonely hours in wretched camps and on miserable marches during the great war to come.

Days of youth blur in old men's minds, especially when little happiness is found there. My years of training as a page run together like water flowing down the burn. Only certain great rocks stand out to impede the flow and recall my footsteps to some slippery crossings. One of these was not long after that gloomy winter and spring of '94. Adela was worried about me, for I had retreated into dark warrens of hate and despair. By my blood, I believe only the singing kept me alive till summer.

I was home for Easter, though only for a week. My father was not well; the winter had been hard on him, and my mother looked ashen. It was a relief to get back to Alnwick, where the peasants were setting up colorful stalls in the

market, and the churchyard burgeoned with yellow daffodils. The lengthening days gave us time outdoors in the
evenings, and I could often sneak away to run unfettered
upon the green hills and through the copses. David and I
would at times play at swords; we were fair matched, though
he was older.

It was one such afternoon in the slanting sun of early
summer that we so played beneath the castle walls. It was
but two weeks until my birthday. The roses in the castle
gardens filled the air with scent, and the sky was blue
without thought of rain. The golden stones of the courtyard
echoed to our shuffling footsteps, and I knew not that I had
been approached from behind until I saw a sudden warning
on David's face. I turned, swinging my oaken sword in
desperation, but the warning was too late. Baldwin loomed
behind me. Cleverly, he used my own swing against me,
wrenching my wattle shield from my arm and using it to
catch the blow. From the shadow of a buttress, where both
boys had been hiding, Duncan emerged as I furiously lifted
my too-impotent sword for another blow at Baldwin. As my
arm came back, Duncan wrested the sword from my grasp.
Laughing, the boys began to circle, waving my poor play-
things and taunting me for a kitchen maid whose white
hands should never touch weapons.

David had set off running when he saw how the battle
was faring. He went to fetch help from some men-at-arms
who were standing lazily in the last of the sun at the far end
of the courtyard. Only part of me was aware of this; the rest
of my mind was tumbling in despair and hate and tears. I
grabbed desperately for my shield; it had belonged to my
father when he was young. Baldwin let me just touch fingers
to it, then roared with laughter as he jerked it away.

Suddenly, all turmoil left my mind and it became calm as
icy death. Blood filled my eyes, and my soul unleashed a rage
as pure as the fires of hell. I saw instantly that the big lummox
had been made off-balance by his jerk. He stood head and
shoulders above me, but I was a righteous David facing a

wicked Goliath. Quicker than thought, I lowered my head and rammed it into his belly with all the force I could muster. He went down as if pole-axed, his breath completely gone. Pent rage knows no bounds. I swarmed upon his great body before he could so much as draw breath, and with hands entwined in his hair, beat his head murderously against the courtyard stones. Fear filled his eyes before they glazed over, blood running from his nose. The blood satisfied me.

Somewhere, I heard David screaming not to kill the oaf, but I was satisfied with near-death. Quickly, as the men-at-arms approached running, I jumped and turned to Duncan. He had stood, I swear, like a chicken in summer, mouth open, watching his mentor bleed upon the stones. Suddenly, he grasped my intent and began running away, toward the moat. I knew what he was going to do even as he himself thought it. Just as he raised his arm to sling my poor sword into the moat, I hit him in the same fashion. Only the wall of his back against my head kept me from sliding into the moat, but Duncan sailed in nobly, feet flailing. Not one of us lads could swim, and I fervently hoped he would drown there amid the sewage and slime. One of the men-at-arms came to his rescue, however, with the blunt end of his lance, but not before I had the joy of seeing his head submerge at least once.

Two men-at-arms carried Baldwin to the infirmary, where the hospitaler monk patched his head with a vinegar poultice. Duncan was removed to the stables for a cold bath, to remove the stench. Me? I was picked up, without a struggle now, and put into a guardroom until my fate should be decided. It mattered not to me. My soul was quieted, and the bleak pall that had covered my life was gone. While I waited, I began to sing quietly, a song about daffodils upon a grave in spring. It was not meet that I should exult, nor did I wish to seem daft to the guards. But the song brought contentment to a mind that was still somewhat dazed by the fury it had unleashed.

It was a long time before anyone came; I suppose they wanted to give me time to regret my sins. They only became sweeter as I sat. Finally, Father Anselm came to succor me. He spoke to me quietly for awhile, but when he saw I was in sound mind, he sent me to the kitchen for some meat and bread, and told me to sleep that night before the kitchen fire. Tomorrow, there would be an audience with King Malcolm himself, who was then sitting at Alnwick. Who would have kenned that the young king would take the quarrels of pages to heart?

I only heard later from David what a rumpus I had raised. Adela and Father Anselm, Garth and the hospitaler, Vincent, had conferred together after speaking with David, the men-at-arms, and the other pages. Duncan was questioned. It seems that Baldwin and I were the only ones not asked an opinion. That was to be reserved for the king.

Justice in those days worked swiftly and economically and usually surely. Certainly it did so in my case. I was subdued but strangely unafraid facing King Malcolm the Maid. There was about him an air of gentleness, almost of holiness. It was from this that he took his name. There were many things I might have said in my own defence, but the resentment of the near-constant abuse had poured itself out upon the cobblestones of the king's outer court. Malcolm's few questions were answered simply. I fully expected to be sent home in disgrace. It would have mattered in a few years; then, it did not.

King Malcolm's last question was couched thoughtfully. "Did ye ken that ye might have murdered this lad?"

I answered truthfully. "Yes, sire. I wished to. I could have. But in the end, I could not."

His sad answer surprised me. "That is well for now, John. But someday, as a knight, ye shall have to commit that deed on men more worthy than this unkempt Norman cub."

All were questioned; all were found lacking. But in the end came decisions that were extreme for that day and age, when children were little thought of and only the toughest were expected to survive. The older pages, from eleven to fourteen, were taken from under Adela's wings and put beneath the direction of a sour old knight, Sir Fergus. Garth and their taskmasters were instructed to work them harder, to keep them from being so lively in the night. The men-at-arms who slept outside the door were instructed to sleep within the dorter. This rankled the pride of the Norman cubs, who regarded the servant's place as outside the chamber. But it was good for their humility.

Humility was also meted out to those of us involved. Baldwin was sentenced to the kitchen for six months. It was such a blow to his pride that when he went home for Christmas, he never returned. I trow his father would have had war with the Scots king, save for the strength at Alnwick. Later, when English Henry confronted William the Lion in siege at Alnwick, Baldwin's father was in the van of the besieging army. Baldwin himself, though his father bought his adubment as a knight when he was twenty-one, never made a warrior. From the day that I almost spilled his brains upon the courtyard stones, he had a certain sense of his own poor mortality. He became what we used to call a Holy Mary knight, whose only calluses were upon the knees.

Duncan was sentenced to the swine herd for six months, a lot for which even I pitied him. Yet he stuck at Alnwick and became a decent knight. As squires, we would at times ride to tourneys together; in the melees, he would ride at my left and David at my right hand. We never broke our rank and we gained spoil enough to later send us to war quite handsomely.

In the days of tourneys, prizes of arms and armor were granted for winning the day. In some ways, it was like to the rodeos of today, only the intent was more warlike. We knights were the professional military of our time, with the need for combat training as telling as now. Though Henry had outlawed tourneys in his English fiefs, they were still held on the Continent. More to our favor, Edinburgh or Berwick, or one or another of the great northern castles, still hosted these games of champions. Certainly, wherever the Scots king came to set his court, pomp required a tourney.

David was sentenced to the byres, which was no punishment for him at all. He liked the warm smell of the cows, and stole extra nourishment from their milk. It was what he needed, as he had been small for his age. He had come from a small holding in the north that was more stone than soil; the greatest crop his father raised was hungry children.

I was sentenced to the stables, mucking out after the horses and carrying them water. It served me in great stead later, as I learned to think like the horses, and to know their moods. Indeed, when my term was up, I requested to be kept on another year, which was allowed because of my age.

Since age had been such a hinge to the whole ruckus, Malcolm decreed that henceforth no pages would be accepted unless they were past six, nearing seven. It was a good rule, and one of the last earthly decisions Malcolm was to make. Within weeks, he was dead, and his brother, William the Lion, came to the throne of Scotland and earldom of Northumbria.

During my punishment, I had most doubts about facing my uncle Kenneth, who had been away on his march, his patrol to the north. But I had no sooner noticed his horse in the stable yard when I saw his red head approach; he must have been told ere his foot was out of the stirrup. He greeted me with great courtesy, taking the manure fork from my hands and leading me to the armory; we soon shared a horn of ale. It was not long before my tale was told, though, truth to tell, my heart lay like lead within lest he be disappointed in me. Beside my mother and father, only Sir Kenneth's opinion had the ability to touch me so deeply.

Despite the seriousness of my offense, which after all was attempted murder, my uncle had no word of blame. Instead, he told me a thing that I have never forgot. "It is meet to be merciful, but never hold pity for the vanquished. God alone, who sees into each man's heart, grants the battle to the righteous. You are here to learn honor, respect for God, and the knightly code. Never judge yourself or your fellow knight; the angel of battles metes out to all as God sees fit."

Then he spoke to me of my ancestors on my mother's side, the Cymry. The Celts, he explained, had been driven from Europe because they were dreamers and poets. Because they felt things so deeply, they too often gathered the woes of those they vanquished. It was like the Welsh, too, he said, to begin a speech, but never finish. Once the thought-arrow left the head, they felt it fly to the listener. There was no need for further words. I nodded even as Kenneth told me. That was the way between my mother and me, always, and with the seeress Annie who lived on our estate. David and I often did the same.

At the same time, Kenneth said, the Celts were fierce fighters. All of the ancient empire feared them because of their blood-frenzy. He told how a few warriors had captured mighty Rome, unclothed except for the torcs about their necks; and all the Romans in their armor had been unable to stand against the force of their battle-frenzy. He told me, too, about the Irish Cuchulain, how he slew the host of the Connacht in his *riastradh* or supernatural frenzy. His every muscle swelled; he quivered like bulrushes in a stream. One eye turned deep into his head, the other stood out, great as the head of a babe. His mouth foamed, and his heart sounded like the roar of a lion. A light shone above his head, and a jet of blood fountained upward from his scalp. Meeting the light, it scattered to the four winds, creating a great mist of blood that enveloped his foes. I listened in awe, for I understood.

Kenneth concluded thoughtfully, "Perhaps you should not have had such patience; all a bully understands is his own blood. But the frenzy had to move you. I trow, it is a boon that you carry that gift of the Cymry in your blood. I, for one, shall rest easier, for I know 'twill come to your aid when needed. And, after all, you did grant Baldwin a mercy he perhaps did not deserve. When the time comes for the taking of life, the blood-frenzy will be your friend. And ye shall sow it in your seed, to come to the aid of your sons and your sons' sons. They shall be warriors of great might"—he closed his eyes, seeing what I could not ken—"and of justice." He opened them again, almost in surprise at his own words. "Not all, of course. There have to be a few bad apples in the lot." He grinned sheepishly and finished off the ale, as I sat in wonder. No greater fighter lay at the court of Alnwick than my uncle Sir Kenneth. Yet here he was, being as fey as Annie. Perhaps that was also part of being a man. I learned many lessons that day.

There were indeed a number of things to be learned during the days at Alnwick, so many an old man might recall that youngsters yet have no wish to hear. But some things stand out because they forged the man I was to become. The winter I was nine, a friar came to us from the Bishop of Durham. On his yearly visit to us that summer, the bishop had noted that a number of pages were at the castle. It was his desire that some be trained as singers for his great Christmas pageant at Durham Cathedral. His singing-master, Friar John, started with twelve boys, one for each day of Christmas, but soon saw that if the pageant were not to resemble the yowling of so many cats, then he needs must choose among the singers. I had always a brave voice for a small lad, and was quick to learn the songs. Singing was my joy, and to be able to sing at Durham, my greatest hope.

I was duly chosen, and we were excused from much of our work to practice for the great feast. The week before Christmas, we rode to Durham under armed guard, to the school that lay hard by the great cathedral. Words cannot tell my awe of that vast house of God, nor of the pure moment when we stood to sing, on Christmas eve, in the gloom of that holy place. We each had a glistening white candle, signifying the Light of God entering the world. There were new white surplices over our red cassocks, and soft leather boots so our feet made no noise on the stone floor as we entered. Only our candles lit the house of God, only our voices poured forth in praise of the Child who was come. When we had finished, candles were lit in each worshipper's hand, and the cathedral blazed with glory. Tears streamed from my eyes like a baby's; yet I saw grown men, battle-hardened knights, also cry for joy on that night. Though centuries may intervene, God's pure gift of love upon that eve will never be forgotten.

When youth attains a certain age, there obtains the certainty that God's omnipotence can be aided by our own small selves. He might be busy, after all, and need a messenger. And who makes a better messenger than a well-trained page? When I was twelve, David and I entered into a conspiracy to turn the workings of mortal hearts nearer to what we thought God might desire. In so doing we almost brought the wrath of the castle about our ears.

David had just turned fourteen, and was new-made a squire. The knight he was assigned to serve was a distant cousin of his, Sir Malwin, a tall knight with a shining grin one could see across the courtyard. Sir Malwin had been dubbed knight in France, in one of English Henry's interminable wars. His family had some holdings near Edinburgh, but Malwin himself was far from a rich knight. His surcoat was often in tatters, but his heart was merry, and he had little thought or care for his appearance when a game was afoot. And wherever he was, there was bound to be a game, whether in the chase or in chess, in wooing or war.

I had been a lady's page for near five years; the last two to Lady Agnes Morton. A lady's page was bound to wait upon his mistress at table, learning manners and gentle speech. He would perform any manner of errands that were too rough for her maid, such as leading her palfrey or taking messages to knights or serving men. In the grey days of castle life, the chief pastime for ladies, other than the interminable sewing, was gossip and intrigue. The knights were not loathe to take part whenever they were in domicile.

It was the custom for a knight to pick a lady—not his wife—to woo with tender words and gentle favors. He would bring her a rose or sing her a song to win her heart, but could never act surprised when she refused to consummate the wooing. Still, the odds were in the knight's favor, unless he were a boor or ruffian. Many sons were born beneath the bar sinister, particularly when a squire rode off to war seeking knighthood, leaving a young wife at home. Then there were the adventurers who wooed young ladies simply for the deflowering. I had heard the women talk of them when they forgot I was standing behind their chairs. It was unchristian, the aspersions they cast upon these men, but still it seemed that some young ladies would submit to such predators despite the sensibilities passed on to them by wiser heads.

When the great tourneys were held, a knight would wear his lady's favor attached to his helm. This token was usually a sleeve, since most of the ladies' tunics had detachable sleeves that could be changed and cleansed without removing the entire garment. Even though her husband might be present, a lady would often bestow her token upon a young knight simply to play to his pride, or to pique her husband. And there were other ladies who faithfully gave their favors to their husbands alone, and the husbands carried them gallantly. But this was unusual enough to set tongues wagging.

Lady Agnes was a de Villiers, from a good Norman family. She had come to Alnwick as lady's maid when her sister wed a northern knight. Agnes was married to Sir Brian Morton who, like my grandfather Rhys, was a knight-adventurer. Though he had been landless, he made a great deal of money from tourneying, for he was a strong and often unscrupulous knight. He was unscrupulous, too, in his wooing of women. He chose Agnes for her heritage and her patience with his charades. Her father settled land upon him when they were married, and he was often in France seeing to their affairs. Lady Agnes had three sons and a daughter, and the daughter was most dear to her. When I came to her service, her eldest son had been sent to English Henry in France as a page in the royal household. The second son, Robin, had just begun his time as page at Alnwick, and the other two children were still in the care of their nurses.

There was no running free for these children of courtiers, as I had run free in the first years of my life at Glororum.

It was coming up on Midsummer in 1171, and great festivities were being planned. There was to be feasting and dancing, and a fair for the villeins. A great tourney was planned, and the prizes promised to be rich. The ladies had been sewing gowns for weeks, and knights were gathering like bees to the plunder of fragrant clover meadows. Lady Agnes was particularly excited, for her husband had been gone some months. She spent much care sewing a new sleeve of brown velvet, with lace trim, for him to wear upon his helm. Truly, she had passed her age of great beauty, for her teeth were going bad from bearing children, and she was often sorrowful, which set upon her face. Still, she was a fair lady in ways which many another was not.

Sir Brian was, however, his usual satyric self. He had singled out a maid, Blanche of Amble, as his game. Despite the ladies' warnings, Blanche began to find herself entrapped in the web of his smooth wooing. Agnes simply bit her lip and kept sewing. But David's young knight, Sir Malwin, was beside himself. His laughter had ceased to light our days. He set greatest store on Lady Blanche; indeed, he had petitioned King William for her hand. She had steadfastly refused to listen to his pleas, calling him a buffoon, which was a sword to his honest heart. When he could become a great knight of battles, as Sir Brian was, she told him impudently, she might consider granting him her favor.

Thus it stood on the day before the tourney. David and I had talked often, gloomily wondering how God could reward such a scoundrel as Sir Brian. 'Twould serve him right, we said, if the ladies' sleeves could somehow become confused and Brian should have to wear his own wife's favor, and Malwin might wear Blanche's sleeve. Yet, to save our lives we could think of no way to effect the change without being turned out of Alnwick in disgrace.

Grand preparations were under way for the feasts and merriment. Fires in the courtyard were roasting oxen and sheep; in the kitchen, bacon and puddings were boiling, and pheasants and peafowl were roasting, to be served in a covering of their own feathers, with feet and beaks gilded. Pastries, too, were being gilded, and innumerable bread loaves being baked, rosy with flower petals, yellow with saffron. The rooms had all been swept, and fresh straw and rushes strewn upon all the floors.

Blanche's sleeve of cream brocade was borne by a young page, Will, who was new-made a lady's page. I bore Agnes' velvet token. We were crossing the courtyard, each with sleeve in hand, on our way to the armourers, where they would be affixed to the helms. We both had the same destination, Sir Brian's helm. The soft brown sleeve in my hand would, of course, be cast to the floor to be trampled upon like my lady's feelings. Though she knew it, still Agnes' faithful heart must make the offer.

David walked by my side, casting side glances at Will and his sleeve. I shall always believe in Providence! Of a sudden, it seemed God was to take part in our plans after all. One of the piles of greasy straw that lay in the courtyard awaiting the dung cart caught spark from a cooking fire. It was hard to our hands.

Without speaking a word, both David and I knew what we should do. "Quick," we shouted at Will, "run fetch help!" I took his sleeve, and shoved him away toward a group of cooks. As soon as his back was turned, we began beating out the fire—with the ladies' favors. Soon both were smoke-blackened and begrimed, though I do say the cream brocade fared much the worse.

When Will returned with the cooks, the two sleeves were lying cast to one side. I ordered Will to help with the bucket line, and while he was busy, David snatched Blanche's sullied sleeve from the ground and hurried away with it. I knew that by the time Will bethought him of it, 'twould be firmly fixed to Sir Malwin's helm.

In time, the boy looked up, poor face all besmirched, and noticed his token was gone.

"Don't worry, lad," I told him, "I sent it off with one of the men. You've done a champion's work here today. Go wash your face, and you may tell Lady Blanche her sleeve was delivered." Unsuspecting, he went to do as he was bid, while I took Agnes' sleeve—somewhat the worse for wear—and fastened it to Sir Brian's helm with my own hands. Of course, the knight had so little intercourse with his wife he recognized the sleeve not at all, and so, in a way, we cuckolded him in reverse.

Sir Malwin became privy to what had happened, for David told him everything. I could hear his laughter echoing from the stables as he and David prepared his mount. The upshot of the tourney was that Malwin sought out Brian and, with rare courage and humor, unhorsed him. He said afterwards that the thought that Sir Brian had been so done for by a page gave heart to his blow.

But the real trouble began when he rode up to Blanche to present her with her favor. So begrimed was it, that she had not recognized it from the gallery, when the knights were in combat. When Malwin rode up grinning, his helm in his hand, she saw at once that the favor he wore was the work of her own small hands. The furies of Hell erupted from beneath the wimple of that young lady.

Agnes had recognized her own sleeve upon the fallen knight, her husband, and she realized that something had gone amiss. She turned where she was seated and looked up into my bland face, for I was standing behind her. Suddenly, I believe she knew what had happened, for never have I seen a lady strive so hard to keep the mirth from her lips. It was, she confided to me much later, just payment for a debt her husband had long owed. Though her token had fallen, it had taken that proud knight with it.

Once again, I was called to face the wrath of a king; this time, William the Lion. He was of sterner stuff than Malcolm, his countenance far more severe. I explained about the fire, how we had worked so hard to put it out, and how, in the confusion, one of the men had picked up Blanche's sleeve and had all unknowingly bestowed it upon the wrong helm. Had not Malwin been wooing Lady Blanche? I asked innocently. No, I did not know who, in the confusion, had done this. Yes, I had fastened Lady Agnes' sleeve to her husband's helm, as none other was in place. William could not fault me for this, though Blanche should cry to heaven. Malwin himself, when called, said that he had no knowledge how the sleeve had come upon his helm, but he was right glad to see it, dirty as it was, for he loved the maid beyond reason.

The upshot was that David and I got off with no more than hard looks. Malwin resumed his wooing and, despite Blanche's wrath, he finally won that maid with his good humor. It helped that he had an uncle who was so amused by the story that he went straightaway to dicker with Blanche's family on Malwin's behalf. And the fact that Sir Brian paid handsomely for his defeat also helped sweeten her temper, for it bought Malwin a new surcoat and the lady enough velvet and lace for a new dress.

Sir Kenneth, my uncle, told me later that if William could have figured out how we had started the fire, it might have gone worse for us. But all testified that we were nowhere near the stack when the blaze began. William could only conclude that the hand of God had intervened to chastise a foolish maid and a lecherous knight. And so it had, with a bit of help from a young squire and a lady's page.

Chapter 3

Iron Men

What relative peace I had known as a lady's page broke on the rocks of the '70's. By 1173, I was made full squire, and few memories recall aught but pain, exhaustion, and constant bruises. I was well-grown at fourteen, but unlike many lads who sprouted like young corn thereafter, my height settled there. Though all the pages had been tempered by toil, the squires were forged white-hot into new steel by the Squire Master, Sir Gilbert. Only hard work could lay on the muscle needed to wear the weight of armour for a live-long day, for the rest of our lives.

As yet, I had no armour of my own. It was expensive and foolish for a family to provide for a still-fleshing youth, save he be scion of earl or king. In the armoury at Alnwick hung a collection of forfeited armour of every size, mostly of ancient date. Much of it had been paid in heriot, that is, death duty. When a householder died, his family owed his overlord a payment of kind. A villein might owe a good beast, such as a cow. A knight's family, according to their wealth, paid at least one suit of armour, one sword, and one horse, and often more. This heriot was shared out to the replacement of the lost knight. In practice, a king might assign a knight's gear to the knight's son, as a sign of the son's succession in the fief. Other times, the heriot allowed a family to dispose of outdated relics of war, which could be used by the reigning lord for the training of squires, or by the sheriff for the local fyrd, the peasant militia.

My first hauberk, or byrnie, from the common armoury, was heavy scaled iron upon a crusted leather jerkin. It had no sleeves, and came only to my hips. That was a blessing, for ancient dirt and bloodstains and rust all had to be cleaned until the byrnie was shining. In addition, we were burdened with the old Norman mail hosen, or cuisses, tied behind the knee and strung to a belt on the waist. They were useful to men on horseback, but clumsy afoot, and David and I vied in inventing new ways of cursing them. Still, as Sir Gilbert pointed out, even with extra weight upon our hips, we learned to move easily and quickly. When the weight was removed, a greater dexterity remained.

We were issued swords, some of ancient make, curiously wrought with plaited steel twisting like ribbons of light along their length. All were blunted, but nonetheless respected, for a sword is a knight's right arm and his honour. At first, we fought afoot and Gilbert taught us to evade the deadly steel, for even a blunted sword wounds. One of his favorite sports was to set two upon one, so that deadly intent would not set our focus in but one direction. We later had melees afoot, to sort out various dangers and counter each most effectively. Besides the sword, we learned the use of axe and mace. I found to my sorrow that the mace can be more deadly than an edged weapon; it crushes flesh and bone beneath the armour, and it can be thrown with deadly aim.

When we began practice ahorse, I had my own destrier from Glororum. The farm was noted for its war horses even in my father's time, and Old Peter was a trainer par excellence. A good horse makes the knight's job easier, for he turns not aside at the wrong time, nor does he flinch with the shock of battle. Yet when called upon to swerve, he will do so with the lightest touch, or upon voice command. Shadowed centuries later, rodeos would require much the same from a horse. Perhaps the skills which came from Spain for working cattle on horseback had roots in our knightly combat.

Riding at the quintain was the favorite sport of all the young men, and my nimble brown destrier made me look good at it. The quintain was used for lance practice. Riding hard, your lance must prick a wooden shield clean in the center; then you must twist your body and sweep by, ere the sandbag on the arm of the shield can deal you a blow upon the back. Only once was I unhorsed by my hesitation; from thence I gave Brown Thunder his head and quintains became play. Then came lance-play with one another, using padded lances, but as long—about ten feet—and as heavy as a war lance. Couched beneath the right arm, great strength of arm develops to hold the beam true. For this, we trained in byrnies such as were worn at Hastings, long to the knee, of chain mail. Above knee and elbow the mail was edged with leather straps, and all was held together with leather thongs. We had bare arms and legs, and no coifs around our heads; only the old-fashioned helms with nose piece set atop a padded cap. Even this light armour weighed about thirty pounds, and we wore it everywhere except to bed, to allow our bodies to harden to the weight.

The weight of other people's power and ambition sat upon us also, and our lives were embroiled in the politics of the day. It was Christmastide of 1170 when the fatal blows were struck to Thomas à Beckett in Canterbury Cathedral. Beckett had opposed King Henry and needled him almost beyond endurance, but Henry's four knights who murdered the unarmed Archbishop at his altar did the English king no favor. Pope Alexander demanded retribution of Henry with a vengeance, and the English crown paid. Common people began to distrust their king, and his own sons went to quarreling with him. The English lands on the Continent—Normandy and Anjou, Aquitaine, Poitou, and Brittany—had been almost constantly at war with one another and with the French king. In 1173, abetted by Louis of France, the king's sons rebelled. Henry had promised each—except for the youngest, John—a part of his Angevin empire. In truth, he ceded no power to any. Henry was a hard man, always keeping the reins firmly within his own hands. Though he prevailed, his quarrels in France once again dearly cost the English.

William the Lion, with Scot's canniness, saw that the time was ripe to avenge English Henry's high-handed treatment of his brother Malcolm. When that twelve-year-old lad had first succeeded to the throne of his grandfather, David I, Henry, new-crowned, marched north, lusting for the land of the Scots. Malcolm had been coerced into ceding Scotland to England, contrary to Henry's own earlier vow. After William came to the Scot's throne, he laid in wait for years, patient as a hunter in a hide. In 1174, he seized his opportunity and marched quickly to Carlisle. Restoring Scot's rule in Cumberland and Westmorland, he then swept south to bring all Northumberland under his control. William kept on the move, and made fools of Henry's few troops. Truth be, the best of them were still mired in wars on the continent. Then word came that King William was falling back to Alnwick. We squires were excited; the news of battle to young men is meat and drink. But at the same time, I had word from my father; I was required at home immediately.

Disappointment did not dull my senses. At Alnwick, I was on the wrong side of the war to be an English fief-holder. What I did not know was that Henry had called my father to France; the royal messenger had reached him after only three days on the road. As soon as I returned home, father put me in charge of the defences of Glororum, which he had organized. Stock was pulled in from the further fields, and guards were posted day and night. Villeins in our home fyrd were sent to neighboring villages to scout. If war appeared near, I was to take mother and the women and children to Bamburgh, where King Henry maintained a paid garrison of some twenty men. Though undermanned because of Henry's constant wars, the great castle was still siege-strong.

Father took only one man of his own, and with the weary messenger, set out for the south. It pained me to see the helm again on his grey head, and the pain that even light armour gave him. I was furious with English Henry for inflicting this on my father, and my heart went that day to the cause of Henry's sons, where it had no thought before.

It was not until Sir William returned, near three months later, that I understood the war plans of that stubborn fox of a king. My father had gone first to Yorkshire, where the High Sheriff, as king's agent, was waging Henry's battle against William the Lion. The sheriff needed every bit of my father's knowledge of Alnwick, its defences and weaknesses. With that information, he made a lightning thrust north, surrounded the castle, took the Scot's king prisoner ere he was aware, and packed him off willy-nilly as hostage. It would be December ere the Lion was ransomed from Henry's "care" in France. All Scotland's strongest castles were surrendered to England, and William the Lion became a vassal of the English king. It was just another move in the chess game of power, but the board upon which they played held our lands and lives.

No one has known till this day the part William Forestrius played in that war, for our aim was to keep good relations with our neighbors. All thought he had been called to Henry's continental wars. Truth be, father was galled in mind, until he died, to have served as spy, such an unhappy and unknightly errand.

In 1175, I returned to training at Alnwick, and though regarded with slight suspicion by some, the days soon set into the old grooves. For my part, I knew I had to work harder than ever, for only our Lord could tell how long I would be able stay at Alnwick under Gilbertus. I had been assigned one of William the Lion's household knights to serve; a poor knight, he often took his malhumour out upon me. Still, I served him well at table, cutting his bread and meat; I polished his arms and carried his bath. Truth to tell, I felt sorry for poor Bran; he had but two virgates of land to support him, and he was a widower with three daughters to dower and marry off. Only as a castle knight could he live, for his land did not suffice.

I would have sooner served my uncle, Sir Kenneth, but he had at last left castle service at Alnwick. His half-brother and head of the family, my uncle Sir Henry of Cornhill, had arranged a marriage for Kenneth with a rich widow of Berwick-on-Tweed. In 1171, we had ridden to Kenneth's marriage feast, and seen him well and truly wed. The widow, Eadra de Mill, had inherited her husband's prosperous tannery and six virgates of land. She was over thirty and childless, but her plump round cheeks were always bunched with a smile. Eadra seemed not to be the sort of woman Sir Kenneth was always a-wooing, but seeing the two jesting with one another, we could hardly doubt but that they were well-suited. Yet his settling with wife and property left my later days as page saddened, without sight of Kenneth's flaming head or the sound of his merry songs.

My seventeenth birthday in 1176 was a noble one. Father and mother both came down from Old Hall, and I was greatly honoured, for my father had been in great pain ever since his enforced trip to France. They brought me my first true armour, which William had been having forged for at least a year. Looking more grey and bent than ever, he fitted it to me himself, using pads of sheepskin to take the pressure off shoulders still not fully callused. I will always remember the gentleness of his hands that day. The resentments of my young years melted away under his touch. I could look at him and truly see the father's love in his eyes, and all was well with us. My mother saw, and knew, and I felt the happiness bursting her heart.

With byrnie and helm came great-grandfather Hugo's sword, heavy but well-balanced in the hand, and polished to a bright keenness. I was proud that my father thought me of enough merit to bear that weapon. I carried it all my life, as I know my grandson Alfred did after me, and none did it dishonour.

It was just after fall plowing that I was called home for good. William had been in the fields, seeing to the work. A cold, wet wind came blowing off the sea, as so often it does in October, and father took a chill. He lingered, with the fever in his chest, for only three days. He was forty-six when he died, an iron man who had lived his life in the crushing grip of pain. He asked me to sing to him as he lay a-dying, and that was the hardest thing I ever had done. But his face softened, and I could see him once again, on that faraway day when he had left Glororum singing, on his way to war.

After we buried father, mother and I were left alone to manage the scattered estate. Since the days of Richard Forestrius, some scattered freeholds and forest had been added to our lands. We held near forty virgates now—nine were under cultivation—and we had twelve plows instead of four. Pasture was chronically short, and some of the waste was being cropped. Wool was beginning to pay well; weavers in Flanders bought all we could produce, at a premium price. William had begun to follow the new practice of turning sheep into the stubble fields, not only to glean, but to enrich the land. For the same reason, he had begun the new three-crop rotation: wheat and rye in winter, oats and peas in spring, then the land left to rest a season. 'Twas far more productive than the old two-field system with one year in and one year out of cultivation. Still, our northern soils were never as rich as the dales of the south, and we had more predators. Great flocks of gulls and rooks stole seed wherever they could; wolves preyed upon the lambs; and wild boar broke fences and took out gardens.

There was never any question of turning our forests to cultivation, however. We were, after all, the Foresters. William the Lion came to hunt with us, and many another man who wore the trappings of power, sheriffs to bishops. Sundry were the affairs that were concluded upon these hunts, small bargains that would change our history. But in 1177, I had no ken of many of these things yet.

My sister, Maud, was just fifteen. After father's funeral mass, she returned to Cornhill, where she had been staying with my mother's eldest brother, Henry the Grey. Mother had no wish to subject my sister to court life at Alnwick, as she herself had been. Part of the reason was financial. To marry Maud to a wealthy courtier would have required more dowry than we were able to raise; nor did mother wish her to marry a poor household knight like Sir Bran. Sir Henry, Rhys' oldest son by a different mother, an heiress from Lincoln, had become a man of power in the north. Maud was able to spend some time at Lincoln, as well as Cornhill, and became more conversant with the life of an English lady. Still, she kept her good country Scots sensibility. But now one of our first problems was to arrange her a suitable marriage, as she was of age, and more. William had been making inquiry, but naught was settled when he died.

Part of the trouble was the Church's refusal to sanction marriage within seven degrees of kinship. We had distant cousins, quite well off, on the Marches of Wales and at Lincoln, but like many of our neighbors, to whom we were related, the degrees of kinship were too close. Hugh, the great bishop of Durham who had known my father, at last suggested to him that he had a young kinsman of marriageable status. Stephen de Essh was heir to a fine manor at Hutton, south of Durham. Like many southerners, our wild northern forests seemed a hunter's paradise to him. William had proposed we give a leasehold of forest land and a cash settlement as dowry. Our man Bors had already investigated and reported that the family seemed to be just as the bishop had said. Yet nothing further had transpired.

A month after father's death, we received an invitation to visit Hutton. Mother sent word that we were currently in mourning and unable to travel, at least until summer.

"That," she said, "will leave the matter in the hands of God. If it be a good match for Maud, Stephen will only grow more anxious. If the Essh's are not of good faith, why, better to know it now!" So the matter was left till summer, but we had enough to occupy us besides.

I was concerned over the heriot, William's death-duty owed to our overlord, King Henry. The usual fee was a knight's horse and armour, but we were sore beset to provide arms and trappings for our own. There were two knights of the house, two lads serving as squires, and four men-at-arms that we called sergeants. The small armoury that stood in what had once been the porch of Glororum church was not overfull. Little of armour or weapons could be spared without being sorely missed. Our horses were in fine shape, for William had traded whenever he thought one was going poorly. Peter thought he had a young destrier that might be spared, especially with pasture so scarce. Money payment would have to make up the rest. With a dowry payment at hand, the timing could not have been worse. To be sure, our tenants would be asked for boon on the heriot, but I was reluctant to squeeze the villeins overmuch. Like mother, I resolved to wait and see what the sheriff would require and what God would provide.

It did not take long to find out. I was outwardly calm but all a-seethe inside, watching the fat, red face of the sheriff at supper. He and his two men ate enough for five; as luck would have it, I had but that day killed a red deer. Bread we always had in plenty; the oven at Old Hall was always full with the baking, not only for the house, but with loaves for the villeins who brought them to old Lucas to bake in the courtyard oven.

February was not a good time for feasts. The bullocks and other animals that we had not enough hay to overwinter were already killed and gone. Red deer and wild swine from the forests made up most of our meat after Christmastide. We had not held full Christmas that winter, because of mourning, but there had been funeral feasts that ate up our winter's meat. Though father had only a scattered handful of cousins left in his family, they all had ridden to Old Hall to pay their respects. But we always had pease porridge a-boil, some with bacon, and new ale. Ralph, the sheriff, did not look displeased.

Mother rose to see that some of our small stock of wine was broached, ere the sheriff took the papers from his pouch. I called Father Cedric, our clerk and chaplain, to read them. It would not do to have Ralph think I was other than a simple country squire, little able to read. The heriot was about what mother and I expected: horse and armour to the value of five pounds silver. Ralph was feeling expansive, especially after mother pourcd his wine. We had it imported from Spain, and it was particularly fine. It was also particularly hoarded for just such times as these. The sheriff would take the young destrier, though as yet untried, and a payment of three pounds silver, deferred for a year and a day. We knew he was making a good bargain of it, as not all would find its way into the royal coffers at Winchester.

What did surprise us was when Ralph pulled a second paper from his pouch. "King Henry saw fit to reward your father—and his heirs after him—for his bit of service in France." He winked at my mother. "This is a deed for a bit of marketplace land in Alnwick, and a house on Bow Street to go with it. Both belonged to a wool merchant who died some months ago, without heirs. As you know, since 1174, all Alnwick property devolves to the crown upon that instance." To say we were amazed would be to make too small a face of it. Cedric read through the papers, and the deeds and grants were indeed all intact.

"However," Ralph went on, "I know that fox of a castellan at Alnwick. As soon as the grant is cried, William de Vesci will contest the deeds; he would like to swallow every piece of land clean to Durham."

I was properly at a loss. "What recourse have we, then, a widow with an unknighted son?"

The sheriff held his cup to be refilled, and I saw my mother's hand shake slightly as she poured. She knew that contested deeds of land were still tried by combat, and we had no great champion in the household; whereas William had his choice of brave knights. We did not want to call upon either Kenneth or Henry, if any other means existed to us. "Mayhap your mother may not always remain a widow," Ralph winked. "Or mayhap the grants may not be read yet awhile, should I not find time. The king's justice will travel this road in a year. I have word from London that he will bring a new form of court, the assize. It will enable a knight of noble birth—or his family—to call for a writ, enabling a jury of peers, knights of the neighborhood, to pass judgment. Henry, may God save him, has long wanted to right the wrongs of judicial combat."

I was amazed at Ralph's loyalty to the crown, but, indeed, this new court of assize seemed a Godsend. I felt the gloved hand of Dame Fortuna touch my shoulder, and it made me bold. "I would like to empower you now on our behalf. When the king's justice comes, if William tries to seize our claim, then we will throw our case upon the assize. Meantime, I am sure that you would like to come north to hunt. Our forests are always open to you." I was hoping it didn't sound too bald a bribe; it was really all I could offer. I knew that if our case went to a panel of peers, knights who held property in the area, it would be decided in our favor. None of our neighbors had much use for de Vesci's greed. The trick was getting the sheriff to stall the crying of the grants till he got word of when the king's justice would be coming. Still, such were the skirmishes of power, that the bad blood that already lay between Sheriff Ralph and William of Alnwick was on my side.

Ralph looked again at my mother—she was still a pretty woman, with all her teeth—and smiled. I knew we had him then, and indeed, he promised to do what he could. But it was autumn of '77 before he came for his promised hunt, and that was soon enough. The grant was cried at Christmastide, and naught could be done till '78. The justice of the crown was due that spring.

The assize went as expected. When a man knows his neighbors and is able to walk the disputed property, the matter of right comes perfectly clear. I was myself to serve on many assizes later. It was a new concept then, though we had had crown courts for years. Not until Henry issued formal writ, however, was the assize accepted all across England. We didn't miss the old trial by judicial combat, which de Vesci had hoped would prevail in our dispute. God again came to our succor. My father would not be robbed of his reward, even though death intervened.

Chapter 4

Rites of Passage

The spring of '77 was especially fine, but with the greening of the year, my mother's face began to set more in shadow. It seemed not grief that hung upon her, for I rarely found her in tears; rather, it seemed more some grey, gnawing worry. At last, I importuned her to tell me the secret of her sorrow.

"Somehow, I have failed my trust," she began. "Through the years, your father—rest his soul!—gave unto me the care of all the deeds and papers of the Forster land. Since the matter of Maud's dowry has arisen, I have searched through the papers in the geld-chest, but can nowhere find the grant for the west forest that Henry First granted to Hugo. It was part of that grant that we were to use for the dowry." She hid her face in her hands. "I have tried so hard to see, see in my mind's eye, just what has happened to the deed. Yet in nowise can I glimpse it. I have even prayed to St. Aidan, but all is dark, covered with a veil I cannot penetrate."

I could feel her distress, but that darkness of soul seemed to me to hold away the very knowledge she was seeking. "I will look also, though I doubt not your word. If the paper comes not to hand, then we must get Annie." I said it with more confidence than I felt, for mother would eat humble pie to call upon the village seeress. Annie was less even than a villein, for no one knew who her father was. Her mother

Ruth held a croft simply by being the best ale-maker in the area; she scraped a small living by keeping the village alehouse. Since our villeins were as well off as any, there was always coin and meat enough in Ruth's cottage. But Annie did little to help put it there.

Mother bowed her head. "I kenned you would say that. Annie does know herbs, but no more so than I. Still, she does have the gift, and she may see what I cannot. But you must make the bargain; 'twould not be meet for me to humble myself before her."

Upon my promise, mother seemed much lighter, but I felt her burden slip to my shoulders. The house search was futile, as we had both known it would be. Next morning, I sent one of the house squires to fetch Annie, and it was near noon before he brought her back. "She was out hunting herbs," he panted, and I knew she had led him a merry chase. Annie knew every ditch and copse at Glororum.

I greeted her with courtesy, though my still-raw voice as lord of the manor held a pomposity I regret to think of today. "Maid, the Forsters ask a boon of you, as your lord and lady. We need your aid in finding something of great importance."

Annie seemed not the least ruffled, but sat watching me as a hearth-cat watches meat being prepared. "According to our custom, such a boon is met with kindness. What will my lord gi'e?" Thus we haggled, and at last settled upon four pence as faith money. Still, she was not satisfied. Closing her eyes, her dark hair untidy and falling from her cap, she began to rock back and forth. "Ere the power comes to be, there needs must come unto me something blue from beyond the sea." She opened her eyes, to gaze square into mine. "I see a great blue bundle in my arms, blue as our Lady's gown in the church." She stared calmly at my face, whilst I tried to hide the sudden vision that had come to mind. As soon as she had begun to talk, I saw the bolt of blue cloth that had just come from Flanders; a cloth of value that she would have had no way of knowing about. What is more, as soon as I saw it, I knew that she kenned the same. Our minds had touched, in a most unholy way.

"You shall have enough blue cloth for a dress if, by God, you find for us what we so grievously need." It was my last concession, and I was turning grim. She knew it instantly. "That I will, but you must make shift on your own behalf. I shall come to the Hall to seek your paper"—now, how the devil did she know that, as I had said nothing of a paper?—"but only after you have made offering to the little folk, whom your father before you forgot." I remembered then, the old custom of setting out food at night, particularly at full moon, and on the equinoxes. Most of the villeins believed in the little folk still, the ancient nature spirits that once peopled all our land.

She went on. "You must take them bread and fresh milk, Tuesday hence, after nightfall. If they come to tell me that the bread was fresh and the milk sweet, I will know that I have the power to grant your boon."

So it was on the Tuesday night after, under the full moon, that I stole from the house like any peasant night-hawking. I had a trencher of fresh brown bread, and a small tass of milk from the day's milking. Beside the path to the great front door of the tower, where it wends toward the stables to the west, and not far from the water of the pond, stood a great rock. Somehow I had always known that this was the place where, over generations, people had laid their offerings to the pixies, the little people of the forest and stream, whose land we now cropped as great, blind strangers. I felt a fool, for both church and knightly training gave the lie to such doings. It was not meet for the lord of the demesne to behave as any ignorant peasant. Still, I went; for in my heart, I kenned that Annie spoke the truth.

I slept but badly that night, nor did I let on to mother what my errand had been. She somehow knew enough, at least, to pretend that she did not, while making her pretence plain. I slipped out to view the stone with first grey light of morning. Sure enough, the bread was gone, and the cup licked clean. I am forester enough to have looked for tracks of cat or hound. I found none, naught but some strange dents in the soft mold toward the pond that were like no tracks I ever saw. After breakfast, I went to sit in the chamber and ponder, for I knew that Annie would soon be there. Now, though I live a hundred lives, I could not explain what "knowing" is. Nor could I explain why, on many nights throughout my life, I felt it necessary to make offering to the little people of the farm. All I ken is that Glororum prospered with their goodwill, far beyond my own small efforts.

I had not long to wait ere Annie appeared. Nor did I need to send for mother, for she glided into the chamber, silent as a wraith. I counted the pence to Annie, for I knew she would not move without silver in her hand. Nor would the blue cloth she coveted be hers, unless she unearthed our papers. She said but little, but asked us to follow as she sniffed her way along the hall, and into the anteroom of the tower. God knows what she found to smell, but she led us to the foot of the center staircase, which led to our sleeping rooms on the second floor. The curtain walls were up to the third floor, but that remained raw and a-building, with no rooms set in. Above the second floor, a narrow staircase wound up inside the south wall. Past the closed door to the unfinished third floor, it led up to the roof, where it was topped by a small cupola. Indeed, the design of our west tower had not the simple symmetry of the old hall, the church of the priors, to which it was attached. But the roof was a point of vantage that served us well, and would serve those who came after us, when ugly border wars became common.

Annie hesitated at the head of the staircase from the first floor. She went to the winding stair to the roof, listened, and smelt the air rising. Shaking her head, she turned back. She then wandered from room to room on the second floor, with mother and I behind her, silent. Once, she got down on her knees, ran her hand through the air just above the floor, and smelt her hand. Mother and I looked at one another, puzzled. Annie didn't seem to notice; her attention was focused on something beyond our ken. She turned in then to the room that had been William's. He and mother had slept apart for many years, due to the near-constant pain he was in.

We had not changed the room, for we had no need at the time to use it. There would be time enough to erase father's memory when the mourning was past. It was a small room, more an antechamber, in the northwest corner. There was little to see for our houses held few furnishings in those days. There was one small open window on the west; we had no glass at that time, only wooden shutters to keep out wind and rain.

His bed was tucked in an alcove, as were beds of old, to keep out drafts. There was a crucifix above an iron-bound chest against the north wall. Next to the door, on the inside wall, was a small prie-dieux, well padded, where William was wont to make his prayers. Above it hung the tapestry of which he had been so proud. Imported from Flanders, it pictured the crucifixion, with Jerusalem-town in the distance. Roman knights stood guard, while the Marys wept. I think father spent much time gazing at that scene, as had I when I was small. It comforted him in his own pain, and reminded him of his own steadfast Mary, my mother. The houses of Jerusalem-town had been my favorite. Imagine walking those streets whose very walls had echoed to our Lord's voice!

Annie entered the room and turned 'round three times, sniffing loudly. I wondered if she would go to the chest, for mother and I had searched it thoroughly. But no. She hesitated only a moment, then walked to the tapestry as if she would enter clean into the picture. Stopping abruptly, she lifted one corner. We could see nothing amiss with the stones of the wall behind, but she spoke for the first time, with satisfaction. "Here, belike you may feel, one stone throws cold from it. And the smell of the pixie's milk is strong upon the air!" Both mother and I held our hands a few inches from the wall; sure enough, one stone threw a cold that was noticeable. What was even more amazing, just as mother and I spoke of it later, there was a definite sweet smell of milk upon the air.

I fit my fingers around the stone, and it came away quite easily, for it was only a front. Behind it was a small cavity, where two papers lay rolled and tied. One was the deed that had so made my mother distraught. The other was a strange paper that I thought best we take to mother's room to read in private. We first went to the anteroom with Annie, where I found a lad to fetch our seamstress. When she arrived, Annie was cut a fine long length of the blue cloth she coveted and, just as she had seen, left with a great bundle of it in her arms. We knew the story of her success—and our expense—would soon be all around the vill and into Bamburgh. Yet we both had gained, for Annie was thence much in demand, which kept her even after her mother died; and we had our papers.

The deed was most important. It allowed us something over eighteen virgates, along the west road that led to Cornhill. The boundaries were clearly set down. It adjoined the king's forest on the west, so was open for game to track back and forth; else such a small parcel would not have had much value. Mother and I put our heads together and, to keep the forest in the family, decided to deed only enough land for a hunter's lodge, with a croft for the caretaker. Then we could cede hunting rights, in perpetuity, without losing the bulk of the land. Along with cash payment, it would make a good dowry for Maud and, to be hoped, bring her a husband of worth.

The other paper was strange indeed. Mother had to cast her mind back, to a time almost eighteen years ago, to explain its origin. "When your father and I were married, the family chaplain was an Irish monk who had first come to serve your grandfather, Reginald, in the time of King Stephen. Father Duns had traveled across the world, to France, to Rome, to Jerusalem, to Spain. He had studied at Paris, but it seems that his Irish impudence caught him up in quarrels with other churchmen. He preached politics in England also, and it was a weary bishop who sent him here as clerk." She paused, remembering.

"Duns was far too educated for such a small place, but he cast his mind toward many things and kept to his ways, alone. My mother, Gwynlyn, was the only friend he had, and when she was here, they would confide in one another as much as seemly. When you were born, Duns was an old man. Mother was here to help with your birthing. While she was busy with me, Duns sat upon the roof and watched the sky, for it was his contention—as it was hers—that the stars held portent for a man's life. Belike the church would disagree, but Duns had studied books that were old in Roman times. After your birth, those two put their heads together and, like fairy godparents, wrote you a scroll that held the auguries for your life. Your father was aghast. Such nonsense, he would say, has no part in the life of a knight. 'John's duty will be to God and king, and to our land. There is naught else.' I often wondered if he had destroyed that precious scroll, but no, he dared not, after all. He simply hid it away."

"But why, mother, was the deed with it?" That was what made no sense to me.

"I think he had fetched it from the geld-chest, to think how best to make the appropriation for Maud's dowry. He was so sick at last, feverish and not of his right mind. I am sure he forgot that he put it in the cubbyhole for safekeeping. Had he not, we would never have found your birth scroll." We were both silent, thinking how the hand of God works in wondrous ways.

It took many evenings, after the day's work, to puzzle out the Latin of my birth scroll, but we did not feel Father Cedric should be called. That straightforward clerk had not much more Latin than I, and much less tolerance for things arcane. As near then as I can recall the words and bring them to English, it read thus:

"Mary began her travail an hour to midnight, June 28, *anno Domini*, 1159. Both dippers in the north were then pouring grace upon the earth, the smaller completely emptied.

On the horizon below the North star, the Twins stood ready to receive the blessings. On the southern horizon opposite, Neptune stood in Sagittarius. The midpoint of the child's life will be a journey across the water as a great warrior. From thence began a stately parade of omens; let him who understands read what he will.

"The moon, held in the claws of the Scorpion, descended beneath the horizon, near an hour past midnight, where she became a silent watcher. The Scorpion opens men's eyes to see, but below the horizon, the child will ever be in darkness as to how the seeing comes to him. The next hour brought the great Bull over the eastern horizon, crowned with the Pleiades, the favors of Fortuna. With him he drew Mars, to make the child a strong man, with the seed of many generations of warriors hot in his loins.

"Just as the child began entering the world, at three hours after the midnight watch, Jupiter and Mercury, conjoined, rose above the horizon. They stood in Gemini, and it was upon them that the blessings of the dippers had been poured out. The greater blessing was upon Mercury, to give the child a quick and keen wit. The lesser blessing, only partly poured from the great dipper, was upon Jupiter. As a man, the child will gain wealth, but not extravagance.

"Just after the cord was cut, scarce an hour later, Sun, conjoined to Venus, rose above the horizon in the sign of the Crab. The man-child holds a loving heart, and love for his own fair lands. And women will find him fair. As guard, mighty Orion stands beside these, his birth stars, the Hunter rejoicing in the son of the Forestrius.

"Yet on the other side of the world, grim Saturn opposes this grand panoply who have come to bless the child. All his life, this John shall know sorrow, and will work hard to earn the gifts Heaven has bestowed.

"God's blessing upon the household. Done this fourth day of July, 1159. Duns Hibernius, clerk."

Beneath this amazing gift was written a few more words, which I recognized as being from my grandmother.

"Look to the stars, your Guardian stands nigh. Life will end when he falls from the sky."

I often watched mighty Orion, with a great sense of peace, but never could I make sense of the latter line. But on the whole, these voices from the past—Duns had died when I was scarce two, and my grandmother not long after I had gone to Alnwick—brought sense to my life, if not always sensibility. At the time, I was most ready to get about the siring of sons, for indeed, youth fired my loins. But we were still in mourning, and there was my sister to marry off. Would there be no end to waiting for a marriage of my own?

Chapter 5

Venus Rising

Our year of mourning passed like a gale from the sea, blowing on hurried winds of much to-do. In July of '77, after the hay had been gathered, mother and I traveled south to Durham, to the manor lands of the Esshes. Stephen's inheritance, at Hutton, was a fine farm, and not far from the sea. It was close enough for mother to go and take over the household when Maud came to childbed, as her mother Gwynlyn had done for her. But the land was more cultivated than at home, with little forest, and Stephen liked to hunt. He was a tall lad, with hair bright as corn and the long legs of the Vikings; yet his family claimed descent from Norman knights. Like myself, Stephen was not yet knighted; we were what was later called valetti. Though lords of country manors and accorded the same honor as knighted gentlemen, valetti were still squires, because they had not yet seen service in war. Only the very richest families could buy grand ceremonies of adubment for sons who did nothing to earn the honor of their knighthood. Like political appointees to any officer corps, Holy Mary knights were thankfully few.

Stephen, like myself, would win his spurs on Crusade. We liked each other instantly, and though at first I had not the camaraderie with him as with David or even Duncan, with whom I had grown up at Alnwick, eventually he would become even closer. Stephen had served as squire at Richmond, and his ways were more English than those of our border knights.

Mother, however, was impressed. "He will do for our Maud, and she will like him." Her mind seemed to be straying back to when my father had been a young valetti, tall in his armor, riding off to Wales. She sighed. "We must ensure that Maud is properly taken care of, should anything befall. The Esshes have other manors; we must see that Hutton stays with Maud, should she be widowed." So it was done, with much haggling, and mother and I thinking we made the best of the bargain.

Betrothal could not be announced until the end of our year of mourning, after Advent. Maud's marriage would take place after Easter the year following, 1178. To give her opportunity to meet Stephen, we set a betrothal feast at Glororum for New Year's, in the midst of the Christmas season. In time, all came to pass as we had hoped; Maud and Stephen made a loving couple. It was a blessing of wisdom that mother had foreseen to her daughter's inheritance, however. Maud was to be long years a widow, outliving even her son, Henry. Her strong north country upbringing, coupled with the self-same sensibility that my mother always held, stood her in good stead. Few were the times I had to ride south on her behalf. She had, too, the benefit of a strong and honest steward, Sir John de Hawthorne. Her grandson, also Henry, inherited and held the property for many years. So great was his tenure that the farm village is called Hutton Henry to this day.

The first two years after William's death were tough meat to chew. Often I wished I had that hard, uncompromising man beside me. My days as lady's page in no wise prepared me to deal with recalcitrant villeins, wild north country customs, divers accounts and documents, and headstrong retainers. All tried me sorely as I struggled for control. I was like a man riding a nightmare, a great runaway beast humping and rattling beneath me, threatening at every turn to unseat me. It was with great relief that I gave to Sir Bors the duty of the manor court for six months, while I was yet a-learning. But Bors himself was part of the problem.

Sir Bors was one of those knights who were younger sons, left without property and little money, to make his own way in the world. Bors acted as our seneschal, or steward, overseeing the dispensation of work boons and fines and suits to court, as well as acting as general agent for the farm. He was an intrepid knight, though scarred and bitter.

As the son of a smallholder, Bors had earned his spurs in Wales, like my father. In those days, even a serf might be knighted by buying his freedom and showing a gallant heart in war. Bors' father was already a freeman, but the only training the youth had had was in service to Fountains Abbey, and in the Welsh wars. A strong fighter, he too had been injured in '63. A sword cut had taken his left ear, and badly scarred his face. It had also cut into his shoulder and made his left arm near useless. However, Bors was one of those great strong men who could manage despite hardship. He had come home from Wales with my father and been there ever since. Younger even than my mother, he seemed a great deal older than us all. Certainly, he was more chicanery-wise than I, which he never let me forget. He had been devoted to my father; they shared a certain ruthless loyalty to one another and to the estate. With Bors, I was John the Child again, treated with faint respect, and a thinly disguised disdain.

If William had become Bors' good left arm, then certainly Bors was my father's strong right hand. As seneschal, he seemed to be everywhere, in village and field and forest. He made miserable the life of whomever was elected reeve for the year, for no accounting would suit him. A good reeve is the heart of any manor; as one of the established villeins, he is responsible for work gangs and boon days, for apportioning everything that needs must go to the peasants, and accounting for everything that comes back to the demesne. I suspected that the only way our reeves could get along with Sir Bors was by geld-payment. Still, the manor could not run without Bors.

My father, due to his disability, had two knights in the household, where other country knights might have one or none. Our other knight was Sir Giles. Giles was also a younger son, and a Holy Mary knight. His family, from Yorkshire, was quite well-to-do, but they sent him packing north when it came about that he was causing dissension among both his brothers and the household knights. My father had required the services of another knight, as he himself could not well bear arms. Giles' father, one of the company who had marched to Wales, bethought himself of William's estate when attempting to find a place for his son. Giles was near as old as father when he came to us, with a payment for his keep, not unlike that of dowry. His great failing was that he eschewed the company of women for that of men, which had caused no end of holy uproar when he was young.

Giles and Bors became fast friends at once. The iron-grey head and the round, scarred face nodded together over many a horn cup of ale. The two shared a room over the forge, apart from the dormitory for the squires and men-at-arms, which stood over the kitchen. There they would bicker and fight like any married couple. It was wondrous to hear them. Bors would at times become exceedingly wroth with Giles, and go a-whoring at Bamburg; it would then take weeks for the arguing to cool down. But I sound like an old gossip. Giles was likeable, and performed his duties well. He took over father's marches to the west and north, those road patrols known then as cornage, that the country knights performed to keep the king's peace. Thus were the roads kept open and the countryside unsullied by renegade bands of outlaws.

Since marches were made on irregular days and routes, so that no man might know when a knight was a-riding, Giles spent many days at Old Hall. Father had made him master of squires, and, indeed, of pages also, though with firm admonition. Giles had never betrayed his trust. Mother abhorred father's faith in the Holy Mary knight, and ever looked askance when he approached. She prayed regularly for Giles' soul, though I never felt need for such niceties. He was a man as any other, flawed perhaps, as we all are, but true to his bounden duties. But a man is only as good as his master. I looked often upon Giles and his works, and though his slowness of wit at times drove me to distraction, he performed for me as he had for my father.

It was the custom at Old Hall to hold manor court every month, to hear grievances and collect such fees and fines as might have at last come due. A villein might be reprimanded and fined for such things as allowing his cattle to stray, or refusing to come to boon-work, when he was required to perform service upon our demesne. He might be called up by a suit from his neighbor, for anything from stealing hay to assaulting a daughter. Still, it was another matter to collect the few pence in fines, which might be held in abeyance for months whilst the culprit scraped together the justice-money.

We have been adjudged harshly by men of other generations who have little understood our lives. Our society was no harder on the laborer than many another; for a fact, I believe it kinder. Authority in those days had a name and face, and could be soon appealed to. Later men have had no less authority over them, but their masters wear a thousand faces and a hundred disguises, and to right a wrong now requires far more than petitioning your landlord. Nor were our court decisions rendered arbitrarily by the lord or his steward, who mediated the court. Judgments were arrived at by what was customary on the manor, how the villeins themselves saw their rights by precedent in each matter. These rights were presented, usually by the reeve, to the curia, which was the total assemblage of the villeins of the estate. Each man might then add his witness as to what was customary. When all had been heard, the curia put their heads together to decide on the matter. They then informed the court, through the reeve, as to their decision, and fine would be set. Yet custom also decreed that the lord had certain rights which took precedence in certain circumstances.

On some matters, even local freeholders were called upon to make up part of the curia. As estates grew larger, and the assembled curia became unwieldy, a jury came to be selected from the landholders, just as it was for knights in the king's court of the assizes. In every case, if justice had been badly done, there was always right of appeal to a higher court, under the king. All worked well, though lawyers were beginning to ply their trade. Then, as now, they could confuse even the simplest of cases in order to line their own pockets.

Life then, as life in all times, required toil, both by master and serf. Yet those of us who held the land held the greater responsibility, to the soil as well as to its people. The fines and fees that came to the manor by right of custom and law were just as taxes today, a web knitting together society to bind the common good. Nor were we exempt from tithes to the church, or taxes and fees to the king.

Holding court was not one of my favorite duties, but I soon took over from Bors, for I adjudged his bullying of the reeve and the curia to not be in our best interest. But the tedium of constant complaint over very little—the trivialities into which man's nature ever seems to lead him—made me irritable also. Had I not spent the court imagining that all the villeins were children or clowns, I should have been as roughshod as Bors.

My third court, at the end of June in '77, was an example of the usual uproar. It seemed the whole village stood sullenly beneath the court oak, to the west and north of Old Hall. Bors was seated at the table where Cedric kept the manor scrolls. He had just laid upon Richard, the reeve, the requirement to assemble every peasant household for three days, to lay in the hay for the demesne. These were boondays, where the workers would be provided with ale and two good meals, according to custom. Bors expected their assembly three days running, which gave the peasants no time upon their own holdings. Now haymaking is best done at once, while the weather is fair, for if it rains upon the mown hay, it is apt to spoil. Yet the villagers had their own plots to gather, as well as other chores. Truth to tell, they had been grumbling and shirking over haying for some years, and William had cut short the custom of giving the workers a sheep for a feast at the end of the boon-work.

I looked at the circled faces of reeve and villeins, with not a few of their wives, and stood up. "Bors is right to demand boon-days in succession," I told them. "If the hay spoils in the field, meat will be short next spring." Their stubborn faces told me they already knew this, that it made little difference. They were set for defiance. "But to grant you time upon your own plots, I ask for one full boon-day, in accordance with custom, then one half-day. You will receive a noon meal only. Then I ask for one more full boon-day, followed by another half. If we start on Monday, weather permitting, then our hay should be in the barn by Thursday, and your hay in the sheds by Saturday noon. If all goes well by then, you shall have a half-day holiday, and a sheep."

Bors looked at me sourly. The villeins looked confused; apparently, they had expected a fight. Richard asked permission to withdraw the curia to deliberate, which I granted. I took the opportunity to tell Bors that I felt he was right, but I wanted no quarrels with the farm labour at such a busy season. When the people reassembled, Richard spoke slowly, but with some trace of defiance still. (They would not have been my villeins had they acted overjoyed at any grace from Old Hall.) "We will do this, in accord with custom. But the small commons we will not hay, as we will not have time nor labour."

I had forgotten about the small commons at Bamburgh. A triangle of ground, it stood in the center of town. My ancestors had held the right to the hay of the commons since we came to Glororum. It was a nuisance, half a league away, and no bigger than a handkerchief. But it always yielded well, and at this time of year required mowing. It needs must be done. I looked over the crowd, and as God is my Savior, He gave me inspiration; one of those great, bold ideas that comes swooping on angel wings.

"I myself will see to the mowing of the commons. Bors will oversee your work here. (Did I see a face or two cloud and fall? Good.) Give me your children, such as normally do little to help with the haying. With their help and St. Aidan's, we will hay the commons."

So it was the following week that I found myself upon a palfrey, watching over the haying of the commons. Two lads, one well-grown at twelve, and one near ten, struggling with his scythe, cut the small plot. Rafe, one of our men-at-arms, grumblingly fetched ale and the noon meal of bread and bacon and cheese. As the day wore on, I found myself honing the scythes for the boys, and taking over some of the weary work for the youngest. We joined in small jokes, which were not unlike those I had known as a page. The girls raked the sweet grass into great sweeping windrows to dry. I can see them yet today, gracefully bent to their work. There was one girl near ready for marriage, perhaps fourteen. Two younger ones were as graceful, but children still. All the girls were dressed the same, like small nuns in grey gowns tucked up into a cord at the waist. Each wore a white head-cloth to shelter from the sun and keep the dusty hay from her hair. My eyes kept straggling to Kate, the eldest; the bloom of her face and form and the grace of her movements held me enchanted.

The next day, when the hay had been cocked, Rafe helped the lads load it upon the cart, and the oldest boy drove it to the barn. At nooning, there was much merriment, for the children were rightly proud of their day's work. Bors sneered at the small commons as "the children's meadow," and so it remained in local memory for generations. Custom had been new-set; every year thereafter, the villeins' children hayed the "children's meadow," and it became a sort of holiday.

But I had not seen the last of Kate. At Michaelmas, the end of September, threshing was held upon the floor of the great barn. The harvest had been good, and the folk were in better humor. At the end of the last boon-day of harvest, a

*The children's meadow at Bamburgh
now overgrown with trees*

hearty dance was held upon the threshing floor. All the doors stood open; the night was warm as milk, and the moon lighted the farm like day. Perhaps I allowed more ale than necessary, but I was coming into more confidence, and was exceedingly glad for the bounty of the harvest. Even the villeins seemed to forget their usual grumpy demeanor, and abandoned themselves to pleasure.

After the music was done, and the last villagers had gone to their cots, I made a last turn of the great barn. In a corner, I found Kate asleep upon some sacks of grain. Too easily I recalled how I had danced through the night with my villeins, seeking especially the golden hair and rounded body of young Kate. Her flushed youth, bright with life, called to mine. Her kirtle was the same blue as her eyes, and she opened them as I called her name. There are some things that happen without thought or plan, and making love to Kate was one of those. There upon the threshing floor, both of us were broken.

I ken not how mother knew, but she drew me aside next day. "I understand that you have become a man, John. That is the course of nature, but reason needs guide you now. Kate is a villein, daughter of Andrew the ploughman. She is unfree. If she should bear a child, he would have no future save as farm labor. Perhaps we could set him up as a small freeholder, but he would have no true right to a patrimony. Your firstborn child deserves celebration, not shame."

Of a sudden, I realized the greater responsibility of my lust, no matter how heartfelt. Kate had been placed in a terrible position. She could be sold as wife to the least desirable man of the village, for she was no longer a virgin. I had no desire to keep her as the master's whore, for I pitied her too much to lead her that kind of life. I hung my head. "I pray she gets not with child. What must I do?" I was John the Child again, asking the advice of my mother.

"We will wait awhile. I may call her to the Hall, to help with the winter's spinning and sewing. But you must not lie with her again, if your intention is truly good. By Christmas, she may be ready to be wed. Alan, the smith's son, would be a good husband for her; he is young, but well-grown and lusty. You can inquire of his father, as I will of the maid. It will keep both of them on the estate, and we may thereby lessen Andrew's merchet." The merchet was a price paid by a villein when his daughter was wed, and was larger if the marriage took her from the home village. Merchet had become largely a token, but we could not break with custom altogether.

Seeing Kate near daily, upon her work at the Hall, was the greatest torment for me. My dreams were full of her. I longed to put out a hand, to touch again her wondrous warmth, but dared not. Nor would she raise eyes to mine; though once, when our eyes met by chance, they told me again of her love. But that Christmas, just before Maud and Stephen's betrothal was announced, Kate, her womb still untouched, married Alan and moved into the smith's household. But in that passage of time, it became more pressing that I find a wife. Mother set Bors to help with the search, for my father had made but little inquiry. My life was to soon change. But a man's heart changes little, even over the years. A part of Kate stayed with me, soft and rosy. On shipboard, going to the Holy Land, it was her face and warm body that fed my mind. The first love of a man's life remains always, at the center of his soul. I can see Kate there yet today.

Chapter 6
A-Tourneying

As the flaming steeds of heaven drew the days of 1178 across the summer of our lives, I began to grasp the reins of Glororum more easily. It was a hot summer, which meant the haying went well. Now that manor custom was more on their side, the villeins grumbled a little less, and haying the children's meadow was a time of great merriment. Though we had lost Kate, we gained three more youngsters, two boys and another girl. I began to see a proud toss of heads when they told how they had worked with Squire John, who sharpened their scythes and brought them good ale with his own hands. Never did I regard work as just for simple men, nor the teaching of children for women and priest only. The new custom of the children's meadow was already as well-accepted a precedent as if generations old, and it sowed goodwill for the morrow.

The heat, however, worried me. Too little rain would mean a poor harvest, and we had many mouths to feed. Never were our stores abundant from year to year, and the wolf of famine lurked always beside the door. Sure as its omens, the summer continued, burning crops and meadows and withholding its rain. Barley and oats were scant, the peas small and dry, and the winter corn would make but half a crop. The waste was drying also, and the animals of the field found little pasture. Milk became scarce, hence the store of cheese was meager. Faced with the paltriness of winter rations, my mind began to cast for new ways to keep us.

Peter had two good destriers near trained. It broke my heart, but summer was tourney season, and I took them to Alnwick fair ere all the pastures of Northumberland became too dry. Men may covet a horse they think they can feed, but when they themselves face too little, no great shining beast can tempt them. We still had four mares in foal, and I pinned my hopes for a destrier to replace Brown Thunder to another year. The horses were our backbone of wealth; a good destrier then might cost a man as much in resource as an auto costs you today.

Lambs, too, were sold or soon eaten. Sheep were another cash crop, for the demesne as well as for the villeins. Northern wool was by far the finest, much in demand by the weavers of Flanders. Drought today cast the shadow of poverty for years to come. More to my heart, the animals of the forest also suffered. Even the wild swine, who dined on the mast of the great oaks, had but small litters, a bad sign. Meat would be scarce in winter, and the pease pottage scant.

The great accounting of all the stores of the farm took place every year at Michaelmas, at the end of September. Before that, mother wanted to visit Maud at Hutton. It was fair weather for travel, though hot. I worried along as we rode (young men worry more than those whom age has made wiser) but mother bade me to be of better cheer. "God never sends more than we can handle. If we but look, every travail ends in a birth. Something yet will come..." And so it did.

Stephen was anxious to show me his new game, coneys from the continent. In France, he said, hares multiplied in all the hedgerows and fed both lord and villein. His were yet enclosed, producing prodigious numbers of young, all busy jumping over one another and frolicking in the short grass. When we rode back north, it was with a gift of two pairs of the soft brown creatures. Mother was especially taken with the gentle does, and declared that we must set aside a piece of waste beside the pond for their new home. Indeed, I had the selfsame spot in mind. 'Twould only take small hurdles, woven of alder or willow, to keep them closed.

Another benevolence from Stephen was his promise to send Alfric the mason to me before spring. Alfric had become master mason during the building of the Galilee Chapel at Durham cathedral, initiated into the guild with all its secret arts. Bishop Hugh of Durham had sent him to work on Stephen's manor, as a wedding present. That work would soon be complete. It would mean an expenditure, but with the selling of the horses and the extra lambs, we could afford to finish the third floor of our west tower at last. Indeed, if I were to be married, it was pressing to do so. I had no wish to rout mother from her accustomed rooms on the second floor, though they, too, needed furbishing and repair.

So it was that we rode back toward sultry Bamburgh in a somewhat better frame of mind. But young men can play at farming only so long, and then the heart grows restless for war. I had taken to riding the march with Giles, usually once a fortnight if all was still; oftener, if outlaw bands were rumored to be about. We would ride north, to check the fish weirs and the mill at the weir-pond. Thence, we might turn west to Spindlestone and Belford, then south by west to the new farm that Chatta had established on the River Till.

More inn than farm, and more fortress than inn, Chatta and his wife and sons had built a wayside stop for those of us who needs must travel the long road north to Scotland. Just to the west of Chatta's, the way led into forest, yet untamed, thence up into the Cheviot hills. It was wild country then, full of wolves, some with four paws and some with but two. I greatly admired the landlord's courage in assarting a homestead in this inhospitable place, and stopped to check their welfare at least once a month, for the rest of my life. 'Twas not easy work, assarting, cutting back forest and grubbing out brush and heather to create pasture and plowland. I admired their courage, and helped in what small ways I might. Chatta was good to me too, passing on information about the road and its travelers that I could have gotten no other way.

Indeed, 'twas he who passed me the word that in mid-October, after all the manor accountings were done, and after the hot weather at last gave us forbearance, there was to be a grand tourney at Edinburgh castle. William the Lion had called all knights and valetti, and their squires, to a feast to celebrate the birthday of his wife, Ermengarde. My old enemy, Duncan, was castle-knight at Edinburgh. Our war as pages long behind us, we had often tourneyed as squires, side-by-side, along with David. We were a bold triumvirate. None of the knights or squires at Alnwick had been able to unhorse us in a melee. I foresaw that perhaps we might turn this old trick to our advantage. I knew not where David was; he had not found employment and was wandering in search of a settled berth, what later was termed a knight-errant. Truth to tell, 'twas also in a sense for adventure, for young men without lands are freer to seek the wiles of Fortuna.

I sent two men-at-arms (one alone was too much at risk through the forest) at once to Edinburgh, to seek out Duncan. They returned with the joyous news that I would be welcomed, and that David was already in the castle, armed and raging at the quintains. Mother bade me—I swear—a relieved farewell. Without a wife, and chafing under the tedium of the farm with all its problems, I ken I was becoming a bit of a bear. Not even the hunt seemed to cool my passions.

I bade Giles to redouble the marches, for with so many knights away, the rats were apt to play. I could not however, in good conscience, leave Sir Bors at home. He was eager for a fight, to renew old friendships, and remove himself from the tedium of the farm, just as I was. I think that from the time of that tourney, Bors at last became my friend. He took as squire, Carl, the son of one of our freemen, who was under our training. With him went also Crinan, a younger squire sent to us by my uncle, Sir Henry, for seasoning. At my back, I had my faithful Andrew. It behooved me to finish his education as squire, for none other could handle the horses as well as he. He had become passable at swordplay and better at quintains; the manners required of a knight were all that needed finishing. Truth to tell, I craved also to find once again that easy camaraderie we had held as boys.

The skies were bright and blue, with low-flung clouds racing in on the wind as we arrived. Banners fluttered and snapped on every tower and turret, and the smell of baking bread and roasting meat filled the air. It was a glorious time and a splendid reunion. David, Duncan, and I put heads together and decided to place Bors at the center of our small battle unit. He was pleased at this. Though slower than we younger men, he had enormous strength in his one good arm. Like my father before him, I would be his left hand. His horse, too, like my own Brown Thunder, was one of the sturdy destriers that Glororum produced, far outstripping many of the lean mounts of the border knights.

David and Duncan would be our outriders. After the center took the first shock, they would close quickly from the sides to sweep away any who remained unhorsed. Pulling quickly back, they would then lead the second wave into the maw of similar destruction. We had practiced often with three; the center was by far the most critical, requiring great strength and a sound horse. In Sir Bors, we found new strength, as well as giving us the patronage of a war-honed knight.

We did not rely, however, on plans scratched in the dust. The first morning after we arrived, long before most of the lazy knights had left the warmth of their sweethearts, we were in the field, a-practice. This was critical, since working with Bors was as yet an unknown to us. After some cursing and bumping and false starts, we began at last to work together. We then went to care for the horses, and feed ourselves. As supper was being assembled, we went out again, thinking it no great loss to miss a meal, if by so doing we might polish our skill as one precision fighting cadre.

During the night there was rain, blessed rain. While good for the country, it boded not well for the tourney, for the field would be slick and treacherous underfoot. King William, indeed, put off calling the opening until near ten o'clock. All who were to ride in the tourney paraded by the gallery, where William and his courtiers were gathered with their ladies, not only from the castle, but from miles around. Indeed, I looked hard at that fair gathering, but none I saw who were not spoken for or else pining for some great champion. David and Duncan each wore a sleeve as token; even Bors wore one from my mother, as sign of his respect. Alas, I felt naked, but with eagerness for the battle, saluted King William and my Uncle Henry, who sat near him, and all of that gay crowd of rustling laces and satins that adorned the ladies' gallery.

The first day was devoted to single combat. Only skillful knights, apt to be great champions, dared risk horse and armour and prestige upon the joust. There were a few older men, moneyed enough that the glory of single combat meant more than possible loss. More like, these were men like Sir Brian had been, seasoned and flushed with manhood. None took thought that he might be unhorsed or wounded. Though lances were dulled, men were sometimes crippled or even killed in our war-games. Yet for a poor knight, winning a joust meant taking the loser's war gear, or perhaps a money payment. It was worth the risk for a strong and desperate knight.

Of the knights in the combats the only one I knew was—surprise!—Sir Malwin. His fair Blanche had contrived to make him into another Brian, after all. He won his match handily, but through all the days of the tourney, I never saw him smile as before. I did see, for the first time, that he wore one of the new great helms in his combat. I later tried one on in the Edinburgh armory, and wondered how a man might fight in the accursed thing. I was to find out, in coming years.

Due to the shortness of the days, the melee was reserved for the morrow. First, there was a tourney, with two lines of opposing knights, such as is usual in battle. We joined in that tourney, though saving our greater strength for the melee. My uncle, Sir Kenneth, was one of those battle-knights of the line. He carefully chose for us a position on the south. (The field ran east to west, so that no man might have the sun in his eyes; still, in autumn great Sol tracked enough south to wish to keep him at our back.)

Kenneth kept us to the western end of the line. The greatest damage to man and horse was apt to be in the center, where the press was strongest. After much turning and wheeling, cat-calling and cursing, the two lines were formed, twenty to a side. Near instantly, the flags were raised, and the trumpets called. Never had I been in such a host of shouting men and thundering horses. Garth's training paid well, for I let not the tremendous noise and confusion divert me from the knight opposite. His shield loomed larger; I noticed near idly that his horse wanted to shy right. He carried a great black shield with no device, and my lance point held firm at its center. Just before we struck, Brownie turned left, into the other horse, which had shied right just enough to throw off the black knight's lance. It whispered across the front of my shield as my point went true to center. The force of the blow, with all Brown Thunder's charge behind it, threw the unfortunate knight over the high cantle of his saddle and laid him a-sprawl in the grass. As soon as I could turn, I saw that all was over. Far more remained horsed in our line than in the northern line, which had been commanded by one of King William's bastard sons, Sir Edward. I alighted softly beside my fallen adversary, to render what aid I might. He was greatly dazed, having had the wind knocked from him in the fall, but other than bruises and a pained back, he would well survive.

Bors had wisely refrained from the tourney, saving his strength for the melee. Duncan had also unhorsed his man, but David and his foe had simply grazed one another in passing. We were fortunate, for had one of us been hurt, the melee would not have gone well. The trumpets sounded again. Our line, under a great northern lord, Sir Killeen, filed by the royal gallery. William the Lion presented Killeen with a handsome dirk, on its pommel a great shining ruby. The rest of us received a small gift, shillings enough to pay for our trip, and more. I was pleased. Bread and meat and ale were brought to the field, and each man could eat his fill. After the repast, the melee would begin. The four of us gathered to look to horse and armour, and ate but lightly. We edged quietly to the south side of the field again; the lowering afternoon sun made it even more imperative. This time, we positioned ourselves in the center of the loose line that formed. The horses were quiet; they had quite forgotten their nerves after the first battle. Bors' old charger especially was too wise to waste energy fidgeting.

When the trumpets shouted, 'twas as before, except the noise more terrible, for now there were full thirty men to a side on the field. At the first shock, our little cadre held well. We had held the horses to a trot, and relied on skill with the lance to unseat our opponents, rather than the force of rushing horse. The mounts need must be saved, for much was yet to come. Three of the four who came at us fell; the other wheeled and gathered to him three more bold knights. Again they rushed, and again we swallowed them. Our first adversary, though still a-horse, was shaken, and he rode from the field. Again, rearing and wheeling, four more knights materialized from across the field. I could hear Bors whistling softly to himself; David was laughing, but Duncan as usual was silent. Of a sudden, we all knew that the confidence we had going into the melee would be justified. We would take the day.

The next four thundered by, one wheeling away to avoid Duncan's lance, one hit hard but not unhorsed, and two fallen upon the sod. We slowed, wheeled around as one, and quietly awaited the outcome. Only five knights were left upon the field; all had overcome more than one knight. It was plain that they intended to charge us *en masse*. This was to be a trial indeed! We settled our lances and began our rush, not holding back this time. Bors and I were in front, and we took a great shock. Both our opponents were unhorsed, but though their lance blows had not hit entirely true, we had both been spun in our seats and suffered a tremendous impact. Indeed, Bors would have fallen, had I not reached out to him. David and Duncan, a half-length behind, had done the same for their foes, though one stayed a- seat and spurred back to meet the fifth knight, who waited but a little behind. They sensed blood now, as Bors was still reeling. On they rushed, at us in the center; then, most marvelous, David and Duncan came from behind us to close with them. We stopped our mounts instantly. In confusion, our foes swung their lances, but neither could hit true. Our nimble destriers jumped aside, letting them pass as they fell, while David and Duncan wheeled away to either side as the last two knights tumbled from their saddles.

All of us were twisted and bruised, and the horses lathered. But from the gallery we heard cries and hoorahs, and the sounding of trumpets. Surprised at our wholeness, but not at the victory, we rode slowly to the gallery where King William waited. Slowly also, we unhelmed and awaited his words.

"Never have I seen such cunning and war-skill," William began. "You four have taken the day, well and truly. What are your names, and to what house do you belong?"

Duncan replied first, that he was castle-knight at Edinburgh and had trained at Alnwick when William was still there. David then said the same, except he made bold to say he was looking for a worthy lord to serve. The Lion nodded. I told him I was John Forestrius of the berwick at Bamburgh known as Glororum, then also reminded him of my days at Alnwick. I always felt somewhat outlaw, held in fief to English Henry among my Scots neighbors. Bors, too, introduced himself as of Glororum, but could add, "knighted in Wales in '63."

King William stood, musing for just a moment. "I might have known. The squires who defeated Sir Brian—I see you still have your wits about you! And, you sir," he turned to Bors, "have fought better than many a man who entered the lists whole in strength." I approved of his accolade for Bors, but who would have thought he would still remember David's and mine youthful prank? Amused, he must have read my face. "Yes, Cock-o'-the-woods, and I remember well the time you near drowned poor Duncan here, too. It is meet that a man should come to unity with those with whom he fights. We are all blood and bone and bowel underneath, after all. To you four goes the honor of the day. Where it is usual for the victor of the melee to receive one silver mark, you each shall have one. Indeed, I might donate two to you, John, if you could tell me how you started the fire that day!" He looked at me and laughed, but I could only smile and shake my head. "Ah, well. But David and Duncan, I need men like you in my personal guard. Strong arms there are a-plenty, but clever heads are, alas, too few. If you join me, we will have a ceremony of adubment at Midsummer next. What say you?"

It is hard to say who was more overjoyed, David and Duncan, or myself. I could not have wished better for my friends. Indeed, they humbly thanked William and entered his service that very day. I went to their adubment on Midsummer day of 1179, as happy at their good fortune as if it were my own.

The day following was one for binding up of wounds, salving bruises, and preparing for the great feast that would end the tourney. So, too, was it a time to renew old acquaintance, and though I spent part of the day visiting friends and paying respect to Uncle Henry and his family, the best part was spent with Sir Kenneth. His flaming head was already a-graying, but his remarkable voice had weakened not a whit. By late afternoon, we had already surrendered our dignity to Lady Wine. He told me of his marriage, and things of women I would need to know when wed. His goodwife, while jolly and easy in bed, had no desire for children, nor had she any from her first marriage. That was beyond my ken, for the Forsters always felt succession to the land was our greatest responsibility. Yet, Kenneth confided in me, he had a son by a villein woman, by name of Robin. The lad was a sturdy four, and soon would need his schooling. Would I take him on when he became of age? I replied that

I would be honored, regardless of his blood. Was not the great King William, who conquered all England, the bastard son of a tanner's daughter? So it was settled, and time would prove the fortuitousness of that decision. Between such solemn talk, we sang together every maudlin and bawdy song we knew, till men came at last, laughing, to pour water on our heads so that we would be fit for the evening's honours.

The feast that marked the end of the tourney was a wonder to behold. Verily, it delighted my heart for long years after, especially during the war. When a man is on an arduous campaign with little between belly and backbone, sumptuous feasts remembered or contrived are often all that keeps the will alive. And William the Lion's feast was sumptuous indeed! It was all the greater for that David, Duncan, Bors, and I were honored to sit at the King's table, along with Sir Killeen and the champions of the first day's jousts. Queen Ermengarde, whose birthday feast it was, sat in the place of honour. The only other women were Sir Killeen's wife, and the wives of the six champions, resplendent in satin and fur. Now, you must understand that this table, set on a dais, received the choicest of the victuals, many reserved for the King's table alone. So while the boards groaned for all, the high table rumbled especially sweetly.

Behind us was a wondrous tapestry of the Garden of Eden, resplendent with lions and tigers and many strange animals; with curious birds and great exotic flowers. With the afternoon wine still warm in my head, it seemed to enfold me like a vision of paradise. We were all laved by our squires with perfumed water and clean napery, and duly the victuals were prayed for by the King's chaplain. Sweetly, then, came the pipes playing, the players like satyrs dressed, and with them came the soup. A delicate soup, with cherries and cinnamon, served with wafers of herbs; it cleared the head and honed the appetite. Next came an enormous salmon, seethed and gilt with silver. Parsley he trailed like seaweed, and he swam in a sea of pureed leeks, colored blue-green. Maidens accompanied him, with lutes trailing notes like water, and voices plaintive as those of the sea- people.

The end of this first course was marked by the maw-money, which was always brought to wish prosperity to the host. It was white capon boiled in almond milk, thickened with egg and bread crumbs, lightly seasoned with spice, and covered with almonds fried in butter. Mawmoney was always colored yellow with saffron to signify gold, and formed into rounds like coins. With the mawmoney came a huge golden lion, made all of bread, also colored yellow, and glazed. His fearsome teeth were of marzipan, and the eyes held real gems. When carved, the King and Queen each received a jewel, wondrously shining and marked like a great cat's-eye. My portion was one of the paws, and belike it was sweeter in the mouth than one from any real lion.

Next was a short play by mummers, with St. George slaying a huge red dragon, who slithered around the floor on ten silken feet, breathing smoke and bellowing with fearsome noises. Satan himself came leading him, and the imps of sin cavorted and tumbled about. Sir George and his marvelous horse, which stamped and pranced in a most unequine way, chased away the imps. Whilst St. George fought the dragon, his white destrier kicked and bit at Satan, until he, too, was driven away. All went as expected, with God's forces triumphant, and the servers brought in the main course right on the heels of the expiring dragon.

Before each two of us was set down a roast suckling pig, wreathed in baked apples and surrounded by roasted small fowl. With it came small loaves, made pink and toothsome with rose petals. King William and his wife had a larger pig to themselves, which when carved was found to contain a cock, which when carved was found to hold a lark with gilded feet and beak. Their loaf was formed like a summer rose, at its center, a golden heart of butter. Minstrels played softly, for this was the *piece de resistance*, which all soon set about enjoying.

After the main course was a pageant of dancers. I sat, near transported, as women dressed as water kelpies, those fearsome spirits that tempt men to drowning, glided and shimmered across the floor, their pale silken dresses moving like the very waves of Budle Bay. Acrobats, then, played among them, as fishermen and sailors might, rowing their boats, and listening to the murmuring that arose from the waves. One sailor, deep in his cups, fell from his pretend ship and was enveloped by the "waves," never to be seen again. I ken not how they did that! When all had drifted out the door, a great swan was brought in honor of Queen Ermengarde. Made of marzipan and sugar and spices, every feather glistened as if newly wet. So real it looked, that only tasting let me know of what it had been so cleverly crafted. Around its neck was a golden chain, set with a great blue stone—a gift from William—that exactly matched the Queen's eyes. All had a taste of that fabulous bird ere the third course was brought.

With much trumpet fanfare, a great pie was set before the royal pair. Its sides had been cut to resemble the castle walls, and the banners of both King and Queen flew atop its savory mince. When our own pastry was brought, I found it to be an excellent mince, tender beef with suet, tempered well with oranges in sugar, apples and pears, and raisins of Corinth. Spiced with ginger and cinnamon and boiled in wine, the toothsome beef still held sway. Never again have I had mince as well assembled; and you know how fond I remain of it.

With the mince was served Queen Ermengarde's favorite frumenty. This was very light, white wheat boiled in milk and thickened with egg, much adorned with sugar and mace and almonds. It made a fine counterpoint to the richer mince. All the while, lute and psalter and flute played delicate airs, to help the digestion. When we sat groaning, unable to stuff another morsel into our mouths, the minstrels were called and the hippocras wine was passed. King William called a toast to his fair Queen, and to the great land of the Scots, to which we owed such plenty. Then the bards began a frolic of roistering songs. The hippocras made its rounds again along with sweet wafers baked with cheese and honey. Ere long all were singing noisily enough to drown out the minstrels. William, however, at last signaled for towel and basin, and when he rose, we rose with him, willy-nilly. As the royal house made its stately way from the dining hall, most of us fell in behind. Next morning we would be sore of head and gut, but on this night, at the high table of the King, we were honoured as never before or since.

Chapter 7

Marriage in the Making

Red poppies sprinkled the fields of greening grain in spring, but still the growth was scant. On Mother's advice—for she had seen these lean years before—we had planted half rye instead of all the wheat, since rye stands more drought. Through the mud of spring it came, sucking vigourously at the earth from which it would so soon be weaned by summer's heat. By this time, none of us had meat, neither lord nor peasant. Even the peas had gone, and oat gruel was our constant diet. Women and children dug endlessly for cockles and mussels at the shore, some of which I traded for, for our table at Old Hall. Perhaps once a month I killed a deer from the forest, but pressure on the wild game could not become too severe, lest their numbers decrease beyond recovery. Our woods, after all, were not extensive. There was no need to admonish us to fast for Lent, and the salt fish I bought to extend our diet was dear.

With Lent came also Alfric and his wife, Jene, both uncomplaining of the hardship. Even the rich Bishop of Durham found himself in straitened circumstance due to the drought. We still had barley enough for ale, though since before Christmas I had ordered it watered. Christmas itself went well, as I had specially held back one ox so that we might have our traditional feast. All the farm—cottars, labourers, villeins, and house servants, as well as our knights and men-at-arms—were party to the Christmas feasting. We knew there would be little enough to eat in the months ahead, more reason not to skimp on the great feast of our Lord's birthday.

All accepted these trying times as God's will. We had been through them before, and would do so again. There was little any lord could do to keep hunger from eventually knocking upon the door when times and tides turned the weather to mischief.

I was surprised that Jene accompanied Alfric and me as we inspected Old Hall and the New Tower. She seemed as knowing as he of details needed to bring the building to full strength and usefulness. At that point, I was not concerned to make a showplace, only to provide quarters for myself and a wife, and to keep the place from tumbling down about our ears. We should not have had the money to do otherwise, even had I so wished. But Alfric was agreeable to so small a commission; he had work elsewhere when our tower was finished. They agreed that the undercroft looked sound, and that water had damaged the masonry of the tower stair which would need repair. Also, a new stair needs be built to the third floor, where our rooms would be. "Even a rat builds a back entrance to his burrow," Jene had said. One stairway into living quarters was a danger in case of fire.

I can see them today, as we sat at table, conning our plans. Alfric, slight and white of hair, always sat quietly, head in hand. Only once in a while would his scarred face liven, and he would disagree vigourously with what was being said. Jene did most of his talking, turning the possibilities 'round and 'round. She disdained wearing a wimple or head cloth; her brown curly hair bobbed as she made this point or that. Stocky of build she was, and I soon found that she was strong as a man, though poor-sighted and apt to squint disconcertingly. Alfric was the true technician, though. In other times, he would find his cunning caught up in mending marvelous instruments, with Jene still faithfully at his side.

The first thing we did was measure the great empty space of the unfinished floor. Jene told me we had seventeen by seventeen feet, plus a smaller space on the south side, on the other side of the new stair. There was only one place for that stairway to go; up and out of the minstrel's gallery. None of us were happy about that, but we could ken nothing else. The second floor, where my mother's rooms were, was already built up. Only major removal would give us a stair in any other place. That second-floor plan was itself dependent on the placement of the ground-floor supports beneath it. Only in the undercroft was a stable beginning.

Up and down stairs we tramped, over and over. When at last we arrived at the decision of the stairway, all else fell into place. An anteroom had to be provided in the southwest corner, where the old circular stair to the roof lay. This would give a place for servants to come and go, and to bide on watches. There was a similar anteroom on the second floor, and a guard room and chapel on the south side of the ground floor. A small fireplace in the new anteroom, said Jene, could be easily vented to the roof, and provide coals for our braziers on winter nights. This new fireplace would be above the garderobes—the privies—on the floor below, and adjacent to the servant's narrow stair. The grand new stairway would end in a short hall into the anteroom, dividing the remaining third-floor space into the large area on the north, and a small room perhaps ten feet wide in the southeast corner.

Good, I said, haughtily, seventeen square will be enough room for myself and wife. Leave the small room for a nursery; there is bound to be a child. Jene protested. "But you must have room for a nurse; caring for a child requires constant care." I shook my head, lost in some vision of a perfect wife and mother who could manage a child in that tiny room, and still care for my every whim, lolling in comfort in a room fit for the king's castle.

Alfric exploded my dreams. "Even so, that the small room may be used for a child. A man, as he comes to his senses soon after marriage, requires a place of his own, away from whining wife and mewling babe and fussing nurse. You think now to chase her around your apartment in constant games of love. Believe me, you will change your mind."

I hit ground with a thump after my flight of fancy. I had been guilty of those very imaginings! Of course, real life would be different. I agreed to a division into two apartments, one sheltered on the east, and one facing the mountains to the west, which would be my own. How glad I was in later years for Alfric's wisdom! I only wish he hadn't been so prophetic.

It was Sir Giles who at last found me a wife, for which in later years I was wont to curse the poor man's memory. He had been patrolling to the south—not a usual march, but there had been rumours of a covert outlaw band working through the area from Brunton Mill to Ditchend. I set Sir Bors to watching the forests, along with our sergeants. Giles was making survey, to find which of our neighbors had suffered losses, and if anything might be known of the gang. When he stopped at Ellingham to visit with Sir Randolph de Guagy, he found the household in an uproar.

Randolph's wife, Agnes, had been deceased for many years, since the birth of their son, Hugh. Hugh was now a page at Alnwick, but, indeed, I had no ken of him before we visited Ellingham. He was a thin, pale boy, marked all his life by an air of helplessness and careless indifference. I wondered if his mother had not been the same, as I saw the woman in him. Sir Randolph himself was not a neighbor with whom we normally had dealings. A strong, red-faced man, he was given to drink and bluster and little else. His demesne was woefully mismanaged; he had not been able to keep a steward who would put up with his drunken rages. Sober, he was cheerful and of good wit; drinking, he was apt to be a fiend from Hell. Still, Giles stopped on the outside chance the man would be sober, which indeed he was. The house servants were turning to in frenzy, trying to tidy up the pigsty that was Ellingham Hall. Unbeknownst to most of us, Agnes had also had a daughter, some four years older than Hugh. She had been named for Randolph's haughty Norman mother, Herleve.

As time came for Agnes' childbed with Hugh, she must have had some premonition of disaster. She sent her four-year-old daughter, under escort, to her sister at Poitou. There the girl was raised until the sister herself died when Herleve was eleven. An uncle had been sent to Ellingham to consult the girl's fate with her father. Randolph, according to rumour, had at that time a whore in the house, and the uncle was extremely displeased. He convinced Randolph that Herleve would severely cramp his lifestyle, and should be sent to a nunnery until more mature. Randolph reluctantly parted with the money; his comfortable Norman inheritance was crumbling away into the seas of his drunkenness.

As with most of our well-placed families, the de Guagy's had once been Norman nobility, and their lands at Ellingham were extensive. Granted by King William after 1086, the de Guagy demesne, or home farm, had been much more extensive than at Glororum, and their villeinage alone ran to over thirty virgates, with as much more in waste and forest. They retained ties to the continent, and the family enjoyed the favors of the church, which added to their power. One of the de Guagy's was Bishop of Chartres, and cozened the ear of the pope.

Then, as now, politics bestowed power and privilege. A grant of land was made for a church at Ellingham, and Sir Randolph's father, also Randolph, became benefactor of the new church of St. Maurice built there. Truth to tell, the tithes of the local peasants all went to the new church instead of Rome, with some left over for the de Guagy pocket. As often happens, a strong father built up the estate for a weak son to destroy. Herleve's father had never shown inclination for either farming or politics. He was like the reivers of old, a strong warrior with little wit except for war and rousting. In that, he was like his grandfather who had ridden north with William, burning the land and slaying thane and peasant alike as if 'twere sport.

Herleve was more like her grandfather than any of the living de Guagy's. Had she been a male child, who knows what grandeur might have returned to Ellingham Hall? Instead, she received her share only in wit and arrogance, and her life became one of frustration and rage. In the end, I truly believe her woman's mind became slowly consumed by that rage.

At age sixteen, Herleve had to take the vows of the convent, or return to secular life. Randolph could have been persuaded either way; either way, Herleve would cost him money. But it was decided for him when a letter from the Mother Superior came, stating that Herleve, while pious enough, had no real vocation as a nun. Willy-nilly, she was being shipped home to her father.

It took much inquiry and some little prying to discover this much of the secrets of the de Guagy's. Other, darker rumours are best left untold. Both Giles and Bors spent much time ferreting out the story of Ellingham; Randolph himself was undiscerning of the truth much of the time. The one overweening concern of Herleve's father was to marry her off to a sound knight of the neighborhood, of good blood and better-than-average management skills. When Giles mentioned that my lady mother had been looking for a suitable bride for me, Randolph pricked up like a pickpocket on Fair day.

He lost no time sending a messenger, saying he would like to come to call. Mother put him off a bit, while we gathered what information we could. Cooling his heels only made him more eager. When finally he rode up to Old Hall, Randolph looked about him with undisguised satisfaction. Despite the drought and the sorry state of the pastures, Glororum looked like Paradise beside his own neglected estate.

Randolph also lost no time tendering an offer; 'twas plain that the girl meant nothing to him save as an investment with which to buy more time for his dissolution. I felt sorry for the poor baggage. Mother put him off with feigned indecision; such bargains are not to be rushed into.

Later, we called the household together to discuss the situation. Neither Giles nor Bors were impressed by the de Guagy name or situation. Giles, however, who had seen the maid, said she was slender and fair, with both russet hair and eyes, and rosy cheeks. I could imagine her then, and my heart burned within me. Mother was dubious, but no other lass was in the offing. "Perhaps," she said, "we might make a bargain of this marriage, John, if you are willing. God knows we need money, what with the drought and house-building following so soon on Maud's dowry and the heriot. But you must be satisfied; marriage is for a very long time."

Father Cedric, surprisingly, was the only one who spoke out strongly against the union. "'Tis true that she has good Norman blood, but it is tainted. There was dark sin in that household ere her mother died, and dark sin afterward. The Word of God holds that those whom God hates, He will hate for generations, for the sin they carry is in the blood. Mark my words, the burden you will bring to the Forster blood with that maid will bring sorrow unto your own generations."

His words sobered us mightily. Once again, we racked our brains to think of someone else suitable. Yet after two weeks, no inspiration had come, and courtesy demanded that some kind of answer be made to Sir Randolph. Mother asked me once again in private, but I was growing testy. Brutally, I answered. "If I have not a suitable woman soon, I ken not what my body may drive me to. 'Tis well for priests and old people to cry caution; they have long forgotten how younger blood surges and cannot be denied for aye. I care not if she be witch or whore; I need a wife." How I was to regret those words in time!

Mother made the best of a bad thing. She herself went with Bors to meet the lady, and found her manners impeccable, if haughty. With shrewd northern cunning, she let Bors make the arrangements, knowing that Sir Randolph would treat her own efforts with nothing but contempt. In the end, it was decided that until Hugh came of age, I was to manage Ellingham as my own. All profits would accrue to our household, in the name of Herleve, as my wife, but she was to have no actual share in the land. In exchange, Randolph would receive a small annual rent, dependent on the productivity of the farm. This last was because we had estimated that it would take at least five years for the land to begin to be fertile again, after its years of neglect. When Hugh was twenty-one, he would take title to the demesne of Ellingham, less twenty virgates and one fishery, which would remain with the Forsters. Ten of the virgates were in villeinage, that is, under cultivation by the Ellingham peasants; and ten were in waste, pasture and woods. This was not so much dowry as it was repayment for restoring the estate. There was little enough for dowry; the drought had reduced their livestock as it had ours. Though their villeins were accustomed to pay merchet, that is, a marriage-price assessed upon the tenants, still, where there was nothing to begin with, nothing much could be expected. Sir Randolph had all but drunk his land dry. Just enough was left for Bors to obtain a cash payment, which would pay for a small wedding and one year's wages for Herleve's handmaid.

In the end, the settlement left some cash in Sir Randolph's coffers, bargained against what future profits the land might hold. It would be up to me to make of it what I could. Such pacts can only be made with youth and enthusiasm; I would need all I could find of both. Herleve's personal inheritance proved quite small, some jewelry of her mother's, and a tenth of the profits from the estate of Ellingham for as long as she should live. I felt sorry for her and would have liked to see her better placed, but as in the case of my sister, Mother's shrewd negotiations held great wisdom for my future.

In truth, pity and passion are poor bedfellows to bring into a new marriage. Herleve, on her part, was to bring to Glororum a life-long insecurity and a guilt for worldly sins (imagined or otherwise) that the nuns had told her could be expiated only by spending hours upon her knees in chapel.

There would be no patience born of love and respect for one another in our alliance, as there had been for my parents. There would only be the lonely struggle against destiny by two people separated by marriage.

Our wedding date was set for three weeks after Michaelmas, in October of 1179, just before the anniversary of William's death. It was not an auspicious time. Annie, when the news had been bruited about, came to find me one day, in the stables. "I bring you merchet for your wedding," she began, "so that neither mother nor I should have to pay more."

"I will take merchet from you in prophecy," I replied, "but I cannot excuse your mother." Annie was just agitated enough that I was sure she would tell me her vision if I but stuck to my resolve. Finally, she gave in. Rocking back on her heels, our seeress began a rambling chant. "The woman brings with her sons, but poison enters the blood thereby. With a bird, she will fly away young, and unsainted she will lie." Opening her eyes, Annie looked around the stable in wonder. "You are lucky. You will find much happiness here."

Methought it little enough she had said, but I had already forgiven the merchet. Later, I wrote her words, and found they ran deeper than the shallow pool they appeared to be on surface. Some, of course, I never kenned. Only after generations, looking back at the seed that was sowed in the Forster line with Herleve, could I see the poison of alcoholism trailing from her father into our own blood. But Fate decreed our marriage, I swear; looking back, I ken not how I might have escaped it.

Summer wore on, with just enough rain to bring us half-crops once again. The old people all swore that drought years come in three; the dryness would only begin to abate with the coming year. And so it was. This second year was the worst, as the live chattels were sold down as far as they could go. We did have a good run of fish, however; they were salted and smoked for winter, when they would be much welcomed. And the lively little hares became a problem.

At manor court in May, I listened to angry villeins complaining how the hungry creatures, long ago 'scaped from beneath their hurdles, were eating gardens and crops. Their burrows also held danger, especially for the horses. A new precedent needs be set. At last, after talking with Richard, the reeve, who brought me the demands of the curia, I set the law for Glororum. No villein might poach coneys upon the sheep pasture or in the forests, for those belonged to the family. However, in hedgerows or garden, or upon the villeins' own holdings, the hares might be trapped at will and used for food. In the horse pasture, however, the hares must be run down while no animals were upon the land. There could be no traps, nor any running of the horses. From scourge, the coneys turned out to be a welcome source of meat and, had they not been protected in the forest and sheep pasture, would have disappeared altogether; such was the hunger of the labourers.

By August the new rooms in the Tower were completed. Had not the summer's work intervened, it might have been sooner. Our craftsmen were those of the farm, except for a pair of masons who came up from Durham for three months to do the stonework. They left the day after my twentieth birthday, in 1179, and our local carpenter finished the woodwork. Jene bossed all the labourers impartially, but none of the men resented her, for she had a fine knack of turning a jest upon herself as easily as upon another. Alfric hummed after them all, correcting where needed, and setting up their references from lore buried in his head. In all, it was a splendid job that served through several lifetimes of Forsters.

The adubment ceremony for David and Duncan at Edinburgh was a welcome respite in midsummer. William held a small tourney on the afternoon after the ceremony, and again, I made a pittance toward my expenses. The hospitality of the castle was strained, however, in this second year of drought. Though David and Duncan and three other lads had their feast, 'twas a more solemn gathering. It was in the power of kings to knight worthy men, even when they had not been yet to war. Usually, they were the king's own guard, but perchance there might be a Holy Mary knight, whose father had enough money to pay for the ceremony. There were none this year. The five new knights were all members of William's own household, as alike as peas in a pod. They were bathed by the older knights, and sent to spend the night in church, praying; perhaps repenting of past sins or looking forward to others.

After Mass, we broke our fast with a modest repast of smoked fish, bread, and ale. When hands were washed and the napery all removed, King William began by calling each man's name. Each candidate then left his place at the board, walked to the throne, and knelt. William laid his right hand on the young knight's head, and put the royal dirk against his neck. This signified the loyalty and courage required of a knight. Placing his hands between those of his king, each new knight swore fealty to the crown of Scotland.

The lads then stood a-row upon the dais and were dressed by their own squires with sword and belt and, lastly, spurs. 'Twas the spurs that more than anything signified their knighthood, men armed and trained to fight on horseback, above the plebeian foot soldiers. More than all else, knighthood signified those whose blood and training made them worthy stewards of the land, keenly aware of their code of honour and their place in the great chain of life. 'Twas a simple ceremony, withal, but how I envied my friends on that day!

After the tourney, and the night's feasting on venison and kid, it was a late start we made toward home on the morrow. Julian, my man at arms, with young Crinan the squire, held back to let me dream along the road in peace. Now that the wife business was almost settled, nothing seemed as pressing as earning my own spurs at last. God save me, 'twas well I could not see how far in the future that would be!

Chapter 8

Ripened Fruit

Mother was clearly exasperated at me. "It is not meet for Andrew to be your groomsman. Mayhap he is your friend, but Sir Randolph would consider his inclusion as a slap in the face. I beg you, do not throw down the gauntlet before your father-in-law, though he be a wicked old man."

It was hot, the crops were burning, an outlaw gang was harrying the countryside, and I was being tested as to my resolve. Rarely did I quarrel with mother, but neither did I wish to lose another battle, no matter how small. Silence aided my composure, but at last I explained again, as if to a child: "I stood for Andrew when he married Margaret, the maid of Alnwick. I promised that he should do the same for me." On our trip to Alnwick Fair to sell the horses the year before, Andrew had tumbled for the younger daughter of our innkeeper. It took little to arrange the marriage, for both were free and unencumbered by many chattels. Indeed, Peter was glad to have a daughter-in-law in their erstwhile womanless cottage. The young couple made a loving pair—Andrew, tall and slim, dark of hair with grey eyes, and Margaret, short and busy, like a little brown hen. Salt-of-the-earth, these were people who savored their land and loyalty. One could not help but love them both.

Margaret's family was large; hard work had been their constant companion. Peter, his hands full with the horses, scarce had time to farm his half-virgate; nor was it any help for Andrew to be following me as squire when his land was so often needy. Margaret had been a godsend. Mother seemed to be following my uneasy thoughts. "Why you insist on raising that young man into nobility, I do not know. He would be happy as a yeoman, tending his fields, and helping Peter with the horses. Nor do I know how Peter manages so well without him."

What she said was true, but pricked to the surface by my own feeling of guilt was a deep persuasion that yeoman and gentry were one. I had seen enough of the barriers that men's bloodlines and virgates set between them, and I told her so. "Besides," I added, "I love Andrew like a brother."

"So I had remarked," she said dryly. "But mark my words, you will regret it if you push this insult onto the de Guagy family. Andrew is but a yeoman, after all, no matter how you exalt him."

I was fair angry then, for I knew her to be right, but would not back down from my principle. "I shall live to see him knighted," I stormed, "and the de Guagys in Hell!"

Mother looked at me keenly. "Be careful for what you wish, my brash son. Someday it may come true, to your sorrow." She swept then from the room, leaving me fuming. It was not just Andrew; it was a growing feeling that our lives were simply pawns upon a board. I wanted better, and I wanted it now. Knight training empowers a man, or so we had been told. I had not yet learned that we crawl about upon the silken web of our days, flies trapped by our times and ways, subject to the invisible hand of God. Older people learn that to struggle is futile, that one can only move slowly from strand to strand as the opportunity arises; and they become happier thereby.

Andrew himself brought good common sense to aid my quandary. Though his wont was to speak little and follow resolutely, he made shift to tell me nay. "'Tis not meet that I should be your groomsman, though you do me much honour by asking. Your friend David, new-knighted, would bring greater distinction to you and your bride. I should be happy to simply guard the church door on your behalf."

So it was done. I sent messengers to David, and to Duncan, who also agreed to be door-guard. Bors and Giles would be included in the guard of honour as we left the church. Father Cedric declined to marry us, but the Augustinian prior, Gulfrid, then at Bamburgh, agreed to sing a Mass and to bless our union. It was but a matter of weeks after that, Gulfrid turned frail, sickened, and died, as if eaten away by worms. Father Cedric, that most practical of priests, only shook his head. He preached the prior's funeral Mass, then blessed the old stone church and all of us who stood in it, paying our last respects. Herleve did not accompany us.

Poor Herleve had neither relative nor friend to stand for her at our wedding. Her only confidant was her handmaiden, Nicolette, who was also a castaway daughter, of an impoverished knight. Both Mother and Maud offered to stand as bridesmaid, but Herleve refused them with scorn. It was as if she envied us our family, and wanted to show she needed none of that. Nicolette would do. What, I wondered, were we to make of it? Should we have been insulted, as mother said Sir Randolph would be over Andrew? Still, in pity, I saw no other way, else the doleful bride be without comfort at the altar.

In early September, we had ridden to Ellingham, that I might meet my promised wife whilst final arrangements were made. It was great excitement for me, to come face-to-face with Herleve at last. I made up a little song, something I had not had time for in a while, and practiced it while riding south the league or so. Bors, who rode along with mother and me, laughed and told me it sounded like the trumpeting of a love-sick swan. "O, summer rose," I sang "come sweetly scent the air. Treads my lady unto thy bower, fair unto the fair. Your golden heart her own heart will ensnare; with love in hand, I'll meet her there." 'Twas but a small ditty, but it satisfied my heart on the journey.

I never had the opportunity to sing my song—foolish lad—for all our time was taken with formal speech and I had but a moment alone with the girl, when we parted. She pulled the veil of her cap shyly across her face then, but I caught a glimpse—almost of terror—in her eyes. 'Twas only for a moment, then she wished me a cold farewell and Godspeed on the journey home. Fair she was, as Giles had promised, with skin like milk and strong locks of hair, colored like autumn apples, curling out from beneath her pointed cap. Her eyes were a curious brown, more near like rust than honey. She spoke in French, which gave me struggle, but her breath was sweet as April meadows. I was satisfied to await our wedding.

Sir Randolph had not proven the ogre I expected, simply another old knight, grown coarse with advancing age, the way some old boars coarsen. Yet his speech was courteous, and it was only riding through his ruinous estate that I could believe all the stories about him were true. Even Ellingham Hall was tumbling down from neglect. I would be glad to rescue the maid from this misery; but when I had whispered this unto her, she bridled like a skittish horse and shook her head. Nought else was said, but I felt my blunder keenly. Riding home, I wondered mightily just what all this might portend. I was soon to find out.

Truth to tell, I can remember little of our wedding in October, or the succeeding days, the way a man often cannot remember battles or embarrassment. By God, I believe it was both! I was gentle with my bride, or so I tried; but she was fickle of mood, sometimes running away and crying, other times attacking my manhood in a fervor born of anger. 'Twas then I learned that only in subduing her by strength did she become meek and satisfied. And we spent much time hawking, for she had a splendid goshawk. To set it working was her greatest joy in life; indeed, she would do little else unless constrained. As a wedding present, I arranged for her to receive a young peregrine, an eyas, to train. These were oft known as priest's birds, as they took much time and cossetting. Also, I presented her with a gentle hound, pied in colour, to retrieve her game.

With palfrey and dog, bird upon her wrist, Herleve was happiest. When I could spare the time to accompany her, she seemed glad of my presence, too. At Old Hall, though, she was most often sullen and silent, or cursing the house servants. It was a wonder where she had learned to curse so, until later I heard her father, deep in his cups, berating his servants with the self-same words.

Just such an incident, the week before Christmas, began a pattern that would abide between us for years. Mother had kept much to herself, attempting only upon occasion to teach Herleve the routines of the household. Near always she was rebuffed, as Herleve was set upon her own courses, her own times. Mother had a seamstress, a widow of the village with three mouths at home to feed. The poor woman toiled unceasingly in the making of our serviceable but plain garments, often straining her eyes by firelight to finish a piece when needed. Herleve had decided that she needed a new dress for Christmas, but was put out when she found that we had no suitable cloth. She never wore any colors but russet or brown. By the time the cloth was ordered and sent, there was too little time before Christmas for the gown to be finished, even had Ingrid worked day and night.

Herleve might have had it by Twelfth Night, had she any patience. Instead, she entered the room one evening as the seamstress was leaving for home to tend her bairns. Mother had brought Ingrid some extra bread from the day's baking, for the poor woman's efforts had been all for us, with little thought for her own family. Herleve became a shrew, cursing both Ingrid and, worse, cursing my mother, in her own home. That insult was more than any decent woman should bear, and rankled me beyond measure when I heard of it. Heretofore I had stayed out of the household quarrels, holding that the good common sense of our people would recognize that my wife was simply high-strung, as the French often are.

I can still see Herleve as she was on that winter's day when I found her in the Hall and approached her, for the first time, as a husband to be obeyed and a Christian to be respected. Both concepts most often seemed foreign to her nature. Sternly, I demanded her apology to mother. I required that she learn sympathy for our household help, and spend time learning the routines of the house. I threatened, as one might a child, to take from her bird and horse and dog, until she made amends.

She turned then, almost as if fleeing from me. Her gown of russet velvet trimmed with white fur flowed behind her as she moved away, flinching. I can still see the colors, her beautiful ashen face. It annoyed me, even as I was heartsick. As if I would lay a hand upon her! "Leave me," she shrilled, "I shall control what I will in this household. And touch me not, thou coarse hound of a bastard Englishman!"

Furious, I tried to reason. "We must talk. You must understand what being a mistress entails. You must learn proper ways..."

She looked back at me then, with a countenance I shall never forget: white, haughty, frozen. "I have only *my* way," she said; then added, "and that is the way of *my* family." Angry, fear-ridden, near mad, she screamed for her horse and rode off, though dusk was falling. It was not my first brush with her unreason, but this was a defeat that marked my soul. What man, who needs must beget sons to hold his land and lifework for the coming generations, can do so with such an unwilling wife? What home can maintain itself with an angry, hate-filled mistress?

Grey-faced, my mother stepped from the shadows into the hall. "It is not good for girls to be raised by nuns. They have no ken of life as we must live it. But 'tis no wonder the Mother Superior said Herleve had no vocation. She is haughty and rebellious, and takes no heed of any but her own unthinking counsels. Albeit, she must learn that Glororum is too large a stake to waste on the whims of a petty girl."

"Mother, my heart is saddened over that piteous damsel, but somehow she nourishes no affection, save such as a wild animal might hold. There is no sense of 'other' to rouse her to pity or love. There is only a blackness that turns her into her own heart and eats away at her soul; and she pulls anger around her like a cloak to hide it." I spoke slowly, finding words for thoughts which had dared emerge for the first time.

"May the mercy of God not remain an unknown country to your wife! Still, I rue the day we decided to make her your bride." Mother seemed torn between sympathy for a fellow woman, so hurt by life's reality, and by our own plight. Unspoken, the issue of an heir lay between us. She sighed. "You have known her. She may have conceived, even if unwillingly. And you must ride forth to speak again with her father, and pray he not be too deep in his cups. But not soon. Give her time. Meantime, send Nicolette to her right away, in company with Giles; she will need the comfort when her rage cools. But we must hurry, for night falls. Giles must spend the night, so tell him to 'ware in that mouldering house." How often mother's words echoed the thoughts of my own head!

So it was done. I was determined to leave Herleve to the comfortless cheer of her father's house over Christmastide, at the very least. Laughter crept gradually back into Old Hall with her departure; 'tis strange how we creep around when one in our midst is of sour humour. What meat we had for our Christmas feast was of the woods, wild boar—and gamy and stringy he was—and hares. With the plenteous catch of summer's fish, all made a meal. If our bread was brown and coarse, our hearts were merry for awhile, alight with candle fire and good ale.

Strange year, there had been no snow, when two days after Christmas, William of Lucker, the house in the hollows, rode up in haste. "Bring your men," he cried. "We are upon a hot trod! The outlaws have beaten and robbed an old woman of my vill; they were hungry and looking for food. They came out of the forest to the west (our forest!) and we have that way blocked against their 'scape. But we have not enough men to cast 'round and comb the heather hills where they are holed." 'Twas a mark of the times we lived in that Glororum had two knights, three squires, and four men-at-arms, as well as myself, all ready to ride within the hour. Two of our sergeants must bide as house guard, and we needs draw straws to see who was left behind, so keen were they all upon the manhunt.

The heather where the men were holed was a large pasture, perhaps twenty virgates. It held a stream on the south end, and two or three scattered copses. The heather was brown but of good stand; no cattle had been upon it this autumn. A row of villeins, armed with staffs and bills, stood along the edge of the forest to the west, along with some of their women. It looked to be most of the folk of William's vill, and angry they were at the brutal beating of one of their own helpless women.

By the time all available mounted men had assembled, fifteen of us, more than two hours had gone into their vigil. It was decided to move slowly across the pasture from east to west, flushing the hidden gang like birds, toward the waiting peasants. It was the work of but an hour. Two outlaws were run into the waiting arms of the villeins, and were near clubbed to death ere we could rescue and question them. One miscreant crept toward the end of the line, then disappeared into the forest, with six men tumbling after him. I did not think it belike that they would catch him, for never before or since have I seen a man run with such fear.

When we questioned the two partridges caught in our net, they denied wrongdoing. But one had the old man's shoes upon his feet, and the other had bread in his satchel that the daughter said her mother had just taken from the baker that morning. We withdrew to let the men of the vill wreak their vengeance upon the wretches, and they cried for mercy and the King's Justice. At our impassive faces, they admitted guilt, saying that their leader was one Dirk, who had gotten away. I started, for Dirk had been a villein of ours. He had been up for poaching several times, and still owed fines, but he was an all-'round bad sort who would never do right when wrong was at hand. He broke his old mother's heart, for she had tried to teach him aright. But some there are who enter this world with less morality and more cunning than any outcast wolf, and such a one was Dirk. I was sorry he had slipped our net, for here he was William's problem, a thief caught in the act upon a sovereign estate. Loose, he was more my concern than any other landholder's. It was a problem I could well have done without.

With dogs and determination, 'twas but a day before the escaped outlaw was run down. To my great surprise, it was not Dirk, but another peasant of similar ilk, from Ditchend. Times were hard for all our folk, so the man's whining about hard times fell on deaf ears. His lord, Warren de Millhouse, might have had him hung, save he was not taken in the act of plunder. With his two fellows, who had implored the King's Justice, they were taken to York under armed guard. At the next riding of the Justice, all were ordered hanged as incorrigible. None there were to come forward to ransom them, for they had cast aside their families for their own evil counsel.

Dirk remained at large, and by his violent nature and desperate situation, more a threat than ever. I determined to lure him if I could. While Stephen's hunting lodge in West Forest had not been finished, the caretaker's croft was complete. One of our sergeants, old Will, was quartered there, along with his three strong sons and their wives. I ordered all to return to Glororum, latching the door securely, but leaving the stock for the nonce. I then set two men watching in shifts, under cover of the forest. It was not a week before Dirk crept to the door of the cottage, unlatched it, and began rummaging for food. Finding none, he took Old Will's billhook and slaughtered their only sow. It was then Bors and Julian took him, red-handed.

I called the curia together immediately. The manor court of Glororum had always retained the ancient right of infangentheof, the right to hang any thief caught in the act upon manor property. Only once before that I ken had it been invoked, and that was in the time of Reginald, my grandfather, when thievery abounded. The curia concurred that such was my right. As formality, I questioned Dirk sternly, and by the venom of his own mouth he stood condemned. Nor was he repentant, for his last words were, "Had you not tricked me, I would be a free man yet. Now you think to hang me. I have no fear of you, John, nor your noose. Hang away, and we shall meet in Hell."

[In 1975, there came an incredible testimony to John's story. Across the round, bland face of a much-troubled woman I had been counseling, Dirk's countenance came stealing. Twisting, the face sharpened, hungry and thin, gloating. We heard once more Dirk's words, issuing from that unlikely mouth. "I know who you are, John, so high-and-mighty! You and the fine lords, who thought you were so powerful, so smart. Yet I led you all a merry chase, for nigh nine months. And with your grand horses in the pasture, you kenned you had me then! But you, great stupid John, passed right beside me as I lay still as a ferret in the heather, nor did you see me, just as I willed. And I can fool you again." Dirk's gloating echoed across the centuries with the force of a blow.]

Yet I could not be angry, only saddened at the futility of the outlaw's wasted life, by the willful refusal of grace that would follow his soul, fouling life after life. My prayers commended him to God, but on the day the King's coroner came a month later, to certify his death, we hung Dirk without regret. The hanging oak stood at Bradford, where it would continue to perform justice for many hundreds of years. I declared a solemn holiday, and the folk of our vill and most of the countryside 'round came to watch Dirk hanged. Herleve was back at Old Hall by then, and I held her beside me and forced her to watch the ripened fruit of obdurate wrongdoing. She was white and subdued, and after, vomited her heart out. It was the first sign I had that she was with child.

Chapter 9

Wellsprings

The year 1180 began a decade that was marked by the events that introduced it, times more trying and drudging, and, yes, rewarding, than any young and yet fearless valetti could dream of. Being lord of a well-run estate made any man as worthy of knighthood as battle; unfortunately, most of the scars were inward and the glory nonexistent. Yet pride in the land, pride of our blood, compelled, as it had for my parents before me, true service to that which God had rendered.

After the first capture of outlaws in Lucker field, I decided it was high time to claim my bride once again. Who knows what dangers lurked on the loose-kept estate at Ellingham? Dirk had not yet been taken; no man could say where he had gone. With one of our sergeants, Blaise, I rode south on a bitter cold day, two days after Epiphany. There had still been no snow; Blaise complained that it was too damned cold to snow, as he wrapped his cloak tighter against the wind. That self-same wind was howling about the corners of Ellingham Hall when we arrived, and the place was cold as death inside. I set Blaise to roust the household for fire and food, then set about to find Herleve.

It was in her old room that I found the two of them huddled, mistress and maid. Nicolette said they had been there for nigh a week, cold and hungry. An old manservant would bring them food at night, after Randolph had passed out in his cups. During the day, the raging knight periodically threatened at their locked door; nor would he allow comfort to be brought them. They were under siege, he roared, and he would starve them into submission to his will. Only God knows what that will might have been, so drunken was he.

A wife I might have to endure; her savage father, upon whom she wasted her adulation, was another matter. Pent rage exploded into blood anger as I slammed from the room in search of the old wastrel. I found him in his chamber, calling for wine, and fear filled his face when he saw it was not his servitor who answered. Like most men who bully women, Randolph was a coward, and no true knight at all. I seem to have been shouting all this as he stumbled to his feet and drew his sword. Like many men who affect their knighthood, seldom was he unarmed, even at home, but paraded the trappings that he sullied with wearing.

I had been idle from the arts of war too long; great relish overtook me as my own sword answered. Somewhere I heard a maid shriek, and Blaise's answering growl as he guarded the doorway. Fear filled Randolph's eyes and his breathing became labored; truly, he was too drunk to scarce swing a blade and his plight dug home on him. He assayed one feeble blow as I knocked the blade from his hairy hand. As he reached for his dirk, I laid the flat of my sword against the stubble of his wine-puffed face. Blood sprang from the cheek where one edge had cut flesh, and he bleated like a frightened ewe. Contemptuously, I laid aside sword and took to him with bare hands. 'Twas but the work of a moment to lift the dirk from him, another moment to send his head spinning. Despite his bloated body weighing near twelve stone, so great was my anger that I lifted him like a child and pinned him to the wall with his own dirk, inserted through the rings in his armour. Full of drink and fear, his eyes lost their comprehension.

I called for an ewer of water, and for assembly of the household. When all had gathered, the blood-rage left me, leaving icy determination in its place. I poured water over Randolph's head until he sputtered into some sensibility, then fixed him once again, this time with strong speech.

"Sir Randolph, and little right you have to the title, I declare to you this day that only because you are my father-in-law have I spared your life. Henceforth, there will be no wine in this house; if you have any left it goes with me to Glororum. So too, does Herleve. I know not what claim you make upon her as father; I do know that if you threaten her or her maid again, your miserable life is forfeit." I heard the daughter gasp; she too got the point. Turning, I fixed her with a gaze that brooked no reply. "You, my lady, will visit this hell-hole of a home only when I concur. And you," I turned to the servants, "will scrub this pigsty as well as you are able, it being cold winter. Come spring, the whole house must be turned out, the linens and napery boiled and aired. You have lived like swine for too long."

"By terms of our agreement," I continued, "I am steward of this property until Hugh comes of age. Every man and woman of you, 'ware. You will live and work like Christians henceforth, and I will set a beadle over you as overseer. I myself will hold manor court every month"—I groaned inwardly, my least favorite chore—"and justice will prevail among you. You will pay homage to Sir Randolph as he deserves that homage; your lands are still forfeit to him." I could not rob him of every shred of dignity, nor of his rights as landholder; despite all, he was a knight of good blood, though in wine he had dishonoured it. Besides, my anger was cooling into a profound weariness.

That very day, Herleve and Nicolette returned with me, though I left Blaise behind as a mark of my resolve. Turning on my bed that night, tossing all the day's events into a stew, I realized I was already spread too thin at Glororum, without the burden of Ellingham on my back. The invincible confidence of youth died with but a whimper. It was patent that I must find a beadle—an under-steward—for Ellingham, and that as soon as possible.

I knew no knight who would take on such an unreward-
ing task on such a demanding estate with so little profit. A
young squire would have neither patience nor cunning to
deal with Sir Randolph and his crew. The answer might lie
with one of our own older sergeants, Blaise or Julian. Old
Will was needed at the West Lodge, and his son, Young Will,
whom he was a-training, had not yet the experience. Our
fourth man-at-arms, Rafe, could not be counted on except
in a pinch; he moved only under direct order, and that often
accompanied by a well-placed shoe.

On the morrow, I called the two men-at-arms into the
Hall. Both Julian and Blaise, as sergeants, held dependent
crofts, and received a yearly wage as well as other boons.
Our two house knights, while not landed, were better paid,
and received clothes and armour as well as their keep. But
both Bors and Giles were sorely needed at Glororum; a
man-at-arms would be easier replaced. I told the men that
Ellingham required a beadle, responsible only to me, whose
loyalty I trusted. The hours would be long, the pay small.
But I did have one compensation that might be made. Of
the virgates accruing to Glororum from Ellingham, as part
of the marriage agreement, I was willing to deed one virgate
of prime ploughland at the end of seven years service. Few
of our yeoman freeholders held as much.

There was frank talk among us. Mother sat, to give her
concurrence, but she entered into no part of the discussion.
In the end, Julian seemed willing to decline. He had not sons
enough to work the virgates, and his wife would be loathe
to move from her rounds among her sisters. Blaise, too, was
torn. He had seen Ellingham first hand. But the temptation
of the land was great. I insisted that each man consult with
his family, though hunch informed me that Blaise would be
my man. God knows who I could come up with if both
refused.

Blaise indeed answered aye, and we rode to Ellingham
again, just after Dirk was taken. We were waiting for the
coroner to come north, so that Dirk might be hanged legally.

I was anxious to put a man in place on Randolph's demesne, lest my inaction make the old knight bold once again. Snow clouds threatened; for the cold and wind-dried land, moisture promised at last. A fair blizzard struck while we were entering Blaise on the manor rolls. We had called the Ellingham curia together in the Hall, but many had refused to brave the worsening storm. I was forced to make my little Latin serve, as Ellingham had no clerk. It was all a simple formality, but I wished the curia to reelect another reeve. With blank or even hostile faces the villeins regarded me; it had never been their custom to set one of their own above the others; every previous reeve had been appointed. We had the devil's own struggle to get one man to accept the reeveship, and then only by promising the old reeve the position of hayward, a job near as important. All wanted no responsibility, only boons. Even children were not as slothful as those Ellingham villeins. Blaise would have his hands full.

As it turned out, Blaise did begin to turn the estate around, though it was slow. Yet after two years of naught but slow country ale, Randolph's thirst as well as his pride had all it could take. Ellingham Hall was put up for sale. When it was finally sold in 1185, Randolph took his money and went to Newcastle. There he died of drink some few years later, intestate, unshriven, and without a word to son or daughter from the time he left.

We had the devil's own time over the deeds, and once again, an assize was called. It was adjudged that our virgates, and Blaise's, were duly sealed. The demesne of Ellingham, with its ten virgates of plowland, and an equal amount of wood and waste, was confirmed property of the new owner. The remaining land, thirty virgates held by the villeins, had not been deeded with the estate as sold. Hence, Hugh had some patrimony, though more by default than by any intent on the part of his father.

Blaise continued to act as beadle for Hugh; the lad was as ineffectual a man as he had been a squire. He continued to live in Alnwick town, scraping by on the rents of the few poor acres left to him. Had it not been that I pitied him, and continued stewardship of the farm, or that Blaise continued his honest work, Hugh would have starved.

Though spring held late in 1180, it did bring snow, then rain. The drought promised to be over. The plowmen were late getting into the fields for spring plowing due to mud, but we had seen so little rain for so long that no one complained. April brought the dry winds normally carried by March, and ploughing and planting went on apace. All of us were vitiated by two years of poor food, the cold winter, and the sad hanging of one of our own. Mother looked drawn, but poor Giles was positively haggard. His age was beginning to tell, with too many hours in the saddle. He even neglected his regular quarrels with Bors, who had become almost maternal. We were both riding most of Giles' marches. That was no burden; it took us from the petty whining and day-to-day tedium of the estate. I knew that I particularly was becoming shorter tempered by the day.

Poor Herleve was sick much of the time. Pregnancy did not agree with her; there was not the joyous bloom some women seem to acquire. Nicolette, too, was worn out from the constant demands upon her. I kept to my room at night—bless Alfric!—and went abroad early. Truth to tell, I felt the weariness and the downcast hearts of all.

About the time of the plowing, mother came to my room one evening, as she hadn't done for months. "John, all Glororum seems to have become sad and weary. The hanging of Dirk especially has cast a pall, as if evil was released upon the land with the departure of that outlaw soul. Herleve worries me; she will take no nourishment unless Nicolette coaxes; 'tis no way to grow a babe." She paused. "We need a pilgrimage."

My head entertained the idea at once. What a wondrous way to heal our many wounds! "Belike. But where would we go? Hexham?" Hexham, nearby, was the battlefield where St. Oswald had died; a stone cross and small chapel had been erected there. It was a shrine dear to Northumbrians.

What mother answered made my head spin. "I was thinking of ancient Bath. The old buildings of the Romans are near tumbled down, 'tis true, but nowhere else in the world can such healing water be found."

"But Mother, Bath is the length and breadth of England away! And it is no Christian shrine." I stopped to think a moment. "Though health now may more be found in the waters of Bath than in our sad prayers. I suppose if we take a large enough party, and make the journey joyous, the outing itself may hold reward. Have we money enough for such a venture?" Mother held the purse-strings more tightly even than I.

"Money is cursed if it does not good. I have a pittance that was mine from my father; 'twould be a shame to be buried with it unspent. I am strongly called to go."

That put an end to it; if mother's wisdom called her to the journey, it must be made. "Then we shall go. Two weeks hence should give us time to prepare. We will take two tents, one for the ladies, and one for your honor-guard." I smiled, realizing that it had been weeks since I felt so light-hearted.

"I am sure there are inns and hospices along the way," mother answered, "but to be sure, the tents shall go. That means not more than four women; we are three, who shall be the fourth?"

I knew her well enough to know that she had an idea a-hatching, and told her so. "I first thought of Maud, but she is heavy with child and will be in childbed in June, mayhap upon your birthday." That was glad news, but she went on. "We surely might stay at Hutton one night on our way south; when we return, I will remain there." Sly-boots, she already had that worked out. "However, Andrew's wife, Margaret, could certainly take her place. The girl works overmuch; no marvel it is that she has been unable to conceive. The waters at Bath are said to open the womb, also." I had noticed that mother had taken a liking to young Margaret; in some ways she was more like a daughter-in-law than Herleve. It made me glad, for in accepting Margaret, she had become more accepting of Andrew.

"Then I have little need to plan further. Bors and Julian needs must run the farm whilst we are away. Young Will can come over from West Forest to help out. With Giles and Andrew, I will take young Carl. Before Michaelmas, I shall have to make him a full sergeant, with a croft of his own, now that Blaise is at Ellingham. The trip will season him."

So it was, the second week of May, amidst much baggage and turmoil, we set out for Bath. Stephen wistfully looked after us as we left Hutton; the thought of adventure had stirred his blood. Our road ran first to York, then down the old Roman way to Lincoln and Coventry, thence to Cirenchester and Bath. There were many great abbeys along the way, such as at Tewkesbury, where we could stop a day or two and rest the weary women and the horses. Indeed, the food improved as we got further south. I had not realized how close to the bone our rations had been. Even Herleve began to eat a little; the trip was agreeing with her, even if it did little to allay her petty tempers. Mother said that often women become nigh unbearable in pregnancy, and that we should ignore it. So our trip went well, and we used the tents near not at all.

How can I explain my thoughts upon entering Bath at last? Coming down the hill into the town, all was familiar, as if I had been there long ago. Indeed, all I could call to mind was the Roman soldier that Annie had told me of, so long ago. Where he had trod, I was now striding, every ancient stone still in place calling forth dim memories. "*Aqua Sulis* at last," I told mother. But I dared not let loose the paean of praise that filled my head. 'Great Minerva,' it exulted, 'bring us to your waters for blessing. Let us feel once again the softness of your flowing love. Let Father Sol bring his heat and health to our bones through your waters. Our hearts rejoice!' Upon reflecting upon my pagan instinct, I could nowise see that Minerva was much different than the Lady we now call Queen of Heaven, nor was great Sol much different from any other saint to whom we might pray. Still, my joy remained silent.

Though much of Bath was tumbled down, part of the great pool was usable. As the warmth of its healing waters folded around me, I felt again the great softness of Minerva, and I emerged weak but confident of renewed vitality. So also it seemed to affect all of our party; Giles especially seemed to come to his old self. There were hawkers of the waters also, said to cure every ailment known to man or woman. Especially prized was the ability to bring pregnancy to women, and to enable men to sire sons. All this was told behind the hand, with a wink; indeed, one might think the streets of Bath would be filled with children.

I employed a lively lad to find us a spot to set the tents, in a high meadow by the river. He was useful in dealing with the local mendicants and cripples, who clustered 'round the bath asking alms. It was he that I asked about buying some of the healing waters, for, to be sure, I trusted not the local peddlers overmuch. It was as I feared; much of what was for sale was taken from drains and other fouled sources. "Aye," said our lad, Caedmon, "but I can take you, sires, to the great bubbling source of the waters, and you can fetch your own. 'Tis not an easy search, for it lies buried deep in the ruins, not a trip for the fearsome. Some claim there are ghosts deep in those caverns; all I know is that 'tis eerie beyond belief. But if each gentleman were to take a flask, and a rope as well, for a few pence I will take you to the very beating heart of Bath."

As he threw the gauntlet, so we picked it up; Andrew, Carl and, myself. Giles was far too old to be clambering about in dangerous ruins, more like to lose his life than gain his health. The trek was all that Caedmon said it would be: dirty, difficult, and dangerous. It minded me of the catacombs of Rome the old knights told about on winter evenings about the table at Alnwick. Still, nothing had prepared me for the sight of that great heaving pool of steaming water; how the Romans had managed to girdle it with stone was a miracle. With care, we managed to cast our flasks into that great eye of a spring, to take water ere it slid down the stone troughs into the bathing pool. More than ghosts seemed to reside here; it was as if the gods of the underworld frolicked around us, their mocking laughter hidden in the bubbling of that awful beating heart. We were glad to leave, uncomprehending mortals stealing from the buried terraces of mystery and sacrifice. Unbeknownst to the others, I, too, had left sacrifice, two pence to the waters. It was the least I could give toward blessing.

Before supper, each took a sip of that hard-won elixir. A sip was enough, for it was foul-tasting indeed! But medicine must bite deep, and not cosset the innards. We carefully packed the remainder to take back to Glororum; it sustained us for many years. Caedmon knew where we might buy food in town, so we ate at leisure, and, after, walked the meadows and the peaceful countryside. A great renewal seemed to come over the whole company; even Herleve left off complaining and walked peacefully by my side in the evening.

The other great memory I have of Bath is of the bakers. Caedmon showed us how the guild—for they had increased beyond the family who first began the baking—artfully turned out the many buns for which Bath is famous. In the warm water of certain drainage troughs, large pots half-full of wheaten dough were placed. When the dough had risen to the rim of the pot by the nurturing of the warmth and moisture, it was taken out and rolled in spice and sugar and raisins of Corinth. Placed over the warmth once again, on great trays, the buns were soon ready for the oven. Never had we tasted anything like that bread, quickly raised and always light. We were soon spoiled against the hard, dry, brown crusts of home. Still, all things pall after time, and home began to loom more in our minds, and mother must needs be soon at Hutton. Stocked with both buns and the precious water, we retraced our steps, rejoicing in the blooming countryside of early June.

Chapter 10
Children

Maud's baby, a girl, was born just a week before my birthday in June of 1180. Mother was justly proud, for she was not only midwife, but namesake. However, Maud and Stephen bestowed two names on their infant daughter, unusual enough in our times. Mary Rose was the symbol of the love that had flowered between husband and wife. For a wedding present, Stephen had brought for Maud a rose bush from Provence. A lush, shining pink, full in form and fragrance, the Provence rose bloomed all of June and into July, love embodied. It was fitting that this fat, pink girl-child carry the name of Rose along with her down-to-earth Mary.

The christening was in July, at Durham. As godfather, I rode down, unaccompanied by Herleve, who herself was ripe with child. The ceremony was brief but fitting, and Mary Rose cried when given the salt, a good sign. I cannot describe how I felt, holding that child before the priest. I was as proud as if she were my own; and indeed, for all her life, Mary Rose excited affection in all who knew her. I vowed to keep her safe and to teach her of God, as did her godmother, Stephen's sister, Suzanne.

Mother reluctantly rode back with me to Glororum. Leaving the love and happiness that flowed from every cranny of Hutton for the screaming and complaining of

Herleve at Old Hall must have been a sore cross for her to bear. Yet she tightened her lips and came along, rather than leave my wife to childbed with none but Nicolette and Annie's old mother, the village midwife, to aid her lying-in. Some mothers are as worthy of knighthood as their sons.

Our eldest son came lustily screaming into the world in mid-August. Herleve was quite exhausted, but looked radiant, far better than she had throughout pregnancy. She insisted, by custom, on naming the child for her father and grandfather, Randolph. It pleased me not at all, but to keep peace, I agreed. The lad grew sturdy, and I was minded of myself at an early age. Yet sons change as they grow. Though we sent Randolph to Alnwick when he was seven, rather than becoming more noble, his intellect dimmed and his boldness melted before the discipline. I despaired of his ever becoming a true knight, though some years after my death, with his patrimony in hand, he rode with the courtiers of Prince Richard, and for camaraderie rather than valor was knighted in France. Thank God, our son never became another man like Herleve's father; but too often I was reminded of his ineffectual uncle, Hugh. In truth, Randolph visited that poor reed whenever he was able, and worshipped him as I had my Uncle Kenneth. 'Tis a pity how life turns. Still, never was our Randolph quite as weak of will or mind as Hugh, though Glororum prospered not under his hand.

In September, our new son was christened at Bamburgh. Maud and Stephen stood for him, despite Herleve's bitter objections. It was well that I insisted, for they took his interest at heart through the years, and gave him a strength in God to compensate for the inherent imperfections of his nature. It was after the ceremony, as if the devil driven from the baby had taken root in her heart, Herleve became near wild. Weeping incessantly, she would not be comforted. The fact that she had borne a healthy son meant nothing; she took to her room and refused him care. We were all afraid she might take either her own life or the baby's, so distraught was she.

My fair and buxom Kate, mother of her second babe, was brought in to nurse our son as well as her own. I also brought in the daughter of Richard, our reeve, to wait upon Herleve, as Nicolette became more haggard with each passing day. Though no great beauty, she was beginning to resemble a death's head; I could not have her slow demise upon my soul. I sent her to sew with the rest of the women, and to exercise Herleve's horse and hawk and hound whilst her mistress was unable to do so. Carl was assigned to watch over her; he might have performed those chores himself, but that Nicolette needed the outings.

From this house of busy women, I fled. Truth to tell, it did not do for me to watch Kate nurse our son, or be too much around her. I had given up my room for the nonce, and had a space cleared in the undercroft, beside the window and near the stair, and it was there that I slept when at home. I spent much of my time patrolling the marches, even at times as far as Berwick-on-Tweed. Giles was becoming more feeble; long marches were out of the question for him now. Still, he could teach and was diligent in the care of the pages and squires, though mother continued to watch him like a hatching hen.

At manor court at Michaelmas, I formally made Carl a sergeant, a man-at-arms of the household. It was now incumbent on me to find him a croft of his own. With the consent of Old Will and his family, who were now firmly rooted in West Forest, and by judgement of the curia, the old croft in the village that once belonged to Will was ceded to Carl for his sergeantry. Richard's younger son, Thomas, was promoted to squire; Giles had spoken for him though he was but thirteen and a half. This left Glororum with but three pages. Old Will's sons were all too well grown to begin training, and they were needed at home. None of the villeins had sons to spare to be trained to the arts of war. I put the matter in abeyance till some future court, but had little idea as to how to revitalize our needed defence force.

The curia consented to boon days at the end of October, to raise a new cottage for Carl; probably out of eagerness to set a glorious bonfire. Will's old croft was in sad disrepair after many years of use. So it was that we cleansed the land by burning of the old sties and pens, and the tumble-down cot. In two days, we had the great timber cricks of a new cottage set, and a habitable room built and plastered. Provision was made to add another room, should Carl marry, which he had not yet shown inclination to do. Our people were often slow in this regard, not wanting the responsibility of family until the need for labour or the call of nature became too pressing. With some fencing up, Carl was given the month off to improve and stock his homestead. With his wages, he was able to buy a sow and three bred ewes to put on the common pasture. In time, and with diligence, he would prosper.

It was not two weeks later that Providence answered our need of a page. When I was told that a rider from the north was coming with a child and one man at his back, I remembered my promise to Kenneth. It was with joy and feasting that I greeted my uncle and his son and their man-at-arms. Mother, too, was delighted to see her brother; Herleve's illness had drawn her into its maw of gloom. I made mental note to send her back to Hutton after Kenneth left, so worried was I over her health.

Robin was a well-grown seven, near eight; and though his head held none of the old fire of Sir Kenneth's, still there was the glint of June strawberries in his cap of golden hair. Kenneth himself had grown near white of pate. When I remarked upon it, he laughed and said it was the price of his sins. Yet when he joyously ruffled the hair of his young son, age fell away from him and I saw the vitality still in his eyes and speech. The boy meant youth to him, in a way that my sons never quite did for me. But Robin—he had been christened Robert—was like Mary Rose, one of those sunny souls that light the life of those who know him. I was to owe my life to his loving strength one day, but that was yet for the future.

Robin brightened our house; nor would mother budge toward Hutton with a new page to watch over. I put him under her special care, and Andrew's, when he was not riding the marches with me. There was scarce a week I was not in the saddle, always with Rafe or Julian, or sometimes Carl, behind me, or Andrew. Crinan would usually make a third, or Young Will, unless one of the pages had been unusually good—or bad. High spirits that cause boys to find mischief can be well allayed by hard work or long hours in the saddle. Requiring a boy to act like a man oft makes a man of him.

Andrew, whose Margaret had meekly sipped of the waters of Bath, at last came with the news that his little brown hen was with child. We were joyous, and little did I call him to ride, knowing he was more needed at home. The drought showed every sign of being broken, and the land needed much attention, with fields and flocks returning to fertility once again.

Bors, too, was glad to stay at home more, with Giles often ailing; and indeed I needed him as steward in my place. Also, he often rode south to Ellingham, to succor Blaise. His presence made the villeins uneasy in their small rebellions, and he enjoyed confronting Randolph, counting the ale kegs to make sure no wine had slipped among them. Randolph hated him, which gave Bors much mirth. By his aid, I only rode to manor court at Ellingham six times a year, which was more than enough for a saint, much less a natural man.

After about six months, Herleve began to recover, enough that I set her to hawking again with Nicolette and Carl. It did her wonders, especially after the gloom of winter had passed. When Randolph began to walk, she took great interest in our son, and set to raising him as a mother should, though often to my detriment. My orders she countermanded, and she literally would snatch the child from my arms as I held him. Mother refused to interfere, but on this she agreed with me; 'twas better to let time and education teach the child respect, than to scrap over him as dogs over some poor bone. Perhaps we were wrong.

In midsummer, too, Margaret was delivered of a son, whom they named Ralph after her father. He was a delicate child, though handsome. 'Twas with great sadness we buried him at Bamburgh, after the summer plague of '87. That was a bad year; the farm lost many children and elders to the griping sickness. Old Peter was especially dispirited; the lad meant the world to him. Often you would see Ralph in the saddle before his granda', even before the baby could walk. Indeed, I was afraid we would lose Peter, too; he cared not if he lived or died. Margaret it was who cheered him most, though old Peter began to lean more and more on Andrew. The couple's own grief was unassuaged by the appearance of more children; Margaret remained barren till her death in 1199.

It was not often that any of us knew our grandparents; death often claimed them ere we were born. So it was with my grandparents. Thus it behooved us to carry their memory carefully in our traditions, and was one of the reasons precedent was so important in our lives. Every man, too, be he peasant or knight, knew his genealogy at least three generations back. Grandchildren, at least to the country folk, were a treasure; nor could we understand how kings might slay those of their own blood. Such tragedies were mourned for centuries, in the ballads of our bards.

I had little enough time for singing in those days. Indeed, Chatta often saw more of me than did Herleve. My regular course was to ride three leagues to the west, to Chatta's farm, and remain overnight. The ale was always good, Chatta's son Simon was fond of chess, and would play me a fair match. There might be troubadours from France, or messengers on the King's business, or any number of mountebanks on the road to Scotland. Chatta always gave us the hospitality of his house in return for protection, though I brought meat to him several times a year, and such goods from Bamburgh—shoes, cloth, and suchlike—as he was unable to garner for himself. No man ever proved so true a friend as Chatta, and many were the stories and rumors he was able to tell that I might not have heard otherwise.

Chatta's Twelfth Century Barn, Near Chatton

From Chatta's, we would set off early in the morning. The great dark forest started just beyond his door, and the way wound up the hill through the trees. On the side of a fair hill overlooking the valley of the River Till, there ran a spring of cold water. Men had been stopping to refresh themselves in this lonely spot for years beyond my ken; but as yet, none dared live here. Not two leagues west of Chatta, the welling spring made a fine place for nooning. From thence, we might return for another evening at Chatta's farm, or we could ride northwest to Sir Henry's demesne at Cornhill, or due north to Berwick. Either road would bring us at live-long last to Edinburgh, where I fared near once a year to visit David and Duncan.

Often, I would meet some of my Uncle Henry's knights at the high spring, riding the march down through the Heather Law, that wild upland of rock and heather, girdled by the great forest of oak, and ash, and beech. Between Cornhill and Chatta's, except for the brooding spring on the hillside, there was little comfort. Some monks, enticed as Chatta had been by this lonely land, were building a new church near a league above the spring, and there a man might find some scant provision and a bed for the night. Needless to tell, too often I turned back to Chatta's after a noon drink from the welling waters.

Never could I hide from the problems of Glororum for long. Summer of 1182 brought a new plight. Herleve confronted me at the very door of Old Hall one day, just after I rode in from the march. Rafe and Crinan were seeing to the horses, but had they wished, they could have heard my wife clear to the stables. "What games do you think to play with me, now, m'lord?" she shrilled.

"Woman, I have no idea of what you are speaking, but if you will come indoors with me, perhaps I can ken what your noise is all about." Such times as these let me understand I had not got off altogether devoid of William's temper. Yet it was as nothing before Herleve's flaring wrath. "I suppose you thought your bestiality could run unchecked, and none would know. But God punishes sinners! The woman is with *child*!"

"By God's holy blood, will you tell me what all this is about? I am no sooner off my horse than you are screaming at me like a woman gone mad. Can you speak sense, or must I have you pond-dunked?" The thought of holding her under water until she came to her senses was at that moment enticing.

"Nicolette, my Nicolette. Oh, you don't fool me. You have got her with child!" At last it was out, and I groaned inwardly. What some lout had taken in pleasure, I was being blamed for. Now I needs must not only settle Herleve's accusation, but make arrangements for her maid and descry the lover. As my mind cast about, I thought that he would not be too hard to find.

"Herleve, I have never lied to you. You must know that if Nicolette is with child, it is not by me. There are a fair number of men on this estate," I added sarcastically, "some of whom might lack the discretion to leave your maid to die a virgin."

"If not you, then who?" She was defiant still, but sensed that she had got it wrong in her irrational jealousy. "How dare a man touch my maid, without my permission?"

"You have been sick for months. What would you ken or care what happens to those around you? If Nicolette has found some happiness, then it were well-earned. You dare not risk falling ill again, over such a slight affair. Randolph needs you now, now that you have your wits about you again. I shall take care of the matter."

And so I did. It needed but one call and I found the right man, my faithful Carl. With a house of his own, and young blood surging in his veins, even plain Nicolette had been a charming princess. He was not sad, either, that she was with child. A wife and son would make his croft a true home.

Nicolette was feared out of her mind when I called her to me. Herleve had filled her head with threats of unholy punishments for her sin, all of which I was supposed to carry out. I never thought of love as a sin, I told her, and I wished her all the blessed pleasure she might find away from the demands of my petulant wife. I was firm that they should marry; the child needed a family. Nicolette had thought that impossible, because noble Norman blood ran in her veins, while Carl was of simple, sturdy Northumbrian stock. I told her all people bleed red before God, and He judges them on merit alone. The doughty knight who was her father, who had abandoned her and her mother, the gentlewoman who died before her daughter could be set in life, both were as nothing before the love that had redeemed her. So the two were married by Father Cedric in the chapel of Old Hall, quietly, with mother and Giles attending, and Bors and I as witness. Herleve was still in a snit. She was not missed.

Her child set Nicolette free. A boy, she named him Carl, after his father; Carl, Carl's son. So he was known all his life, even after he had become a squire. Though Nicolette continued to work with Herleve, never would she be tyrannized by her again. Most amazing, with Nicolette's new stouthearted confidence, Herleve began to treat her with something akin to respect.

Herleve herself began to settle into country life and take over some of the regulation of the household. Yet always was her face set against me, and she gave me battle every day for the control of my own heritage. She made every complaint against me public and I was forced to do the same. If maid or manservant came with witness to their mistress' unreason, I usually decided against her, to her great fury. Yet she knew I would lock her away, should she continue, away from her beloved hunting and hawking. So we kept uneasy peace, though the complaints of her tongue followed me everywhere. I was often minded of Sir Gareth of the ballads, who endured such abuse only to find great happiness at last.

Our second son, William, was born in November of 1183. Herleve refused him any comfort whatsoever, and it was high summer before she became well enough to go about her rounds of the house. Randall, as I had taken to calling our eldest, was a comfort to her, but she pushed William away from the time he was a babe. Often he was naughty, trying for her attention, but she would call him a base-born cur and turn away. I became father and mother both, except when mother was home, for she took him to her heart. Still, William had my father's high temper, which caused him grief all his life.

I sent mother to Hutton, to preserve her health. Robin, whom she adored, I sent with her as lady's page; his schooling could be had at Hutton as easily as Glororum. The boy adored his young cousin, Mary Rose; had there not been such strict regulation of consanguinity, they might have even married. Regardless of all others, Robin was to remain her true knight all his life. Nor did she ever marry; the girl's heart lay always with her childhood friend and succor. Many were the mock battles Robin fought for her, and Mary Rose learned her childish songs to please him alone. They were often Maud's despair, but mother told her, never mind, they understand their lot in life. And so they did. I often envied such unsullied love, remaining in childhood's innocent mould.

Mother came home in spring of '84, at least for awhile. Giles had been taken with pain for some months, and had wasted to a shadow. He died in May, 1184, and we buried him at Bamburgh, with daffodils all a-bloom in the church-yard. Death was a blessing to him; it was more Bors that I worried over. Yet our steward seemed to be lighter when his old friend's suffering had at last been cut short. Bors' lusty days were over, the drinking and quarrelling and wenching, and he was content to keep with work and memories.

No matter how many years may intervene, I mind well those last months of Giles' illness. Near every evening, he and Bors would sit at a small table set up in the kitchen, playing draughts and drinking ale. Often I would sit in my corner near the door, watching their slow shuffling moves, playing with their thoughts as much as with one another. Bors, his round face ruddy in the flickering firelight, dark hair curled under upon his brow, would often reach up to scratch the well-trimmed salt-and-pepper beard that wreathed his face. Neither man wore a mustache such as I affected later in life (a lesser evil than a beard, which did indeed itch). Giles was white of hair and beard, which he kept always trimmed to a small point. His skin became like parchment, but Bors saw to it that even at his weakest, Giles was shaved, with hair trimmed neatly. The dying firelight cast no ruddy glow upon Giles to hide the pall of death he carried. Yet overshadowing even that, like a spirit hovering between the two old friends, was a certain rough devotion that lighted the whole room.

I had no heart to replace Giles. Indeed, in the flush of invincibility that youth bestows, I was confident of being able to take up the few chores that had remained to the old knight. I myself became master of the squires, with Julian to teach arms, and Andrew, protocol. Andrew also oversaw the pages, though oddly enough, Herleve became mistress to them all; and while she was demanding, they learned of French speech and manners as they might not have otherwise. Even Andrew, whose quiet obedience managed to win over even my imperious wife, told me he learned much that I had not been able to teach him. He, like myself, was eager for knighthood. It was well we could not see the future, as Annie might. That great hardship would be over six years yet in coming.

Chapter 11

Button

'Tis strange how we look forward to the morrow, each day, in disdain of the blessings that already lie upon our heads. In the cycle of days that held the life of Glororum, in healthy sons, in the strength of family and tradition, our days were hallowed. Yet too little did I stop to thank Our Lord for what we had; instead, in eagerness, charged toward what was still aborning.

Dame Fortuna preserved Northumbrian country knights from the overweening politics of royalty that were destroying estates across the continent: in Provence and Anjou, Flanders and France. Yet we were men of war, trained for war; and the occasional skirmish with border outlaws by no means sated our appetite for war. Mother bid me be thankful for this. With all the demands of the demesne and its vill, with all my riding of marches and overseeing Ellingham, discontent still hid in my soul. To ease it, once a month I turned out the villeins and freemen of our home fyrd and set them to, with bow and arrow, and playing at quarterstaff. Andrew and I would test the strength of their line by riding upon it; any who broke and ran would be thumped with a lance. They soon learned to nimbly jump aside as we rode through. They were allowed to tag us then, and sore bruised beneath the armor we became on those days. But they were not allowed to strike the horses.

The great horses we raised were the pride of Glororum. While not clods, like so many of the horses of Flanders or Normandy, they were large and heavy enough to stand the force of charge when lance met shield head-on. They had been bred with smaller, nimbler horses, and could wheel and feint with no pressure but from knees and body. Most possessed a certain keenness of mind, and delighted in the tricks of war. Often a good horse would put his knight into position of his own wit, and any man with a horse like that was a fool to overcontrol him. Stallions were our men-o'-war. Prime mares we saved to breed, or sold. Some colts were gelded and used for pack animals. A few mares were used for palfreys, women's riding horses, though usually the geldings were more reliable. A mare that threw stud colts regularly was more valuable than one who ran to fillies. Thus management of the horse herd was of prime importance, and a great part of our revenue. Under Peter's steady hand, our destriers were the pride of Glororum; indeed, of all the countryside.

Glororum Stable, Tumbling Down After Nine Centuries.
The Road to Chatton Led From Here.

Through the drought, the herd by necessity was reduced. But Brown Thunder, my destrier, was past his prime, and I desperately needed a new mount. In 1179, we raised four foals, three colts and a filly. Two of the colts were poorly from the drought, and we gelded them. The next two years gave us more fillies; only two middling destriers were started. But in 1182 God smiled upon our animals; we had three prime colts. One was black, unusual enough, but he was also eager and strong. I marked him for my own, and called him Black Stone, for the strength of his bones and the hardness of his muscle. I began his training in 1184, albeit slowly as he was still a-forming. Andrew, too, picked a prime colt, a bay. So the two of us worked out our battle-hungers in the stable and horse-lot, and 'twas well we did so. Our mounts were in their prime when the war came.

Much has been bemoaned over the lot of the villeins, yet they worked no harder than myself or my men-at-arms. Nor had most peasants either judgment or responsibility to control land and life; those who welcomed such were made reeves or sergeants, or even brought to knighthood. And none of our people went hungry, save when those of us at Old Hall felt hunger too. There was a good soul to our estate, despite grumbling. The man who does not grumble abides in another world, one of either pain or ecstasy. Few of our people were given to ecstasy! 'Twas not the same at Ellingham, where no manner of reform could sate the villeins' sullen defiance, which distressed none but themselves. It was as if the land itself had been accursed.

Many evenings I sat alone before the smouldering fire of the kitchen (which was never allowed to go out), hatching plans, or worrying over some new trouble. Sometimes Bors would come to sit silently beside me, staring into the flames, lost in memory. Other evenings we would sit with Father Cedric in our old family chamber at the east end of the Hall, drinking ale and speaking of the wonders of the world. Often we spoke of celibacy, and we were an unlikely trio—a priest, a bereaved old soldier, and a weary young lord with an unwilling wife. But the things I learned from those men helped me through many a hard day and night.

I was determined not to let Randall suffer what Fate had meted out to me. I would provide a wife for him long ere his body called for him to settle on someone unsuited. On every journey, my ears were pricked to learn of a girl child who might be of proper age and blood, so that I might negotiate as soon as possible. I was confident that appealing to Herleve's pride would garner her acceptance, though I had no intent of bringing more Norman or French blood into the Forestrius family.

'Twas easier than I had suspected. In 1181, my old friend Duncan had taken to himself a wife. I had thought that David would be first married, for he was of good heart and the ladies loved his innocent air. Yet I had reckoned without Duncan's lifelong canniness. As castle knight to King William, only lack of an heiress wife kept him from becoming a lord. In typical diligent fashion, he set about remedying that lack. One of the royal courtiers was a distant relative to the king, a descendent of William's great uncle Alexander I, by a son born on the wrong side of the blanket. This son, in turn, sired Sir Ethelred whose daughter, Aethelfritha, had the royal blood of both Scotland and England in her veins (and money in her dowry-chest). Indeed, both Aethelfritha's mother and grandmother had been daughters of noble English thanes displaced by the Conquest. Duncan had lost no time a-wooing this most eligible lady.

In October of 1181 I had ridden north—the weather was miserable, raw and blowing—to attend their wedding. Duncan looked justly proud, for he had taken the day from more accomplished knights. Aethelfritha, though only sixteen, was one of those strong, big-boned lasses that always look breathless and ruddy, as if from running. She promised to be a good mother, and both David and I were content to see Duncan so well and truly wed.

It was not until 1185, when David finally married, that I saw Duncan with his family. Though I had known that he and Aethelfritha had made a child in 1183, a daughter, the significance had not entered my ironclad skull. Now, as I saw them standing together after the ceremony, a thunderbolt cracked upon my pate. In the child, Margaret, with her strong bones, set little mouth, and great blue eyes, I knew we had a wife for Randolph. After the feasting and before we rode back south again, I tested the waters. It did not do well to set upon Duncan all at once; he needs must have time to think upon a new idea and take it for his own. So it was that I made delicate mention of the affair and left it to grow with time.

David's wedding was in May, alight with sunshine and new bloom. My old friend had found a maiden willing to put up with his insouciance at last. Glenda was like the winds of May; dancing, fair, and bonny. Her golden hair hung, I swear, to her knees; no cap or veil could contain it. Many were the envious looks cast at David! But her face and none other held her fortune; she had been raised in the Highlands by her grandma, an ancient crone. Her father was of Norse blood, descendent of a family of reivers. A giant of a man, able to kill a sheep with one blow of his fist, he had come to serve in the King's bodyguard. So delicate was the maid, his daughter, that one wondered about the poor lady her mother. 'Twas said she died in birthing the lass. Glenda had been brought to court when she was ten, after her old grandma died. She was a great favorite with the ladies, I garnered, with willing hands and a clever mind. Rumors had that she pleased some of the men also, but she was one to charm the very ring from your finger, and never come scathed. She even learned to read a little, and though her dowry was poor, I kenned that her wit and looks would eke David greatly, if he but held a loose rein.

It was not to be so. By whatever artifice, Glenda never came with child. Her carefree youth never seemed to diminish, while jealousy came to gnaw more and more upon David's heart. He moved her from court, and they took residence in a croft upon his brother's stony estate in the north, the very estate he had been born upon and worked so hard to leave behind. Thus in trying to destroy Glenda's golden light, David began to destroy his own. The sour peasant women called Glenda a witch, for her ways were different, and their menfolk fair ogled her. When I saw David at Edinburgh Fair in 1188, the pot of his sorrows was already seething. Soon it would run over completely.

It was in 1188, too, that Duncan approached me with *his* idea for betrothal of our children. In truth, 'twas just as I had hoped; the match was advantageous to us both. That same autumn I sent Randall to Alnwick, just as I myself had been sent. Herleve was heartbroken and sulky, but still paid no heed to William. Instead, she began to shower her attention on the baby. Henry had been born on the last day of February in 1186, and of my three boys, he was the keenest and most charming. He was always so pleasant and uncomplaining that often the whetstone at his core went unremarked. He toddled behind me, too, in a way that Randolph had never been allowed, and that William was too restless for. Henry was everybody's darling on the farm; even the villeins' children looked out after him.

It was spring of '86 that held the strange encounter that was to later change my life. With Herleve just out of childbed, and suffering her usual illness, I spent as much time on the marches as possible. With Julian and Crinan, I had stopped at Chatta's one night in late April. My host told me that slave bands were beginning to be seen again on that wild frontier. They stole the tough Scots' children and sold them to the large dairy farms of some of the priories and abbeys in the south, for cheese-making requires many hands. Most of those farms were run by stewards, working for fat prelates who spent near all their time in Normandy or Flanders. A sharp steward could line his own pockets with cheap slave labour. Money was the true god of too many men, then as now, annulling any claim made upon Heaven.

There had been some delay the day we left Glororum; Crinan's cinch strap had broken, then a maid came to tell me that Herleve was refusing all food. We set it all to right, but I fumed at the delay, not remembering that God sets our feet in motion in his own time. We had clattered into the little rock-walled stable yard just as Chatta's boys were shutting the stout gates against the night. After much ale, I felt little like resuming the march up the steep forested hill to the west in the morning, so we stayed slug-a-bed till long after our usual hour to depart.

Splashing in leisure across the ford, we began our road up the hill. Just where the track ran into the darkness of the forest, an old crossing trail ran down from the north. Near obliterated, it came from ruined camps up in the hills. Some men said they had been built by Romans, others said it was the work of the little people. When I first visited them, I saw they had been made by men like ourselves, albeit very ancient. These were no Roman ruins such as abide at Chollerford, but works of a people wild and free, who left us their tracings in stone and no guide to ken them. 'Twas such a place as gives a man shivers, unless he has no sense or feeling.

I had just yawned and stretched in the saddle, when I saw a furtive movement down that haunted trail. It was not imagination that peopled the shadows! Without hesitation, we charged, and four men burst from the trees and ran. They headed south toward deeper undercover, where they could disappear. One of them was slowed; he dragged a pitiful wretch of a child behind him at the end of a dirty rope. Without thought, I spitted him like the beast he was. Julian, too, had edged toward the forest as he ran one of the miscreants through. Young Crinan, with the quickness of youth, sprang from his horse and swung into the dark forest in pursuit of the others. We heard his staff crack upon head, then silence. It was not long ere he returned shaking his head; the fourth, he said, had gotten away in the thick brush.

Waiting for my men to return, I sat my horse in the middle of that God-forsaken track and surveyed the pitiful scrap of humanity before me. Standing as tall in the dust of the road as it was able, the child stared at me with hollow eyes. The fair hair, neither short nor long, was matted with twigs, framing a face streaked with dirt and tears. Brambles had scarred the thin arms and legs, and the child's feet were broken and bleeding. Only a dirty shift covered the bony little body; I had no idea if 'twere lad or lass. A short length of rope had cut a burn around the waif's neck, and now hung limp by its side. Yet there was a pride of defiance in the blue eyes that blazed up into mine, as if daring—or perhaps welcoming—death. A knight could not dishonor that bravery by words; instead I quietly sat my horse with compassionate demeanor until Crinan returned and reported. He then lifted the child to the saddle before me, and cradling the poor scarred body gently, we wheeled and returned to Chatta's.

The innkeeper's wife took my bundle quickly and disappeared. When she had washed and dressed the child, she came to me with the news that it was a girl, possibly eight or so years of age. What little memory remained to that broken and starving lass was what we had already suspected. She had been stolen from her parents farm, and knew only that the slavers were taking her south to work in a dairy. They had fed her just enough bread to keep her alive, and she had shivered through the cold spring nights in her thin shift. Afraid of the wood spirits, the slavers traveled only by day, through the thickest cover. They had holed up for the last night at the ancient camp to the north; had we not been delayed, we should have missed them altogether. No, she had no ken of where her home had been, but thought they had been traveling perhaps four days. After some coaxing, she shyly said her name was Allie. Later, she was to tell the name of the village in which she had lived: Neather Lea. Over the years, she was able to recover little more than this, her curtain of memory shut down by the blow of her abduction.

Although the lass was to become a prize beyond any inkling I might have had that day, it didn't dawn upon me until we reached Glororum that now this rescued slave was mine to deal with. I first left her with the maids to coddle, until her strength should come back. We found new clothes for her, among which was a short cloak that had one of those newfangled buttons at the neck. It looked near as large as her head, and I laughed and called her "Button;" a nickname that stuck through her childhood. Herleve, roused by the commotion, came later to insist the waif be baptized a Christian by Father Cedric. She disdained the good Scot's name of Allie as uncouth, and said it sounded a heathen note. She picked the name Ellen for the waif, and though I felt it unfitting, the lass bore it for the rest of her life.

Eftsoons the clamor died, and I left Glororum once again upon the regular marches, and thence went to Ellingham to hold my regular court session. With the arrival of Ellen, Herleve had come to be her usual self, and began riding again and managing the household. I interfered little in the day-to-day affairs of the Hall when she was well, for she was better with our people when I kept away. All efforts on my part she regarded as a challenge to her sovereign authority; it seemed often as if we were two knights in contest for the field of honour. Never had I known a woman so combative.

Thus it was by chance alone that I went one day, during daylight, to the kitchen. Entering the dark room from the sunshine of the courtyard, I needs must stop to adjust my eyes. With horror, I saw the pitiful waif, Ellen, bent over the stone slop trough, wrestling a huge kettle, much too heavy for her. Her poor stick arms scrubbed at caked soot and dried porridge; her new clothes were wet and besmirched. She looked up at me as if betrayed, her grimy sullen face scarce holding back the tears. Of an instant, I cast the kettle from her and clasped her in my arms, pity disarming anger for the moment. Thus soothed, she began at last to weep, great sobbing tears, the first I had seen from that brave child. At last, I was able to quiet her. The cook came then, and told me all I needed to know. Herleve had ordered the child to the kitchen, and demanded she be given the hardest, filthiest chores, "as befits her station." She herself came often to see that her petulant demands were carried out, and woe to the servant who showed the child mercy. The poor lass's only failing had been that I had rescued her, had showed concern over her. That and her helplessness were enough for Herleve.

Anger became a cold, hard wedge of iron in my soul. This was enough. Yet I dared not let Ellen sense my anger; she was distraught enough, and believed as Herleve had told her, that her innate wickedness had brought her to these straights. Something had to be done to remove her once and for all from the torments of my wife. Suddenly, I thought of a place for my foundling.

"My child, I should have known sooner what had befallen you. You are not wicked; 'tis I should be faulted for trusting a woman whom I well know is of unsound mind. Come, I know of a fine place where you may stay, away from this kitchen with its vile smells." I myself remembered but too keenly the stinking kitchen at Alnwick. Stooping and holding to the thin shoulders, I looked into the child's clear eyes. Though her pride had been shaken, I saw there a stubborn tenacity that held hope for her future. "But you must never come to the Hall without my accompanying you. You must stay safely away."

Button never asked once where we were going, but put her hand in mine. I took her then to the stables, and to old Peter, and told him what had befallen. He, more than any other man upon the estate, free or villein, would take no words from my haughty wife. The only time she had come to interfere in the stable, he had chased her off with a hayfork. I told her it had served her well. She never went back, always sending a page when in need of her palfrey.

"I want no trouble with my lady wife," I told Peter, "but the child must stay here. Margaret may bring her fresh clothes and food, but I do not wish her to abide with any of our people, for fear of vengeance from Herleve's twisted mind. As she is able, the child may help with the horses. We will make her a pallet above the harness room, among the spare blankets and trappings."

"None can harm you here in the stable, Button. Remember that Our Lord himself was sheltered as a babe among the animals in a stable. This will be home to you, and Peter will be your guard. Remember also, you have a powerful angel that stands by your side to guide and protect you, else you would never have come to be here. I swear, also, upon my word, that any who try to harm you henceforth shall answer to my authority." I held her again for a moment, and felt that she was comforted. Climbing the narrow ladder to the loft, I saw to her bed among the horse blankets with my own hands. That became her refuge for as long as we both did live.

Returning to Old Hall, I sought out Herleve. Finding her spinning with some of the maids, I dismissed them all, intending a quarrel. Herleve always preferred to air her grievances before an assemblage of servants, knowing it would add to my outrage. This time, I took the field first. Nor would I grace her despicable behavior by addressing her as "Lady," as was my wont. "Wife," I growled, "why did you send the waif Ellen to do man's work in the kitchen?"

"Ah, she has come crying to you, has she? I'll see to that. She is naught but the runt of a litter of wild swine. Why did you bother to bring her here? Now I have another mouth to feed."

"You seem to forget, Wife, that it is my land that feeds us, that I am the master here. I ordered that the child be protected, and when I walked to the kitchen this morning, I saw her bent double with the work you assigned. I did not rescue her from slavery to have you make a slave of her! No, quiet, I say"—Herleve was opening her venomous mouth—"I have taken that innocent child from this house of iniquity. And I swear to you, Woman, that if you so much as lift a finger in her direction, I myself will beat you and turn you out penniless. Then you can join your father in the gutters of Newcastle, like the proper whore you are." It was going too far, but years of forbearance had burst their bonds at last. I was through with that woman, and told her so.

"From now on, I will bide in the undercroft, as far from your presence as possible." I turned on my heel and strode off, leaving her no chance to reply, for I was heartsick. If she screamed and berated me, we would return to our old ways, scrapping like animals. Staying beside her tarred me with the brush of her evil nature, nor could I feel sorry for her any longer.

Thus the pattern of our lives changed with the coming of the foundling, Ellen. In just three short years, the war would come to change us even further.

Chapter 12

Pestilence

1187 was the year the Devil walked abroad upon the land. In spring, the cattle birthed but few live calves. So many dead half-formed calves lay in the waste that great numbers of rooks gathered for the grisly harvest. Unsated, they then took to robbing the fields of their greening seed. Every child was set to watching the fields and gardens; it was grim play, for our winter's food was at stake. Not since the drouth had we been so threatened.

Little would Satan stop there. Upon the First of May, the ancient feast of Beltane, a cold, wet wind descended upon all Bamburgh. Rain and sleet filled the whole miserable day. The Maypole in the vill was drenched, nor could the lads and lasses celebrate the coming of spring. It was inauspicious; so much so, that I threw open Glororum's great barn and brought an extra measure of ale. The sturdy youths reset the pole within the barn, but the hard-packed floor resisted, and the pole set not well. During the dance, the Maypole collapsed and had to be abandoned. All tried to put a good face upon the matter, but the omen made us shiver.

The Forster barn was the wonder of the land, from Alnwick to Berwick Town. It was near-round, lagged with great timbers like a ship, and towered into the sky. Twenty yards across, it was greater then any barn yet built in the northland. It had been raised in Hugo's time by Danes

164

captured in the raid upon Bamburgh—seafaring men. The barn was set about like the points of a mariner's compass, with sixteen sides of four yards each. In each cardinal direction was a wide door, so that the wind might draw through to aid in winnowing or drying of hay in wet weather. Upon the crest of the roof was a cupola through which the great structure might breathe, it being left open upon the sides. Nor did the lofts where hay was stored impede that breath, but always stayed fresh and sweet-smelling. To the west, in an ell, lay the sheds and byres, the slaughterhouse and tannery. The smell was oft noisome, even at Old Hall, which lay yet westerly.

The unseemly cold rain of Beltane, blown on the northwest wind, joined our dance with gusts of fulsome smell, especially since the tannery was overfull with skins, laid in from unfortunate beasts which had died in the fields. Later, when the Maypole was to be laid upon the Beltane fire, we had the Devil's battle to keep the bonfire going. Nor could we hold the Beltane fire upon the village common, as was tradition, but instead, kindled it upon the road in the lee of the great barn. Now all folk ken that roads bring ill, but it was either put the fire there or have none at all, which would have been worse. Nor could the ancient Beltane rite of fire blessing be performed; but when it was observed, it was oft done on Midsummer's Day anyway.

Not long after, the griping sickness came among us, and many a funeral we had, of old and young. Margaret and Andrew's little Ralph was not the only child to ascend to our Lord in Heaven; full one in three of our bairns was taken. Annie's mother Ruth died, as did one of our housemaids; our man-at-arms, Rafe; and two other men and an old woman. Had an enemy come, the rest of us could not have held him off, so sick were we all.

Richard, our reeve, asked for a meeting of the manor court. I sat, as Bors was deathly ill. 'Twas the end of June, just before Midsummer's Day, which is the feast of St. John, my saint's day. The weather was just beginning to dry. We had not been able to think of haying, so wet had it been and so devastated were we. The curia asked that we set the Midsummer fires as was done of old. These great fires were kindled and all the animals of the farm passed through the flames to cleanse them. It was a ritual lost in time. Since our woes had begun with the cattle, I readily agreed. But we had no strength among us to perform the ritual at Midsummer Beltane. I set the day forward to the Feast of St. Swithin's, July 15. It was an auspicious day for all England, and if the weather turned dry, the rest of the year would be good. If it rained—which I misdoubted, for we had had our fill—there would be forty days and nights of more wet and miserable weather.

When the men had garnered more strength, I ordered all rotted byres and sties pulled down, for even our sturdy swine had been afflicted. Before the cleansing of the animals, Father Cedric made procession through the village. First, a man went before, carrying a torch into every cot in the vill, nor did they neglect Old Hall and its New Tower. The fire, we believed, would cleanse the vapors from the air which held the sickness so fiercely among us. Then our priest, accompanied by the statue of the Virgin from the church at Bamburgh, entered and blessed each house. All believed that if Holy Mother were only to see our misery, she would have mercy upon us and our poor beasts.

So it was done. Then one by one, every animal both of vill and demesne was driven through the squeeze fence and hence through blazing fire. Great was the fury and clamor of those animals! Only the horses were left uncleansed, for fire upon a horse will ruin him. After, new whitewash was spread over the houses, and lime upon cesspits and all stinking ground. We did not ken then what caused sickness and death, but we had wit enough to know that cleansing stopped most plague.

By July's end, only a scorching wind reminded us of the Devil's passing. He left us mourning, and went to seek other mischief. It was not till nigh Christmastide that we learned whither he had gone. A minstrel traveling to Berwick Town brought us word that in July, Jerusalem had fallen to the Saracens. Prince Richard was enraged. He vowed a Crusade, much against the wishes of his father, King Henry. The winds of winter were not as bitter as that news, and the storm clouds piled upon the horizon were portent of the war yet to come.

The year 1188 brought hiatus. Men fumed that the holy places were being defiled, but kings move in devious ways. It was not till May that we received word that in January a great shining cross had appeared in the sky over Gisors, where Henry and Richard were meeting with Philip of France. Those great kings fell to their knees before the portent of God, and both Henry and Philip took the cross of Crusade that Richard had already espoused. More un-likely allies in war could not be imagined; they had fought one another across the face of the continent since Philip had come to the throne of France, eight years before.

So amazed were we at this miracle, that many of us began consideration of taking up the Crusader's cross. And serious consideration it was. A man gambled life, limb, and the resources of his patrimony against fervor for Christ and the honour of knighthood in a Holy War. It was not a decision made lightly. I ventured on the road to Hatton in July, after haying, to speak with mother and Stephen and Maud.

A sadness hung over Hatton, for the heir of the house, young Stephen, had also died of the griping sickness in 1187. He was William's age, but taller and better mannered. I felt their loss deeply, more since my own sons had survived. But Maud had been delivered of another son upon my birthday in 1188, and I agreed to stand godfather to him as well as Mary Rose. We christened him Henry; he was to be the last son in that family, as Henry was in ours. In later years, we often called him Hutton Henry, to distinguish between the cousins.

Stephen, like myself, was anxious about the Crusade. His eyes shone when he spoke of battles to come. War was what we were all about, what we had been trained and prepared for all our lives. The fact that we were naught but English country valetti, much looked down upon, added fuel to our fires. Yet the weight of vill and demesne stood upon our backs, and had to be accounted for. I went to speak with mother, and it was like the old days before Herleve had driven her to stay at Hutton.

She was anxious. "I have had many an evil dream because of this war; always I see it sucking men and horses into its great bloody maw and spitting forth bones. Yet I, too, feel the cross calling to us from Jerusalem Town. But I know English Henry of old; because he fell to his knees once does not mean that he may not repent him of the vow. Nor do I like an alliance with France; that self-serving domain has always sacrificed its good intentions for presumptuousness."

"I, too, am restless for those reasons, Mother, but my heart is calling me, as I know Stephen's is. Yet so much remains to be arranged; my head hurts thinking of it."

"First thing is to make a will," she quietly said, "and leave it with the Bishop of Durham. The same for Stephen. If two of you go, belike but one shall return." Her face was sad, and I knew that what she kenned was true. "You must arrange for your sons, and for Herleve."

I told her then that Herleve and I were living apart, albeit in the same house. She shook her head. "I saw it coming to that. But God will send you consolation. And all the more reason to hedge her unreason about with lawyer's words. The clerics at Durham will help; you both should ride that way soon. For I am very sure that this Crusade will envelop you."

Our minds, half made up, found surety when we rode up to make our wills, for we had begun to come to grips with the details our long absence would require. Then I rode home to plan and ponder, waiting to see which way those clouds of war might blow.

Fighting broke out once again between Henry and Philip, with Richard as instigator. The hate between the King and his sons—the rage and hate that filled every dukedom on the continent—promised to delay any Crusade indefinitely. Finally, Count Theobald of Blois and other counts who had allied with Henry refused to fight any longer. The battle, they said, should not be among Christians, so long as Saracens held the Holy City. Yet even the Pope could not settle the quarrels between those three, and their fighting broke open the old wounds again in June of '89.

Henry, ill and old, was defeated at last at Tours in July. He died then, at Chinon, granting his throne to Richard with great bitterness. Men said that when the old king died, his very servants stripped him of all he owned. One young squire—may God bless him!—wrapped Henry as well as he was able in his own short cloak, and begged a ring of common metal to put upon the king's finger for his burial. It was ill portent for the barren days to come.

In July, Queen Eleanor, released at last from prison and exile by the death of her husband, sailed to England. In a series of marches, she herself visited many prisons; and across the land, all manner of felons were released, owing only homage to herself and the new king, Richard, who had always been her favorite. Stephen wagered this would lead to much crime, but I argued that the most hardened criminals were already hanged; only grumblers and debtors remained. They and their families belike would be enough grateful that peace would remain. Thus it proved.

Richard was crowned in London on September third. Every lord of the land, so it seemed, was there. Stephen and I rode in the entourage of his kinsman, Bishop Hugh of Durham, who was awarded a position of honour in the coronation. It was a long affair, climaxed by a huge banquet. Though Stephen and I sat at a lower table, our senses were dazzled by the wealth and sumptuousness of both ritual and feast, exceeding well what I had known at the court of William the Lion. All was marred only by a senseless uprising of the people against the Jews. Richard attempted to put a halt to the rioting, but Jews everywhere began to be robbed, murdered, and burned alive.

Finally, Richard stirred himself to put down the riots and hang some of the ringleaders. We saw then that he would be a strong king who would hold the land in his fist. A sinewy fist it was, too, for Richard was tall and strong and comely, and a fighter with no match in the world. Truth told, he was impulsive and had a fierce temper, but he was also a man to inspire loyalty in all who knew him. Stephen and I agreed; this was a worthy king for our days.

The kingdom was turned topsy-turvy while Richard searched for money to wage his Crusade. Men were not cheap; a knight might make a shilling a day for as long as he was in service. Then there were horses and equipment, ships and fittings. The thought of all that money was beyond the power of my reason. Still, we bided, waiting for the call that would send us to arms.

Sooner came the call of the Saladin tax, a tithe of ten percent of all the estate produced, to be collected yearly. It was a wracking burden, added to the tithe already sent to the Church. We had thought Henry's taxes were harsh! Richard squeezed us even further, and the whole kingdom became for sale. No prelates were confirmed unless they bought their sinecures. Heriots became ruinous. All sheriffs were removed from office, and had to buy their way back in again, which gave the common folk many a jest. Any man with enough money might own power. So it was with our Bishop, Hugh. 'Twas whispered that he paid King Richard 10,000 silver pounds to become justiciar for Northumberland whilst Richard was on Crusade. Knowing our Hugh, the silver would float back to him like bread upon the waters.

Stephen and I had vowed to take the cross at Durham, but waited till the friars sent out by Richard, two by two, should come to enroll our people also. Many wished to take the cross, but it was a solemn undertaking, and I preached against the friars. Too often men are swayed by honeyed words into what they will regret. But the excitement of war inspired our young men, and the two pence a day for infantrymen called to many whose gray heads should have been more sober. All, however, were fired to redeem the Holy Places from the Saracen.

In the end, pledged with me were Andrew and Crinan, young Will, and Carl. In vain did I try to discourage Carl; when he insisted, I could but promise Nicolette that we would try to bring him back of a piece. Julian, too, clamored to take the cross, but I forbade him, and so did his wife. His gray head was of better service to Bors at the farm. The friars promised that the king's agent would come from Durham soon, to seal the bargain.

I mind well the day that Anselm the clerk came upon that errand. As was so often my wont, I had taken the boys to the stable. It was warm September; William was ruddy from running, coursing ahead like a hound. I sent him to Margaret's for water, knowing full well that he would make for there anyway, to see if there were any bread to spare. William was always hungry. Henry chattered by my side; his incessant "why?" was evoked by everything he spied. I was glad when Peter came to take him. Button came to keep me company; as I leaned upon the pasture gate to watch the horses, she climbed up and teetered by my side. "Ah, Sire, see, the dark mare will foal within a day or two. I ken the signs as well as Peter."

Amused at her wit, I asked, "And what else can you tell me of the herd?" In a year, she had become conversant with every beast; she was a natural with the horses, and Peter's chores had been made lighter. So she told me of the well- or ill-being of each, and I remarked upon the astuteness of her answers. We stood silent, then, each dreaming in our own way, but in perfect comfort. I felt more solace here than I had known in many a day, though I came often to let the healing of the paddock sink into my bones. My will provisioned that the lass be sent to Maud at Hutton, should I not return to Glororum. 'Twould be a pity, for her heart lay here with the horses.

Of a sudden, I was minded of the handsome palfrey that stood in the pasture of my neighbor, William of Lucker.

Scarce larger than a pony, the dapple-gray gelding with dark eyes was as gentle as he was willing, as if thereby he might make amends for his diminutive size. Dapple had belonged to William's youngest daughter ere she married and moved to Edinburgh; he had grown fat with idleness. He could be had cheaply, the perfect horse for a young lass. Button will trim him up, I thought; it will be my going-away present to her. A great contentment filled my soul.

But peace was born only to be shattered; a page came running from the house to tell me the clerk from Durham had arrived. He had come up the coast road to Bamburgh, enscribing all our neighbors upon the way. Gathering my sons, I went with some growing excitement to see what King Richard's Crusade would mean to a country valetti of Northumberland.

Anselm stayed a full three days, for each man upon the manor who took the cross must needs be enrolled. Long and hard was what you now call dickering, for many privileges of war had to be negotiated ere signing the king's pledge. Rather than allowing Anselm to sign our men as infantry, I insisted that they be registered as squires. This doubled their wage to 4 pence a day. As to our horses, the King's writ required the manor to supply two beasts to the Crusade; all others were to be paid for from Richard's war chest, along with silver for arms and provisioning. To supply us with destriers as well as pack animals, ten more horses were bought by the King. In addition, ship passage was paid to France, and thence to the Holy Land, with meat and drink provisioned by the king. In return, if any man were slain, half of his estate would go to a common fund, held in trust to pay the debts of the Crusade, and only then would his heirs be satisfied according to will.

Even nobler incentive was given by forgiveness of the Saladin tithe. All duties of the realm, such as our cornage, were suspended till a Crusader returned home, as were all debts. Since the Forster's neither were owed nor indebted, this made little difference to us, save as recognition of

Richard's generosity, which we would have occasion to taste in later matters.

I had forgotten one detail that was to cause much bother. Stephen came riding to Glororum near a week after Anselm had left, bringing Robin with him. To be sure, I had forgotten that Robin was my ward, since he had been biding at Hutton. "He insists," said Stephen, "upon taking the cross and riding with us. Since he is legally beneath your protection, you must sign him with the king's agent."

What Stephen said was true, but I was annoyed for a moment. What trouble I should have now, running after Anselm! Nor would I be in position to bargain favorably. I tried to dissuade Robin, largely because of his youth (he was but seventeen), but he shook his head stubbornly, and I was minded of his father. I bethought then that the oversight was mine, and not the fault of the boy, and welcomed him as I should have done. With that gesture, his faith in me remained, and I all unwitting laid my life in his hands.

Too many are the details of preparation for an old man to relate. One scene that fills the mind, as certain meaningless things oft do, is of our pages sitting in the courtyard, between the kitchen and Old Hall. Upon the courtyard stones, well-cleansed with wet dough which was then thrown to the swine, they rolled stiff bread dough into thin strands perhaps a foot long. When these had risen some, Nicholas the baker baked them slowly till hard. We had countless of these near imperishable bread sticks, sprinkled with salt, and wrapped in linen packets sealed with wax. To go with them, we carried kegs of salt herring, which were always plentiful at Bamburgh. These were to serve us in good stead, as the King's provisioners were oft careless about our rations.

We were fortunate to have a good harbour at Budle Bay, in the shelter of great Bamburgh castle itself. It was to here that the Vikings first had come, and it was from there that we sailed a week after Easter of 1190. The king's own ships had come for us, and fair crowded they were when we left.

From Glororum there was myself, not yet knighted; Andrew and Crinan and Carl as freehold squires; Will, Will's son, as villein squire, and my nephew Robin. Joining us was Stephen, the brother-in-law I had grown to love. With him were two men of his estate: Odo, a sergeant, whom he too had enrolled as squire; and Mark, a freehold squire of just sixteen. Alan, a freehold knight in the service of the Esshes, also came with Stephen's party. With us were twenty horses, three tents, provisions, and enough arms for a dozen men. Small wonder the ships did not sink! But these faces of home were to sustain us through many a trying day ahead.

Chapter 13

Crusade!

In the fortnight after Easter of 1190, the ships of Richard the King gathered in Calais harbour. Our ships from Northumberland were among the last of the stragglers. When the army had all assembled, the horses were exercised one last time; then that tremendous fleet set off down the coast of the land now known as France. It was a relief to be at last on the way to the Holy Land. Every evening we anchored for fresh meat, and to give our poor beasts the pleasure of treading upon firm ground once again.

Richard's provisions were adequate, and we had no care save to ready our war gear, sing ballads, dice, and jest. All was still well among us. We were to meet Richard in Marseilles, and the war seemed very far away. The ships must needs sail around the Iberian peninsula and enter the Mediterranean Sea to reach our trysting-port, but because of the animals, our pace was leisurely. In Portugal, we were warmly greeted by the King, and invited to stay. In truth, he had our sharp swords in mind, for we were invited to assist him against the Moors of Iberia. We were glad of the exercise after the boredom of the ships, and we swept that small country clean of Saracens. It was the first time I had experience of serving a foreign king, of putting my sword to hire, and it felt pure strange, so used were we to service only within our ordered system of land tenure.

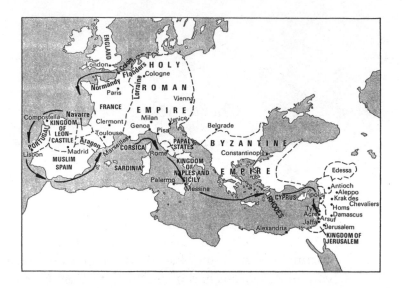

Europe and the Holy Land — 1190 with Route of the Third Crusade

We docked at Marseilles on the 22nd of August, the feast of St. Sigfrid of Wear, and found that Richard, impatient as always, had sailed for Messina the week before. He had hired more boats, and went fuming off to rendezvous with Philip in Sicily. It behooved us to be under way again, and so we were, after a rest of but a week. We set sail again on the feast of St. Augustine—an auspicious day for us sinners—and reached Messina harbor some time before the King's party actually arrived. He had made many stops in Italy; as with all armies, we hurried only to wait. We stood upon our ships, and after a short while, Richard's small fleet arrived. Messages were sent to all that our landing was to be made as impressive as possible. We polished armor (once again!) till it reflected the rays of the hot southern sun, and all debarked together to march into Messina as the greatest army the world had ever seen. Our trumpets blared, and we were instructed to clash our arms as we walked or rode forth. The din was nigh unbearable.

Richard was met by the nobles of Sicily, and by his old bed-fellow, Philip Augustus, who had already quietly landed with the French army. There was much feasting and diplomacy among them for the next month, whilst we set our tents outside the city walls and began to organize a sort of rough city. More out of boredom than anything else, some of the English knights, with their followers, began a series of skirmishes with the townspeople. It was October, and we had been idle too long.

Richard admonished us at first, then conceived the grand plan of conquering Messina, more as a show of political power than from any real grievance. Two thousand of us were chosen, along with 1,000 archers. It required only that we wait out the hail of Sicilian arrows. Then while our own archers kept the defenders behind their ramparts with good English arrows all abuzz, we took a battering ram to the gate. It was open in a heartbeat, and we swarmed into the town. Only the fortified houses of the nobles were entered; all else was spared. In the nonce, others of our men were burning the Sicilian fleet in the harbor. King Tancred's palace and King Philip's quarters were spared, but all of Tancred's Sicilian knights were taken hostage and held for ransom. A great amount of gold changed hands, and went into Richard's war chest.

For the first time, I began to see much of what war is all about. Upon entering the nobles' houses, we were told by our field commanders that we could keep whatever loot we might find, and passing strange it seemed to me to be lifting money from another man's house. In England, we would have called it stealing; here, it was reckoned as part of our wages, and the man who did not fill his hands when he found opportunity was a fool, for the man behind him certainly would. I did not fare well, being hesitant; still I did find one cache of silver that helped to sustain us.

It was after that skirmish that Richard assembled and knighted those valetti who had taken part in the battle. Both Stephen and I received adubment at this time. Being at war, the ceremony was not as grand as what had been accorded to my friends Duncan and David. Still, we did receive a hot bath and a fine feast. I cannot well describe my feelings at prayer that night, for it seemed a lifetime had already passed in service to king and country, a life spent in hard knocks, desperate training, and crushing responsibility. Yet I could see my mother, also kneeling in prayer on my behalf, and great strength invested me. I am proud of you, my son, she seemed to say, and the peace of angels filled my heart. I felt fulfilled at last by knighthood; Sir John meant more to me than any name; it was a badge of honour. When I tried to explain all this to Stephen, he concurred readily enough, but I misdoubt that he felt as deeply as I, his nature being more forthright and practical.

It was after this that we built for Richard the tall wooden tower he called "Greek Killer," for it had been chiefly the Sicilian Greeks who had set their faces against the English. The Mategrifon tower would be disassembled and sail east with us, and we were to foray with Greeks again in Cyprus. Richard never trusted a Greek. In the meantime, we settled outside the walls of Messina, as winter was coming on, and no ship captain would risk the sea at that time of year. The Kings, in strict concord, regulated both prices and gambling, and our commanders enforced order. Many of the men railed at that long, dreary winter, struggling constantly with wind and rain in our thin tents. It was the devil's own chore to keep equipment dry and clean of mud, and the latrines from caving in or overflowing. The dull routine enforced boredom. Yet I found much to do ere we began battle in earnest.

It had become readily apparent that to fight in this war, a knight needs must rely on a great helm, as the arrows came so thickly. I bargained and obtained one, and set about on its padding, to remake it with as much comfort as possible. Stephen, in the fashion of the southern knights, already had one of these encompassing helms, but Sir Alan did not. He, too, set about equipping himself, then we jousted a bit with one another, to test both vision and the judgment of our arms. It was strange, peering through the eye slit and trying to fight with this escaped cooking-pot inverted upon our heads.

Due to the concealment of a knight's countenance by the great helm, men began decorating their shields with divers devices by which they might be recognized. All the noble knights' shields had been gilt and glittering for our entrance into Messina, while tradition required squires to carry a plain, white shield. Many of the knights added a simple cross or band to their golden shields, and required their squires to adopt the same design. It soon became apparent that simple designs, even of divers colours, would afford little recognition. I had much time for thought that winter, and finally decided upon a mason's square, its apex pointed toward heaven, centered upon my shield. Alfric had made me believe that the mason's art was akin to the Mass in offering pleasure to God. I left the shield a shining silver for ease of polishing, but the chevron I coloured green, for the hills of home. In the three sections thus formed, I had an artisan depict the hunting horn that had belonged to my father and to his father before him, and to their fathers before that. It was the ebony horn of some great ox that wandered upon the earth no more; it was twice the width and heft of a common horn. Always the great horn was hung from a baldric of green, for the forests from which we took our name. Three were my sons, and three horns were thereon inscribed; one for Randolph, one for William, and one for little Henry.

I missed the boys, and the green rolling hills and forests of home. I missed Button, and wondered how she fared with her fat Dapple. Yet we had concern enough over the younger squires with us, for soldiers away from home oft fall into the ways of sodomy, and boys are prime meat for men's appetites. Even worse, Richard himself, like Giles, gave his love to men, so that no knight felt shame in doing likewise. It became an evil camp, nor did we venture far seeking neighborly gossip, lest we give false reassurance to those seeking new consorts. When not exercising the horses or ourselves, or cleansing equipment and fixing meals, we spent endless hours at draughts or chess. Andrew and Robin, particularly, who kept to my tent, were always at draughts. This suited me, as oft I simply wished to ponder, as I had while devising the Forster shield. Little did we ken that such devices would become the art of heraldry in years to come. Many ballads came to mind then also, something I had not had time to indulge myself with for years.

Stephen, too, worked a design for his shield: a single ash tree. The Esshes were called for that tree, and Stephen had but one son as heir. It was fitting. With Stephen abode our Crinan, and the boy Mark. Alan kept the third tent, with Odo and Carl, who became fast friends, and Will's son. Thus all our youths abided under protection of a made knight, and were also kept from hatching small plots of their own. Well we remembered our own days as squires, and the mischief idle hands could find when abetted by several heads.

It was near Christmas when Richard (some say upon the advice of his angel guardian) hied him, barefoot and in sackcloth, to the chapel of Sir Reginald de Moyac. There the King asked his chaplains to scourge him for his sins, and he renounced sodomy for all time. Odo grunted what we were all thinking, that sooner might a leopard change his spots. Still, Richard made every effort, and God must have seen into his heart, for when we sailed at last for the Holy land, fortune followed the English crown.

It was at the great Christmas feast, when many of the captains and noble knights were invited to dine with Richard, that we learned that Stephen's great-uncle, Bishop Hugh of Durham, was no longer one of the King's justiciars. With his demotion, we too fell from grace. So we made Christmas cheer among ourselves, as family should, and envied not the golden plate from which the other knights ate, nor the jeweled cups from which they drank. Too many heads were uneasy that night, for Richard was in foul mood.

Not long after Christmas, the famed seer and preacher, Joachim of Fiore, came to tell Richard of his visions. Full learned was he, upon the stories of the Apocalypse, and he turned them to our Crusade with holy fervor. Saladin, he said, was one of the monstrous heads of the great beast; he would fall in battle at the hands of Richard himself. His words made us shiver. Many of us were there, crowded into the hall to hear Joachim, but Richard himself had much to say upon the Antichrist. All who heard him were amazed at his wisdom and his prophecy, which rivaled that of Joachim himself. Truth to tell, both were proved wrong; but then, no man truly knows what lies within the mind of God.

Not long after the worthy abbot left Messina, rumours began to circulate throughout the camp that Prince John had returned to England and was planning to assume the throne in Richard's absence. He had not dared, had his brother not been on Crusade, for John was ever a coward with a villainous heart. These rumours had more truth than the prophecies of Joachim; so much so, that Richard began to fret to be upon the march, so that we might speedily conclude this Crusade. A kingdom was being held as pawn.

It was the Wednesday before Easter, 1191, before we actually sailed. It had been near a year since we had left Budle Bay. On Good Friday, there was a great storm at sea, and many of us were sick both of body and mind. When we finally docked at Crete, we found some twenty-five of the King's ships had been blown away. Many of us knelt and gave thanks, but we were quickly ordered back into the barks, as a fair wind was blowing for Rhodes.

We bided ten days upon that island, not least because Richard himself was sick. Hope entered our hearts once again, when we found that Richard had been making inquiries about the isle of Cyprus. It began to smell like a battle, and we were sore overdue. It seems the despot, Isaac, who ruled Cyprus, had taken power by wile and the presentation of forged documents. The common folk of the country were murmuring against him, accusing him of all manners of blasphemy. More to our purpose, he was reputed to be an ally of Saladin.

Richard found too, that some of our men had been shipwrecked upon the shores of Cyprus, and as was common in those times, were being held for ransom. Even worse, the ship carrying the King's sister, Joan, and his fiancee, Berengaria of Navarre, had been blown into the harbor there, and was standing just offshore. Isaac entreated the women to visit his palace, but they sent back soft words and hoped that Richard would soon come. Their position was precarious.

To make a long story short, we soon arrived and took over the port of Limassol. There Richard and Berengaria were married at last, but Richard had no time for a honeymoon. Isaac, while entreating for peace, stole secretly away by night to Famagusta and ordered us all to leave. His temerity was met with the sword. At Nicosia, our well-trained ranks held against his scattered troops, nor was he able to break our lines. It was a preview of what we would find in the Holy Land. Also as forewarning were the petulant letters from Philip, requiring us to be soon at Acre and leave off the diversion we had found in Cyprus. Yet later events proved Richard's wisdom in securing that fortunate isle, contrary to prevailing opinion.

Sir Alan, Crinan, Carl, and Andrew had gone to the battle of Nicosia under King Guy of Lusignan. So successful were they, that King Guy endubbed all those squires who were with him who were not yet knights. Too, in Isaac's castles was much treasure, and having learned our lesson at Messina, we lost no time in making up our wages. Richard himself extracted a toll of half the goods of the land, and the riches of Cyprus thus paid our expenses whilst in the Holy Land, and for long after.

The army was treated to a great feast and a short rest; each knight in the campaign received a silver piece from Richard. The squires and common soldiers also received gifts, so all were content. There was special rejoicing in our tents over the new-made knights. All the men of Glororum had given luster to their training, but I was especially proud of Andrew. Indeed, my prophecy to my mother had come true; Andrew was now not only my brother-in-arms, but made knight as well.

We sailed from the pleasant land of Cyprus on the feast of St. Boniface: June 5, 1191. As Crusaders, our vows would be fulfilled at last, when we set ashore upon the Holy Land. Yet in our first attempt to dock at Tyre, Richard was turned away by the fortress garrison. That was Philip's work. Fuming, we spent the night upon our ships and resumed sailing in the morning, south toward the siege of Acre.

Upon that venture, we had a battle at sea. Never would I have thought to be tossing about in those small ships, plotting to sink another vessel. Upon land, massed in a row, with a discerning destrier beneath, a man has a chance in battle. Here, I could see naught but a watery grave. A huge ship, carrying the flag of the King of France, had run across our bows. We soon found that the ship belonged not to France, but was flying a captured banner. Our own galleys began to ram that great ship, and the sailors to engage in hand-to-hand conflict. It was not long ere the enemy ship, rolling in the water and badly broken, began to sink. Richard had the devil's own time keeping our troops from slaughtering all the Saracens who washed about at the mercy of the waves. Finally, some were pulled aboard Richard's flagship, and the King ascertained that the ship had been a Saracen troop-carrier, going to the relief of Acre, where Christian forces had been sitting in siege for two years.

I have oft been asked why we followed Richard so loyally, when he had so many grave faults. To answer that, I can only point to the Providence that always seemed to nurture him, and to his own boldness in seizing that Providence. We never felt abandoned by God when we were under the banner of Richard the Lionhearted. And Lionheart indeed he was, both in bravery and fighting skill, and in his generosity. His great Destiny washed over our own, making us also chosen, knights in the service of the Kingdom of Heaven.

On June 8, the besiegers of Acre welcomed us to the Holy Land, with much clamor and triumphal procession. Our tents were set, and within a few days, we began the final siege of that near-impregnable city of Acre. Richard's natural ability soon made him Commander-in-chief. His strength alone fetched awe among the troops; once he carried a siege engine up to the walls when two struggling men had scarce been able to budge it. Philip had tried to buy the loyalty of his knights by offering them three gold pieces a month; Richard countered by offering four. Thus all rallied around the English banner and siege machines. These we had brought with us, along with Mategrifon tower, and they were the greatest ever yet built. It behooved us to defend them well, as Saladin, who was encamped outside the city walls in vain effort to save his people within, made foray upon them with fire. Philip's machines, lightly guarded, near all went up in smoke, whilst ours came through the attack unharmed. Saladin then withdrew to con his plans, and 'twas a good thing.

A bout of Arnauldia fever hit the Christian camps, and soon spread to the Saracens also. We called it Arnauldia, for it began in the tents of the Arnauld brothers, of the French Auvergne. With the summer heat upon the land, the fever was even more deadly, as men simply dried up and died. Richard himself was sick near to death, as were many of the rest of us. Some lost their hair entirely; while both Stephen and I succumbed, neither of us suffered that peculiar loss. Yet the Arnauldia left us weak for many days, nor do I believe I completely recovered strength until long after I was home.

In July, Richard had his servants carry him to the siege engines in a silken litter, and thence began assault of the walls of Acre in earnest. Sappers dug under those strong walls, shored them with timbers, then set fire to the supports. With missiles rocketing into the walls above, and the foundations collapsing below, a great section of the wall was reduced to rubble. But this very rubble made an obstacle to any attack on our part; behind it, the defenders waited grimly.

Richard withdrew and pondered how he might widen the breach. The siege engines could not be used, for they would simply raise the obstructing pile of debris. At last he came up with a plan to offer a gold piece to any man who would creep up to the wall, loosen a stone, and bring it back. This impressed us all as certain death, and the King had no takers. Next he upped the ante to two, then three, and finally, four gold pieces. A few foolhardy men began to take him up on his offer; it was a miracle any came out alive. I forbade our men to take part, but Carl could not resist the temptation. He told Odo that he could creep up just before dawn, whilst there was still no light for the enemy archers. I, like a fool, knew nothing of this and was still asleep when they brought his dying body back.

Another foolhardy man, Hal of York, had the same idea as Carl. He, too, went out in the dark predawn, a few yards behind our man. As Carl bent to detach a stone from the rubble pile, a dark, crouching figure suddenly detached itself from the shadows where it had waited, unseen. Before Hal could cry out, the Saracen buried his dagger in Carl's back, then slipped back into shadow as Hal shouted and ran to apprehend him. It was bootless; the demon Muslim disappeared as quickly as he had appeared. It was the first time we knew that the Muslims were posting guards at the breach at night.

Hal, half dragging, half carrying, managed to get Carl within earshot of our camp guards, who carried him to our tents. There was little life in him. A chaplain had been sent for, and whilst Odo cradled the poor carcass of his friend, the priest anointed him and said the prayers that would open the gates of Heaven. I held his hand, and told him I would tell Nicolette that he had died a knight's death in the service of Our Lord. I felt his hand but twitch in answer, then he was gone. We buried him there, outside Acre, commending his soul to God. We sorrowed, particularly Odo, and I truly dreaded taking the news to the wife who had adored him.

As was the custom, half Carl's gear went to our field commander for use by Richard's army; the other half we packed to send home as soon as it were possible. Saladin soon moved off from Acre, and went to the other side of the bay, where he destroyed Haifa to keep it from falling into our hands. Meanwhile, he sent gifts of fresh fruit to the Christian kings, hoping to negotiate, but neither Richard nor Philip was disposed to do so. Perhaps a thousand years of warfare would have been saved had all agreed to an honourable partition of the Holy Land at that time, yet we were blind to all that was yet to come.

Saladin was one of those great leaders of men who are too often tarnished by being on the wrong side of history. Against his advice, the defenders of Acre, largely Turks, negotiated a ruinous peace with Richard and Philip. Because of the extreme hardships suffered by the defenders, Saladin could do naught but agree with their surrender. They promised us not only the True Cross, but 2500 freed Christians prisoners, and untold ransom for the war coffers of Richard and Philip. In addition, they left behind more than two thousand Muslim hostages as guarantee that all would be done as agreed.

Empty-handed, the Muslim defenders left their city, and we who arrayed to watch them go were amazed at their dignity and courage. Despite our sorrow that one of our own had been killed in the siege, we could not help but admire the unconquerable spirit of those Saracens.

Stephen lost no time commandeering a noble house for us in Acre. It had belonged to a rich Muslim, for it was larger than Glororum, and built with great beauty. Even in hot July, its earthen walls remained cool. Around a center courtyard were arranged the many rooms; all opened onto a portico where the breezes played across a pool in the center of the courtyard. The house was cleverly arranged to catch rainwater to fill that pool, which never seemed to go dry. Flowers and plants scented the air, and the thick plastered walls kept the noise and heat outside. A deep well provided sweet water, and we all began to recuperate from the hardships of the camp.

Along with a house, again we were able to summon riches for our pocket. I carefully began to hoard what money I could towards our return journey. Jewels I traded, for those pretty baubles were hard to dispose of. Silver was better by far for us common knights, but that, too, was traded, for gold. Only silver enough for our expenses went into our pockets. After much clamor, we finally received our back pay in gold pieces from the army paymaster. Alan remarked sourly that the man treated every sovereign like a virgin daughter.

It was at this time that the English knights began wearing robes left behind by our enemies; rich, silken robes that not only kept the sun off our armor, but became a mark of honour. We had freed Acre, and the robes were the badge of that campaign. Also, when at home and unarmed, the Saracen dress proved the most comfortable of garments. Those silken surcoats, though originally worn only by Crusaders, became widely copied; till today, none knows how the custom began.

No sooner had the city of Acre fallen than merchants gathered like vultures over a carcass, importuning the Kings for special trading privileges. Largely Italians and Jews, each group called for its own section in the city, and for protected trade agreements. Surprisingly, either from weariness or greed for revenue, the crowns of England and France acceded to most of the demands. In no time at all, Acre became a new Babylon, a city wherein silk, spices, slaves, whores—any desire of the human heart—became for sale.

But this was not what we had come for; we had come to free the Holy City from Saracen rule. Richard, though often sick, became impatient to resume the campaign. Yet it was still July when Philip announced his intention of returning home, pleading illness. His army was furious; they too had Jerusalem as their goal. English and French alike had worked into a cohesive fighting unit, universally called Franks or Latins (or Infidels) by the Saracens. While many nobles returned to France with Philip, Hugh of Burgundy and

Henry of Champagne, among others, stayed under Richard's leadership, and were a valuable part of our forces. There was universal disgust, even among the vassals of Philip, at his cowardly action.

In mid-August, impatient to be on the march, Richard moved us back to our field camp. We had never bothered to strike our tents, which were becoming worn and sun-faded. The King had been in ill humour since Philip had departed; now Richard was quarreling with Saladin over fulfillment of their agreement. At last, we were ordered south to near the well of Tell Kaisan. The hostages went with us. In a fury, Richard ordered the army to surround and murder those chained prisoners, in violation of every law of war under Heaven. I held our people to the rear, though there were many like Odo, who had lost dear friends and sought revenge. Then the dead bodies were hacked open and gutted, looking for gold coins the prisoners had swallowed. Our army seemed to have gone mad. Odo first railed at being restrained from the butchery, but came later to thank me quietly. As he said, 'twould not have returned our Carl to life.

With that slaughter, Richard felt he was free to march south again. But certainly he lost favor with God by his dishonourable and unholy actions, and it went not well with us from then on. Muslim troops had endeavored to rescue their fellows, but to no avail. They would not forget Richard's atrocity, however, and many a Frankish knight later paid for it with his own agony.

While the Saracens were burying their mutilated dead, we retired once again to Acre to make final preparations for the push toward Jerusalem. I left Crinan and Robin, Mark and young Will at Acre. Crinan was still recovering from fever, being too weak to ride. Nor after the slaughter of the Muslims was I eager to bring along lightly armed squires who would be prized as slaves by the Saracen troops. Though they entreated me, I told our squires quite truthfully that our house was subject to being raided, and needs must be protected whilst we were gone. It was to their woebegone looks that we rode out of Acre on August 22, the very day we had arrived in Marseilles just one year before. Besides myself, there was Stephen, Andrew, and Alan, now all knighted, and Odo as squire. Little did we know we were marching into Hell.

Chapter 14

Jerusalem

Memories of the last half of the war are blurred and indistinct in my mind, like the endless swirling dust that everywhere rose about our feet as we marched south from Acre. With the same dogged determination that made our yeoman infantry slog forward then, I shall move back into the misery and heat of those sad, chaotic days. But even now, unutterable weariness overtakes me as I try to bring some order to that devil's brew of a campaign.

As we moved forth down the coast road, Saladin's army, on our east, moved south beside us; near always within shouting distance. On the horizon, the ships of our fleet also sailed south down the coast of the Mediterranean. The brilliance of the water dazzled our eyes when we glanced after them, nor was the sun abated upon the sands which we crossed. Metal armor upon leather, padded with sheep's wool, is not ideal when marching into the gates of Hell. Indeed, some fool of a knight, when we stopped one noon, cooked an egg upon the top of his great helm. Little could we eat, for the dryness. Some men had brought wine from Acre with them; it only served to inflame thirst. Our water was carried upon the ships and it was scummy and brackish; twice a day they were beached so that we might drink. Those who had brought wine out in skins turned them to better use, filling them with that terrible water for the march. I swear, the foot soldiers suffered the worst. Even the horses endured great hardship, with too little feed and water.

The Saracens, on lighter horses and without armor, buzzed about us as blowflies upon a carcass. Their taunts mocked us without surcease, as annoying as the constant chafing of the sand beneath our armor. One young French knight—may God rest his soul!—at last had enough. 'Twas only the third day of march, but he broke ranks in great fury to chase a tormentor. The man teased as he rode away, luring Brevard ever further. Suddenly, when our knight was too far for us to succor, a great mob of the heathens broke from their wolf-pack and cut him to pieces. It was a grim lesson for us all, for not one among us would not have liked to shut those taunting, lying mouths for good. Yet that was the way of the Saracen in battle: scorn and harry, and run away.

In four days we reached Haifa, which Saladin had burned, so there was precious little resource for us there. We rested one day, enjoying what shade we could find, and I hasted to find a skin to carry water. We had not had good ale in near a year, though the Egyptians in Acre made a decent beer that served us better than the strong wines of the East. We dreamed away the hours of the march, thinking of that beer, and the cool, shaded courtyard of our house in Acre.

A week after leaving Acre we crossed the River of Crocodiles. Hundreds of the great animals swarmed upon the river banks, and their stench was unbearable. We killed a number, just to be able to cross safely. Even so, the evil beasts lurked beneath the waters unseen. Two of our infantrymen, uncautious in crossing, were dragged beneath the water and devoured. 'Twould have done us well to have been able to bathe, even in those murky waters, but those fiends of Hell denied us that slight comfort.

Our skin was raw, oft bleeding; and many were bleeding from their noses due to the heat and dust. Most wrapped a silken cloth about the face, just to be able to breathe. Many were the men who dropped from ranks, burnt up with heat and delirious. Our Odo was one of those. Just before crossing the River of the Dead, we needs must stop, as he swooned from the saddle. We wiped his face with water, and poured some into his mouth, praying that he not retch. We knew that those men who dropped and began retching soon died. When the ships beached that eve, we put him aboard with the rest of our sick. There were a great many, for griping sickness was coming among us too.

At the River of the Dead, we buried many of the sick who had died on the galleys, as well as others who had simply dropped from the saddle, lifeless. Truth to tell, we the living had begun to envy the dead upon that cursed march.

At last, upon the feast of St. Remaculus, September 3, we halted for two days beside the Salt River. There was shade, and water for bathing. Horses that were completely spent were butchered for food, and Richard ordered some Egyptian beer brought out, which he had hoarded upon the ships. The nights were cool, and beneath more stars than any man might think existed, some of the men began singing. We caught breath, and began to believe we might live.

Our respite was short-lived. On the 5th, we began marching again, coming into the wooded country of Arsuf. By night, we reached the River Rochetaill, and Saladin's army was disquietingly near. Indeed, Saladin began talks once again with Richard, which was always bad news for us. It soon became apparent that a battle loomed. The Saracen army blocked our passage to the city of Arsuf, where we needs must march for supplies. On September 7, the battle of Arsuf was joined.

Richard, by dint of many battles, was a commander like none other, save perhaps the great Alexander. He cannily sent our baggage and infantry to the shore, to act as anchor for our lines. Before them, we mounted knights held the main line of defence. The English were in the center; to the south were Bretons and Angevins and Guiennes. The brave Templars held the south end and flank. To the north were the Flemings and French, and knights of the Holy Land. The north flank was anchored by the Hospitalers. Saracens had never been able to pierce a line of our armor as long as it held steady. Before us were deployed the archers behind a wall of shields.

We stood our places from sunup to near midmorning. Screaming like animals and pressing fiercely, the Muslims at last joined the battle. Their first wave was a line of Turkish light cavalry, with bows and light spears. They were followed by Negros, and Arabs on foot. Thousands of arrows they shot, high into the air, so that they might rain down upon our infantry. In the terrible press of their assault, our shield wall began to give way in many places. Some were simply overwhelmed by force of numbers; other men, frightened, threw down their arms and ran for protection behind our lines. Everywhere our armor held, and repulsed such of the enemy as came through the shields. Still Richard would not move us out. He rode up and down the ranks, encouraging all to hold fast. He wished the main force of the Muslims, which still held back, to come nearer.

Of a sudden, the Turkish cavalry charged again, this time with swords and battle axes. With terrible slaughter, they broke through the shield wall on the north, and brought pressure to bear upon the Hospitalers and Flemings. They attacked and withdrew, then attacked again. The master of the Hospitalers sent messengers to Richard to beg that they might break ranks and engage the Turks. Richard refused, for he wanted the whole ranks to close at once, to save casualties. The Hospitalers held through two more assaults before two of their knights broke ranks without orders, and began to charge the enemy. The rest of the Hospitalers were not to be held in check longer.

This was not Richard's plan; he had wished the center of the line to take the initial thrust, then the Templars and Hospitalers could close around the ends. It was too late now to reform our lines; Richard ordered us forward toward the weakest point in the Saracen array. He himself took the foremost position, rallying men around him. No other man possessed such an arm; his mighty sword swept like a grim sickle. Before it, enemies vanished, heads and limbs cut off, bodies scythed in twain. Woe to the Muslim who lay in his path! One man he split clean in two; others with faces sliced off became grinning skulls in an instant. Little time did we have to watch, however, for we were surrounded by lance and sword and war-ax, and hundreds of brown faces screaming "Death to the Infidels!" The dust rose so thick that scarce could we see to tell friend from foe.

Suddenly the enemy fell back, and we were able to reform our lines. The horses of the slain Muslims wandered the field, nuzzling at the severed bearded heads, looking for their masters. It was a scene from Hell, but we had scarce time to take a breath before they were upon us once more. It had been better had we not time to gaze upon that horrible field, for in that slight weakening of resolution, the Saracens gained strength. They near broke through our line; beside me, I saw Andrew fall with a lance in his throat. My own straits were desperate, as I had two Turks upon me, one with lance, and one with sword. I parried the lance quickly, but it took poor Black Stone in the flank. The sword disappeared as in desperation I sliced away the hand that held it, then the head. The lancer foolishly threw himself upon me with naught but a dagger; he too fell lifeless in the dust.

From the edge of my eye, I saw Richard take a small force, and wheeling quickly, charge the enemy from the right flank. Hacking away behind their lines, he threw the Muslims into confusion. This time the hesitation was theirs, and the resolve ours. We renewed the attack, and though Saladin himself attempted to stem the rout, the Muslims fled from that bloody field, leaving us victorious.

Our strength was at an end, nor could we have pursued the enemy further. The historians wrote what a glorious battle it was for Richard, and truly, never had mortal man fought as he fought. Saladin's reputation of invincibility was forever broken. Yet the battle of Arsuf was not without great cost. Though some seven thousand Saracens littered the field with their bodies and blood, many of our own had fallen also. Among them was my beloved Andrew, and the King's great friend, James d'Avesnes. We brought our slain into the town of Arsuf, and a solemn funeral mass was sung at St. Mary's. My beautiful black destrier was also led away to the butchers because of his wounds, which had I been at home, he surely had been cured of.

To say I was sick would be to say too little. Heart and mind were sick nigh to death; the body near followed. The griping sickness came upon me in earnest, and I had no more strength than a mewling babe. Stephen insisted that I be put on board a ship for Acre, to be allowed to recuperate. Odo and I thus returned to our home there, for that old stalwart had never yet regained strength from being sunstruck, the heat being harder upon the older soldiers. To replace us, when next the galley ventured south, we sent Crinan and Robin and Mark, though I kept Will at home for the nonce, as our nurse. Had not at least one able-bodied man remained with us, the ruffians who roamed Acre would have turned us out and stolen both house and our belongings. Odo recovered first, and went in search of a physician for me, as I was faring little better. Finally he returned with an old Jew, and belike, no greater physician could have been obtained. He ordered some of the peculiar resinated wine of the country, and mixing in it some bitter powder, made me drink. At first I retched most out, but gradually, I began to hold down more and more. After three days, I could once again begin to hold down food, and the running of the bowel ceased. Still, I was weak for many days, so near death had I been.

Many were the weary knights who had returned to Acre, and Richard himself rode north in October to collect us. Alan, too, came at that time, he being ill of wounds and fever. He said that Stephen was still holding up, and had obtained quarters in Jaffa. Our squires were with him, having safely arrived there in a returning ship. Richard himself had been near killed by the Saracens while hunting, Alan said. Only when William de Preaux shouted in Arabic that he himself was the King, did the Muslims divert enough for Richard to 'scape. It was too close a call, yet one which was to be repeated, thanks to Richard's habit of foraging the countryside with only a small company. Yet I understood, for the hunting and hawking in open country was healing his mind and soul from the terrible battles.

Will and I returned to Jaffa with Richard, whilst Alan and Odo remained in Acre. Stephen had a very pleasant little house of three rooms, and a palm tree for shade across the front courtyard. It was from that very palm that we later cut fronds to carry home, as Palmers—pilgrims to the Holy Land—were everywhere protected in Europe.

Though we were some crowded, we continued to wait while Richard and Saladin negotiated. We had not yet received the True Cross, and all were impatient to at last free that holy relic. At the first of November, there was another small battle outside Jaffa, which history has dismissed as only a skirmish. Though the Saracen forces were not as large as at Arsuf, the battle was in deadly earnest. Stephen was unfortunate to take an arrow through the slit of his great helm. An inch to the left, and he would have taken it in the eye. As it was, it cut a gash across his forehead and temple. When we got to him, he had fallen from his horse from lack of blood, for head wounds spurt like fountains. It was only with great difficulty that we got the wound stanched and carried him home.

All able-bodied men were then ordered out, first to Ramla, thence to Latrun, about halfway between Jaffa and Jerusalem. Heartsick, I left Robin to nurse my dear brother-in-law, who had been such a succor to us all. It looked as if Richard's negotiations with Saladin might at long last bear fruit, but the skirmishes never ceased. We spent a miserable Christmas in camp at Latrun, with cold and wind and rain searching out every rent in our well-worn tent. With me were Crinan and Mark, and we remembered well when we had filled three tents at Messina. Our comrades were dispersed, dead, or ailing, and we ourselves were heartily sick of this war. Only the nearness of Jerusalem kept us from deserting and going back to Jaffa. Jerusalem was the goal of all our dreams and I wished to see it, not just for my own heart's ease, but for William my father, for Andrew, and for Carl. And for Stephen, too, whispered a voice, for I began to misdoubt if his strong Viking nature could recover from such a grievous wound. So I prayed, more for my friends than for myself, that I might be granted one glimpse at least of the Holy City.

Father Cedric might have said that when you wish, wish large, for prayers are granted in the largesse with which you define them. Two days after Christmas, quite by chance, I was selected to ride forth with the Templars, to scout the Holy City. There, high on a hill outside the gates, we beheld Jerusalem in the distance. There was much murmuring among the Templars, to the effect that our tattered army could not hope to take those strong walls. 'Twere a matter for negotiation they said, whatever concessions Richard might wring from Saladin. We had too little lifeblood left to pour out.

And so I sat my jaded horse upon that stony hill across the valley from the city of all our dreams, and knew I would never in this lifetime come nearer. I wept, broken-hearted with broken dreams. What was life after this? So many of those I loved had gone, destroyed by this single glimpse of the City of God that I alone was afforded. I near swooned in despair.

On January 10 of 1192, we scouts rode with Richard to Jaffa, so that he might confer with his advisers. Representatives of the army clamored to march at once upon Jerusalem, but the Templars and Hospitalers insisted upon caution. When Richard asked us, his own English knights, for confirmation, we could only nod assent. Richard became gloomy, and began to ponder. At last he announced to all that we would begin moving back to Ascalon, which the Turks had completely destroyed, leaving not one stone upon another. His plan was to cut the Saracen supply route from Egypt. The whole army was dispirited, each man cursing the day he was born, but the French troops were furious. First their King deserted them, then Richard, to whom they had transferred allegiance, turned away just short of the goal. Many deserted to throw in their lot with Conrad de Montferrat in Tyre, who was expected to continue the battle.

Whilst in Jaffa, I abode with Stephen and Robin. It was plain that Stephen was growing weaker; his wound was fevered, with angry red lines running from it across the white of his face. He was as sound of mind as ever, however.

"My dear brother," he told me weakly, "I shall not live to see my beloved wife or the fields of home again. You must look after my family when I am gone, as I know you surely will." He stopped awhile, being short of strength. "I know the king's agent will come for half my property: wages and arms. There are ten gold sovereigns here with me, and twenty more buried beneath the floor of my room in Acre. Take them to Maud, for the children and my estate." He closed his eyes, and I thought that he slept. After a long while, I rose to steal away, when he opened his eyes once more. "As soon as you can do so with honour, get our people hence from here. There is nothing more you can do, save bleed and die. God requires no more English blood upon this sad land." I nodded, unable to speak without betraying myself. Clasping my hand, as if it were a benediction, he gave his farewell. "My prayers from Heaven will be with you." Our one consolation was that those of us who died in battle for the Holy land were rewarded immediately in Heaven.

So it was I stayed with him till he died, slowly and in great pain, a fortnight later. With Andrew, though he were older than I, I felt as if I had lost my younger brother, for so many years had I taught and encouraged him. Now with Stephen, my grief was even greater, for though he was not much older than I, he had been like an elder brother in his care of me and of Maud and mother. So in this land of screaming devils, stinking heat and bitter winds, this land of death and blood unending, I had lost two brothers; the two men I loved most in this world. So, too, Carl, a friend from childhood whose happy nature had enlightened our days. All gone, and with them, my great steed Black Stone, whom I had raised from a frisking colt. I became utterly determined to get the rest of us hence from this bitter country.

Whilst hearing mass before returning to the army at Ascalon, I met two friars of St. Brendan. Both were Celt, though one was Irish and one a Scot. They had come to the Holy Land under the patronage of one of the Irish de Courcys. Suffering with us throughout the war, they administered to the sick and dying, at great hardship to themselves. Now John de Courcy had just died, having contracted the lung sickness during that terrible, wet, cold Christmas at Latrun, and the priors were without a patron. Their hopes still centered on Jerusalem. God, they said, would not send us through such a terrible scourging without reward. Though the knights were disheartened and despairing, those men of God still trusted in miracles. Indeed, they were later proven right, for an uneasy peace was at last negotiated which allowed Christians some access to the Holy Places. It was not to be whilst I was yet in the Holy Land.

Though I could in no way support those holy men as de Courcy had, I offered them Stephen's little house, to be used as a refuge for pilgrims. To give them some living, I added seven of my own hard-won gold sovereigns; 'twas enough to keep them for seven years. That done, Robin and I rode to Ascalon, where we found the entire army, knight and foot, at work hauling stones. Even Richard helped shift and lay stones, as ably as any mason. I was determined to speak with him as soon as possible, to obtain permission for our little group to return home.

During one of Richard's hunts, I was sure that the time had come, for I was selected to ride patrol with the hunting party. My hopes were dashed, for though he spoke fair to me, never had I a moment to snare his ear with my petition. The King then rode to Acre for more negotiations, leaving us to labor like slaves upon the harsh stones of Ascalon. God, however, heard our pleas; perhaps it was Stephen, praying for us in Heaven, as he had promised.

Richard returned to Ascalon at the end of March; following him two weeks later was Prior Robert of Hereford, who brought disquieting news from home. England was in crisis, thanks to the loving ministrations of Prince John, who had robbed the treasury and hatched any number of seditious plots against the crown. Philip of France was licking his chops, like the jackal he was, making overtures of alliance with John. The situation was serious. Richard was first furious, then cold. He summoned the leaders of the army to him, and made preparation for his own possible departure, though many negotiations yet remained.

It was then, at last, that I was granted audience with the King, and given the means to negotiate our honourable departure. Kneeling before that fearsome monarch, I first offered my fealty, and that of the men who rode with me. Richard only nodded, impatient. I knew that no story of hardship would move him, as he had partaken equally of our adversity. Instead, I minded him that Bamburgh was a royal castle, and as such, should be secured for the crown. Also, I gambled that his falling-out with Bishop Hugh of Durham had not incurred lifelong enmity; I proposed to secure for him the backing and goodwill of his former justiciar.

It was but the work of a moment, for Richard was ever swift in decision. "Take your men and depart for England," he said, "and mind that you are my agent upon these matters. Tell Walter, the warder at Bamburgh (Richard's memory for men was prodigious), that I am making you castellan until I return. The clerks will give you a paper with my seal, and a letter for Hugh. Contact the paymaster for your full wages, and travel expense for the return voyage." He then dismissed me abruptly, and turned to other matters, but my heart was overjoyed. Truly, prayers are answered, and I knew then that Stephen, and Andrew and Carl, marched beside us.

With Crinan—now Sir Crinan—and Robin and Mark and Will as seasoned squires, we rode back to Jaffa. It was but a short distance, and I wished to say good-bye at Stephen's grave. The St. Brendan friars good-naturedly put us up for a day, though we overflowed into the courtyard. We cut palms to signify that we had indeed been to the Holy Land, and the friars blessed them, as our protection for the return trip. We then rode north as far as Arsuf to pay our respects at Andrew's grave, and the graves of many another of our fellows. From thence, rather than relive the horrors of that coast road once again, we took ship to Acre.

Once again, aboard ship, I felt the griping sickness come on, but dismissed it. We were all worn; armor hung upon us loosely as bacon sacks, though the younger men fared better. A rest at Acre, and some of the Jew's medicine, I felt, would soon put all to right.

Yet in Acre, time became precious. There was much to do, and Richard's bidding needs be carried out as quickly as possible. Seven horses were left to us, four only of the ones that had been raised at Glororum. It was decided, to save battles for our small and weary party, to travel home as pilgrims. What armour was left, we packed, and from three worn tents, cobbled together two that would serve. I went forth to trade away two of our jaded beasts and buy smaller Arab horses; indeed, I could see that they might well fit our breeding ventures. I obtained two well-built mares; one brown with white markings, and one gray, that minded me of Button's Dapple. With them I bought two strong geldings. Every piece of gear that was unneeded was sold, as well as some of the robes we had confiscated. In each man's pouch was one well-folded silken surcoat, a few silver coins, and some small packets of pepper. Pepper was by far the most valuable spice of the East; by twisting some up in paper, and waxing the ends, we carried a fresh supply that would be worth more than gold in Europe. It was light and easily traded for. Our gold coins, Robin cleverly sewed up in the hems of our coarse robes.

Alan and Odo both were fit, and eager to return home. To Alan did I entrust Stephen's equipment, though not his gold, reserving that for myself to carry to Maud. Each man, however, carried enough to be wealthy when, with God's Providence, we would reach home. At last, we sold the house in Acre, to a noble knight desirous of staying in that land of warmth and luxury, and we divided the money fairly. I entrusted Robin with my geld, and 'twas well I did so.

It was near our last day at Acre, while bartering on the waterfront for our passage, that I was set upon by thieves. I was but lightly armed, carrying only a falchion, a short scimitar much like a machete, well-suited to work in the cramped quarters of town. Will and Mark had hied them off to see to our provisioning. All went well, for I sent one thief to Paradise and was routing the rest when a stranger joined the fray. He was suddenly upon me with a paving stone, which I took upon the forehead. As I fell swooning, I saw Will and Mark come running, or I should not have lived to see the voyage home. 'Twas a cruel turn of Fate that I had come through all our battles unscathed, only to be felled by a paving stone upon the streets of Acre. The scar lies with me yet; long after the holy palms have turned to ashes, that memento of our Crusade still marks me as a Palmer.

At last, a month after Easter in 1192, we boarded ship for Marseilles. So much had befallen that it seemed more like ten years than two since first we had sailed from Budle Bay, young, eager, and confident. We were returning home rich men, but aged and weary, sorrowful at leaving behind three of the finest knights whose blood and bones ever enriched that cruel land we called Holy.

Chapter 15

Alyse

It had been better had I taken from Acre more of the Jew's potion and less pepper. Dame Fortune had smiled upon us since Richard granted us his blessing to return home. Perhaps she blinded me to the real hardships yet to come.

Our ship, under the flag of Genoa, was one of the largest freighters plying those seas. The captain was skilled, having made many trading ventures. Still, I had not accounted for the volatile Genoese temperament, nor for the superstitions of sailors in general. As we wended slowly across the Mediterranean, my old fevers began to return. I would shiver with cold, though the weather was warm, and lay up close to the dappled Arab mare, for she was the gentlest of horses. In her warmth and strength, I found comfort. We stayed an extra day in Cyprus, and an extra three in Rhodes. The captain was becoming anxious, for soon the winds would be more against us, and his crew were already a-grumble. Nearing the coast of Sicily, a storm overtook us and blew us south, where we were scarce able to make the refuge of Malta.

The captain, a burly bald man with a circle of dark beard, came to me as soon as we docked. He made no bones about why he had come. "My sailors refuse to further work the ship with you aboard, lest all die at sea. 'Tis well known that sick men bring a curse, and you have laid heavily upon us throughout this voyage. We must leave you here, ere this ship sails again." Little did I feel like further voyaging, and indeed, it was the hand of angels once again that had cast us upon this isle. Here dwelt the Hospitalers, men dedicated to the care of sick and wounded knights.

"Grant me two days to make arrangements," I told him, "and you and your crew may leave. You will leave with only half your bargained fee, however, if you leave without my friends." Illness made me worn and testy; I was in no mood to be tried by a seaman, even a clever Genoese. We had given him but half our agreed-upon fare, with the other half to be paid in Marseilles. I did not envision him wishing to lose his geld.

Upon his agreement, our knights and squires began preparations to leave me behind, installing me in the castle of the Hospitalers. They made shift to exercise the horses and quickly repack our goods. I put Sir Alan in charge, as he was senior knight, but Maud's gold, I divided between him and Sir Crinan, lest something befall one or the other. To Alan, I gave the paper for Bishop Hugh, and to Crinan, the paper for Walter at Bamburgh. 'Twas all I could do, as my strength was spent. I gave them loving messages for those at home and bid them Godspeed. Truth tell, I was groaning inwardly, for I so longed to see the hills and forests of home. The pain of homesickness was near greater than my foolish heart could bear.

Robin refused to leave me. "I have lost Sir Stephen, who was like another father to me. I will not leave you, Uncle, for the love I bear you. 'Tis not seemly to leave you a stranger in this land, with none to care for your needs, or to bury you if you die." All knew this was important, nor did any flinch at hearing the words spoken. We had been marchers with death too long.

So it was decided, and the ship sailed without us the following day. Later, I learned that the party landed safely in Marseilles, and made its way home by God's grace, upon the feast of St. Stephen, September 2. By this token, all the family knew that Stephen was indeed in Heaven, and praying for our welfare.

The Knights at Malta were kind, and the room where Robin and I abode was sunny and cheerful, yet cool in midday. I did little save sleep, for I was worn beyond telling. The priests gave me tisanes and herbs to drink, and Robin tempted me with choice foods, of which I could but partake only a little. The summer whiled away, and I became more anxious to be upon the road home. Northumberland was in all my dreams; I would wake from a night spent hunting in our forest, or riding upon the shore at Budle Bay, or visiting Chatta, only to see the stark walls of the Hospitalers before my eyes. At times, I wept, bethinking that mine eyes would never be eased by that fair country again. Then Robin would cajole me, and tell me noble tales, or sing a fine ballad. He had his father's voice and love of music. As a mark of respect, he ever addressed me as "Uncle," though we were cousins by blood.

Oft in the hot afternoons, I would amble slowly to the great church of the Hospitalers, to feel awhile the peace of God. Though the Mediterranean sun was white-hot outside, within it shafted through the small portals like arrows of Heaven, and illuminated the windows of colored glass in shifting cycles of rainbow hue. One of the pictures was of Abraham about to sacrifice Isaac, with an angel staying his hand. As I thought about our Crusade, it seemed to me that God's grace had come to us; not through our deeds, as the Church had promised, but in our simple desire to serve Him, and our willingness to take up arms to do so. Yet as the angel stayed the hand of Abraham, perhaps our love of the Lord should stop us short of murdering our fellow man. When I told my thoughts to Robin, he but laughed. "You are becoming a philosopher, Uncle. All that is well and good, save when a Turk is coming at you with lance and war-club raised." At which I conceded to his wisdom.

One August afternoon, while the swallows wheeled about the bell-tower, disturbed from their midday rest, I entered the church again to pray. More than any single thing in the world, I wished to see the fields of home again, to embrace my mother and children, and, yes, even my wife, poor Herleve. I understood better now her battles, she to whom life had always been unkind. Yet I was nowise better prepared to heal her mind and soul than I had ever been; that was up to God. So I prayed to Our Lady on her behalf, more perhaps than for anyone else. Though Carl and Andrew and Stephen, too, were in my prayers, it was with a certain contentment that they had simply reached Heaven before us.

Whether I then dozed, or whether the vision came to me awake, as I was certain it had, a certain transport of mind enveloped me as I sat. The shafts of light in that great church dimmed, and I was once again in the churchyard at Bamburgh, all enshrouded in a fog of dim green light, blowing in like mist from the sea. Suddenly, I saw a sepulchral monk, face hidden in his hood, rise from the ground of the churchyard. I knew it was St. Aidan himself. He appeared in that mist of death's decay to lead me to something; I knew not what. Silently, I followed him into the church, the one that my forefathers had helped build when first they came to Glororum.

Quiet, we watched, as a great gray wolf, large as a man, came stealing through the old north transept and into the chancel. To my surprise, at the very spot where Holy Aidan had died, which we had marked with a cross, a spring of clear water appeared, bubbling from the stones of the floor. The huge wolf looked fearfully 'round, then lay him on his belly and began to lap the water. I held my breath, lest I disturb him. He began then to rise, and as he rose, the wolf became a fair knight, circled with a halo of light. Slowly, he walked to the high altar, and to my amazement there appeared behind it a glorious window, shining with morning sun in colors of blue and red and gold. The knight then walked into that window, where he stood in sunshine as part of the picture. When I looked around for the monk, Aidan, I saw that he, too, had disappeared, only to reappear upon that heavenly window. As I watched and marveled, the scene began to fade, and I found myself kneeling upon the stones of the Hospitaler church in Malta. Shaking, I returned to my seat once again, weak as a child newborn.

Robin soon appeared, through the shaft of light that marked the door, anxious as to my whereabouts. Indeed, I had been overlong at prayers this afternoon! When I spoke to him of my vision, he shook his head. "Methinks, Uncle, the Saint himself has called to you. Do you ken what it is he wishes you to do?"

Slowly, the words formed, as if of their own will. "The wolf was the symbol of the people before Christianity; the knight was St. Oswald himself, who with St. Aidan brought the Holy Cross to Northumbria. Together, they shall become the glory of a new church at Bamburgh, and I am called home to build that church. God willing, and by the intervention of those saints, I shall yet live to do them that honour. We needs must be on the road home."

Thus slowly mending, I set my face toward home. Both of us knew we had to be hence from Malta ere the winter storms set in, or I at least should never see Glororum again. So it was, in late August, that Robin booked us passage once again to Marseilles. This ship was a small bark, with room for but one horse, and we took the Arab mare. Robin sold his larger beast, who, truth to tell had seen better days, and paid the Hospitalers. Our trip was long, and the choppy seas arduous for a man half-well. We disembarked in Marseilles, and began the long trek up the Rhone River, north toward the port of Calais.

I did well until we reached Arles, when the old griping fevers began tumbling through me again. Robin felt it no hardship to humbly walk beside the horse, steadying me in the saddle. At times, I would doze a little to his voice, then open my eyes amazed at how tall and strong he had become, for I was wont to remember him as a happy youngster, playing with Mary Rose at Hutton. When we stopped, he would find lodging at a church or abby, since we were pilgrims, and bring me gruel and wine with whatever bread I could choke down. Those days blurred, one into another; nor could I tell you to this day how ran our route.

A sad song framed that journey, a worthless ditty that kept time with the soft plodding of the gray mare's hooves upon the road. I refrained from singing it aloud, for Robin had grief enough of his own; but the fever-song remains etched in mind to this day:

"Oh, I have been to Jerusalem town,
Rode the shore road up and down;
The dust it rose, the dust it clove,
Naught can bring back the ones I love."

Somewhere, mayhap near the River Meuse, my little strength ebbed away once again. I remember coming to a ford on the river, unable to sit the mare any longer. Robin propped me beneath a tree beside the road and gave me water to drink; a sip or two was all I could keep down. Then I remember glancing across the river and seeing a meadow so green it seemed to have fallen from Paradise. And upon that meadow, among its waist-high grass and golden flowers, rode a woman upon a white palfrey, coursing as hard as the horse could run. Her cap tumbled upon her back, and her long hair fell from beneath, like Midas' gold in the sunshine. Her dress, a brilliant blue, fluttered behind her. I was minded that perhaps I had died, till I saw Robin go to the water's edge and blow upon a horn that hung upon the tree.

At once, I saw the lady's retinue, who had been standing near, turn and start toward us. The lady herself, spurring wildly, came splashing across the ford and reined before us. As Robin entreated her succor, she gazed down at me with a face filled with pity, a face that belonged upon an angel. Oft angels are frozen in stone in some great cathedral, but this face was alive and warm and kind. She asked my name, and I still had sense enow to tell her: John Forestrius, of Bamburgh, Northumbria. Little do I remember after that. I kenned a litter being brought, and being carried into the castle which stood beyond the meadow. Thence the memory fades.

It must have been some days before I awoke with any sense, in a clean bed in a sun-filled room. The lady herself sat beside me with a basin; she had been washing my face.

When she saw my eyes a-flutter, she ordered one of the two maids to help me sit, whilst the other spooned broth into my mouth. Robin told me later that they had been doing this for near a week, though I have no recall of it. "Begone," I muttered, "a man must feed himself." I tried to take the spoon, but my hand shook so, the ladies laughed at me. Between us, I managed to sup the bowl. Alyse told me later that it was the first she knew that I would live.

A great weariness overtook me; I stretched and yawned and returned to sleep, but this time the sleep was of the living, rather than the senseless stupor of a man near death. Robin also remained by my side, and when I awoke, he helped me rise to relieve myself. Never, he said, was it so welcome to watch a man piss. My skin was taut and dry and yellow, and I had lost so much flesh the knobby bone ends stuck through everywhere.

As soon as they ascertained that I could begin to hold down food, the ladies came plying me with delicacies. First there was milk with spice, and healing herbal draughts, then custards, and finally some mawmoney with finely chopped chicken. All came over a great space of time, and in small amounts, for my stomach could scarce hold down two spoons of anything. Between feeding, I slept the livelong day and night, only rising to relieve myself and shuffle across the room on Robin's arm. Each time I rose, I tried to make the distance further, the standing longer.

Alyse came each day to hold my hand, and in her touch was the sort of healing that my mother had. She told me of her life, bartered away to a proud knight who much preferred the company of King Philip and the rousting of the tourney. He too had been in the Holy Land, nor had he returned with Philip, but remained there yet. He was one of the French who had deserted to Conrad de Montferrat when Richard made the sad decision to forbear the siege of Jerusalem. I recalled the man, as dark of hair and eye as Alyse was fair.

Two daughters they had, fair maidens both, who often came with their mother to visit. They sat quietly at their stitching whilst we talked. Both were dark of hair, the elder with her father's dark eyes, and the younger with eyes of bright blue like her mother. Their names were Eleanor and Anne, and no man ever had finer daughters. Alyse told me privately, however, that their father would have naught to do with them, furious that he had girl children instead of sons. Alyse, too, was blamed; he had wed her, he said, to sire sons, not throw useless girls. I should have been delighted to have such daughters, I told her, for I had no girls of my own, save the foundling Button. I told Alyse of Allie's rescue, and she shook her head over Herleve's rejection of the waif.

On sunny days, though it was now coming winter, and the leaves had fallen from the cherries and plums, Alyse and I would oft walk in the garden or orchard. As she had when first I saw her, my lady disdained the company of her retinue. She still rode near daily upon the meadow, though often the grass was wet and slick with rain or frost. She needed the run, she said, or she would explode. Her servants knew far better than she what ailed her restless nature; 'twas not thus, confided her maid, when the master was home to see to his wife.

I swear, both Fate and the servants conspired against us. Even my faithful Robin disappeared upon errands of his own, leaving me often alone with the fair Alyse. As my strength returned, so grew my love for the lady. Nor can a man returned from war remain a monk for long. One warm November day as we sat alone in the garden, she at her spinning—the women of my day were endlessly spinning—and I singing fair songs to gladden her heart, she put her spindle upon the grass and turned to me. "John, you need not sing of love to me, for already I love you with all my heart. Since first I saw you, lying so pitiful beside the ford, I loved you. I dared not hope, for there was so little life in you. Now, by God's grace, you are here singing to me of love, and methinks you feel as I."

Had I dared hope? She entered my arms as eagerly as I sought her. I had been a husband eluded by love for thirteen years. Now, upon this green land of France, came a passionate woman offering me her love, and I loved her dearly in return. Beyond the amour sung of by the troubadours lay this, a new realm of heart's ease, a realm I entered as a stranger. I could not hold her tenderly enough, nor could she bear to be parted from my side, even to tend to her daily affairs. Thus we lived in a fool's paradise through the high holidays, and into February.

We learned then that Richard, on his way home from the Holy Land, had been taken prisoner by Leopold of Austria. England was in turmoil, they said, with John taking every step to bring himself closer to the crown. My sleep became uneasy, thinking of my commission at Bamburgh. Philip, too, was on the move, calling together his knights, many of whom were beginning to trickle back from the Holy Land. I liked it not; the affair had an ominous cast.

Two things happened, then, that set me upon the sad road homeward, away from my beloved Alyse. The first happened the night of February 10; I mind it well. I woke out of a sound sleep, to know that there was a presence in the room. I heard Robin snoring upon his pallet next the door, but someone seemed to be standing near the window, watching me. I had no fear, only a great sense of peace and love. Then I saw the form, as of a woman, and I smelled again the sweet herb scent that always followed my mother. I knew then that she had departed this life. I slipped to my knees upon the floor, to pray for her, but she interrupted me. Though she spoke, 'twas only in my head I heard the words, for not a sound broke the cold stillness.

"John, it is time you were home. Affairs there can wait no longer. And Alyse's husband is less than a week away. Be of good heart, you leave behind a son." I felt a breeze then, and she was gone as she had come, silently in the night. I knew without being told that she had prayed for me every day, and her prayers had helped to bring me thus far. Now I would have to fulfill them on my own.

So many thoughts tumbled through my pate that sleep was impossible. Of course, I had known that I would have to leave my beloved Alyse, but my heart had refused to face that agony till now. We were tolerant, in my day, of courtly love between knights and ladies, who often were wed unsuitably and, like Guinevere, found love in the arms of a devoted champion like Lancelot. But some husbands, like Alyse's Arnaud, were not tolerant, preferring to lock their wives away. Neither of us wished to confront him.

And a child! She had said naught to me of it yet. Certain it was that I must make plans, for Alyse's life would not be worth a taper if Arnaud thought she had thrown a wood's colt. I felt fair ready to burst with the hurt, the pride, the love, the defeat that whirled about my head. Slipping from bed, I went to walk upon the cold battlements.

'Twas some hours yet to dawn, perhaps the fifth hour after the midnight watch. I heard the house guards clank and shuffle and spit as they watched while the household slept. The early sky was dark and clear, with no morning star yet arise. Then stealing softly over the horizon came a pale moon, hiding the baleful face of Saturn, low in the Eastern sky. I minded the little star lore my mother had taught me, and knew that thus in the sky was the mark of her passing. Again, I kenned she was near, and of a sudden I knew that all would be well.

As soon as rosy morning dawned, I sought out my fair Alyse. Alone, I held her softly, until small sobs betrayed her tears. "John," she began, "you have come to tell me goodbye. I see the sadness in your face."

"Not sadness alone, Alyse, happiness too. Why did you not tell me about the babe?"

She collapsed then, as a soldier after battle, and I held her for a long while and kissed away her tears. "I had thought not to tell you, John, for the struggle will be mine. But I swear, whatever happens to me, the child will stay safe." I could tell then that she had been worrying over it for days, and I was amazed again at the courage of women, a-clash in the subtle but deadly battles that lay within their lives, far beyond the ken of mere men.

She started then, and asked, "But how did you come to know? I have told no one."

"Mother told me," was my answer, and I told Alyse of the visit in the night.

Solemnly she replied, "It is meet then that you be hence."

But I could feel her fear at the news of her husband's approach. I tried to comfort her; something would come to her succor, for mother had so reassured me.

And so it came about that very day. When Dame Fate begins to move the pawns upon the board, she oft moves more swiftly than our wit can follow. Philip Augustus had come to Alyse's cousin's manor, not four leagues away. Denis sent a messenger, asking her presence, and that of her daughters, at court within the week. As important vassals of the French king, Arnaud's daughters need be suitably presented at court, and arrangements made for their marriages. Alyse shivered with fear. "I tremble to face the French king. Oh, John, take me away with you to England! I cannot bear to deal with life without you."

My heart wept, but I needs must don a stronger armour than ever I had worn in my life. "Beloved, were I to take you from your children, you would only grow to hate me. Nor could I find livelihood away from my lands, where unfortunately there already abides a wife. But kings are only men, I assure you, and I have known a few." I paused whilst an idea rattled across my brain. It came, I swear, not of me, but from Above, where lovers are specially protected. I held Alyse from me, the better to gaze into her beautiful, tear-stained face.

"You must go to Philip," I said slowly, "and be as pleasant as ever you are. Show no fear, but at some proper time, contrive to loosen your cap and let your hair fall. That will be his downfall, for he is a man like any other, and no man can see that fall of hair and not desire you. Though it pains me to think of it, you must smile upon him. The smile of an Angel to be wasted upon a cur! The court will then take up with rumors a-plenty. Arnaud will be able to do naught but fret if his King was the man who wantoned with his wife. You have great courage, and you can do this thing; it may mean your life, and the life of our child. Remember, when each day's battle is joined, the morrow will bring surcease. You will have to toady to that bandy-legged runt for but a day or two, at best."

"I do not like to even think of it, John. I am but a weak woman, how can I fight such battles?"

I laughed at her. "You are weak like the she-wolf is weak, when her cubs are threatened. I would help you if I could, but the best succor I can give you is to be from hence as soon as possible."

"But why, John? Of what purpose is it to try to seduce King Philip?"

"When our son is born, Alyce, you must name him Philip. Arnaud will never dare lay a hand upon him. I have seen the evil in men's hearts when faced with a cub they suspect is not their own. This is the only armour I can bequeath him. If he be of such a bent, send him to school with the monks when he turns seven. (God willing!) 'Twill do both of our souls well to have a son to offer to God. In about a year's time, I will send a messenger to you, to see how you fare, and to bring you his inheritance in gold. I dare not leave it now."

Thus we prepared, and Alyse sent the messenger back to Denis with fair words. We crept together to spend our last night in tears and kisses, for ever were we careful not to cause undue whispers among the servants.

So it was, on a miserable, wet French morn two days before St. Valentine's, when birds begin to mate, Alyse and I rode away in opposite directions. I never saw her again, save in my dreams.

Chapter 16

Boots

Robin and I arrived at Budle Bay on the first day of March, the year of our Lord, 1193. It had been near four years since we had ridden from home, off upon Crusade. No words can tell the joy of my heart when once more I beheld the hills and fields and forests of home.

The family that greeted me, so dear in my memories, had all changed. Henry had all but forgotten me, and hung behind the skirts of Father Cedric. Nor did he make up to me for some days, for I had left when he was but three, and he was now just seven. I was startled too, to see William, who should have been sent to Alnwick with Randolph, some three years ago. The lad had grown tall, and quieter; indeed, he stood behind a corner of the wall as if to shun notice. Watching him, I felt a great sadness come over me.

Randall was at Alnwick, since there had been no notice of my coming; nor would I have wished any. 'Twere far better that I see unadorned how my estate had fared in the absence of the master. I would ride to Alnwick shortly, both to see my eldest son, and to check on our town property.

Herleve looked older and worn, her hair graying slightly at the temples. But her eyes were suspicious and sharp as ever, and her strident tone little altered. What greatly surprised me was that her worthless brother, Hugh, stood beside her, as if he were lord of the manor. He greeted me effusively, but with fear in his eyes, and I knew the two of them had been up to no good.

All looked so much older than my memory had enshrined them, especially Cedric and Sir Bors. Bors particularly seemed full weary, as if he had been through wars of his own. It took not a man of genius to surmise that the trouble lay with Herleve and her brother. Indeed, when I got Bors and Cedric aside—which I did both separately and together—heir tales told me all that I had feared.

As long as mother was alive, with the help of Bors and the priest, she had managed to circumvent many of Herleve's wild-eyed schemes. Mother had been at war fully as much as I. But she was old, and growing weaker with each battle. What misery she must have endured each day, trying to mend what my wife so easily undid! 'Twas on the eve of February 10th, they told me, that she simply slipped away in her sleep, leaving Old Hall for other stout hearts to defend.

As soon as mother died, Herleve had called in Hugh, and the two began looting the estate. Had I been another three months a-coming, all would have been lost. Villeins were fined for no offense whatsoever, and all who protested were pilloried. Hugh had just enough knight's training to be able to bully the peasants with sword and staff. Short of murdering him, Bors had not known what to do. Richard, our reeve, had finally left his family and run away to Berwick-town, leaving Glororum's vill to limp along with no direction whatsoever.

Over Father Cedric's protest—for he still kept the manor rolls—Herleve had begun to sell down the stock to near what it was in drought times. The forests were in ruin, for no one stopped the poachers (and some of them were wellborn), or the wood cutters. There would be many months of work to restore what greed and ignorance had destroyed.

Still, that first day or two, when I felt such joy at being home and Herleve being on her best behaviour, I resumed my place as her husband, despite the vow I had taken before the war. Indeed, I felt some pity and tenderness toward her, for full many had my prayers been on her behalf. She, too, seemed truly glad to see me, but much of her welcoming air was dissembling. I misdoubt if she herself knew her own mind; one minute glad, and the next fearful.

Inside three days I had got the picture of the ruin of Glororum, and had come face-to-face again with the strange ways of my wife in love. I began to recoil once more from her presence. The third night, as I slept by her side, I woke suffocating in the dark. A huge dark bulk, like an evil cloud, lay over me, pulsing, sucking away my strength and very soul. It had origin in my sleeping wife, a force of evil so strongly possessive that it crept upon me to feed, swallowing my energy as a snake might swallow a coney.

Gasping, I tried to move but was unable. Calling upon Michael the Archangel and St.Oswald, I at last managed to roll from her bed and crawl from the room. No battle I had ever fought took so much strength from me.

Shaken, I went to my corner in the kitchen and poured a cup of ale, where I sat till morning, mulling over the evil force that had proceeded from Herleve's sleeping form. In the end, I was minded that while she might deny its presence to herself, still she must have been aware that it existed, that she had indeed welcomed it by her brooding hate over every grievance, imagined or real. Feeling unclean, I drew a basin of water and washed, shivering like a wet cur in the early morning moonlight. As soon as dawn had broken the sky, I went to Father Cedric and was shriven, though he found my tale too gross to believe. I was but dreaming, he said, and as a Christian should not harbor such evil thoughts against my wife, no matter how mad she might be. I was silent, for I knew what I had been through. There are those who believe not in ghosts, or evil spirits, or little people. Then, recalling these, our ancient friends, I promised that I would take bread and milk to the stone near the pond the very next night. The little people had been neglected too long.

I decided to move to William's old room upon the second floor; its plain furnishings suited my ways. Yet, entering there, when I turned from the door to view my father's tapestry of Jerusalem-town, I found it cut near to tatters by someone wielding a knife, tracing its patterns. Fury possessed me. Once again I sought Herleve for explanation.

It had been William, she explained. She had locked him in his grandfather's room for some offense. Many hours later when the servants went to free him, they found that he had taken vent upon the tapestry. It was because he was a base and evil child, she assured me. I was minded of rescuing her and Nicolette from her room at Ellingham. I trow, she was as mad as her father, even without the drink. The boy would have to be taken in hand at once.

Herleve told me then, too, why she and Hugh had so looted the estate. It was to buy back Ellingham, she said, so that she might be buried upon her ancestral land. Her weak-minded brother was easily talked into helping with her feather-brained scheme. That eve at supper, I banished Hugh from Forster lands for the rest of his life, upon pain of death. I cared not where he went, or how.

After we had finished our meat, I called Robin to me, and Cedric and Bors. Many were the measures that would need to be taken to restore Glororum, yet most pressing of all were my sons, and my faithful men. Bors looked so old and weary that I misdoubted he would ever recover. Father Cedric, too, was worn, but his practical mind was as keen as ever. Robin had been many years from the company of his father, my Uncle Kenneth. He needs must go home, and then decide where his Fortune lay.

We four conversed near all the night through, ere any decisions were made. In the end, much depended upon Sir Crinan. Crinan had ridden to Glororum from Bamburgh as soon as word reached him of my arrival. He had been acting as my agent at the castle, working with Walter, the warder. He had been unable to stay at Old Hall because of Herleve who treated him like a page instead of the knight he had become, honour-won in battle. There was always work a-building then at the great castle, and Walter seemed not to resent a new master, but was glad of the succor.

Our meeting after so many months was warm; Crinan said he oft wondered if I would live to see my native land again, but was right glad that Robin had managed to pull me through. Little was said about my long stay in France; some memories are too cherished to be soiled by speech. Robin, too, never spoke of my adventure there. I asked Crinan to remain as my agent at the looming old castle until he himself should settle upon wife and home. He promised to do so, and seemed content when he rode back to mount that great grim rock where the sea splashed without surcease upon the roots of stronghold.

As yet, I had not inspected Bamburgh Castle myself. In the name of Richard the King, I decided to ride forth on the morrow upon that task. It would give opportunity to ask Sir Crinan if he would bide at Glororum whilst Bors, Robin, my sons and I ventured forth. We proposed to ride first to Ellingham, to consult with Blaise about the ruin there (for it was certain to be at least as bad as at Old Hall), and from thence to Hutton. Robin had been adamant about wishing to visit Maud, before riding north, to pay his respects to Sir Kenneth, his father. All knew that his mind was less on Maud than Mary Rose. I could but concur, remembering the heart's-ease of love.

Sir Crinan agreed readily enow, but only upon the stricture that Herleve be constrained. I was only too willing to see to this. One of the saddest duties I ever had was visiting Nicolette, but she seemed grateful to me for what cold comfort I could offer with the stirring memories of her husband. Her son Carl was a strapping ten-year-old, and there was, besides, a girl of six, Elaine. Carl's son had been a page at Old Hall since we had ridden away to Crusade, and soon would make a fine squire. I enlisted the two of them to watch over Herleve whilst we were absent, and my lady wife was promised strict punishment if ever she meddled in the affairs of vill or demesne again.

Even sadder than my visit to Nicolette had been the encounter with Andrew's family. They were still mute with grief when I arrived home, for Andrew had been the hope of their lives. Margaret in particular, with no living bairns, pined to a shadow. We buried her in 1199, dead of a broken heart. Old Peter, also, first broken by the loss of his grandson Ralph in 1187, had become a bent and shuffling old man with the news of Andrew's death. He held so little interest in living that I marveled at how he had managed to keep so well the few horses that Hugh had not taken away to sell. But even by my second day returned, the answer came plain. It was Allie's doing.

She it was who had groomed and cleaned and exercised the horses, seen to their pasturing and breeding. She thought like a horse, and felt them with her soul. She bullied old Peter gently, and was his strong right hand. In some small way, she made up for Andrew's loss to his father, if not to his wife. Old Peter would live to be an ancient of days, dying of a sad old age in 1206.

Allie was the greatest wonder of my return. No longer was it fit to call her Button. We hung upon the pasture gate and visited, as if it had been four days instead of four long years; but my eyes kept stealing to her, most amazed. This was no more a rustic child, but a woman grown, long of leg and hair, and a-bloom in face and body. Yet her speech had not changed; it was of the horses and the farm, and every other word was "Yes, Sire," or "No, Sire." The look she turned upon me was plain adoring, and her smile made me feel as tall and strong as Richard the King.

At last, I remarked upon her growth, and she shied like a filly. "No, come," I enjoined her, "and measure 'gainst me." So it was that I found her just as tall as I, for she had likely come from that tall northern stock that held Norsemen as ancestors. We laughed when she placed her slender foot next mine, for it, too, was fully as long. Her old shoon, however, were cobbled and patched and near in tatters, and I made resolve to remedy that as soon as ever I might.

"Try my strength," the girl challenged, and we gripped arms right there upon the fence. Though I bested her, the

strength in her slight arm was a wonder. Beneath her coarse
linen shirt and under the patched old leather jerkin that had
once been Andrew's, I saw the small breasts swell with the
exertion. I turned away a moment, berating myself for an
old fool, to have been so taken.

"You have become a woman whilst I was gone, lass.
Knowing the farm lads, have you not been troubled?" She
knew what my bent was, for she answered instantly, with a
chuckle, "Wouldst care to joust with quarter staves? No one
here will meet with me, save young Will. He and I joust for
the play of it, and right quick and strong he is becoming. But
not as strong as I."

When I questioned Peter later, I found that she had taken
to the arts of war like a lad. Villeins were largely armed with
the heavy quarter staff, or with bow and arrow, and dirk or
short sword. Many older men carried the bill, a large axe
used for felling limbs of trees or men. Peter himself had
taught her the rudiments of quarter staff play, and whenever
not needed, she spent hours in practice. He had come 'round
the end of the stable one day, to find her with torn shirt and
one of the village lads lying in the manure pile, near dead
with a cracked head. Nor was she repentant. After that, Peter
said, the lads thought her too dangerous a sport and left her
in peace. But my Will would slip from the house to train
with her every chance he could get. I learned later that this
was the reason he had been incarcerated in his grandfather's
room, locked away for hours with only hunger and thirst
for companions.

As soon as possible after riding to Bamburgh Castle and
settling things with Sir Crinan, I sent for William. I was
seated in my father's old room, musing upon the tapestry,
when he entered. I swear, he was afraid unto death, but he
held his chin up and made no show of his dread. Yet when
fear comes that deep upon a man, its scent follows him. Every
dog in the kennel can smell it, as can any good huntsman.

I kept him standing, small fists clenched, face wooden.
How like my father he minded me, with his iron resolve.

Suddenly, I saw him as a knight, and I knew he would be redeemed. It was as if a message had come to me from William himself.

"My son, I am sure you realize how you have dishonoured your name. To destroy the tapestry of your grandfather is beyond petty, beyond what even a sulky maid might do. You are a man-child, and though you have not been sent for training as is proper to your station in life, still you must have had enough instruction at the hands of Julian and your grandmother, Mary, that you know a man endures, even when that which faces him seems wrong or cruel. What have you to say for yourself?"

Young William was not eager to talk, but at last many things came tumbling out. How his mother, when she noticed him, told him he was naught but bad in the blood. He would never be a knight, she promised. He might make a monk, if he didn't become outlaw first. Thence she proceeded to fulfill her own prophecy, driving him away at every chance; for an outlaw among us was one whom no family member would redeem. He crept through his young life, hand to mouth, since Mother died, for Herleve begrudged him the very bread he ate. Nor was he entitled longer to sit with the villein pages that Julian and Father Cedric were training. Only Allie had given him succor and encouragement, and this had infuriated Herleve even further.

No one on the farm missed my mother like that lad; she had been a shield to him. Bors was never long on patience with any child, being a man of war and having no family of his own. But Will was sturdy, and he hid his grief when his grandmother died, and began the grim task of survival. Less than Christian I trow, but at that moment I could have cheerfully seen Herleve hung upon a tree, as we had hung Dirk. They were of the same ilk.

I explained to the lad, then, that his mother was quite mad, and not responsible for her actions. The fault of her rejection lay not in him, but in her anger at the world, and at me. (In truth, she was destroying my son because she could not reach me.) "You are of good blood, and your arm will be strong to serve God and King. We will yet make a knight of you," and I told him of my vision. "Still, a man-child must learn to control his passions, for anger will destroy you, as later will lust." And I told him of my own father, and the pain of his life, due to a moment's anger. I admitted then, that not always had I understood that iron man, but how much I had missed him upon his death.

We then looked at the tapestry, and I determined a punishment for him; for he would not have forgiven himself, had I not given him strong penance. "I shall have Nicolette come to repair it as well as able, for her stitchery is the best in all Bamburgh. And you, small sir, shall act as lady's page unto her, fetching all she needs, holding together the cloth, and threading her needles. You will learn yourself how to sew upon that tapestry, for as you have behaved as a maid, so a maid's lessons become you. Yet all men need be able to sew somewhat, for in a war, there are tents and clothes and leather to be mended. I myself learned to sew at the feet of Lady Agnes, whilst still a lady's page."

William first hung his head, then glanced at me in wonder. Little did he say, until I told him that all had to be completed in three days hence, taking no time for aught else, for we were making preparations to journey forth. I proposed to leave him with Maud, where I knew he would find love, and strict training under her steward, Sir John de Hawthorne. Will was excited, as he held much the same regard for Maud as he had carried for his grandmother. I warned him that any misdemeanor on his part would return him to Glororum.

I then charged him to forget the woes of the past, and bend all his efforts toward becoming an honest knight. We knelt then, together on William's old *prie-dieux*. As I raised my head upon finishing our prayer, my eyes fastened again upon Jerusalem-town. "It looks naught like I remember it, from my hill so far away," I told my son, idly. Then a sudden light came upon me, and I turned to him once again. "I charge you, by the Holy Blood, to make the trip to Jerusa-lem-town. You will enter there, in my place. Knights are welcome in that land, and a squire may be knighted by the Count of Jerusalem for his service. It matters not if he be a younger son or country-raised. Richard treated with Saladin, or so I heard whilst in Malta, and Christians can now go unto the holy places to pray. As soon as you are able, get ye hence and light a candle for me, and for my father, at the Holy Sepulchre. And light one for your grandmother, Mary, and all the noble women who bear such suffering in this world. In this way, your every sin will be atoned, and we who have gone before you, and pray for you, will sleep the sleep of peace." Thus he promised me, his hands between my own as signal of his service, and I was content that this poor child would become a man of pride.

We were soon upon our way. Ellingham was as I had imagined. I could only leave Blaise with some encourage-ment and no real succor, for that would have to wait. But a plan was beginning to shape itself in the corners of my mind.

Hutton was as always, so much so that I near expected to hear Stephen's footsteps once again in the Hall. Maud, too, said that his presence oft seemed near her, and a great comfort it was. She was sure that he was helping look after their children, for both Mary Rose and Henry had had curious escapes from accident. She greeted William warmly but sternly, for if he misbehaved, the peace that lay over Hutton would be broken. He seemed to understand, and to know that this was for him a last chance at deliverance. Mark promised to see to his training, and a monk from Durham, Bede by name, came to stand by William's side as friend and confessor. I was content that this was the best possible place for the lad's healing. Maud's young son Henry would go to Richmond in two years, as had his father before him. The wealth that Stephen had gained in the Holy Land ensured his estate and the noble education of his children.

From Hutton, we traveled back to Durham, where I had audience at the great cathedral with Stephen's great uncle,

Bishop Hugh de Puiset. Neither of us liked the smell of Prince John's politics, but the scrabbling to raise ransom for Richard was galling. It made the Saladin tax look like a child's game. Still, one always knew where Richard's mind lay, nor was he a coward like his brother. We agreed to bide in watchfulness, and Bishop Hugh promised troops for Richard's cause, should it become necessary.

Our road fared first to Alnwick, where I found Herleve's worthless brother had already exerted himself to hunt out my eldest son, to fill his head with untruth. Being second to bear a tale holds little advantage; Randall only hung his head through our visit. Little Henry was the only one of us he seemed pleased to see. If truth moved not my son, then he would have to bide in his own darkness. We left, hoping that time might grant him some wisdom.

From thence, we rode to Chatta's farm. What can express the pleasure of meeting my old friend once again? Four year's gossip was ours to spin, many kings to crown and songs to din, over horns of good Northumberland corn ale. After staying three nights, we rode north toward Cornhill, to my Uncle Henry's estate at Colin's Wood.

That man was a wonder. Elder by seven years to my mother, still he was hale and strong. He was right glad to have news of Maud, who had bided under his care for so long. I petitioned him to also raise my youngest son, Henry, to knighthood, as he were able.

Henry the Grey simply shrugged. "I intend to hold here for many long years to come, and your son is welcome. Mayhap he will some day be a succor to me, for my eldest son, Sir Brandon, was killed but a year ago. Surely you heard?" When I told him I had not, having just returned from Crusade, he told me that Brandon had been drowned in the River Tweed, whilst attempting to rescue a villein lad who had been swept away. I saw the ache in his father's heart, for his only other son, Malcolm, had gone to be a monk in Ireland. I touched his shoulder gently to let him know I understood his pain, and was rewarded with a flow of strength as seldom comes from any man. I knew then that he would do as he foretold, being determined to raise up a knight of his blood once more.

So affairs were settled between us, and Henry remained with his great-uncle. Indeed, so much like him did he become, that upon the old man's death at eighty-six, our Henry took his name, Sir Henry Grey. He was to remain at Cornhill the rest of his days; though knighted by Alexander of Scotland, he eschewed the service of war for greater service, that of the land, and the people who toiled upon it. In this, I was content, for I understood the true valour of those who sustain our estates.

At last, we wended our way to Berwick-town, and great was the rejoicing when we came under Kenneth's roof once again. More ale we drank than I can ere remember; more ballads we sang, and telling of tales that passed all belief. Yet for awhile, I left father and son to rejoice alone, whilst I scoured the town for a certain pair of boots. Berwick had been known of old for its crafters of shoon. There was a certain lass who would not go much longer without the pride of decent boots. As she had become my hostler, so should Allie be rewarded.

Robin declined to stay at Berwick. His place, he said, was now at Glororum. Certainly, I sore needed him. The trip had done Bors well, but he was an old knight, and often in pain. 'Twas plain that soon the Forster lands would need a new steward. "Uncle," Robin told me in private, "my place is beside you. If you will have me, 'tis where I derive the greatest comfort." I read in his thoughts, too, that Bamburgh was far closer to Mary Rose than Berwick. He instantly saw that I kenned what was in his mind, and grinned. Thus we came to the years ahead, one in mind and effort. I could sooner lose my right arm than Robin.

The other great pillar of my life came to be my young ward, Allie-christened-Ellen. I scarce could wait to present her with her new boots. As soon as we had arrived back at the home farm, I cornered her in the stable yard. Holding them behind me, I called to her to guess what Beltane had brought. She darted behind me then, near splashing me upon my knees in the muck.

Boots' Lair inside Glororum Stable,
Now Roofless and Overgrown with Weeds.

"Boots!" she breathed, and clutching them to her, was gone in a flash up the ladder to her cubby in the loft. Like a lady, then, she came down, rusty, tattered skirt tucked up to show the shining black boots that rose to near her knees. They would protect her whilst working the horses, and when those wore out, another pair would follow. And never again would she be called aught but Boots, even unto lives that still lay far away.

Chapter 17

Communion

It was August of '93 ere I was able to walk forth and make peace with the land again, a peace too long a-borning. Yet 'twas all the sweeter for the wait. With William at Hutton and Henry at Cornhill, Old Hall seemed miserably quiet; but that lonely quiet was a boon whilst tramping the fields and riding the forests. My very soul began to hush also, and memories of the war grew dimmer. 'Twas as if the ground itself gathered and held the mischief that war had done, and burgeoned because of it. What few crops as had been planted grew lustily; the harvest promised a full ample blessing.

Yet peace is ever a distant vision, like some great cathedral looming before the eyes, even while the feet are ensnared by pitfall and bramble. I had not two weeks of healing ere a lone knight was reported riding in from the west. On hunch, I myself went to meet him, and found it was my old friend, David; but what a sad and haggard man he had become! We bid him welcome, but neither feast nor wine could dispel the gloom that encompassed him 'round.

After dinner, so nervous he seemed in the company of our table, that I walked forth with him across the tilt-yard and to the stables. 'Twas a soft night, with tipped moon arising. David stopped and cast a stone into the pond, disturbing both the moon's reflection and a family of ducks, who set up a concert of squawks and peeps. As we leaned upon the fence of the horse pasture, he unlocked the misery that lay in his heart. Indeed, he had become not the David I knew from so long ago, but a different man, one turned inside out by the Devil.

It began, he said, after he had become jealous of his shining wife, Glenda. Rumors filled Edinburgh castle, because of her gay nature, her beauty, her sympathetic heart, but most of all, because of her cleverness. She had naught, he said, eking out a childhood with her ancient grandma'. When her father had been forced to bring her to the castle where he served with King William's bodyguard, he abandoned her to the ministrations of the women of the court. They were entranced with her beauty, her long and perfect hair. They treated her as a doll, a live dancing toy of innocence. Thus she was ill prepared to deal with the ardor she raised among the men of the household, both squire and knight. Yet she cleverly escaped their many small traps, and they adored her for it. When she married David, many were left sighing; but some were undiscouraged and continued to ply her with favors and entreatments.

At last, David had enough. He packed up Glenda and returned to the home of his birth, Ingleterry. His brother Fagin had inherited that rocky estate, and grudgingly granted David and his bride a cottage in the vill. There David tried to settle, but his brother was as penurious as he was honest, a typical Scot. That was in 1188. In 1189 came news of the Crusade, and David saw it as his only chance to recoup his fortune. Perhaps you know; David, in a company of Scots knights, held with us through the battle at Acre. Wounded and sick, he returned home with but little gold to show for his endeavor.

What he found at Ingleterry broke him completely. He had left Glenda in the care of Fagin and his wife, Erma. Erma was a good soul, and Glenda's only friend. But Fagin grudged Erma the time she spent gossiping when she should be spinning and doing chores, so Glenda had but small chance to visit her friend. When Erma could steal away to the vill, she always took Glenda extra food. Fagin was to provide for her, under the terms—and money—which David had left behind. Yet he cut short all the measures he sent to her, and what little bread and pease Glenda had would scarce keep a rabbit.

She was a clever girl, despite her beauty, and remembered well the lessons of her impoverished childhood. She kept her cot clean, prayed at the church every day for her David, then hurried to the fields and wayside to gather what she might. Without a man in the house, her little flock of chickens had been stolen, one by one. She took birds' eggs wherever she could, and gathered wild strawberries. She dug roots and gathered wild pot herbs; even at our worst in the famine, I could not imagine living in the straits that poor girl had come to.

David told me this with tears running down his face, a face already deep-grooved by their unremitting torrents. Though she became thin as death, still her beauty shone, and as she passed by, some of the villagers would mutter and cross themselves. The girl was a witch, they said. How else could she stay so happy (it was her faith in David that made her so) and so unworn by the cares that life had thrust upon her? Look, at her, they said, with her delicate bones, her little feet and hands, her slim neck. And look at her hair! The women regarded her with envy, and the men with their lust, both awed by her ethereal beauty.

It was but a month ere David came home that Glenda's fair young life was ended. She had been digging herbs on the verge of the peasants field, when one old crone came out of spite and threw a stone at her. "Begone, ye witch, from our fields," she screamed, and soon the other beldames joined in the sport. Spattered and bruised, Glenda began to run for home, when the men came running from the fields. The village priest also hurried from the church, but not in time to stop the riotous mob from driving their field forks deep into her innocent body. "Ha' done, ha' done, ye murdering louts, ye have slain the lady!" With the priest's reason, unreason disappeared; the mob slunk away to hide in their cots till justice might come to visit them.

The priest gave Glenda such comfort as he might, and she died in his arms and prayers. Her last words, David said, the priest came to make known to him alone. With death filling her eyes, Glenda whispered, "I would ha' left, but I love Davy so." They took her to the Hall, where Erma laid the poor child out, with much weeping. She was dressed in a pure white linen shift, with her long shining hair wrapped about her for a shroud. Then a most extraordinary thing happened.

Before they could hold the mass and bury her, a great storm arose. None had seen its portents; it seemed to come from nowhere and return it did to the Devil. Even sour Fagin was on his knees praying, so dire was that storm. Many of the villager's cots lost roofs or collapsed altogether. Sheep drowned, crops were flattened by the immense wind and destroyed by the hail. Then, at the height of the storm, lightning struck the church and destroyed its tower. Not even the eldest could remember such a storm; it was vengeance, all said, for Glenda's murder.

Even that was not all. Glenda laid three days in the Hall in her coffin ere she could be buried. Yet even though the weather turned warm after the storm, no sign of corruption showed upon her body. Most surprising though, was her hair. After death, the hair that had once grown down as far as her legs began to grow again, so that when they buried her, the golden shroud was down about her ankles. All witnessed the miracle. Many were the villeins clothed in sackcloth with ashes upon their head when David returned home.

Yet God saved his most awful punishment for David, for He struck him in the heart, and he was eaten every day of his life by the worms of remorse which lingered there. Erma, too, suffered, for not taking the girl's part more strongly with her husband. After the funeral, she turned to Fagin—for the first time in her life, people said—and spoke up. "You are in part responsible for this murder, Fagin, and may God forgive you." She turned on her heel and walked off, and never shared a bed with her man from that day hence.

"I am the true murderer," David groaned, "nor has a single day gone by that even the blessed sunshine itself does not accuse me. I have gone to wandering, nor do I know how many days since. I have found no peace, for the light has gone from my world."

His tale stunned me. Of a sudden, I realized I needed another knight in the household. It was something I had stubbornly refused to face since the time Giles died. "David, my friend, what is past cannot on this earth be undone. You and I both know that death comes to all, we have seen his awful work. Some meet him bravely, and some as cowards. Your Glenda was as brave as she was beautiful, as kind as she was light-hearted. She would not want her death a pall across your life. Just as she was sunshine, so you must let her shine upon you once more. You are shutting out her holy essence in sorrow and guilt. Remember her with love, not tears, for to do else besmirches her memory. Stay with us, I beseech you. I have work a-plenty; work and time are the healers of the human heart."

"Ah, John, your words are a comfort. So also have I tried to tell myself. Yet in her death I have been completely unmanned; I can never work as knight again, never deal in death even once more. That is a punishment God has bestowed upon me, nor have I sought it for myself. But there is something more for me, somewhere He wants me to go. I have only to find it."

We stood quietly there in the night, the breeze bringing the familiar smell of horse from across the pasture. Low clouds scudded across the moon, bright edges enlivening their gloom. Of a sudden, the knowing was there again, that sudden sure touch of God that had not been with me since early in the war. "David, you must go to Holy Island. It is there you will find peace for your days."

He turned to me, surprised. "Why do you say that? It seems that is the one place in England I have not yet been, here so close to home."

"I know not why I say it. It runs through me, and is not of me, like our seer, Annie. But I am sure that on Holy Island your quest will end."

And so it was. David rode to Edinburgh once more, as if cradling still the smart of his memories, but slowly and irrevocably he turned his steps toward Lindisfarne. There the search for his Grail ended, in the chalice of the monks of Holy Island. He cast off all his knightly trappings and became their servant, tending the altar and the chapter house. His days ran out there, in 1216, at the age of fifty-eight. I went to his funeral mass; the monks of Holy Island had esteemed him highly. But they could not fathom his last words, which were, "I am coming, Sunshine." I had a stone set for him, with the sun upon it for reminder.

David's coming set a pall across my heart. I took to riding more, and less often wished to be alone. Sir Bors at times clinked along by my side; but usually, when not riding far, I took Boots, for the grace of her company. She was content to ride and listen, and remembered well my words. Indeed, she kept tally of the many works needed, which, like the sins of man, were legion. Other times she chattered like a hen, bemused by all the foolish tales heard at every peasant assemblage. Long did she tease to be able to ride to great Bamburgh castle with me, which I refused; for I felt it not seemly to ride into that fortress of men with a maid at my back. Yet at last I succumbed, but only that she might tend the horses of Julian and myself as we visited Sir Crinan and Walter.

Bamburgh Castle, that stronghold of last resort for desperate men, was in nowise a place of comfort. Most of the men-at-arms that garrisoned there found more comfort in the homes of village lasses, whom they took to wife. Walter held them by dint of constant building, for men without work are discontent. The great Keep was plain and without accouterments, except in the guard room. Indeed, 'twas the only place a fire prevailed through the damp months of winter. Yet the fortress must needs be kept always ready for the English king, and out of the hands of any reiver baron. As I inspected the new stonework of the inner bastion, a gloomy parade of warriors seemed to march beside me, from King Ida who built the stronghold, to King Oswald who saved it from the pagan hordes, to Earl Mowbray who based his bootless rebellion 'gainst the English King William here. I always felt a trespasser in Bamburgh Castle. All seemed to be in good order; however, when we returned to the horses in the courtyard, Boots was nowhere to be found.

Alarmed, we struck out in divers directions to search for the girl. It was Crinan who found her. Off the guard room was a walled cubby wherein lay the ancient draw well, water for the castle in case of siege. It had not been in use since Mowbray's time, a hundred years before, and 'twas old then, having been dug from the living rock—so it was rumoured—by Merlin himself. It was a place to shun, for magic hung 'round it, and the water itself was said to be enchanted. No man would drink of that water, except in desperate circumstance, though it were sweet and clear. In our day, the well was sanctified to St. Elmund, but boarded away and near forgotten.

Boots had somehow managed to slip through the boarding, being slender as a wraith (and as determined), and was hanging over the well, from which she had inched away the covering. Dangling from her hand was a piece of rope which she had brought from the stable, unbeknownst to me. Attached to it was a torch, with which she attempted to light the darkness of that shaft. Who could miss my mischievous sons, when this imp of a ward behaved so?

I demanded explanation from Boots on the spot, and most of the garrison crowded 'round to hear the sport. They were disappointed, for that firebrand lit like her own torch, and refused to speak. There was naught to do but repair the damage, and order her home beside me. Julian, bless him, rode ahead, so that he could not hear our words as we quarreled along.

I berated the girl for leaving her charges; but though the horses had been tied, they were in no discomfort. Asked again the reason for her strange behaviour, she at last told her story.

"I have heard often the story of the Glower Worm, that loathly creature, that kept the countryside so feared. Was it in your Grandda's time?" I shook my head, amused at her innocence, and she continued. "Ah, well, many years ago, at least, the people of the country were sore afraid, and brought the Worm the milk of seven cows to drink each day. They poured it into a stone trough, and the ugly creature would slither up and drink. Some say that the Worm lived nigh Old Hall. When I looked, there was an old and broken stone trough, buried among the stones of the courtyard. So, you see, I kenned the tale to be true."

"I have heard the tale, to be sure, the old story of the Laidley Worm, or Glower Worm as many are apt to call it. 'Twas said to be a dragon, such as was slain by St. George. But the stone trough proves nothing. The country is full of old stone troughs." I shook my head. "Dragons such as the Worm no longer exist, if ever they did, outside men's imagination. 'Tis but an old-wives tale."

"Ah, but hear me out!" she cried. "The Worm was given its shape by the Wicked Queen, a woman very like your wife. Surely such a thing is possible! And then the Prince came, a man just as yourself, to rid Glororum Hill of the loathly Worm. The Glower Worm hastened to the Spindlestone, and many are the times we have ridden beside that stone ourselves! The Prince drew his sword to cut off the head of that fearsome monster, but she found voice to plead with him. At last, he believed her, that she was really a Princess, grown loathsome by enchantment. Some said 'twas Merlin himself gave her voice; he was then a lad and lived on Budle Bay. Annie says that Budle was an ancient holy site, that its very name means it is a place of power."

I interrupted her tale, which I had heard before without such embellishments. "Most say that the Spindlestone itself granted her human shape once again, as she coiled about it. Such stones hold great sway. I have felt the strange power humming within Spindlestone myself. In the south of England and in Brittany are many standing stones; to touch them makes the hair stand on end. But what has that to do with your breaking into the old well-shaft?"

"Ah, that is where Merlin comes in. He hastened to the castle, where dwelt the Wicked Queen. 'My art has saved the beautiful lady, your stepdaughter,' he said, 'and now 'tis your turn to feel enchantment. Be thou turned into that which you most resemble, a monstrous toad.' And so it was done. The Wicked Queen sought out the depths of St. Elmund's well, and there she is said to still abide. No metal can touch her, for the enchantment. So I bethought me of my common knife, which I crafted myself from stone and is sharper than any blade of iron." Indeed, in our time, the peasants still carried blades of flint, which they would carefully flake out on winter nights before the fire. Though easily broken, flints were truly keener than iron blades, apt to slice the flesh of maker or user. For that reason, they were often blessed with blood, then water.

"So you thought to creep up to the well and hunt the fearsome toad out with your torch, then kill her with your stone knife. No wonder you pestered me so to go to Bamburgh Castle! And tell me, did you see that awful toad?"

Boots hung her head. "No, Sire. The well was too deep and dark. And it took too much time to move the cover; I had not time to devise a way to lower the torch further. The men would ha' laughed at me, had I told you there," she blurted out.

'Twas all I could do to keep from laughing. The lass was so serious; but it was very like her to search out the truth, and devise a way to explore what no other person would think of trying. It was like her too, to take stock in such a story. Boots knew only that there are things upon this Earth that lie outside of mortal ken, but never had she the sensitivity of my mother, or even myself. If she had, she would have known, with a knowing beyond human ken, that there was no toad at the bottom of St. Elmund's Well.

"Ah, Boots," I said at last, "you have a keen mind and courageous heart. Still, what you did was foolish beyond belief, and I must devise a punishment. The greatest wrong was in betraying my trust, leaving the horses alone and sneaking away, leaving us to search for you with our hearts in our mouths."

We were unsaddling in the stable ere I could think of a suitable punishment for the lass. "Your Dapple stands in the waste growing fatter and fatter, and little do you exercise him. You only spoil him like a dog. He must go."

"But, Sire, he was your present to me! Yet he is too small to ride; my lot lies with the destriers now."

I detected almost relief that care for the fat little palfrey would be ending. We had neither time nor resource to waste on useless stock. "On St. Bartholomew's Day, the week next, is the great horse fair at Elsdon. Horses from both Scotland and England will be gathered there. I needs must ride forth to buy new breeding stock. Crinan and Will are riding at my back; you are welcome to come and tend the horses. If you bring Dapple, he will be yours to trade. But mind you, I expect you to fulfill your duties first."

"But Sire, have you no need for poor Dapple here?" Despite having outgrown the little grey horse, she was still reluctant to part with the first thing she had ever owned.

My mind had already been made up. Dapple was nigh twelve years old; he needs must be sold soon. I had been aware since returning from Berwick town that Herleve was once again with child; there was no mistaking the symptoms. But it was bootless to expect that any child of hers might accept a horse that had once been owned by a stable-hand. 'Twere better by far to let Boots try her hand at horse-trading; all other horse-arts she had already mastered.

Thus we came to Elsdon town, an ancient place of pasture for the Celts, who gathered here upon the Motte Hills opposite the castle, to fight and feast and pray their pagan rites with fire and air, earth and water. The waters of the stream circled 'round, and lush were the pastures of Elsdon. Several score of horses might be staked here, and the land would shrug off their passing in a fortnight. The people of Elsdon and neighboring Redesdale were known for their wary and war-loving nature; little contact had they with outsiders save on Fair days; then they took opportunity to skin every outsider of his pence—bread and meat were dear beyond belief at the Elsdon Fair. The lord of the castle was as remote as his villeins, nor did we call upon him, but pitched our ragged tent in the meadow next the horse hurdles and open-air stalls. The Fair lasted four days, and we made shift to return in two, since we had naught to sell.

I bought a young stud, black in color like my old Black Stone, but shorter coupled and stockier. I had in mind to breed him with the gray Arab mare, to begin a line of horses for merchants and gentlemen: sturdier than a palfrey but more stylish and swifter than a destrier. I also bought a large young stud from a farm at Lincolnshire; he had good legs and an intelligent nature. New blood was good for our herd; destriers would remain our stock-in-trade for another fifty years after I had departed Glororum. I saw no mares that I would trade for; besides, the studs were dearer than I had ever remembered. The loss of horses to the war and the back-breaking taxes had driven prices to the sky.

I staked the new horses with our own near the tent, and began to look for our people. Even Boots had disappeared. Curiosity made me search for her, and sure enough, where a crowd of men was gathered, there I found her. "What is happening?" I asked one onlooker.

"Ah, the fool lass has just traded a right sound child's horse for the worst beast ever to be born in the Highlands. Old Jock brought him to the Fair, hoping to unload him on some dolt; the horse is worthless."

My heart sank as I strained for a look. "Why, that horse looks sound," I replied. 'Twas a skinny, long-legged beast, but with good legs and a glossy red coat; a young animal, with a nervous air. Nowadays you would call him a Thoroughbred; then we had no such breed.

"Oh, aye," my informant answered. "And he can run like the wind—so much that none can catch him! But worse," he lowered his voice, "the red devil is a man-killer. Killed his handler and maimed nigh every man who's tried to mount him. It was bring him to the Horse Fair or feed him to the hounds. I wouldn't have the blood on my hands if 'twere me; I'd ha' had him slaughtered. But some there are as greedy for money. The little palfrey, 'twill be easy for Jock to sell. But I suppose that since 'tis a mere girl that traded for the killer, 'tis no great lookout." He shrugged.

Times like these, I knew I had William's temper, but would not let it rule me. If I could endure the taunts of Saracens, I could endure the countryfolk's ignorance. Waiting till Boots had the halter of the wild-eyed horse firmly in hand, I moved forward to help her move him back to our tent.

Out of earshot of the crowd, I exploded. "Fool girl, what abides in thy head? Do you not ken that the beast is a man-killer?" To which she looked at me coolly and replied, "Ah, Sire, but I am not a man." And she walked on leading her prize, leaving me shaking my head. Well, it seems her foolhardiness will give her punishment in good measure, I told myself. I will not intervene unless her life depends upon it. And I went to search for Will.

I found him deep in conversation with a woman, a widow by the looks of her weeds. Will introduced her as Elna, a freeman's widow. Her husband had been killed on Crusade; though I remembered him not, he had been an archer at Arsuf. The poor woman had no sons to tend their land, fifteen prime virgates. Until news reached her that her goodman had died, she and her brother had made shift to work the fields, buying extra labor when necessary. Now, both her money and her brother's patience had worn thin. The land must sell.

For our yeoman farmers to be quit of their estate was no small thing. All life centered around the cycle of days held by the land: plowing, haying, reaping. Nor was there elsewhere to go for most of us; only a man as desperate as Richard the Reeve would run away to the stink of a town, where life hung by a thread. Elna needs must find a strong yeoman farmer with geld enough to pay for her living, and kind enough to leave her to remain in her own cot till death. Will, on the other hand, had been searching for virgates of his own, for the gold he had brought back from the Holy Land could free him to begin his own life, away from his family's cramped croft.

The deal was all but done when I arrived, but there were still many details to be seen to, and the clerks must needs make the proper deeds. I told Will that we would return when once the horses were safely home, and we would bring our own chaplain, Cedric. The local cleric, Cowan by name, I trusted not overmuch. He appeared to be one of those meagerly literate priests who were sent to remote, tumbledown churches such as abided at Elsdon.

So it was done. Within a month, Will, Will's son, became lord of his own small manor. A new cottage was built by Will and his brothers; in a few years, it would be replaced with a larger home of stone with a good slate roof, for the virgates were prosperous. The croft of the widow was left as her biding place, for which she paid rent to Will in eggs and chickens. Truth to tell, she paid with her one daughter also, a lass by name of Brenda. Though but twelve when Will bought her mother's property, a fondness grew between the squire and maid. I was soon godfather again; their eldest son was named John, Will's son. The Wilson family endured at Elsdon, where it is known even unto present days.

But between Sir Crinan and me, there was not the usual bond that ties old soldiers. Indeed, 'twas upon the ride home from Elsdon with the horses that Crinan asked me for his year's pay. Bamburgh had stifled his soul, he said. Nor had he been able to return to Cornhill with us, to see how fared his old home; a lack he deeply resented. His surliness dampened the ride home more than the light rain that was falling. Even the horses felt it, and trod subdued.

There was naught I could do but grant his request and thank him for his service. When next I visited Henry at Colin's Wood, I found that Crinan had indeed ridden there to visit, but remained restless. 'Twas many years ere I heard of him again, from a traveler stopped at Chatta's inn. The footloose young knight had at last made his way to the Continent, where he settled in Poitou. He married the daughter of a knight made near bankrupt by the constant wars, but who possessed both a castle and an ancient name. The old knight was glad to find a battle-tested knight with gold in his pocket for his daughter. From what the troubadour said, I gathered Sir Crinan paid dearly for his new status, for the woman was as haughty and near as mad as Herleve, scorning the country knight from England who had redeemed both her and her ancestral lands. Ah, well. I said a prayer then for Crinan's heart's ease; 'twas all I could do.

A daughter was delivered of Herleve on December 18, 1193. After our sturdy sons, 'twas a wonder to me when the little pink fist of the girl-child wound 'round my finger with such strength as to never let go. Always I had marveled at the strength of women, now I kenned that they were born with it. Too, Venus was just peeping over the horizon as she entered the world, and the moon met Mars higher in the early sky, in the sign of the Virgin. 'Twas an omen, as was Jupiter beaming upon her from high in the southeast. Had I been less preoccupied, I would have recognized that her Sagittarius sun had also overtaken dark Saturn. The baby's Fate was there foretold upon that frosty Northumberland morn. The stars ever brought to her both comeliness and a quick mind, and a stirring independence rooted in her father's love.

Herleve insisted on calling the child Agnes, after her mother, and 'twas a fair reminder to me, too, of Lady Agnes

Morton of my childhood. The good Christian name flew away after the lass was just a year old, however. Nicolette made the babe a little fur tippet for her birthday, to keep her warm through the winters. Agnes was five ere she had worn that tippet completely bare with loving it. Winter and summer, 'twas always on her neck or in her hand. We began to tease the child about her Tippie, until no one henceforth thought to call her anything else.

Herleve was very ill after this child; she was older and the devil's fury lit upon her with greater vengeance. Oft were the shutters to her room barred to keep her from throwing her body out the window; naught could drown her screams. It cost dear to keep village maids always near her side to prevent her doing away with herself, and the babe needs must be kept away from her except at rare times when she seemed dully rational. Annie brought herbs that seemed to calm and soothe her fevered brain, and Father Cedric said many a mass for the health of her soul.

The extra work and the strain of Herleve's lying-in took toll on me, for I was still far from being as strong as I had been when I rode to Crusade. Through the dark months I could scarce make myself go my rounds, and oft the marches went unridden, for Bors, too, was frequently unwell. Many times I lay shivering upon my sheepskin pallet before the fire, long into the day; when I would try to rise at nature's call, often I fell, shaking. 'Twould all be well by ploughing, I told myself. Spring and the blessed sunshine were not far off.

Nor was King Richard. Good news spread like wind across the country in March; Richard was redeemed and had gone to Canterbury to offer thanksgiving at the shrine of Blessed Thomas a'Becket. Before the end of the month, we heard that Richard was marching north to Nottingham, a stronghold of John's rebellion. When the king had heard that the castellan and his henchmen had killed honest warders simply for pledging their allegiance to Richard, the Lionheart's fury knew no bounds. Great siege engines the king had erected, and a gallows for the rebels. In two days,

Nottingham castle surrendered in great fear, and the back of the rebellion was broken.

Messengers had gone north to William the Lion; they had stayed at Chatta's, hence I heard their news. William was to ride south and meet with Richard at Southwell, in all haste. Since the king of Scotland owed fealty to Richard, he obeyed immediately, largely with the mind that he might negotiate a return of our border lands to Scotland. That was not to be the case, though Richard, glad of an ally in the north, agreed to pay William compensation in geld.

As King William swept south to his meeting, I snatched at a bold scheme and joined the court. Lying ill upon my pallet, many ideas had come to my head, and one concerned the vow to restore the church of St. Aidan at Bamburgh. 'Twas plain as your nose, that of itself Glororum could not bear all the tariff involved in building the new church. Even Crusader gold could only seed the structure. There must be a land base to finance the new church; of labor, we had surfeit. I could see no way of gaining that necessary land, save by grant from the Crown.

The grants of living at Bamburgh church were in shambles. King Henry, Richard's great-grandfather, once granted the living to the Augustinian canons of Nostell in Yorkshire. Yet by his own proviso, they must wait until the priest at the living, one Algar by name, died. Algar lived fifty years longer, only dying in 1171, whilst I was at Alnwick. Henry II, Richard's father, agreed the canons should have the living, but first, it needs must go to his own clerk, Mudac.

Nostell sent then their own prior, Guilfrid, the priest who had married Herleve and me. (Rest his soul!) Mudac himself died in 1185, and no priest was there, save our Cedric, from hence. Richard, worried with Crusade, had neglected to confirm Nostell to the living. Now, at last the king was back in England, and there could be no better time to settle the fate of Bamburgh church.

I had excuse, also; for there was the great castle to report upon. So it was, after the negotiations between the kings were completed, I was granted audience with Richard. Like a true commander, Richard forgot no one. He greeted me with a deal of pleasure, as a comrade-in-arms. I reported forthwith, not only on Bamburgh Castle, but upon the disposition of Durham, which was loyal to the crown. The king seemed glad of the news. Then I apprised him of the vow I had made in Malta, to rebuild the old church at Bamburgh. Richard nodded; oft, he himself had made repentant vows to God, and understood the need to repair the church. "I shall grant you a deed of living at Bamburgh, to be used for revenue for the new church. Nostell shall be confirmed, but with only half the living that was granted by Henry I. 'Tis a rich house, nor do they seem to be doing else but getting fat from their proceeds. I charge you, build there a church, not only to the monk Aidan, but to the warrior Oswald also. Therein you may say prayers for my soul and safe-conduct, and the priest and soldier may carry them together to Heaven. For what have we old soldiers to hope for, if not God's mercy?" Those, I swear, were his very words to me.

Many were those who came after us who resented the Forster overlordship of Bamburgh church; time dimmed the memory of how the church was built. Only the family seemed to carry some faint recollection that we were stewards of the property as much as the Augustinians. Indeed, the papers that shewed our obligation were later deliberately destroyed by weak and petty men. But 'twas from this time that the Forsters were established upon church land at Bamburgh, and the great new church began to be raised.

Chapter 18

Monk and Warrior

Even in my day, it behooved a man who wished power to meddle a little in politics. The only power I ever desired was to serve well both Our Lord and his saints, and the welfare of our land. On behalf of both, I undertook to visit, once again, Hugh de Puiset, the Bishop of Durham, as soon as Richard's commission was in my hands.

Durham was the most powerful See in all the north of England, holding many rich manors and much property. We ourselves owed fealty to them for our south plowland, and for the southern forest. As long as Hugh lived, Durham's wealth stood to aid the Forsters of Bamburgh, out of mutual esteem and our shared love of Stephen. Not that the bishop was particularly open-handed, but whate'er he could grant at little cost to himself, he was right glad to do. Hugh had come of good English stock, noted for their fair and slender men. Durham's living had in Hugh's advanced years given our good bishop, never tall, a roly-poly look, so that one might never know if he were more broad than tall, or vice versa. Men now called him Hugh Pudsey, or Hugh the Pudgy, rather than Puiset—Hugh the Puny. Still, his keen mind remained as shrewd as ever, and his energy was that of youth, ever a-building.

When I told Hugh that half the living at Bamburgh had been granted to me, to fulfill my vow to rebuild the church, his round face wreathed in a smile. "You ken, of course," he said, "that Henry I originally granted the living to the Nostell canons to spite Durham. As long as Algar was there to oversee the flock and fill their coffers at no expense to the canons, they were well content. Then Mudac came, and began ravishing the living. For a man of God, that man was pure thief. That is why Nostell sent Guilford; they were in anguish over the lost rents and tithes. I swear to this day that Mudac poisoned him; he had been to medical school in Paris when younger, but failed his exams for laziness and high living."

I had not quite known the extent of Mudac's greed, though much, of course, was obvious. One could not look at the tumble-down church with its roof in tatters without wondering whose pocket was filling with geld.

Hugh went on. "Henry II was a far more clever man than many give him credit for. Mudac, as his clerk, performed many unsavory tasks for Henry, but the king apparently never quite trusted him. Mudac had been to Rome, and Henry and the pope were at outs, particularly after the murder of Beckett. I do believe that Mudac knew more about that than was seemly. But Henry managed to keep his unsavory clerk at arm's distance, whilst buying his good will. Even you must admit, my fine Northumberland stalwart, that Bamburgh is the furthest toe in the sock of England. But be that as it may, you have enriched my day to tell me that half the living has gone from Nostell. I advise that you begin right away to build; take the old stones from the church and make of them a new Hall for yourself, right upon the steps of the chancel door. That will seal your rights. Do not, by any means, disturb the churchyard where so many saints sleep, nor remove the great beam 'gainst which Holy Aidan died."

"What you say, Sire, is wisdom. But is Alfric still alive to con the plans for the new church?"

"Aye, though old and bent, but with mind as full of plans as ever. His good wife is still his strong right arm. He has, too, a new apprentice, near a master by now, by name of Manfred, a German mason. Set the villeins to quarrying stones immediately; 'twill take some years to cut enough. The quarry lies upon Durham land; you shall have a claim."

So we haggled over price, and details of the new church. It was to be larger than the old one, which had been built at behest of the Conqueror himself and overseen by my ancestor, Sir Robert. Had not the ravages of greed overtaken the building, 'twould have remained there yet; for 'twas soundly built of good stones, though they were small-cut, easily handled and brought up on horseback. Next, I appealed to Hugh to send me another clerk, as Cedric was growing old, and the extra work of construction would need another hand to keep the records and assist with mass.

Indeed, the bishop said he would, though 'twould be up to Bamburgh to pay him. Many were the young men who settled 'neath the wings of the church—younger sons and poor yeomen. Clerks were to be had for the asking. My next request was some harder.

"Your Grace, I sorely need another knight to help me hold the border peace. Mine own sons are still in training; poor Bors can scarce sit a horse due to age; and Sir Crinan has left me to go seek his Fate. My own health has been poor, and the extra work is like to kill me."

He enquired then as to my ailments, and promised to send a clerk who was also skilled in medicine. "I believe I have just the knight for you. He is young, but earned his spurs upon the continent. Our palace guard is surfeit, but he comes with strong recommendation by his brother, a wealthy knight of Yorkshire. His father was an old friend; I cannot turn away his son. You would be doing me a favor if you took him off my hands. How much are you paying Bors?" When I told him, Hugh recommended that I start Sir Raynaud at near the same wage, as knight fees had been steadily climbing, whilst I remained lost in yesterday's prices. 'Twas just as it is today. Little alters over the ages, except that our changes were slower to roll 'round.

One last emendation I was to request of him, so far-fetched that I had left it to last. Likely he would think me either a dolt or a traitor, but I needs must ask. "Sire, the villeins on the dowry property of Ellingham—you remember we drew up the deeds to give Blaise title to some of that land for his stewardship, just before the war—the villeins are a constant burr beneath my blanket. They are always just on the verge of open rebellion; a more contentious and lazy lot I have never seen. Too much time is spent settling their quarrels."

"My dear lad, if you wish Durham to purchase the land, you are not making a very good case for it," the bishop interjected mildly.

"No, no. Sire, what I propose is perhaps even more desperate. I would like to offer them their freedom, manumit them from the land." Hugh's eyebrows shot up, and he looked incredulous, but before he could speak, I hastened on. "Those who wish to stay will pay rent for their crofts and any ground they till. For demesne land, that is, land that Glororum owns outright, 'twould be cheaper and easier to pay wages; then perhaps the work would be done instead of hindered. Any such peasants as do not like the terms can go fend for themselves and good riddance. They are all outlaws at heart!"

Hugh shook his head. "It seems a bit drastic. Have you tried punishing the leaders?"

"Aye, but little good it does. The whole vill is as sour as bad soil. By being freed, those who refuse to work will no longer be tied to the land, and can be moved off. If not enough labor remains, I have villeins at Glororum that would think it Heaven to be free, perhaps even buy a small piece of the land for their own." I was thinking of Richard, our runaway reeve. After a year and a day in town, he was already a freeman, but had nowhere to go save to labor in a stinking tannery. His wife told me privately that he desperately wished to come home, but his son was already farming his allotment.

The bishop shook his head. "The villeins' security is in being tied to their land. And you wish to make wage serfs of them?"

"Sire, it is already being done, more and more. In another hundred years, there will be few men still tied to the land.

'Tis simply not efficient. Besides," I added stubbornly, "what security has any man, save in the grave?"

At the end of it, Hugh promised to give me an answer within a fortnight; when he sent Alfric north, the old master would carry his message. With that, I rode away content but exhausted. Most of my demands were well received, and the bishop gratified in the smell of new silver. Too, the comeuppance of Nostell had put him in a mellow mood. 'Twould all be well.

But it wasn't, for my heart knew no ease. Though mind and body labored, as if to erase every memory of France, the warmth of Alyse stole ever upon me, all unawares. Some passing scent of meadow, and I would see her again, plain as here I talk to you, golden hair shining in the sun, the bright blue of her dress fluttering in the wind from the dash of her milk-white steed. The scent of crushed meadow grass would rise, not from a Northumberland pasture, but from under the hooves of that phantom horse and rider. Then I would be sick again, as weak as when she came splashing across the ford to save my life. Every burn we plashed through upon our rounds minded me of her headlong charge.

Worst were the nights, when I would wake trembling from a dream of love, all sleep gone till morning. The hollow, the empty pain where a heart should be, oft gave rise to unmanly tears. My mind would speak to her understanding a hundred times a day, even knowing it was foolish. I was sadly comforted that somehow she might know, might feel my words within her heart; might know that I would love her always. Might know that I was as lonely as I kenned she was. Ah, but she had a babe, whilst my life centered around naught but work and pain and memory.

As soon as the spring weather became clear enough for journeying across the Channel, I sent Robin back to France. I sorely needed him, but his voyage was more important by far. Tied up within his clothes was a small bag of gold, that which I had promised Alyse for the raising of our son. Never had I the slightest doubt that it was a boy she bore, as my

250

mother had foretold. I dared not send a letter, but instead entrusted Rob with what words of esteem as would not betray me as an utter fool.

It seemed a lifetime ere a message returned. There was much to be done: preparation for building, spring plowing, courts to be held and roads to be patrolled. I drove myself near beyond the limits of mortal clay, trying to not remember the wanton willingness of true love, nor worry over the mishaps of childbed. So worn had I become that Chatta's became for me a place of refuge; fortnightly I rode there for human company and rest. Always now I stayed a night, or two if unwell. To the left of the inn lay the walled stable yard; the heavy gate was swung shut each night. To the right, stretched a small walled kitchen garden for pot-herbs. 'Twas a pleasant place, well-tended, with a stone bench 'gainst a sunny wall, near hid beneath a spreading sweetbrier rose.

It was an evening in June of '94 (a week lacking to my birthday) that I sat beneath that rose, its apple-scented bloom calling forth a hundred tender memories. The afternoon sun shone warm upon the yellow stones of the wall beside me, a peculiar color, not found in the stones at Bamburgh. Both Chatta and his wife kenned that I needs must be alone from time to time; their knowing looks had followed me into the garden ere the tall oaken gate had shut. Where could my Robin be? God forbid that I had caused aught of harm to him. But my thoughts would not stay from Alyse. In the pain of her, my thumb strayed across the rough stone, over and over, round and round, as if abrasion of its flesh might allay the pain in my soul. 'Twas thus that Robin found me, an hour before dusk.

Kneeling at my feet, my beloved cousin put his hands between mine; so glad was I to behold his countenance that I simply reached out and held him to me for a time. "Ah, God has surely blessed me! You have returned safe. I was sitting, berating myself for having sent you. Let me look upon you once again!" I gazed upon his face and saw it tranquil, whilst mine, I knew, was thin and lined with pain.

"Ah, Uncle, all is well. You could hardly have gone yourself, though you would have rejoiced at the sight of your son." He chuckled. "He has the Rhys red hair, which shines like a beacon in that somber French castle! Alyse named him Philip, as you desired, and indeed, 'twas wise. Her doughty husband smells the blood of an Englishman, but in nowise can he discount King Philip's peccadillos. So he is suspicious and torn, though not from any love for the lady. His pride is overweening. Methinks he much prefers the company of soldiers and the pleasures of blood o'er the joys of wife and home."

Questions tumbled from me: How does she look; is the child healthy; how did he find the journey? So we spoke till darkness fell and we needs must retire from the night air. Thick with approaching storm, it blew about us as we shut and barred the gate for the night.

As we drank the goodwife's ale and talked, the thunder rattled and the pelting rain washed away my heaviness and anxiety. I even made shift to eat a little bread and meat with Rob; often I spent my evenings with nothing more than drink. With gladness, I heard that Alyse's love was still mine; she had missed me as I had her. Indeed, I began to think that perhaps my many thoughts had flown across the sea to lodge within her breast, from some of the tales that Rob related. 'Twas uncanny. Yet my fears for her well being were not unfounded. For fear of Philip's wrath—for Alyse was a favored courtier—Arnaud dared not chastise her; still, he shunned her and set small ploys to instill fear within her heart. Beneath the apple tree where first we had made love, she often went to sit alone. Arnaud had it chopped down; 'twas diseased, he said. When home, his great delight seemed to be in thus subtly tormenting her, and she with no one to rescue her.

My heart cried within me. "Alyse," I promised, "I know not how, but some day I shall make it up to you; I will care for you as you deservest. My beloved wife (for so it was I thought of her), may our Holy Mother in her pity bend to succor and bring you peace!" And I prayed each day that

Arnaud might turn from her; loneliness were a far better companion than hate. This, in later years I found to have been granted.

With Rob's return, my pain abated somewhat, and 'twas a good thing. We had much to do. Alfric and Jene had come, and were supervising the dismantling of the old church. The decorative face of the old church was installed in a wall that marked the boundary between churchyard and the new Forster town house. All but the north transept began to be removed. It was the soundest part of the old church, and we needed a place to hold Mass whilst still a-building. It would be refurbished last. Some bit of the nave and south transept were retained; but for the most, the church would be new and grander, as befitted the saints 'twas being built to honor. The holy monk, Aidan, and the fierce knight, Oswald, both had appeared to my vision in Malta and would be remembered here through every vicissitude of time.

North Transept, St. Aidan's. Window at Right from Early Norman Church, Window at Left Rebuilt by John Forster.

There was great need for a house next the work; Alfric and Jene needs must be housed out of the weather, with the respect due their age and skills. A comfortable hall of two rooms was built first, with a small kitchen outside, as it was at Glororum. Later all might be enlarged. Inside six months, my masons and Robin were installed, thanks to the ready supply of old stone. Robin I made beadle at Bamburgh Hall, and he had much traveling on behalf of the work. Too, the new farmlands at Bamburgh needed a master closer than Glororum.

Through many later years, men and women grumbled that Bamburgh Hall was too close to the church, that the Forsters thus gave themselves airs, as if they alone were responsible for the holy building that God preserves and all enjoy. I return to tell you that care for St. Aidan's is in the Forster blood, and not without reason. Many willing hands have aided its design, but none ever held its concern as does my seed, bound still by a vow more than eight hundred years old.

Free men built the church; our villeins supplied the labor with willing hands, for they were paid. I asked not the good bishop, for this was new custom on Richard's grant, and not subject to old laws from the past. We lacked not men, for the farms were burgeoning; since the Crusade, God had blessed us. Too, we had more lads to bring into service, both for men-at-arms, and for squires. Indeed, we sorely needed another knight to help train the lads and oversee the meetings of the fyrd, as well as to aid me in the marches.

He was not long a-coming. Riding north, just as Bishop Hugh had promised, came a sturdy monk, with an eager young knight at his back. Indeed, I had to look twice, for Sir Raynaud seemed scarce older than a lady's page; he was near dwarfed by the substantial man of the cloth. Edwin was the monk's name, and he traced his blood clean back to before the time of the Conqueror. He was of the old royal house of Oswald, he claimed; if 'twere so, then it was fitting that he should come here to assist in enshrining Oswald's memory. All, all down to the least imp who but drew water from the well, regarded Edwin's arrival as a sign of God's blessing.

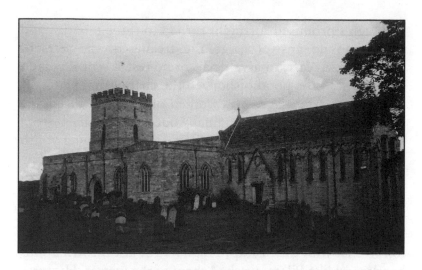

*St. Aidan's Church
(St. Aidan's and St. Oswald's), Bamburgh*

Raynaud was another matter. He was pure energy; in nowise could I find enough to do to keep him from mischief. All Bamburgh soon learned to lock up their daughters and wives; our foxy young knight could sweet-talk apples from off thistles. Despite my many chastisements, he seemed to sit in every court—on the wrong side of the ledger. Withal, he was docked more than ever his wages allowed.

Bors detested our young knight, nor did Raynaud make shift to earn the old warrior's respect. 'Twas constant verbiage between them, oft to the point of blows. I do believe the strife kept Bors alive longer than any of us expected. But no longer could I allow him to sit for me at manor court, or Raynaud would have swung from the hanging oak, with even the curia assenting. Only their goodwives kept the villeins at uneasy peace. Yet both priests and I enjoyed the company of the randy cub; his manners were pleasant and his conversation charming. And he was biddable, being everywhere at once upon our errands.

Hugh's promised fortnight turned to three months, and still I had no answer as to the freeing of the serfs of Ellingham. At last, to give us all some rest, I sent Raynaud south to visit the good bishop, in the chance that he might return with a message. The women of Old Hall threw me surly glances; even Herleve, finally out of confinement from her illness, berated me for sending such a charming youth away upon such a dangerous mission! Bors and I merely gazed at one another across the table with pained understanding, not knowing whether to laugh or cry.

Raynaud was gone three weeks—glorious respite—ere bringing Hugh's reply. I had not done wrong in sending our fox to chat with the bishop; Hugh had at last thrown up his hands, and like Pilate, washed them of the matter. His terse note read, "Do as you see fit. Send me a copy of all the deeds and charters." When I pressed Raynaud as to how he had managed to persuade the doughty bishop, he merely shrugged. "I simply told him that he would be the cause of grievous sin, that you were going to take Bors to Ellingham and put every mother's son of the lot to the sword." He smiled sweetly at Bors, who was choking on his ale. So near did I also. My young friend, I thought, I will repay you for this.

And so I did. Just before Michaelmas, when all the manor accountings were taken, I sent Raynaud, under the firm grasp of Edwin, to Blaise at Ellingham. He was made beadle, to disentangle the knots the Ellingham villeins wove. Edwin had legal jurisdiction, and Blaise, steward's rights; together they had power to nay-say any foolish decision the young knight might come up with. But by and large I trusted Raynaud's wit and felt it only needed responsibility; nor was I proven wrong. Only coming to Glororum for Christmas, the two remained with Blaise till after spring plowing. Richard the Reeve I granted two virgates, at the price of but two sheep a year, to repay his years of faithful service. A fine young milch cow from Glororum was presented, in Herleve's name, as kickerknick, an extra token for his troubles. Another of Will's sturdy sons went also, to settle upon a small plot left vacant. He was right glad of the opportunity for wages and the hope of adding to his acres.

Thus as fall began, the dearest wishes of my heart had been set, like bread to rise. There was time enow to sip autumn's cider, to play chess with Cedric, and to watch the young foals at play in the pasture. Yet discontent beset my heart; nor could I taste of life's small pleasures as a satisfied man. Sleep often eluded me; I would rise betimes with divers undertakings racing through my head, insisting on completion. I worked about the farm on eves when every honest man was home before the fire. Whene'er the pace slowed, Alyse filled my mind and made my heart contract with pain.

One October evening, with blue dusk just beginning to close 'round, I was in the tiltyard exercising a new young destrier. I wore a light coat of mail, to accustom him to the weight. Though coiffed, I bore no helm. When ready to return to the stable yard, I held up for a moment, watching Boots in the pasture. She used evenings for exercising her red steed, Hellfire. 'Twas an apt name, for no man on the place dared go near him, myself included. But she had tamed him enough to be able to ride somewhat, though many were the ploys she used to keep from being unhorsed. 'Twould not do to let the red devil get the upper hand, I thought as I turned my mount toward the stable gate. The moment's distraction was enough; I saw not the great owl swooping across the yard to take a vole from under the destrier's very hooves. The young animal, but half-trained, became a maelstrom, twisting, humping, and lunging in fear. 'Twas over in a moment; he unloaded me upon the earth. Though I have had many falls, this spill took me unawares, and my head struck the wall as I fell. Had I on my helm, naught would have been suffered, but the light coif shunted but little of the blow.

I knew not until later, but Boots screamed for Peter, jumping from Hellfire even as he ran. Her ashen face was the first thing my eyes began to focus on. With one arm beneath my head, I felt her loosen the coif. Blood poured from the side of my head; two inches further forward upon

*The Tiltyard Just to the West of Glororum Tower
Where the Young Destriers Were Trained. It Was on the
Foreground Stones that John Was Nearly Brained.*

the temple, and they might have buried me. Had I not been suddenly so weary, I would have roundly cursed myself for being such a fool.

Somehow a litter was made, and they got me to the Hall. Cedric came to tend the wound, but his cloth had been earned in peacetime; he was not used to the wounds of war. Bors was the only one who seemed to keep his composure, for he was a battle knight. He sent a squire right off to Ellingham for Edwin, and a page haring off for Annie. With his own hands then, Bors cleansed the wound and bound it with clean linen to stanch the blood. I opened my eyes in wonder once, looking at his old scarred face, wreathed in its grizzled beard, recalling how once he and I were near enemies. How long ago that seemed!

Annie had the foresight to bring with her moss to hold the blood and heal the wound. 'Twould be good, she said, that it had bled so, and not pooled dead blood inside the brain-case. Then they managed to get some bitter potion down me, and left me upon a pallet in the Hall for the night. Cedric, chagrined that he had been of so little help, offered to sit by me through the night. Once when I opened my eyes, I saw him kneeling near me, praying. I was well content to let him do so. Rolling onto my side, I returned to deep blackness.

Dawn brought pain, and hard on its heels, Edwin the monk. I made bid to rise, for 'twas long after I should be stirring, but Edwin would have none of it. "Ye shall stay down awhile yet, m'lord," he said firmly. Annie's moss was approved of; 'twas what always we used to stanch wounds and make them heal clean. He ordered a decoction made for pain, but little did we knights regard medicine; we were trained to endure whatever blows Fate inflicted. They moved me then, into Father Cedric's room upon the ground floor, whilst the old clerk retreated to my former lair in the undercroft. It would be near a week ere I was up and doing again; even then, Edwin would not allow me to ride or undertake anything remotely useful.

Robin looked in upon me most mornings, and Cedric stayed beside me every evening. Baby Agnes, whenever presentable, was brought by her nurse to visit, and the tiny girl cheered my heart. Boots, too, stole in to see me whenever my wife went out upon her hawking, which was nigh every day. The poor child seemed certain that I was in imminent danger of dying, and each day needed reassurance that I would indeed survive. Herleve herself seemed more pleased than otherwise at my accident. She had been furious with me for freeing our Ellingham serfs; 'twas an unnatural act, she said, and would be punished by God.

God or Satan, whichever had struck me down, gave me much idle time to spend in contemplation. For the first time since the war, I was forced to come home to encounter myself.

Chapter 19

Grey Days

Within two weeks of my fall from the young destrier, I was once again in William's old room and hobbling about the farm. Edwin had left strict orders that I was not to ride, nor even walk very far. My route lay from Old Hall to the kitchen, to the second-floor bedroom. At times, when Herleve was safely away, Boots would come for me and we would walk to the pasture gate and watch the horses. It was grey November, and only during those short excursions did I feel that there might be any worth to living. A damp pall had settled upon my soul, a blackness that overcame me daily, though I fought as a made knight should 'gainst the enemy in my own mind.

Boots made light of my overweening heaviness. "'Tis but your tumble," she said. "Come spring and the new colts, and ye will be right as rain." Oft I felt her light words were contrived, but nonetheless, my countenance made shift at a smile to please her. It was during this time that I confided to her the small errand I was wont to do for the little people, the setting of milk and bread by the ancient stone in the night. I felt a fool with the telling, but needed an ally to help with those irregular forays. Getting up at night still near overwhelmed me, and I was apt to fall whilst at the simplest task.

"Oh, aye, sire, I too have seen the small tracks that belong to naught I ken. But how shall I help, when I am all but banished from the house?"

So we worked out that upon the second night before each full moon, I would stay late in the kitchen, and she would steal forth from the stable and take the offering to the pixies. 'Twas a relief to know that she believed in me utterly. Oft we would talk about the Spindlestone, and about Merlin. I told her that many of the oldest bards regarded Bamburgh as the Castle Dolorous, from whence Lancelot himself set forth to the court of Arthur. She knew not the sad story of Lancelot and Guinevere, and indeed, 'twas one I scarce could tell for the tears, so minded was I of Alyse. Bless the child, she never asked for that story again, though all the world seemed caught up in the sagas of Arthur and his court.

Those were the few moments of near happiness that life held for near seven months, that and soft moments spent with Baby Agnes. For the most part, the winter dragged with leaden feet, swirling in thick sad clouds like grey goose-down, smothering away life and breath. I could neither sing nor jest. Herleve found many an occasion to taunt my despair; truly, I began to understand some of what she had felt through many a weary year. Still, abject hopelessness and irresponsible arrogance were the walk and trot of my wife's life; the only two paces she knew. No matter how my own pace might falter, never would I stumble into these.

That understanding made me fight 'gainst the despondency with every fiber of my being, but the toll it took was utter weariness. Oft I cared not if I rose of a morning. Cedric, then, would take upon himself to come pray with me; a few days of that and I had heard a lifetime of prayers, and would struggle to rouse myself ere I heard his footfall at the door.

Christmas came and went, yet I cannot con its details. There was a fatted ox, and Edwin and Raynaud and Blaise all rode up from Ellingham, after fetching Randall from Alnwick. William and Henry came not; each was with family and well content. Jene and Alfric and Robin abandoned work at Bamburgh for the joyous season. But I felt a complete stranger at the merry-making, so much so that I went a-field where the bitter wind blew. There none could see, and there I wept.

I cursed my sins, and I cursed God who had ordered such misery for us all. Why the cycles of hardship and suffering, of misfortune and constant battle against human error, that plagued all lives under the stars? I could find no answer, save to set myself against them as best I could. I had no gift for the Christ-child save my knighthood. In the end, I felt little better, but guiltily crept upstairs to bed, exiled from the warmth and cheer flowing below. Thoughts of Alyse pierced my heart with pains as real as any knife thrust, till near dawn, I fell at last into the black pit of sleep, wishing for death instead. Of all my life, no memory holds as heavy.

Thus that grey and gloomy winter passed, each day as sad as its kin, 'til restless spring began to hover over Glororum, sprinkling greening shoots over field and wood. Boots had begun putting me up on a palfrey, and I could ride as far as Bamburgh to watch the progress on the church, which had been slowed by winter. By April, I was feeling near myself again, except for the occasional tumble when rising at night. But a grand obsession overtook my mind, a maudlin passion that filled my idle hours with surmise and new-hatched plans.

I would take Boots home again. Never mind that we kenned not where that home might be; I was sure that riding the back trail would enable her to be united once again with the dear mother who had mourned her for so long. The fact that the lass herself wished not to go was of no import. It was a simple duty, as I saw it, to make restoration. Boots had sighed and agreed, seeing as my heart was death-set upon the journey. She told me later that 'twas her first sign that the great despair of winter was breaking away, and so she hesitantly fell in with my plans.

The first part of April was fine, with a soft wind that called forth the fragrant clover from the land, and startled the pretty buds upon the apple trees. The country had been quiet for months, with not even a rumour of a skirmish. Truth to tell, I heartily longed for a scuffle, to set my heart racing and make me feel as a whole man once again. After months in a dull grey cocoon, the knight was ardent to emerge and fly away. Thus I refused both counsel and assistance. After practicing upon a destrier awhile, I felt confident with both horse and armour, and eager for the journey.

So it was, upon St. Wilfred's day, near the end of April, we two set forth from Glororum upon high adventure. I was upon a tall bay destrier, young but reliable, whilst Boots held to my back upon the small black stud we had purchased at Elsdon. A patient grey gelding carried our pack, which was light, for I wished not to be burdened with a heavy tent. We counted upon lodging at abbeys and inns upon the way; our pack held only a light fly and some tinder for fires, along with such bread sticks as we had once carried to Crusade. Remembering the thirst we had endured in that war, I added a small keg of ale; it was to serve us in good stead.

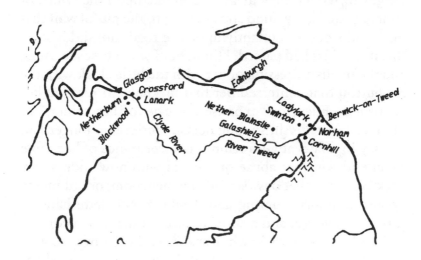

Southern Scotland

Our first leg was to Chatta's, from whence we would journey north, hoping to find country that the maid might recognize. I was in full armour with a woolen surcoat, as the weather promised to turn. The lass was dressed as a squire, with leathern cap and jerkin over a padded shirt. The youthful bloom of her slight figure was well-disguised, her hair rolled under the cap, and tall boots and cloak hiding the shapely legs. I kenned well that should trouble arise, her strength and fury would be equal to any of the house squires; and her knowledge of the horses far outweighed them all. There was always something of the warrior that lay within her, the fighting heart that if found in a squire foretells a worthy knight.

We set upon our road late in the morning, for I intended to stay the night with Chatta; I had sorely missed his company. Little was said between man and maid, but with every pace away from Glororum, memory of the heavy grey weight of winter blew away like smoke upon the winds of spring. Instead, my mind strayed back to the pitiful waif that once had stood so defiantly upon the road; nor did it seem that nine years had passed. I thought of when first she came, and the maids a-dressing of her with the little cloak with the big button that conferred her first nickname. I recalled her baptism as Ellen, to "exorcise the evils of her origin," as Herleve insisted. Ah, so long hence. Herleve no longer had any say in affairs at Glororum; my forbearance of her came to an end with her abuse of the lass who now rode at my back. She spent her days secluded in her room, or out racing upon the moors, hunting and hawking. Nicolette had the care of the house, and a shrewd mistress she had become.

Men's minds work in whimsical ways. I rode away to war, and when returned, expected all things to have stayed the same, as if frozen in the ice of time. I was annoyed to find the eager, tumble-haired girl-child now a young lady, whose budding form seduced my wicked eyes. I thought of Dapple, and Ellen's assayed gratitude, and her trading of him for the wild beast she called Hellfire. I thought of the girl's absolute loyalty, her eager mind, her credulous belief in wondrous things. What would my life be worth without her?

I mentally shook myself. Fool, I said, 'tis too many years you have let go by ere attempting to find her kin. Your duty lies in returning her home; never mind the hollow 'twill leave in your heart. Imagine how you would feel if someone stole away baby Agnes. Does the girl's mother not weep for her child to this very day?

I recalled too, the day I had proposed to her that we should ride north to search for her family. I was idly watching her groom the Arab mare, and begin to braid up the mane, as if the animal were a queen. Ellen's hands flew, gently, confidently. Her thick, dark skirt was tucked up behind, peasant-fashion, to make a sort of pantaloon, revealing the pride of her boots, worn but clean. As I gazed at the long legs, the slender body, I wondered idly about her antecedents. In a rush, the idea came for the journey. But perhaps she had good reason for not leaving Glororum. "Tell me, Boots, have you ever thought of marriage?"

"Never." Defiant blue eyes flashed. "I would sooner die." She tossed her head like a skittish colt, and fair hair fell from beneath the band that tied it. Jerking at the band angrily, the lass clenched it between small even teeth as she rearranged the knot. "Why do you ask me that?" She was indignant. "We have spoken of it before, and my answer is still the same."

My eyes would not leave the petulant mouth, the cruel teeth, the rosy skin. Something very like desire stirred once again; it had been near a year since I had felt such a clutch at the loins. Lecherous old fool, I told myself firmly; be done with that! Aloud, I remarked, "Well, if you will not marry, perhaps I should try to return you to your home and family."

She watched me closely, holding back anger. "My home is here, with the horses. Besides, I do not know how you propose to do such a thing. It was such a long time ago, and so far away. You ken that I have never remembered aught of whence I came."

I rubbed my neck, thinking. "We could ride up the track they brought you down. I suspect the swine could not have come far. Ye said then that the time upon the road seemed near four days. The border is quiet, if ye will go as my squire, perhaps we can track back to where people's remembrance can recall that kidnapping so many years ago."

She seemed torn. Adventure beckoned, and she still held some small curiosity about her childhood home. But she shook her head. "I ken not how we shall find what fled my mind so long ago. But if we should find the place of my birth, you must promise not to leave me there if I do not wish to stay." And so I promised, and began the many hours of planning the search. Boots told me much later that without that promise, she never could have been persuaded to leave. She had no intention of staying in Scotland, but was loathe to extinguish the first glimmer of excitement she had seen in me for weeks.

Thus, each recalling days long gone, in near silence we arrived at Chatta's. As we entered the yellow-rock walls of the stable-yard, a feeling akin to homecoming overtook me. Chatta, too, was happy to see us, for it had been months since I had been able to ride this track myself. Raynaud had instead patrolled this way from Ellingham, bringing to the innkeeper news of my accident and slow mending. Chatta threw an arm about my neck, and led me in to greet his wife and share the gossip over a horn of ale. Simon, his eldest son, at last went out to the stable yard and returned with Boots, who had hesitated to enter, so long had she been banned from the conviviality of the common hearth. Chatta's wife immediately made her welcome, and indeed, Boots remembered her well. Thus we had our meal, unmindful of two strangers supping quietly in the corner.

A full grand meal it was: roast haunch of venison (purloined, no doubt, from the king's forest); wheaten bread with fresh butter and cheese; a salat made with new onions and wild herbs such as the country folk use in spring to thin the winter's blood, dressed with cider vinegar and pepper.

Last came a little mawmoney that Hilda had added in my honour, for luck. 'Twas the height of the feast, for the eggs were fresh, the chicken tender, and all had been well-seasoned with sugar and almonds. Eli, who had become cook at Glororum after Lucas died, was able enough, but such treats as Chatta's wife provided came rare at home.

After Ellen retired to bed down with the horses, and the little inn grew quiet, Chatta stayed behind. I had no desire to sleep upstairs with the strangers, so proposed to roll up before the fire. The innkeeper brought some tanned sheepskins for a pallet, and I was well content. "Ah, Sir John," he said musing, "'tis like old times, having you here. The border has been main quiet; with our knights back from the war, thieves and slavers are lying low. Not like '76, when you rescued the girl."

"God grant they keep from your door! The hardest vermin to control are those that walk upon two legs. But truth to tell, I near relish a fray, so quiet have I been for so long. Know you aught of the road to Lanark?" Lanark was a word the girl hesitantly proffered, as if doubting its taste in her mouth.

"Nay, not after it leaves the Edinburgh track. I ken all of the crossings and roads to Edinburgh, but little of the way beyond. How will ye go?"

"I thought to cross the river at Norham, as the ford is less remarked than at Cornhill or Berwick. We will leave here up the track they brought her down, and stop at Cuddy's Cave to see if aught comes to her memory there. She is frightened of the journey, a small child once again. But as brave as ever."

"Aye, 'tis the most likely way to go. But stop you not at Norham. The innkeeper there is a gossip and a sloven. Go ye a league further, to Swine Farm; Tom keeps a quiet house and a close mouth. 'Twould not do to have the whole countryside whispering of your venturing forth with a maid at your back." After a pause, Chatta plunged on. "The lass has grown tall and fair, and 'tis plain she adores you. But I had felt better about this trip had you a man-at-arms instead of a stripling girl."

I shook my head. The excitement that had been building failed to shred before Chatta's wisdom. "Ellen is wiry and strong, and a master of the staff, as some of the farm louts have discovered with ringing heads. There is none better with the horses." I smiled, in answer to his concern. "We shall be well, and if adventure should come, then let it come and be welcome."

Chatta nodded. "You mind me now of the young John I remember from before the war. God speed you! And now, I ask a boon. There is a merchant upstairs; you saw him at supper. He has with him his daughter; they came here in company of a knight of Alnwick. The man was loathe to escort them further, nor was the merchant anxious for his company after the man cast unashamed eyes upon the girl."

"'Tis not like a knight to be so boorish. What name did he go by?"

"I ken not, but he had a shield with a red chevron. Yet you must understand that the merchant is a Jew, and Christian knights are loathe to regard a Jew kindly."

I was silent awhile, remembering the Jew whose powders had saved my life at Acre. "God's wounds, man, I am sworn to enforce the peace of this road and to aid travelers. A Jew is a man like any other. Were he even a Saracen, I would ride with him. Whither fare they?"

"To Jew-town, at Edinburgh. 'Tis not far out of your way; Ben-Ami has kin there. He has been delayed for two days whilst we waited for a knight willing to succor them; I promised him before supper that I would ask you tonight. I suggest you take the old Roman road across the hills north of Swine Farm, 'tis straight and little traveled. There will be few there to remark upon your passage. A rich merchant is a ripe plum for highwaymen."

"Ah, my friend, we ride with God. Tell Ben-Ami that we will take the road with him, but 'twill be hard riding, two days only to Edinburgh. Plums should not hang too long in the sun."

Chatta rose smiling. "Aye. And may Holy Mother aid your search."

So we fared forth early the next morning, knight in the lead, then the merchant and his daughter, and Boots riding in trail. Her great curiosity led her to often ride forward to speak to the girl. Not often had she companionship with those of her sex; she claimed their idle chatter drove her away. Truly, her experience was like none of the farm girls. Yet here, with this Jewess, she seemed to find a common bond, for the girl had been much upon the road with her father, and had seen many sights along the way. She too had lost her mother when young. Even stopping with Tom, we found much to converse upon. I told the merchant of my esteem of the Jewish doctor who had saved my life in the Holy Land, and he was much gratified to find a knight who regarded him as any other man.

It began to rain the morning of the next day, with grey mist. Indeed, Scotland is a land of grey. The grey road stretched straight before us, across the grey barren hills; rocks and sky and heather were divers shades of grey. Even the men of that country oft are grey. It was near evening when we came to Edinburgh town, but we had not far to enter there ere reaching the house of Ben-Ami's kinsmen.

The night was sour, and we were glad to accept the hospitality of the Jews' house. They made us welcome and fed us with excellent food; the pallets they made for us were warm as their hearts. We sat before the fire ere bedding down, speaking of the Holy Land, an unspoken prayer in every mind for holy Jerusalem. I found, too, that Ben-Ami had access to good Flemish glass; he promised to stop at Bamburgh in a year or so to see what we might need for the new church.

We left in the morning well content. Boots had a firm friend in Devorah, and I in Ben-Ami. The rain had abated and we were off on adventure. The road took us southwest from Edinburgh, and Boots talked away the miles. Indeed, with the riding north, somewhat of her memory had been jogged, as I had hoped. She remembered biding in a stone cot near a river, and her mother. Little did she recall of that lady, save that her eyes were bad from the constant smoke of the peat cooking fire, and that she was ever a-singing. Her father she remembered not at all, only the shadowy figure of a man who came at night and ate and went to bed. No sisters could she remember, but there were older brothers. Indeed, she had been taking the nooning to her brothers, tending sheep upon the waste, when the slavers burst from a copse and struck her down. Her head had been fair cracked with the force of their cudgel; I understood now that she had kenned more than I knew of the weakness after my fall from the destrier. It had not been an idle humouring, but memory of her own hurt that prompted her faithful care. To that, too, could be ascribed some of the loss of memory she had suffered for so long. The longer Boots talked, the more I marvelled at the strength in her, at her devotion to me. How could I ever abide at Glororum without her! Only memories of Alyse held a pleasure as keen as the companionship of that lass.

The track was as barren as it had been going north. The road and its bridges were built by the Romans, the marks of their passing more lasting than any human sign since. We stayed the night at Castlecrag, in the house of a hermit who served the souls of the scattered shepherds of the district. Though an old man, his memory served not to remind him of any kidnapping in his parish; though, he said, such depredations were common enow along the wild border country. To the south stretched dark forest; were the slavers not too afraid of green men and ogres to hide in its depths, he allowed, they would ply their hideous trade more freely.

When we left the next morning, the hermit gave us directions to Lanark, where he advised that there was a large abbey serving the entire district. He told us to ask for Brother Julian, who kept the abbey accounts, and was acquainted with all the families 'round. The weather had stayed its raining and began to blow warm, too warm, and from the south, a bad sign. There was a storm in the offing for the morrow. Boots hurried her horse, as did I, so there was little time for talk. But with every stop to relieve ourselves, she would shake her head. "I remember naught of this. I am sure this is not my country. Further east, nigh Edinburgh, the land held some call for me, as if seen once in a dream. Here there is nothing."

We were lucky to make the shelter of the abbey ere the storm hit; the wind was enough to tear the clothes from your back. The rain soon began, but we were safe inside, waiting for Brother Julian. Another Brother brought us bread and cider, and we supped in peace. At last, Julian came forth, and granted us several hours of his tales. The abbey lay along the River Clyde; to the west was a place called Nether Burn. Not in his memory of the last twenty years had a child disappeared from there, though many came to rest in the kirkyard at an early age. I asked him about the people thereabout, as I had heard the rolling lilt of the Cymry speech in some of the vills we had passed. "Aye", he said, "many were the Welsh who came to settle here, with kin who have abided along the Clyde since time out of mind." Only two kidnapings could he tell us of—one fifteen years ago of a girl from the vill of Crossford, the other, a lad, who disappeared from Blackwood during the war. At last, he shuffled off to his prayers, leaving us little the wiser.

"Lass, I feel we are not in the right place. I ken not how you knew of the word Lanark, but this seems wrong. The folk here have a different speech than you used then; near always I can tell from whence a man comes by the flavor of his talk. Brother Julian may be old, but he seems to remember well. Too, this seems too far for the outlaws to have come. Surely they were afraid to travel much, save by early morning and evening, or upon the most barren of tracks."

"Oh, aye, sire! They did oft stop in midday, when our passage might have been remarked. I was always glad; if there was water, I could drink and wash my feet; or else I would sleep a bit. If only I had marked the passage of the sun! But I was too feared." Boots pondered a bit. "I believe you to be right. This place seems strange to me."

It was two more days ere we could leave, so ferocious was the storm; I had seen few to match it. At last, the good Brothers gave us directions east to Galashiels, and bade us Godspeed. The day we left was fair, but by the time we passed Castlecrag, it became apparent that the storm had a lesser gale riding at its back. To the south stretched forest, to the north, hills and moors and scrambles of woods and brier. The road seemed fair deserted ahead, as the rain began to pelt upon our backs. At last, "This is enough," I said, and led the way up the hillside, where we could look down and watch the road. "We needs must stop now, whilst we may still pick our camp. There is naught before us as far as eye can see, where we might find shelter. Yet I do not wish to be surprised should an outlaw band travel this track under shelter of the storm." So we rode up the ridge, to where a small dale ran, sheltered from the road and the west wind, and surrounded by wet, grey boulders. A few stunted trees had root enough to anchor our fly, and keep the rain from our heads. Despite the hardships of the roads we had traveled, I began to feel confident, saddle-toughened once again. This would not be my first bivouac, nor the last. I remembered the hot, dry road that once led us to the hell that was Arsuf, and in thanksgiving, raised my face to the rain. My very soul felt new and cleansed.

Allie, too, stood quietly, facing the wind, her hair blowing back as she raised her cap to feel the blessing of the rain. There was about her a fierce mood, a primitive, lonely heart that captured the wilderness of bleak ridges and made it her own. Somehow, together, we shared our spirits, fitting as closely as hand and glove about a sword. Our spirits fled into one another; and into the land and into the storm. It was as if we had walked this journey before and were once again coming home.

At last, the lass turned to care for the horses, moving their packs into the lee of a boulder, under one corner of the fly.

I prepared camp, clumping clumsily about in my armour, splitting dry wood for a small fire. I dared not show too much smoke or flame, for we were but two, there upon that wild Scots hillside. Boots gave the horses some small oats, and checked the tethers. I burred a firestick, and with tinder and steel, soon had a tiny blaze. We supped then, on the salty bread sticks, washed down with the ale we had carried so far. Nothing brings home closer to mind than the warm taste of your own ale. As if peering into my thoughts, the girl said without turning, "Ah, John, this is home to me. You, and the horses. Whatever else Fate may will, this is all I ask of life. I care not if we find my family; that is as dead and gone as if another life, another world. This is where I belong."

Her words brought such tender feelings to me that I needs must rise. I patrolled along the slope watching the road; not a fire showed up and down the length of the valley. Below the now-shredding clouds, Venus and Jupiter joined in the western sky. The breeze blew upon the hillside, bringing small showers as the billows passed, silver and grey. Soothed, I returned to our little cove. Taking a handful of wadding from the pack, I wiped my helm dry, and sat it upon impaled sticks, two yards from the fire. We country knights had not the costly court armour that survives even today as remnants of pomp and power. There was only a byrnie of mail, with its coif, light as armour goes, but sufficient for road patrol. Even my helm was old-fashioned; the great war-helms that we had used in the Holy Land were clumsy and awkward. Rather than the old leggin's of mail, tied at the waist, I had the new separate leg pieces, well-padded greaves. Hugo's sword never left my side, and my short shield still bore the Forster arms that I had painted on in Messina. Boots had borne my lance, her own quarterstaff fixed firmly by her side. All were now carefully wiped down and laid upon the baggage, 'neath a corner of the fly.

Three more branches with forked ends I thrust into the ground to hold the wet mail, and Boots helped me off with the byrnie so we could set it to dry. Armour was too precious to be left to rust. I wiped it dry, and turned so the girl could unfasten the ground-clumsy greaves. Riding without them, I would feel naked and vulnerable; too, they kept brambles and mud from the legs. The girl knelt before me, in the small warmth of the fire, unbuckling the armour intently. The wind played across her face, as the clouds chased like lambs across the dark blue pasture of twilight sky.

She looked up. "Ah, sire, your hosen are soaked also."

I knew so, though the woolen knit drew no warmth from the body to betray its sodden condition. "I shall get them off to dry after I clean the greaves. Take your own jerkin and cloak and spread them to dry before the fire, lass; you are as wet as I."

Quickly she turned to as bid, then came to sit upon the ground cloth at my feet. Pulling off her boots, she carefully wiped the stains of travel from them, and set them beneath the fly. With all our equipment, there was little room left for us! "Now, sire, I shall help you with your hosen." I had pulled off the soft jerkin I wore under the hauberk, and stood now arrayed only in linen shirt. Sore from travel and the weight of armour, the breeze freshened body and soul.

Never will I know why I stood waiting for the lass to unfasten the thongs that held the hose to a belt about my waist. Once the tedious armour straps were unfastened, I was perfectly capable of undressing myself. But I waited, while the clouds chased across the moon, and the wind fingered my hair. Carefully, Ellen untied thongs from hose, and unfastened the belt. I felt suddenly freed, free from the grey past, spinning between moonlight and firelight.

Smoothing down the hose, her hands were caressing, soft as birds wings upon my thighs and calves. My manhood betrayed me. The girl laughed as her power struck home to her. Forgetting the hose, she caressed legs and loins, nipped playfully at thighs and belly. How it was consummated, I ken not. It happened in such a rush, rashly but carefully, irretrievably, and with such mingled pleasure and pain that my mind near fled.

Rolled together in sleepy warmth before the fire, I swear I had near forgotten the haven of comfort that loving arms can hold. Yet all the while I was cursing myself for a fool, and derelict in honour towards my ward. Sighing, I raised on one arm to gaze at the lass beside me. The quarter moon had risen, peering through the chasing clouds upon her face. Had she been a kitten, she would have been purring. "Ah, Boots, so easily is a man undone! Not by force of arms or by hardship, but by a maid."

She traced my chin sleepily with one finger. "I, too, am betrayed. Into what I never wanted to be—a woman."

"We must try to find your people." It was a last desperate thrust to break away from her enfolding warmth.

"Ah, master, do you really think I could leave you now? You have brought me to life with your loving; certain now, I shall never leave your side. But I have been yours from the day I first saw you, sitting your horse so vengeful upon that road, the blood of my tormenter drying upon your lance. If, as Annie says, we have lived our lives before, I have loved you through them all. I will love you forever, then a day more." She murmured it sweetly, and my body ached even while my heart was trying to comprehend. It was one moment and all moments; time faded to nothingness. It seemed I had heard those self-same words before, that I would hear them again, life upon life. Nothing else mattered; here was eternity held in one crystal instant of awareness. Then it fled away, in the pain of rolling over upon a stone.

"Girl, 'twill not always be that easy." Discomfort brought me to my senses. I was mindful of more obstacles than she kenned, in the strata of our lives. "But I shall do my best to make you happy." It was a heartfelt vow.

"You always have. I am content in that. But for now..." and she covered me once again with kisses.

With first grey dawn, we broke camp. The rain had at long last gone, and the wind was drying the land. We halted at a little burn that tumbled across the road and drank and washed, then watered the horses. It was not long till we reached Galashiels, and sought shelter in the abbey. Once again we were knight and squire, and once again I needs must inquire as to kidnappings in the neighborhood, some nine years ago. This time the abbot himself came to speak with us, to cudgel memories of his neighbors out from a lifetime of prayers. I was main startled; and Boots, sitting in the corner, straightened her back when the old prelate began to reminisce.

"Aye, there was a lass disappeared from north of here, perhaps nine years ago. My memory holds not so keen on time, anymore. Daughter of a man with a good freehold; some three virgates had he. His son holds the land now; tight with the tithes he is too, not like his father."

I knew what the girl was itching to ask. "What was the man's name, and what the name of his property?"

The prior hesitated not at all. "Blaine, he was called, Blaine of the Nether Lea, the low pasture. A stream runs through it all along; 'tis main wet meadow and waste, with some plowland. Blaine's wife was Carrie; she died not long after the lass disappeared. It was naught but hard work she knew, with four sons and none to help around the house. The girl—Allie, I believe was her name—was a late child, but a godsend to her mother."

"The father too is dead?"

"Aye. And the eldest son. Matthew, Mark, Luke and John they were called, after the four apostles. Matthew took the cross; there was word that he had been knighted in the Holy Land. He was killed at the battle of Arsuf."

With a shock, I remembered the lad well, a yeoman knight not much younger than myself. He had been dubbed at Nicosia, with Andrew and Carl and Crinan; he had fought beside us at Arsuf. Matthew's horse had been cut from under him, and he went down beneath a swarm of Turks. "God rest his soul," I said simply. "He was a true knight. I knew him well." Out of the corner of my eye, I saw Boots look at me, startled. Small wonder I had always found something inexplicably familiar in that lad, some cast of the features that minded me of I knew not what.

"Well, Matthew was the best of the lot. Mark took the cross too, but he was late going out, as his father tried to keep him at home. He stayed a squire at Jafra, and was made knight after the Mamelukes broke into the Christian camp and attempted to make away with Richard the King. He took the eye of Bishop Walter of Salisbury, who went to the Holy Land to negotiate for Jerusalem. A dream that holy man had, that bid him go, and some good came of it, for pilgrims can now go to pray in the Holy Places." He was silent awhile, contemplating the streets that had echoed to the footsteps of Our Lord. I bethought me of the cruel Fate that had kept me from entering the Holy City, and was once again forlorn.

The abbot took a drink of ale and went on. "Walter persuaded Mark to join his entourage, and he bides at Salisbury to this very day. 'Twas up to Luke, then, to stay and farm his father's virgates, but it seemed to sour him. The youngest son, John, could not bide at home under his brother after his father died; he rode away to seek his fortune. I know not where he went, nor how he fares."

"Tell me good Father, of what ancestry were Blaine and his children?" Ellen had the long legs of the Norse, and the pale eyes; though her hair was brown, not flaxen.

"Ah, I know not, Sir John. Methinks perhaps Blaine's English was abetted by Viking blood; the sons were tall and strong. The lass would have been tall also, much like your young squire there in the corner." The prelate's eyes twinkled, and I knew he had seen through the girl's disguise. "But in the main, the line was of the old stock; one of the thanes driven out of England when William took the country. I, myself, am of that stock."

A small voice came from the corner, a mere growl as Boots sought to control her voice. "Do ye ken...was the lady mother a singer?" I knew then that her memory was coming clearer.

"I knew her not well, but aye, so I have heard. She was half Celt, and those folk raise their hearts with song when most unhappy. Her father was Gaelic, her mother a Celt from Lanark." A heavy breath left both the girl and I; her memory had not betrayed her completely. She had heard of Lanark at her mother's knee!

"If you wish to ride north to Blaine's Nether Lea, I can have a novice show you the road in the morning. 'Tis near two leagues by the way you must ride. But I warn you, Luke is a penurious man, and not given to kindness to strangers."

I could not give the good abbot an answer then, but promised one on the morrow. I had not a good feeling about riding north, but the decision was Boots'. After our host left, I went to the corner to sit beside the lass. She had her head buried in her drawn-up knees, surrounded by her arms. It was as if she had turned into the womb once again, and I knew she was possessed by sorrow. I held her then, without words, till she at last unfolded and let me dry her tears.

"They rest with God, Boots. We may go to spy upon the home you once knew, or we may pray in the kirkyard for the souls of your family and return again to our home. The choice is yours." In the end her curiosity won out, and I was secretly glad, as I also wished to see from whence she had sprang. I left pence with the abbot for masses for the souls of the family, particularly her mother. Matthew, I knew, was already with Our Lord in Heaven.

The novice led us by 'round about ways, till at last we spied the grey stone cot in the low meadow. A red-haired woman came to the door to throw out slops; a child played in the dooryard with a gaunt hound. Sheep grazed upon the higher meadows. Boots looked long, then pointed to a copse near the burn. "'Twas there they hid." She turned away, unable to speak further. At last, I asked if she wished to visit her brother. She shook her head violently, "no," and I was relieved. A stingy brother with a red-haired wife would not make a long-lost sister welcome. 'Tis not human nature.

I had the lad show us the road east then, so we might return to the river Tweed. I had in mind to stop in Berwick and visit Sir Kenneth. There had been gloom enough for this trip; I stood sorely in need of his banter and songs. Thus we went, staying the night once again with Tom at Swine Farm. And once again Boots brought her untrammeled love to me, a love that shivered my soul with its consummation. Never again would she stray for long from my arms. Her love burnt with the fire of an awakened virgin, and in it my life was consumed. Sorrows dimmed, and strength returned. As long as Allie was beside me, Glororum prospered beyond the prowess of my energies alone. Some higher force held with us. Not until I lay dying did I realize how very much I loved the girl.

Chapter 20

Banished

After leaving Sir Kenneth and Eadra, we backtracked to Cornhill, to visit the Henrys. My son, I swear, was more glad to see Boots than his father, for the stable had been a favourite haunt when he was still at home. Uncle reported that he was a biddable page, and progressing well, not only in weapon-play, but in Latin and arithmetic. They seemed well content with one another.

We rode once again into the stable yard at Glororum on May 22, 1195. Our journey had taken us many a weary league, but 'twas not just from travel that we rode so weary. New love is a heady wine! Away from prying eyes, the gulf that separated master from horse trainer seemed not so grave. At Glororum, I warned Boots, all was changed; we ever must call upon discretion. Bless her, so tuned was she to my soul that those few words sufficed between us.

We found Edwin and Raynaud returned from Ellingham, the properties there properly seized. Those few whose presence was a detriment to all were resettled on Hugh's virgates, 'midst much grumbling. Raynaud threw the fear of Heaven into them by recounting how I would come personally to have them evicted from those meagre smallholds that remained. Enough stories had gone 'round of my temper when confronted, that the poor villeins held their peace. Still, I was vexed that our young Hotspur had once again used me so harshly in men's eyes. I would bide, till revenge presented itself clearly. For the nonce, I sent the young knight on to Hugh at Durham with copies of the deeds and charters. No sooner had his horse's tail disappeared past the stable gate, than Edwin blew a huge sigh. "That lad has been my penance for taking delight in the priesthood and renouncing the dubious joys of fatherhood. Celibacy, John, holds certain blessings!"

Bethinking me of the problems with wife and children, I could but agree. But Kate then brought Tippie, and the baby laughed with delight, holding her arms out to me. Gazing into that happy face, I knew that the game was worth the candle of my life. Baby Agnes was just beginning to talk; indeed, it seemed she was never silent. She had Herleve's cream-and-rose complexion, her curly russet hair. But she held none of her mother's cursed disposition, and her eyes were the strong grey-green that had marked my mother's. This is a daughter fit to wed a prince of the realm, I thought; then I began to worry once more, about how best to dower her. At last, I laughed with the babe, knowing myself for a doubting Thomas. God would surely provide, as he had for us all!

Haying time was nigh upon us, and I wished Randall to spend some time at Glororum, 'stead of waiting upon some poor castle knight at Alnwick. Accordingly, I rode to Sir Eustace's towering fortress, and obtained permission to bring my eldest son home for a month. 'Twas with great joy that the family had celebrated his becoming a squire just before Christmas; I had been too ill to properly join the festivities. I found him well enough grown, but his head was full of courtly nonsense. The ballads of France had lent a fairy-like air to his view of existence. All women were comely and virginal, all knights courteous and humble before their suzerain. The Holy Grail seemed to him an adventure to be accomplished, rather than the symbol of the human quest for righteousness. Like Hugh, he had a tendency toward indolence; like Herleve, he often lost sight of the common roots of all men.

Randall's hands were little hardened to sword or lance or battleaxe, though he served his knight, Conrad, well at table. His fighting-master, Theodore, merely shook his head when I inquired as to how the lad did. 'Twas not hard to obtain permission from them both to bring him to Glororum for the haying month. When I told Conrad of my plans, he shook his head grimly. "'Twill serve him well to aid in the haying and in the breaking of the new colts. The lad is well-witted, but he has forgotten his roots in the land."

So we began the month with arms-play and horse-breaking, and ended with the haying of the children's meadow. Of all that I tried to teach him, the haying was the only thing that seemed to give him much joy. Knowing his haughty airs, I was much surprised, till I saw him sit for the nooning with a fair young wench of the vill. His anger at me knew no bounds however, the night of the haying dance. I followed him to the house and to his pallet, and posted Carl outside his door. The next day, he requested to return to Alnwick. I laid upon him the condition that first he must joust with Raynaud. Our Hotspur thought it great diversion to run circles around the budding squire, touching him with blunted lance where least anticipated. I swear, Raynaud would ha' made a knight of Randall, had the boy remained at home.

But it was not to be. Herleve was furious with me over the rough treatment of her son, understanding not that a knight's life lies in his strength and wit. Both need to be trained and exercised, not wished for. Never has life been tolerant of tenuous men. In later years, Randall acquired enough puissance to administer the estate, though it slowly went to seed under his hand. And he managed to live out a long life.

So went the summer, with work a-plenty. The late spring storms had wreaked vengeance upon the spring grain; a catch crop of oats was sown to eke out our winter's supply. Bread and ale would both be dear in winter. Work on the church was slow, as the peasants were hard a-labor in the fields, and only the craftsmen persisted. Yet with all these worries, I found time to be with Boots. If I entered the stable and all were clear, I would simply take her hand. We would take the ladder to her cubby in the loft, there to comfort one another in love for awhile. Yet if this were not to be, still we would stand upon the gate and converse, and my world became fair again. Thus we both remember still, though other lives and centuries intervene.

Though the girl's wit and spirit were ever at my beck, there were times I needs must turn away. Too much devotion lays a pall upon the coursing mind, and I had much to occupy me. So it was, when in August I decided to ride south to visit Alnwick for Randall's birthday, thence to Hutton to visit with Maud and Mary Rose, that the lass became petulant. "Why can I not ride forth with you? Was I not a faithful squire?"

Already I had explained that Robin must go with me, not once, but twice. "Leave off, wench," I growled. "It is not to be this time." I turned then to walk away. Furious, Boots took up one of the stones that we put in the manger to make the horses eat their grain more slowly, and fired it at my head. 'Twas as much in play as anger; had I not just turned, I would have seen it coming. It caught me in near the same spot on the head as had been hit in my fall from the young destrier. Though the blow was light, I went down upon my knees in a pile of horse dung. It passed not unmarked, however. Adam, one of the house squires, came running, as did old Peter, who had just come 'round the end of the stable. I had not seen that gaffer move so fast in years! Before I could stop him, he lit into the girl with his staff. Adam was helping me rise; I was bellowing "Hold, Man!" and half the farm was on the run toward us. Peter at last seemed to hear me and desisted; Boots simply looked at us both with smouldering rage. Ah, that temper! But I was minded in an instant of the child who had stood upon the road, gazing at me with fearless eyes. My heart softened; my demeanor must not. "We shall call the curia," an eager voice said. "She should be pond-dunked."

"Nay," I roared. "'Tis my hurt; 'twill be my justice done." The villeins were too eager for sport; Boots, as an outsider, would suffer unmercifully at their hands. "Peter, take us to your cottage, where I may clean myself and confer with you." This the old man did, though Adam still needs must assist me; my legs refused to come right.

Margaret—poor pale shadow—brought a basin and washed my face and cleaned me as best she was able. Boots was subdued now; the enormity of her sin had struck down her temper, and she was pale as death. My shrift was short and sweet. "Ellen, you are banished hence from the stable until foaling time next spring. Adam will take your place as groom and trainer; he has a fair hand with the horses. Peter, do you see that the lass stays from the stable. Her things may be brought here. Margaret, Ellen is to help you with the garden and tend the swine. You have had too little help for too long."

It may sound harsh to your ears now, but punishment for assaulting the lord must be both quick and meet, else rebellion would stir all the land. My vision came clear, there in all the ruckus, as it was wont to do. Angelic guidance always seemed to hold with me in the thickest of a battle.

I had been wanting another lad to help with the horses for some time, but had dreaded the confrontation with Boots. Also, no matter how much comfort her love was to me, my conscience pricked, at times unmercifully. I had been struggling to find a way to hold her devotion at bay, not because I esteemed her not, but rather because I did. 'Twas not a nicety she would have easily understood. It would bid her fair, too, to learn the ways of women from Margaret. God knows, Andrew's poor wife, bereft of both husband and bairn, oft needed succor.

Thus began a time of Hell for us both. The falling, which I had near shaken off, began again in earnest. I was well when straddling a horse, but arising at night or after sitting at supper, my fool legs were wont to give way. As for the girl, she had been banished to slavery, away from all she loved. Yet the thing which hurt her most was the thought that she had so injured me in her peevish humour. I was to return after a month to find her eaten by worms of remorse, pale and sick.

Meantime, I took unto Randall a new destrier for his birthday, in part to make up for the hard use I had meted out to him whilst at home. Our visit was short, but my eldest son seemed to bear me no ill will. For William, I had made a shield with the Forster arms, smaller than full size so that he might practice his sword-play with a shield of appropriate size and heft. I had one made too for Maud's Henry, with Stephen's ash tree upon it. Soon he would be riding to Richmond to become a page; he would need it. I smiled as I remembered my own little wicker shield and oaken sword, lo! so many years ago. For Mary Rose, I took a rosary of blue beads; blue was her favourite color. And I brought her Robin, and no gift could have pleased her more.

As always, staying at Hutton was healing to both body and soul. Maud gave me steeped herbs to drink, and I was minded so much of mother. Indeed, Hutton, as always, seemed rich in the presence of both mother and Stephen. William had shot up like a young tree, secure in the love of the household and in the boldness of his lessons under the justice of Sir John. Privately, Maud admitted he had been a trial, but both of us could see that he had at last turned around. There was pride in his step, even though too often there was fire in his eye.

But I was restless, and worried amain about Boots. I left Robin yet awhile at Hutton, and careless of my own defence, pelted home as fast as ere I might. The stable seemed empty without the lass, though Adam came forward to take my horse. Without bothering to stop at Old Hall, I went directly to Peter's cottage. Margaret was at the everlasting spinning when I inquired about the girl.

"She is at the Spindlestone, I trow. When through with chores, 'tis where she bides."

I asked then if Allie was helping as she should. Margaret gave me a keen look, that I understood not.

At last she answered, "Oh, aye. As she is able."

Had I not been in such haste to see the lass, I might have noticed the faint disdain in Margaret's voice. Later, I was to ponder her words.

At once I left to find Boots, huddled at the foot of Spindlestone, wet from the grass. Had I not been so worried about her, I might have laughed; for Peter's old sow, rooting away, was firmly tethered in the grass, for all the world like any colt. I raised the girl up; her countenance was that of a death's-head. She shivered as I held her. "Ah, my lass, I have missed you so. My heart bid me come find you, as soon as able. Just this hour have I come from the south and set out to find you."

She seemed cold, withdrawn. "And Margaret told you where I was?" When I answered, she refused to look at me, but bit her lip nervously. "And when are you going again?" It would have been impertinent from anyone save Boots. 'Twas plain she was hurt, sick and hurt and dying in the heart.

I sat myself then, upon the wet grass, and pulled her into my lap. I made shift to explain to her why I had done all I had done, as if to a child. My remorse was running over; the girl was well and truly hurt. "Do you not see? I care for you too much to make a whore of you. You belong free, running with Hellfire and the colts. You are my very heart; I can only rejoice when you are unbound from care. As the master, my every day is bound up in care. 'Tis not meet you should partake of it. And I had to give you penance, else the villeins themselves would have done you harm. I would undo it all if I could!"

She hid her face. "'Tis too late. All too late."

Of a sudden, her condition came home to me. I lifted her face, saw the tears. "You are with child!"

She only nodded. I noticed her face then, white and slightly bloated, as was her body. It was not a good sign. She was not a lass made to bear bairns happily. Nor should she have to, I told myself savagely, had I not been such an unthinking brute.

At last the bars between us came down a little, as slowly we found understanding anew. She had been sure that her sickness was divine retribution for wounding me. It was more Margaret's sidelong glances that told her she might be with child, than any knowing of her own. She did not know how she could bear a child, sick and alone, cast away from the only person in the world who could succor her. She cast her fears upon me; dissolved was the anger she always used to cloak them. Her armour gone, she was but a pitiable, shivering child.

I did not let her know how badly I still had the falling. The main problem now was preserving her health and safety. "Ah, Boots, forgive me. Of course you had no ken that you might come with child; the responsibility was mine alone. I can never take back my love, it abides with you; but I would take back my seed if I could. A child is no joy to me when it brings you to such dire circumstance." A mawkish tear fled from one traitorous eye, betraying my steel. "I must send you away for awhile. Life for you here, with a child, would be hell on earth. I misdoubt if either Peter or Margaret will say aught, but shortly all the vill will be abuzz. We must get you hence ere that happens, or I would not give you a candle for your life thereafter."

"Oh, God, you have returned only to send me away again!" Her pain was manifest. Patiently, I told it all to her again. Boots was ever a hard-headed lass; had she not been she had not survived. But at last, she reluctantly saw the truth of what I was saying. "But where shall I go?" Becoming bereft of a home twice in a lifetime was oppressing to her wits.

I shifted her weight upon my lap. "I will send you to Eadra at Berwick. She is a good-hearted soul. Besides, I took in Robin for Kenneth; surely he can do as much for my woods-colt. But I must escort you myself alone; Robin is still at Hutton." And I told Boots of the love between Robin and Mary Rose, and how I could not bring him home so soon, just because a premonition fell upon my heart.

"It is well." She shook her head. "I shall mend also, now I am no longer alone. What God has placed in our lives, we must deal with courageously. I will go to Berwick and bear your son."

"That is more like my Boots! But how know you that you carry a son?"

"Because he is so much trouble." She smiled. "Truly, I simply know. It is a part of me. And can you see me throwing a filly?"

It took me near a week to make arrangements. To Margaret I explained that Scots lasses, such as those of Allie's family, were prone to a strange bloating sickness. 'Twas but a small lie; all women, after all, tend to the sickness that afflicted Boots, including Scots lasses. Peter raised one eyebrow, but said nothing. Next, I hied to Thomas' cottage in the vill. His wife had had more children than nature should allow; one of the younger girls was what I went to barter for. For a small sum, I took a little lass of eight, curiously called Cross. 'Twas a holy name, said the mother; besides another girl child was but another cross to bear.

I brought Cross to Margaret to care for, and to help her with the household work. 'Twas a far better tie grew there than between Margaret and Boots, for the child was a villein and biddable, much like Margaret herself. Boots could never be aught but a wild wind across the empty grey moors. Yet had it not been for Boots, I would have remained near blind to Margaret's slow dwindling, and the burden life was becoming to her.

Allie and I rode north from Glororum on the feast of Saints Cyprian and Edith. Edith was a natural daughter of King Edgar of England. Her mother fled to a monastery for protection when she found she was with child. The girl grew up there in all holiness, and many were the miracles that bloomed from her intercession. As with all that is lovely and holy, she was soon taken to God, living not beyond her twenty-third year. This story I told to Boots as we rode, and we felt it meet. If she should bear a girl, I told her, Edith would be a fit name. Boots only shook her head saying, "'Tis a man-child I bear, and his name shall be John."

The weather had blown in cold from the north, early for a winter's storm. But we had to leave immediately, not only because of Boots' condition, but because the accounting of the manor at Michaelmas was less than two weeks away. Bors was well enough to mind the Hall for now, but 'twould never do for me to be from home during the accounting. Raynaud I reluctantly decided to remove from temptation at Glororum by having him ride as our guard to Berwick. Boots and I had less occasion to speak privately, but I was better able to watch her for not heeding the road so closely. Indeed, she was unwell, her face patchy, her hair dry and unruly. She shivered through the storm; I misdoubted if a week in Hades itself could warm her. Never will I forget the lass, swaddled in wool and linen, wrapped like a great ball with only her eyes showing. 'Twas a misery to see.

As always, Kenneth and Eadra welcomed us. Boots was sent to bed, and I recounted my sad tale to them in private. Eadra shook her head. "There are women who should not suffer birth. Methinks your Allie is one of them. Albeit, 'tis in the hands of God for now; I will do my best to care for her. But I tell you true, young John (how many years had it been since anyone had called me that?), I will give her the lore to keep her from childbed, else your love will kill her." I began to protest, saying I was too feared of the girl's life to put her in peril of motherhood again. "Nay," said Eadra, "when the heart burns with unquenchable fire, 'tis not possible to keep it from consuming. Thy brand will burn hot, and she will answer; some things are thus fated. But I will give her my lore." There was naught else to be said, but again I wondered at the wisdom in the world of women.

When Raynaud and I returned, 'twas to hear a gracious accounting, for Glororum was prospering, as was Bamburgh. The tithe barns were full, despite the poor spring weather. Work on the church was moving apace. All would ha' been well, save the gloom of approaching winter began to set upon me heavily once again. Not only was beloved Alyse lost to me, but now I had driven away Boots, my remaining joy in life. Then came news from Durham that Bishop Hugh, Bamburgh's great friend, had died. But even as I gloomed, little Agnes would come to shake me from sadness and remind me that God's blessing remained after all. Had it not been for her, between the falling sickness and despair, I would have thrown myself beneath the ice of winter's pond.

Chapter 21

Hexham

Allie was delivered of a son on January 25 of 1196. He was early, and 'twas God's mercy, for the lass was sick nigh to death with carrying him. Sir Kenneth sent a messenger, and I returned with him apace. I was much relieved to see Boots beginning to recover, the swelling subsiding and her color starting to return. But 'twould be nigh six months ere she returned to her old self.

Not so lucky was the child, however. He seemed sickly and weak, even beyond the condition of being too soon from the womb. Kenneth found a wet nurse to suckle him, as Boots had neither strength nor milk enough. We brought a chaplain to christen him when he was but a few days old, but like a true knight's son, he fought on for life though hope was small. It was not till after I returned to Bamburgh, near two months later, that I received word that the bairn had died. I rode north again for the funeral. In his short life, baby John had endeared himself to his mother, and often later I would catch her sitting pensively. I knew then her thoughts were filled with him. The stars of his birth should have told us of his fate, for the hardship of Saturn sat upon Venus, the mother; and the ephemeral Moon flitted across the face of Mars, the father. 'Twas only for a time and to our sorrow that young John came.

I left Boots with Eadra and Kenneth till after Easter, for spring foaling would require that she be in full strength. For the high holy day, I myself must make penance, so on Palm Sunday, I visited Father Edwin. There were sins aplenty to confess for the year past, and the sickness still with me that needed allaying. Edwin shrove me, and gave me the penance of a pilgrimage. "Ye need to get from hence, man; commune with God, and ponder on your life. 'Tis a most grievous sin to commit incest with a woman who has been given as ward. Yet no formal papers were drawn, nor any vows made to the church. I misdoubt that in any legal consideration the girl would be considered aught but in a master-servant relationship. The matter seems to be simple adultery. Given the condition of your lady wife, that is understandable, though I am bound to admonish you against it. Still, the will of Heaven oft ties people with bonds that are beyond earthly understanding. You must judge for yourself." The falling sickness, he added, was from a brain bruise, which quiet and leisure might eventually heal with help from God. A pilgrimage, he said, would only be beneficial, and he recommended Hexham as a holy place within easy march.

Much consoled, I began to shake off the desperate pall that had covered my winter, and once again began to make plans for a journey. I would go to Hexham, I decided, and there ask both for healing and for Christian wisdom. Robin needs must go with me; he was ever my strength and consolation, and ought partake also of my solace.

But first, I must bring Boots home. It was with great joy that I rode north with Robin at my back; it had been an age since he had seen his father, Kenneth. Whilst Robin held the attention of his family, I was left alone to make peace with the lass.

First I held her, as we remembered our small son in sorrow. Then she shook her head saying, "But I have seen him being held upon the lap of my mother, Carrie. Both seemed joyous. Perhaps our child was sent to Heaven to make up to her for my loss. I would not selfishly will him the sorrows of this world, when he is so loved there."

"Then I, too, am glad. Your vision comforts me, and makes me see once again the hand of Providence. But we must have no more children. You do not know how I sorrowed over your travail, your body so bloated and ill. Another child might kill you, and I will not be the instrument of your death. I wish no more sons, no more daughters. With God's mercy, the succession to the land is established. Randolph should marry soon; if he has no heirs, both other sons seem able and hearty. There is Tippie, too; she is daughter enough for any man." I held Ellen's face in one rough hand and brushed back her hair. "Ah, my Boots, you are an eagle, wild and free; never were you meant to be brought down and cooped like a chicken. Never again shall I see you pent up. Never again, and that is my promise for all time."

"Oh, John, simply hold to me; 'tis all I ask! Do not send me away again. I have no home save with you, no life without yours. I am dumb and crippled without you. I will work always to make you proud of me, and of my love. I have naught else to give."

"There is naught of greater value, lass, than two lives united in God's love, accomplishing His work as best as able. I went for Easter penance to Father Edwin; he tells me that since you are not legally my ward, we have not the sin of incest."

"Never did I believe so, John. But you are an honest knight, and concerned with righteousness. Never, since that first night upon the Scots hillside, have I ever considered our love as the sin of adultery. I saw the light shining about you, and I felt as if an angel had come to earth to wed us. There will never be another man for me, nor has there ever been."

"Nor bides now the maid who can reft me from you. Still, I must be free to care for the land and its people as is just. And now I am bound to the penance of a pilgrimage; Edwin suggests Hexham. Perhaps there I shall also find a cure for the falling ailment."

Her face mirrored pain at my indiscretion. I had become so used to struggling 'gainst illness, that habit threw carelessness upon my speech. But words once said cannot be brought back; I must now be honest with her. "Edwin says 'tis a brain bruise. Given rest and leisure, 'twill heal. I am taking Robin; he eases the care from me."

"But I am not to go."

I shook my head. "Nay, lass. Another time. You have already expiated your sins, in measure overflowing. This is my penance; 'twould not be seemly for you to partake of it. Besides, you will be sore needed with the foals."

So it was that we brought Boots home to the stable, and even Peter was glad to see her. Adam I set under her as groom, along with his training for man-at-arms under Raynaud. There was work a-plenty in the horse yard for another set of hands. But the first thing the girl did was find Hellfire, to see if he remembered aught of her. It seemed not, for he was wilder than ever, but 'twould take her mind off my leaving to labour toward his goodwill once more.

I sent Bors to Bamburgh in Robin's place, more to put distance between him and Raynaud than for any real need. Alfric and Jene had the new church well in hand, and though Walter, the warder at the castle, had been ill, his second-in-command, Gilbert, was more than able.

I charged Raynaud to ride to Alnwick after Randall, and bid him take the lad in hand as best he was able. If I had not returned by June's end, they were to hay the children's meadow without me. That obligation would bring confidence to my eldest son; but I was cautious to confer with Cedric about him, bidding that young Carl follow him as squire, though he was only yet thirteen. Cedric vowed to keep Randall from straying toward sins of the flesh; and so we rode from Glororum, easy in mind.

Robin and I set out on the road south ere May had finished its flowering. As the year before, we were no sooner on our way than gloom began to lift from my mind, and memories came flooding in—memories of the Holy Land and Malta, memories of Robin bringing me through France, and memories of Alyse. But songs we had now to allay sorrow and keep us company, for Robin was as much a troubadour as his father Kenneth or myself. The road ran pleasantly from Alnwick to Rothbury, where we halted for the night. Skirting forest and crag, it then wound its westering way to Choller's ford, where I asked direction to the cross of St. Oswald.

It was nigh evensong, and the innkeeper at the ford bid us stay, but we both felt high adventure in the air. "Ye ken," the innkeeper said, "that men hereabouts fear to go near the battlefield upon an evening. The cross sits true where Oswald himself first raised it. Believers and pagans alike, his army gathered 'round the rood, and promised themselves to Christ if the battle went their way. 'Twas only with God's help, ye see, that they might win, for Cadwallon had a mighty army 'gainst them. But Oswald was a clever warrior as well as a sainted man. Cadwallon had to come uphill to meet him, and fierce was the fighting. Our ploughmen still turn over the warriors' bones. But calling upon Christ, Oswald pushed Cadwallon north to Hallington, where he tried to rally his men. They broke there, and Oswald's soldiers chased them clean to Denis' burn, three leagues south. Oswald was there avenged of the murder of his uncle and brother in the blood of Cadwallon. Many Christians were baptized after that affray, and the cross still holds the miracle of healing. But 'tis a fearsome place."

The man would have bided us with stories of miracles all evening, had we not mounted and ridden off. We bought some bread and cheese and promised to return ere the sun had well and truly set. It was still some two hours to sunset, with a full moon yet to rise.

The first sight to greet us was the small stone church built to commemorate the battle, and we rode onto the hill directly beneath the cross where Oswald had made his promise to God. 'Twas said that there he had laid him down and dreamed, and St. Columba came and spread his cloak over all Oswald's sleeping troops. As soon as he awoke, the king knew the day would be his; he roused his men and attacked ere Cadwallon had rubbed the sleep from his eyes.

For his vision, and the miracle of the battle, the hill is named Heavenfield to this day—Hefenfeld in the old tongue.

Our horses tethered, Robin wished to sup; but my heart was eager to advance to the cross and pray. Whilst he was setting out our paltry fare, I ascended to that holy place and knelt to ask both forgiveness and healing. Of a sudden, the hillside spun before my eyes; I felt as if smitten by the flaming sword of St. Michael. I fell with a moan, which roused Robin. He struggled to my side; kneeling, he helped me sit up. We both saw him then, an ancient warrior with leathern armour, and all 'round him was a cloud of battle. We could not be mistaken; we had seen such melees before. We heard sounds of "Christus" and "Oswald" trembling upon the air, frightening in their hollow resonance. Stranger yet, we could see those ancient soldiers, even below the brow of the hill, as if they shimmered in the air. The great warrior saluted us with raised sword, and Robin and I both fell to our faces; the vision then passed as quickly as it had come.

"Uncle," Robin breathed, "did you see what I saw?"

"Armed men, in leathern armour, in battle. Aye. And what did ye hear?"

"Noise of battle, far shouts of "Christus" and "Oswald." Robin shook his head in disbelief. "But the words were more in my head than aloud, yet clear. And not of me."

"No. 'Twas the same with me. And the army; I saw them all, though some lay beneath the hill. Yet I could see the evening sky through them, and the far hills."

"Thus with me. And I smelled the smell of battle once again; I ken that smell well. Yet through it wound some sweet and gentle fragrance, not of this world."

We sat amazed that as two, we had one vision. At last I deemed that it was in common blood that we came to see those men without flesh; hear words that had hung upon the air for five hundred years; and smell the blood, the sweat, and the flowers of paradise. We were so shaken that scarce could we retrieve the horses and return to the inn, our bread and cheese hastily stowed away.

The landlord took one look at our faces and began again. "'Tis been many years since the appearance of the battle of Hexham came to living men. The last time 'twas in my father's time; I was just a lad. Two yeomen, brothers they were, and a boy, coming across the hill. One brother was killed on Crusade, the other now farms nigh Erneshaw. The lad became a priest. Full moon it was then, too, and mid-summer. Some there was, thought they was daft; others said they were liars. But from many years ha' come other tales of sightings. They say the cross is the safest place; Heaven bides there and the fray swirls 'round it."

We admitted to the vision, for just so we had found it to be. Other men in other places upon our land would see other great battles written across the sky, places hallowed by men's blood. But this vision was Robin's, and mine. I would like to tell you that upon the holy hill my falling sickness was cured, but 'twas not, though much alleviated. It would take another year for my trembling legs to stop betraying me.

We determined then to explore, like lads escaping les-sons. We rode west along the great Roman wall, and won-dered mightily of the manner of men who had wrought such works. Yet all seemed somehow familiar, as if seen once in a dream. I seemed to know each turning of the road, and feel the presence of men upon that wall, where none had stood guard for near a thousand years. At last, we turned and rode back to Hexham. There was not much love lost between Glororum and the Augustinian canons, so we bided not at the cathedral, the see that St. Cuthbert himself had deemed onerous. Though made bishop there, he bided but two years, then returned to his beloved Holy Island, to that same island church that King Oswald had first bestowed upon the monk Aidan. Cuthbert himself was now enshrined at Durham, and many were the pilgrims to visit there; for Cuthbert—St. Cuddy, as the folk 'round called him—was the most popular miracle worker in Northumberland. His body itself remained, conserved and intact, and, 'twas said, ever warm to the touch. Robin nor I, we swore, would have the temerity to touch so holy a relic.

We spoke, too, of the wrath of that dead saint 'gainst women. So violent had been Cuddy's resistance to having women visit his remains that Bishop Hugh had been forced to demark a line across the cathedral floor, beyond which no woman might step. 'Twas said that the whole building shook if that thin blue line was violated! When Hugh began to build a Lady Chapel 'pon the east end of the cathedral, the building shifted and cracked till Hugh abandoned work. Cuthbert, he said, wanted not even a chapel of Holy Mother next his remains. Nothing daunted, the good bishop then bent his efforts to building a Galilee chapel at the west end, though the site was not nearly so suited. But now the building sat all unfinished, since Bishop Hugh had died.

Cuddy still growled on chance, and chewed at the great cathedral walls. Robin nor I could understand how so sainted a man might be so set 'gainst the fairer sex. We laid the rumours to ill humours amongst the monks, and to bad foundations.

So passed a fortnight gossiping along the road, for we stopped awhile in Newcastle town, to sample the ale and bide at the castle, picking up rumours. Most were of the war in France, where Richard the King struggled to maintain his possessions. He had visited his boyhood home in Poitou at Christmas, the first time his restless nature led him to his mother's castle since the Crusade. Whilst there, he appointed Philip, Bishop of Poitou, to the See of Durham. 'Twas a plum for the old ally of Richard's mother, Queen Eleanor. The English prior of Durham, Bertram, would be left to deal with the problems of the palatinate, and a succession of haughty French clerks sent by the bishop to collect his revenues.

Richard went back to combat. Never has there lived a man as strong or as peerless in battle. Men grumbled at the heavy tariffs levied, first to ransom Richard, then to support his wars. But none wished for the alternative, sly Prince

John. 'Twould be a sad day for England, we said, if ever John ascended the throne. Little did we ken that the day was fast approaching.

News there was of Hugh de Guagy, also. Due to the efforts of a powerful baron who had once been squire-at-arms with his father, Hugh had managed to make a fine marriage. His wife was heiress of the estates at Newark; their son Ralph would inherit both land and power. However, in the time of my own son Randolph, his cousin Ralph would lose near all in vain rebellion 'gainst John's son, Henry. The de Guagy family was ever star-crossed.

Arrived back at Bamburgh, we found the vill in mourning, for Walter the warder had died of the bloody lung not a week after our departure. They buried him in the kirkyard of the ancient chapel of St. Peter, within the castle walls. There once had reposed in that church the most holy relic, St. Oswald's right hand and arm. Aidan himself, upon an Easter feast, had once grasped the living hand and blessed it saying, "May this hand never perish!" For Oswald the King fed and gave alms to the poor, and succored his people as a Christian ruler. From his wooden palace here upon the crag at Bamburgh, holiness filled the land. Truly, the wolf had become a sainted knight.

After Penda later slew Oswald in battle, hacking his body to pieces, 'twas found that the hand and arm which Aidan had blessed remained incorrupt. A silver casket was made for our holy treasure, and it had bided awhile at St. Michael's ere being transferred to the great new abby church at Peterborough. Some there are who can see no use preserving such relics, deeming that Christian burial more befits the dignity of human remains. But perhaps one soul in a hundred may be blessed, and capture something of the sacred energy bestowed within such relics. Then a miracle occurs; many such were attested to by the clerks examining Oswald's influence ere his consecration.

Now St. Michael's was crumbling. As soon as the new church in Bamburgh vill was finished, the arm of Oswald would come in procession from Peterborough to bless it. Or such had Hugh Pudsey promised; 'twould be up to Bertram to affirm it.

Alfric had built a crypt beneath the chancel, with its own chapel, as a biding place for the holy relic, in hopes that Oswald would return once more to bring us grace. A double church we were a-building, with half dedicated to Aidan; without his blessing, Oswald's work had been naught, just as Aidan would ha' had no field of labor save for the benefice of Oswald. The crypt was now finished and the chancel well begun. 'Twas a large chancel, and very fine, though it scandaled the neighbors. A chancel, they said, had in all custom since time immemorial been the prerogative of the church's pastor to build. Laymen were allowed only to bestow the appointment of the nave. Thus folk grumbled at my "airs," regardless that the only priest then at Bamburgh was my chaplain, and that Forster money, with the king's grant of vicarage, was the foundation 'neath their new church. And 'twas my vow, too, in gratitude of my life. But once the cud of slander fills men's mouths it leaves a bitter taste for generations, long after the chewing be forgotten.

Alfric had outdone himself in conning the chancel. A stairway, complete with niche, would lead up from the mortuary chapel in the crypt into the south side of the chancel. On holy days, especially Easter, the priest might rise from beneath the ground with the relic of Oswald raised in blessing. Thus hope of resurrection might be shown to all. The chancel arch, and its following transept arch, were offset slightly to the south so that every person in the nave might be blessed with the vision at once.

The north side of the chancel was reserved for Aidan, with a fine marble slab marking the spot where he breathed his last. The timber crick 'gainst which he had leaned was miraculously spared from flames twice; we would not tempt Satan further. 'Twas to be hung above the baptismal fount, where its blessing might fall upon every generation of our children. Thus from birth to death would our church enfold us, and with God's blessing, see to our resurrection.

Many were the families in the vill even then. As I still held the office of castellan, I appointed stout Gilbert to be warder in Walter's place. Gib, as we called him, was well liked by all, and could move men to his will without their grumbling. His son, in turn, would become warder in years to come; indeed, there are Gib's sons in the area yet.

Raynaud pelted off to Newcastle for me, to invite the sheriff not only to confirm Gib's appointment with the king's seal, but to come and hunt once fall was under way. The wild sows in the forest had o'erbred their feed; we needs must thin some so winter would not take so harsh a toll. 'Twas usual to hunt boar, for of them we always had an excess, and rank was their flesh. Rarely had we tender shoat or sow from the wild swine.

Old Will kept a keen eye upon our west forest still, and he it was who showed me the new litters upon nearly every hillside. His youngest son, Japeth, kept the hounds, some to course for deer, and some to fight the boar. A wild and savage swine is more than a match, both for dogs and the huntsman armed only with lance. With the hills so burgeoning with game, even a fat sheriff might take pride in his skill at the hunt, and have cause to remember our hospitality. And so it came about, and the crisp October forest bought us goodwill for ventures yet to come.

As soon as Bamburgh castle had been settled once again, I sought out Boots. I had missed her company, as she had mine. I was sore torn by my love for her, but she bid me not worry, for from Eadra she had potions to keep the seed from settling. Indeed, so well it seemed to work that only once had she trouble; with a few days sick and bleeding, she then came right. Still, upon these summer days my fears were not yet fully allayed, so much of our time was spent hanging upon the gate, a-judging of the horses. 'Twas a common pleasure, but God surely blesses those whose minds find rest in one another.

One young destrier particularly vexed us. Handsome he was, with a coat black as fresh pitch, and a white star upon his forehead, for which we named him. "I am at my wit's end over Star," Boots began. "At last he will lead, even run the long line. But he is clever, ever looking for a chance to break away. I or Adam can even ride him as long as no trappings are put upon his back. We have even gentled him to stand like a soldier whilst the saddle is put on. But once he feels the rider upon the saddle, he is away; fence or burn halts him not. Adam found himself nigh Brunton the last time we tried it. I finally caught up with him on Hellfire; both those beasts were so spent that they could scarce walk home. It frightened the lad; he will not work White Star again."

"The horse will never make a destrier, despite his size and looks; his mind is 'gainst his rider. We must try to trade him at Elsdon Fair."

Boots looked at me scornfully. "And who do you suppose would willingly take him there to show, knowing what a rogue he is? 'Twould be as much as a body's life was worth, once the new master saddled up his prize."

I gave a whoop, grabbed the girl and danced as if it were the first of May. "Man," she cried out, laughing, "have ye lost your senses?"

"No, lass, ye ha'just shown me a way to repay my upstart young knight. Tell me, does Raynaud come to watch the horses work?"

"Nay, Sire; there are none here he can beguile with sweet-talk. I threatened him with a hiding when first he came." Her face split with a grin. "If ye take me to handle the horse till we get there, then give it over to him to sell, I think we can pull it off."

As always, she had caught the very thoughts of my mind. "So shall we do. What else have we to sell?"

"One handsome bay; he was born a twin with a female; likely he will never 'mount to much. 'Twould be best to sell him young, ere his growth shows up his lack of fire. The mare foal is big and strong, but wild. If she throws twins like her dam, she too should go."

"Aye. But not this year. Let's breed her, two years hence, and see what she will do. We have pasture enough for now. Any old stock?"

So we made a list of what needed to be culled, but for good measure, threw in two fine young war-horses, with not a bad habit between them. 'Twould not do for folk to think that Forster's sold only culls. But with so many to go, we needs must make a large party.

Thus it was we set out, two days before St. Bartholomew's, the 22nd day of August, 1196. I would not lead more than two to a man; Boots had Star and an old gelding to keep him settled. Adam took one of the destriers and a young horse whose breeding had not taken; he was fit only for a villein's cart horse. Raynaud I gave charge of the other destrier, whilst I led the twin colt, who had not yet settled well to halter. With two knights so occupied, it behooved me to take an armed guard, so Bors rode as outrider. 'Twas an excellent pretext; by hook or crook, I wished him to see the fun.

A journey with so many animals to tether and care for was little enough pleasure. As always, the folk at Elsdon made shrift to empty the pockets of all who came. But we had not come to eat and drink, or watch the mountebanks. First, I had Adam and Boots show the old gelding and the patchy young one. They showed them 'mongst a group of yeoman farmers, and we haggled price. They brought no more than I expected. I had Boots then bring the colt forth unto a group of squires, looking for a horse to train for war at little price. The twin sold well, for he looked fancy; nor did I feel remorse. His new owner would learn more from his training than ever the price he paid.

I waited till next day to show the young destriers. Boots was up betimes and worked White Star a little, just to where she thought Raynaud might handle him with no vexation. She then led forth the first of our sound beasts, and after much haggling, a deal was struck with a knight of Cumbria.

Adam brought forth the second, and again, it was sold for a goodly price to a knight who knew horseflesh. I had made sure that my two stablehands would stay busy with the new owners, whilst I called up our third horse, Star.

"Raynaud," I called to our young Hotspur, "I am giving you this beast to show as best as you are able. Wipe him down well and lead him carefully. Mind you sell him well, for the proceeds are yours, in payment for all the loving errands you have discharged on my behalf. Look to yourself, now." So was he forewarned!

I stood to one side with Sir Bors, watching Raynaud announce his beast timorously, for he had more call to ride a horse to death than to care for one. His manner attracted the vultures, as I thought it might. One older knight showed much interest, a man arrogant as Sir Brian. I thought once we had lost the game when the knight slapped Star upon the rump, but luckily Raynaud tightened his grip upon the lead, and the fool horse remembered Boots previous ministrations when he had attempted to bolt at halter. Still, the knight was canny. He demanded to be shown White Star's paces, as I thought he might. I whistled for Boots, who oozed forth from the crowd and confidently sprang to his bare back. With heel and halter, she turned him 'round and showed his walk. The horse was nervous, but he recognized his mistress and was docile enough. At last, the elder knight concluded that if a mere lass might handle him, the deal was sound enough. Though Raynaud's face was bright, I knew the old curmudgeon had skinned him on price.

The crowd began to thin, and 'twas a good thing. The knight was anxious to try out his bargain horse; he had a boy come forth with saddle and bridle. Star seemed to shiver slightly as he was being accoutered, but held well enough 'til the man mounted the saddle. In an instant, the horse was gone; I misdoubted he would turn till he reached the River Coquet. Whilst we doubled with laughter, Raynaud stood staring after them like a man transfixed, and one of the knights' grooms spurred off in pursuit. It was many hours before the groom returned leading Star, but not so long ere the knight returned upon his groom's horse. He made straight for Raynaud, fire in his eye. I made suit to ride closer, but 'twas not necessary; shouts filled the air. At last Raynaud rode to our tents and retrieved his lance, which he shook in challenge at the elder knight. Neither had but light armor, but the knight was mounted 'pon a poorer horse. A joust would not serve him well; only pride would lead him to so foolhardy an undertaking.

Yet a fool he was. I rode forth and gave them warning as agent of the king. Such affrays were prohibited, but men still tried their quarrels by combat, and 'twas often the only way an affair might be settled. So I had a course marked, and announced that 'twould be settled by first fall only. The crowd so gathered (in the space of but a heartbeat) that no barriers were needed. I found six knights willing to hold the sides so that the villeins might not rush upon the field in eagerness.

Our young Hotspur and the old knight rode apart some quarter mile, then turning upon signal, pelted at one another, lances couched. 'Twas an even match, for while Raynaud's horse was stronger, the knight was wary and battle-hardened. In an instant it ended, with both men upon the ground, for lance had struck shield squarely, each on each. Both men raised up with head a-buzz, eager for more battle.

"Hold", I cried. "Ye have both fallen; God thus decrees that both are in error. You, young sir," I turned to Raynaud, sitting in the grass with a most amazing expression 'pon his face, "should know better than to foist such a beast off upon an honourable knight." And I gave him a big wink, ere turning to the proud knight. "And you, sire, need put pride aside and be thankful you learned such a valuable lesson so cheaply. Next time, remember that as ye pay, so do ye receive."

I thought that had done it, but was mistaken. Furious, the old knight strode over to where Raynaud was struggling to his feet, and gave him such a mighty kick upon the arse as to set him down again. The crowd roared, and the knight, satisfied in heart though sore of foot, limped from the field.

'Twas too late to leave for home that evening, so we needs must listen to the jibes of the crowd through all the night. I felt near sorry for our young knight, having played such a base trick upon him. He had trouble sitting his horse all the way home. Bors had no such reservations. "My soul has been surfeited," he nodded, "and justice has prevailed."

Chapter 22

Three in a Row

So passed our days, season unto season, wet to dry; ploughing to reaping. The affairs of the farm were the great wheel of our lives, upon which turned the workings of all our families with their various labours. 'Twas like the new machinery Kenneth had installed in Berwick town, in the tannery. Men of inventive sagacity had begun to create huge mills, wherein an immense water wheel would turn the hammers of the tannery, the saws for lumber, the bellows for the forge, as well as the stone to grind the worker's corn. 'Mazed we were as to how it all worked together to perform more work than men had as yet dreamed possible; yet the failure of one part meant loss to the whole.

So with our little society. As the century slipped to an end, God ordained removal of two of our most vital—and oft unappreciated—cogs. 'Twas as if we were to enter a new century by the sacrifice of those we loved.

We lost Bors first, in February of 1199. I had deferred often to his age; still the old knight would have no taint of pity in my dealings with him. Though he made no long road marches (those being better suited to Raynaud), Bors still acted as steward of Glororum and sore put would I have been without his constant solicitude on behalf of the estate. He had mellowed somewhat with years, but as a true knight, he still was uncompromising toward wrongdoing. When

Raynaud was at a distance, Bors held most of the manor courts; a chore I liked no better then than I had when younger. And Bors oversaw the training of our house squires and men-at-arms, and rousted out the manor fyrd regularly.

Such was his occupation on that fatal day. 'Twas the last day of February, and ploughing had not yet begun. The men of the vill had been cramped in winter quarters, but Sunday dawned fair. Bors deemed that play at quarterstaff and practice with the bow would loosen the snarls of kinked winter dispositions. I myself was watching, and I thank God for allowing me to be beside the knight who had come to mean so much to me, when he was called to Heaven.

I saw Bors crumple to the ground as he was admonishing two young cubs who refused to put their hearts into staff practice. Of an instant, I was beside my steward, who looked at me surprised and said, "My legs are gone dead." Then I saw a look of pain, which was quickly washed away by a softening of his face, and a far look in his eyes. "Giles," he murmured, as if in pleasure, and in that instant he breathed his last. I was glad his old friend had come for him, and knew he felt naught but happiness at his release. Somehow it helped to assuage the grief of his passing. A man who had begun with me as a near-enemy twenty-three years before, had over the years become like a second father. Perhaps it was then I began to understand that the true work of a lifetime lies in learning to love one another, for thus we enter into a Kingdom that passes not with death. Still, 'twould be months ere I had the heart to appoint a new steward; not then would it have been done, save that it was Robin I named, at Michaelmas.

Scarce were we over that blow, when Alfric was cruelly crushed to death when a crane lifting stones to the top of the church fell upon him. It was a wet, raw day, with a nor'east wind a-blowing. The guy ropes of the wooden crane had become sodden, all unbeknownst, and the great machine began to sway with the wind, then buckle. Jene was by his side at the time, and narrowly missed the same fate.

As it was, her mind was near unhinged by the loss of her lifelong companion. Had it not been for Annie bringing her soothing herbs and consolation, I misdoubt that Jene would have lived a fortnight. Somehow, Annie at last convinced her that the growth which had lain 'pon Alfric's face would have killed him as sure, though slower and more painfully. And from the grace that flowed from Bors' death, I was able to reassure the lady that her beloved man lived a better life, where he but awaited her presence. So, slowly consoled, Jene threw herself into the work of the church once again. She agreed that it would be her husband's noblest monument. Manfred, Alfric's chief mason, took over as master under her tutelage; and a fine head for detail the young German had. Some of the columns and decorative arches and pilasters were more originally executed than might have been the case under Alfric. Still, we missed the bent old white-haired figure, pottering 'mongst the stones, conning his angles and braces.

Both Bors and Alfric were buried in the kirkyard, though work was proceeding apace over their heads. I asked Manfred for stones worthy to commemorate those two stalwarts, and he promised to turn to with the stone carvers. Also, 'twas at this time that I asked for a proper stone for both my mother and father. When finished, their simple beauty amazed me; father's with a sword and cross, mother's with key and shears, to denote her rank. To this day you may see their stones at Bamburgh church.

There was a great deal of unease in the air after we laid Alfric to rest. I felt it as well as the humblest of our villeins, for two deaths, one hard upon the heels of another, called for three. Thus we waited for the Angel of Death to bring our sorrow to full measure. Little did we ken what travail that Traveler held in store for us!

On Palm Sunday, Edwin read out the news in church: Richard was dead and his sly brother, John, was King of England. Indeed, Richard was being buried that very day at Fontevrault, next his father, King Henry. The death of that strong warrior, whose patronage had been so vital to the affairs of Bamburgh, set like a lead weight upon my heart. I had followed Richard the King to the mouth of Hell and returned; nor had he forgotten the Forsters any more than I forgot him. Ever when I closed my eyes, I could see him cutting and hacking his way through Saracen flesh, to save the day for Christ at the battle of Arsuf. Many were the prayers I was to say for his soul.

Edwin gave us news of Richard's passing, how he had stood before the walls of the Castle Chalus, marveling at a lone crossbowman that stood upon the battlements. The man had been standing alone, all day, fending off arrows with a frying pan, which he held with his off hand. Richard advanced to the challenge. He attempted to get close enough to the lone bowman for a shot, but whilst still out of normal range, the crossbowman let fly a missile. 'Twas too great a range for most bows; the Devil himself must have lent speed to the bolt. The arrow pierced Richard in the left shoulder, and bit deep. Cursing, he returned to camp, worrying at the bolt.

Ere the surgeon arrived, Richard had managed to drive the head deeper, and break off the shaft, so there was hell to pay cutting it out. The surgeon put soothing medicaments 'pon the wound, but within hours, the cut had fevered. I was minded of Stephen, watching him die in Jaffa. Richard lasted eleven days, dying on March 6. Ere he passed on, he bequeathed the kingdom to John. Chalus had been taken, and the soldier who had fired the fatal shot was taken in irons to the dying king.

"What harm have I done to thee, that you have killed me?" Richard asked the crossbowman.

"You killed my father and two brothers with your own hand, and you intended to kill me. Take any vengeance you think fit; I can endure any torment, knowing that you who have brought such evils upon the world, are about to die." Thus spoke the bowman bravely.

At that, Richard forgave him his death, and sent him forth with a hundred shillings. Mercadier, Richard's lieutenant, seized the crossbowman immediately, and held him till Richard had died. Then he mercilessly had him flayed alive. Nor did Queen Eleanor, Richard's mother, intervene. Old but ageless, her timeless beauty unwithered and her mind yet clear and firm, she had Richard's body carried to Fontevrault for burial. In five years, she would return to sleep beside him.

We had no ken of this yet. Instead, I urged Manfred to hurry the work at Bamburgh church, for grants given in good faith by Richard were not likely to be honored by his brother without much trouble. As soon as possible, I myself rode south, both to the See at Durham, where I conferred with Prior Bertram, and to York, where I found a much-troubled sheriff.

Bertram's advice was that of a prelate who had seen much shift of fortune in the affairs of men. "Kings are men of vice and of blood; their ways are capricious. Yet they hold order in the realm by the authority God bestows, and with the consent of those who form the true fabric of the kingdom, fief-holders such as yourself. Change will come slowly, for John will not altogether work against the advice of his bishops and justiciars. Yet, if he showeth himself inspired by greed, calling upon Satan's powers, then must the kingdom stand 'gainst him. I am not a man of the world, yet as you know, much has touched us here at Durham since noble Hugh passed away, near four years past. I feel trouble coming within my bones, and trouble has been our portion at Durham since Philip of Poitiers was made prince of the palatinate. Yet your benefice at Bamburgh will continue as long as I have sway in the matter. Holy Church is steadfast; she turns not from those whose work furthers the concerns of God. I am no mystic, John, but a man of business; yet I see beside you an angel, who guards your affairs. So will He follow the work of your hands, and it will stand for the centuries. Your seed will be blessed; scattered 'cross the earth, they will pour the consolation of your piety into days of sorrow as yet unkenned."

311

Bertram, as he said, was no mystic but a very able administrator; yet in that blessing I knew he was God-inspired. His voice had grown sure and strong, his eyes fixed on a distance beyond my wit. A sound, as of wings, or wind blowing, filled his chamber. I stood transfixed, in the sure knowledge that indeed, an angel stood there. All would be well, for a higher force would preserve us. In utmost humility, I joined Bertram in prayer.

The High Sheriff of the northern counties was in no such serene mood. "I know not yet what duties ye may owe the crown, John Forster, but be assured that no news from that devil's whelp is good news. He will be squeezing us for money ere long. Never could John hold a candle to his brother Richard, but each thing Richard did, John must emulate, to the detriment of all. He will embroil us in French wars, and squeeze us bloody; England will pay for all his foolishness. For as Richard did, though he was a man of strength, and could at least hold the Norman possessions, so John will try. But mark me, King John will lose them all; 'tis his nature." Thus, too, did the sheriff prophesy, and his prophecy, though mundane, was also proved true with time.

Once home, I took my worries to Boots, for there did I ever find the greatest comfort. "John," at last she said, "you are not a man like other men. God's grace follows you, though you be both profane and mystic by turns. I myself have never found God in churches, but in the fields and forests; yet you were given a vision of saints. As God wills you to build a church, so will He see to its completion." I nodded, for in her faith, my own grew stronger. Yet, fickle as the winds that blow upon Bamburgh's rock, she grasped my hand and covered me with wanton kisses. Setting my passion ablaze, she smiled. "Come, let us love. The gift of life and pleasure is ours to enjoy for awhile. Tomorrow will care for itself." Thus always she wrapped me in devotion, letting her life fold into mine. In her energies, I swear, were mine enhanced; from our loving, benediction flowed upon all that we set upon to do. We would need that strength in the turmoils that lay ahead.

There was a third journey I had yet to make, and I determined to take Boots along as squire. My thoughts had been with Randall, still serving as squire at Alnwick. 'Twas past time he came home. Now that Bors was dead, another knight was needed upon the manor; who better than my heir? Yet, as always, I faced reluctance, for Herleve ever interfered in every decision concerning her son, much to the detriment of his character. But soon he would be nineteen, and we must be thinking of his wedding. I needs must visit Duncan, to begin final arrangements for Randall's formal betrothal to his daughter, the fair maid, Margaret. I had, too, other motives, some of which were not so plain, even unto me.

There was the sniffing out of the feeling toward England's new king, John, in the heart of Scotland's William the Lion. In the politics of the age, men could easily find themselves 'pon the wrong side of authority; allies in other kingdoms were like money in the purse. Ties with Duncan needed to be strengthened; since his marriage to Aethelfritha, he had become one of William's privy counselors. Then, too, there was the joy of a journey with Boots at my back.

Despite the unrest in men's minds, the roads were still safe enough, for the marcher network was strong, and civil justice so set as not to depend upon the whims of kings. Particularly under William the Lion, lowland Scotland was safer of travel than many a road in England. I heard from Chatta that William was sitting at Edinburgh; Boots and I laughed and made plans to retrace the steps that had marked our first foray together. I swear, 'twas not until we were on the road north from Chatta's, with Boots riding as squire, that my little plot was hatched.

For all our comfort together, Boots had never yet been properly laid upon a bed. As groom, her bed was always with the horses, 'pon straw or saddle blankets. Denied the comforts of Old Hall, her life had been utilitarian. She was content, but I began to while away the miles planning a surprise, our first night together in a real bed. Travelers then might sleep several to a bed; inns were kept with common accommodations. For many, this was no hardship, but 'twould not suit my purpose. I must con a way to keep the great bed to ourselves; nor must the innkeeper catch the scent of fornication which lingered 'round my squire.

So quiet was I, that the lass rode forward to catch what I might be thinking. Speaking with her as we rode, the plan set itself. We would stop once again with Tom at Swine Farm, after crossing the river at Norham. The track was not well travelled; like as not we would be the only wayfarers there. 'Twas once again the end of May, and days were growing long. We should make Swine Farm just before vespers. Tom's wife was as pious as he was practical; there would be no meal after evening prayers. Yet I wished no long sessions at ale before retiring; some infirmity needs be invented to allow our retreat to the bedchamber early. Since we wished no hint of any plague, it was decided that I should complain of an unfit back; this would require the services of my squire throughout the night.

Boots seemed satisfied, but curious. As always, she was full of questions: what are beds made of? why would several people wish to share one sleeping space? was it warm? The one vital question she should have asked, we both over-looked at the time.

All went well. Boots ate quietly in a corner, holding to her disguise. She even suffered through the householders' prayers with me, albeit making faces behind our backs. Turning once, I caught her at it, and frowned my displeasure. Later, I was to rebuke her, for there are many honest folk who derive comfort from the simple unthinking rituals of the church.

At last, blue twilight began to fall over the grey Scots countryside. I sent Boots ahead of me up the stair, and made the fatal mistake of accepting my host's invitation for a turn in the road ere he locked the inn for the night.

'Twas a soft night, but there were no flowers beside the road, as at Chatta's. Instead, the dour little inn fronted the road itself, with only a narrow bench betwixt the house wall and the dust churned up by passing hooves. Thank God, there were no windows on the ground floor fronting the street, for the house ran narrow, front to back. But there was one upstairs beside the traveler's bed. Just as Tom and I turned toward the door, the shutter over that window was thrown open. In surprise, we looked up as Boots stuck forth her head. Capless, with long hair a-flying, she called out. "Oh, Sire, you never told me. Do you wish me to take off all my clothes?"

Beside me, Tom doubled over in laughter, as I tried vainly to signal the girl back inside. Instead, she called out more loudly, "Do you wish me to remove my clothes?" At last I held my finger to my lips, and she stared at me a moment, then turned back inside.

"I think you need go tend to your squire," Tom whispered, "ere my lady wife is roused. Her hearing is keen, and her ways are narrow. But I do believe she is at the back, locking away the chickens. Haste ye, now!"

There was no answer to be made. Furious, I rushed up the stairs as Tom bolted the heavy front door. "Girl," I cried, "where are thy wits? Do you wish us to be ejected into the night by the innkeeper's wife? No man takes a woman in disguise up to bed, unless he has fornication in mind. These God-fearing people judge very harshly of that!"

She hung her head. Nature's child, unspoiled by the artifices of polite society, Boots was never to ken the predicaments she put me into. "How was I to know, Master? I only wanted to know, for it seemed I might spoil the linens, wearing my clothes upon such a fine bed." Like all the villeins and house carls, Boots usually slept in her clothes, wherever a nook presented itself. Bedtime formality was unknown to the peasants. Yet 'twas the custom for lords and ladies, even in our time, to be undressed by a servant, and cosseted into bed, nude. That such custom would be unknown to her had never entered my head. Anger at my own thick-headedness—and hers—near spoiled the night for me. Though the road north had been enlivened by my daydreams, reality demanded that I never try that escapade again.

Tom's wife had the last say, after all. That pious and thrifty woman had neglected to air the bed chamber and wash the linens after the last travelers. So it was, we had no sooner resumed our march than the presence of unwanted guests was detected. "Fleas!" cursed Boots; "the damnable things will even make the horses miserable. So much for your fine beds, m'lord." And she slapped at her back roundly.

I was doing the same, and cursing no less. You who say we ancient folk knew no better than to live with such creatures need be ensconced awhile in Tom's bed. There was naught for it but to stop at the nearest burn, remove clothes and armour, wash all that might be washed, and hang the rest in the sun. Even the horses we unsaddled and led into the water, then tethered them in the sun. Our washing of one another soon turned into a splashing match, until weak with laughter, we collapsed in each other's arms 'pon a mossy bank. "So much for your fine beds," Boots murmured. "What could be better than this?" And for that I had no answer.

Yet in Edinborough, I made sure that Boots behaved as befitted a true squire. She pouted, but I had business to tend. Duncan and Aethelfritha made me a warm welcome, as did William the Lion himself. I assured them of the friendship of Bamburgh Castle and of Glororum, regardless of the vicissitudes approaching with the reign of John. In turn, William granted peace between us.

It went not so well with the maid, Margaret. Aethelfritha moaned that the lass was but sixteen; though most of our girls were wed near that age, still Margaret had been slow to come into womanhood. 'Twas so with many of the north country lasses, Duncan assured me. In the end, they asked me to bide for two more years, whilst Aethelfritha imparted greater woman's knowledge to her daughter. There was naught I could do but agree, for Margaret's life at Glororum would be hard enough. Herleve would never accept her gracefully, as my mother had accepted her as my bride.

So we rode home, and despite Boots sanguine humour, I felt a vague dissatisfaction. All efforts at retreat from the coming winds of change were in vain; we teetered 'pon the edge of an abyss that for all my care might open before us. Life loomed as a series of skirmishes, not the sort to be settled with sword and lance, but the harder ones of diplomacy. War is a simpler art than politics.

So as not to face Tom again soon, we went by way of Cornhill, so that I might stop at Colin's Wood to see the Henrys. Boots was miffed, for it gave her no chance to be alone with me for any time, but I missed my youngest son. He was now nigh fourteen, and would be made squire at Michaelmas. Before our own manor accounting, I planned to ride north to invest him with new hauberk and sword and shield. His manhood was becoming unmistakable, as I watched him work the quintains. Then he cleverly beat me at a game of chess and made me pay pence! Henry would be a man for the new century; clever, relying not only on skill at arms, but upon trade and industry. The world was a-changing.

But 1199, the bitter end of the century, was not finished with death and endings. Andrew's little brown hen, Margaret, wasted away in October, just two days after the anniversary of my father's death. Cross brought us the word: Margaret had gone to join Andrew and little Ralph ere dawn broke across the sky. Weeping, Cross vowed to remain and care for old Peter. In his grief, the old man could but mutter, "Why did Ye not take me? What have I left? All is gone! Why did Ye not take me?" After Margaret was sung to her rest, I needs must help the old man from the kirkyard, else he would have laid him upon her grave and never stirred again.

Tippie had ridden to the church with me; Herleve, as usual, refused to have anything to do with church services, even burials. Raynaud, seeing my plight, offered to take the child home. I saw his care as he held her before him on the saddle, and her proud look as she surveyed the world from the vantage of his tall destrier. Suddenly, a pang squeezed my heart, a foreboding that I had no art to ken. All I could do was turn and try to mend the affair at hand.

In this, at least, there followed some success. Peter swallowed his grief and remained head hostler for another three years; work was antidote for his sorrows. As was Cross, for she stayed with him as a daughter. In the end, 'tis work and love keeps the human spirit alive.

Chapter 23

Marauders

John Lackland was crowned King of England in May of 1199 by Hubert Walter, Bishop of Canterbury. Most of the lesser English landowners, knights like myself, were otherwise occupied and stayed from the coronation. John little noticed, for he was a-fever to hie him back to France, where he was embroiled in wars with Philip and his minions over the scraps of Richard's territories. Some of John's Norman barons favored Arthur, Richard's nephew, for the succession; indeed, his claim to the throne was as valid as John's. 'Twas a pity the lad was but twelve, for he was pawn to the French and the barons of Brittany.

England, however, remained quiet, as long as scutage was sent to pay for John's wars. Archbishop Hubert Walter was left to rule the kingdom; under him law and custom held the peace as it had always done. Yet tales reached us of John's cruel nature, his starving to death of any dissenter he could lay hands upon, even women and children, and of his murder of young Arthur. 'Twas said that after he captured the lad during the battle of Mirabeau, he threw him into the dungeon to starve. One night, in a drunken rage, John had the unfortunate boy brought unto him. Before the throne, he abused and finally strangled his young prisoner, then cast his body like so much rubbish into the Seine. Across all the realm, both churchmen and honest knights condemned that miscreant king—most silently, but many aloud.

Philip of France was not one to lose the edge when John's troops were most disheartened. Moving swiftly, he destroyed what small advantage John had taken. By 1204, Normandy had fallen, and John fled to England for his life. By 1206, all the possessions of Henry and Richard on the continent had been lost by John, save a small portion of Aquitaine. Now he might devote his attention to misrule in England.

Yet Glororum continued to prosper during the first few years of the century. The work on Bamburgh church went on apace. As promised, Ben-Ami the Jew stopped to survey the work; 'twas in 1198. From thence until his death in 1218 he helped us find the Flemish glass for the windows and other small treasures to furnish the church. I gave him the hospitality of Bamburgh Hall, and kept two men-at-arms hard by, to face down any grumbling. Ben-Ami worked with Robin, and my steward made many trips to Flanders, selling wool and buying glass and other luxuries. Young Henry often went with him, and learned to drive a shrewd bargain. For my birthday in 1204, they brought back enough glass from Flanders to fill the window of my upper chamber. 'Twas the first glass at Old Hall. I remember well, standing looking through those small panes, surveying the land west, clear unto the Cheviots. Behind me, in the narrow, light-filled room, stood a new carven table covered with a gold-embroidered cloth, upon which rested a Book of Hours. Its prayers were often a comfort unto me, and solitary hours spent here were more precious than the trappings themselves. A bright tapestry covered the wall, picturing the Garden of Eden. It satisfied my soul to consider that in some small way, I was honourably continuing the work that Adam had begun.

Indeed, 'twas the sheep that made these luxuries possible, for the industrious Flemish were crying for good wool to weave. We had every foot of land possible into pasture, both at Glororum and at Bamburgh. By buying out one or two small-holds, our lands at Bamburgh now extended near three leagues along the coast, from Budle Bay to Bedehal (Beadnell). Even the shore grass was pastured. It became apparent that soon we would need more cropland, as our ploughland was worn and would better serve as pasture. I had no ken then as to how this might come about, for good land was firm-held and did not change hands easily. On one of his many trips to the continent, Robin continued east to visit Alyse and see how fared our son, Philip. Alyse had sent the lad to monastery school at age six, and her life became somewhat easier without his presence at home. Yet by the time he was eight, the boy was so miserable that Denis petitioned his sister for the boy. Knighthood was in his blood; he took to training at arms as a duck to water. Robin laughed and said he would have recognized the lad as a cousin anywhere, for his red hair, his love of arms, and his sweet singing voice.

William, too, was becoming a most doughty knight. In autumn of 1201, I had Sir John de Hawthorne and William up to the west forest to hunt. We stayed a fortnight in the little lodge I had built for Stephen, and our fellowship knew no bounds. William shot a prize stag, then ran it to earth and himself dismounted to cut the beast's throat. Though weakened from the arrow in its side, the great stag fought gamely on, but was no match for the cunning and strength of my son. For many years his antlers stood above all the rest in west forest lodge as tribute to William.

In 1199 there had been another call to Crusade by the pope, Innocent III. Many indulgences had been promised, and William had never forgotten my advice to seek his fortune in the Holy Land. In 1201, Robin, just returned from Flanders, brought news that a distant relative, Count Baldwin, was gathering knights to accompany him on crusade. William asked my permission to join Baldwin in Venice, in preparation for the Fourth Crusade. I could not deny my second son this chance to seek his fortune, so I saw him well-armoured and well-advised, and sent him away with blessings in March of 1202. He seemed so young, yet he was well-grown and strong at eighteen. He took as squire the son of Odo, who had accompanied Stephen and me in 1189.

After many adventures, William was knighted at Constantinople in 1204, the first of my sons to earn his spurs. He served Baldwin for several years, till the death of Sir John de Hawthorne called him home to Hutton. There he served Maud, and her grandson Henry, as steward till the day he died. Of all my sons, William was the one who accorded me the greatest respect. He never forgot his promise to light a candle for us at the Holy Sepulchre, and it was he, after my death, who commissioned the carving of the stone effigy that lies in Bamburgh church. Thus he honoured his father as patron of the new church, and 'tis the only monument that survives, though now its significance is all but forgotten.

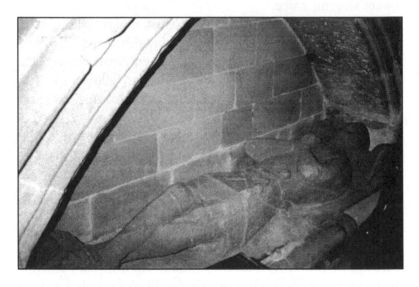

Knight Effigy, St. Aidan's Church, Bamburgh
Commissioned for Crusader Sir John Forster (d. 1220)
by his son William.

Randall was another kettle of fish. I brought him home to stay in October of '99, and some disgruntled he was, away from the trappings of luxury and ease as castle squire at Alnwick. And I liked not his open admiration of Eustace de Vesci of Alnwick, for the man could be a formidable foe when crossed, as his father had been before him. But Randolph had a fine eye for adornment, and often I found him gauging some small detail on the church with Manfred. My eldest son also had an eye for the delicate points of women; it was evident that soon I must return to Edinburgh to finalize his marriage.

In the nonce, I gave Randall charge of the household squires and men-at-arms, to give him experience at working with men whom he naturally—after the manner of his mother—considered his inferiors. 'Twas a burden on me, guiding him in the courteous control of our housecarls and fyrd. But Edwin stepped in. I had given the younger priest charge of the pages, as Cedric was inclined to be short-tempered with them, now that his years were well over three score. Randall seemed to listen to Edwin, whereas he shut his ears to me, so I let wisdom flow in its natural channel. Eventually, my eldest son made an adequate instructor for our young men. His knowledge was up-to-date, and his hard-to-please air made the lads strive harder to win his few crumbs of praise.

I had the last laugh, however. With great pomp and ceremony I turned the manor court over to my proud son, knowing full well the demands of the curia would soon drive him distraught. Yet I had had to take the reins of manor affairs at an even younger age. 'Twas good seasoning for a bland sauce.

In early May of 1202, as soon as Easter was well and truly behind us, my eldest son and I rode north to Edinburgh. I had sent Raynaud on ahead with a formal announcement of our coming, for this was to be the final settlement of the younger de Ros's marriage. I could brook delay no longer, for my son had already sired a child by one of our villein maids, which caused no end of trouble upon the estate. Most courteously I asked Herleve to accompany us, but as she was dead-set 'gainst Randall marrying, she refused us her company.

'Twas as well; her ways had deteriorated into incomprehensibility. A maid was required at all times in attempt to keep the mistress clean; the lady simply adored being filthy. Julian—God bless his faithful heart!—followed Herleve near everywhere, save into her chamber, lest she injure herself. Still she went out with hawk and hound, and the household breathed a sigh of relief on fair days when she rode from home, granting us respite from her trying ways.

These things I made known to Duncan and his family, in the gentlest way, lest the maid Margaret enter marriage blindly. Randall was much taken with the lass; tall and strong, she was as bonny as any man might desire. The dowry was harder to settle, for Duncan was ever the canny Scot. Yet Aethelfritha, being of royal blood, could scarce allow her daughter to marry penuriously. Indeed, the lady was my strongest ally 'gainst Duncan. At last, we settled on a handsome sum in silver, part to stay with Margaret as allowance, part to go to the estate for the furbishing of suitable quarters for the newlyweds. That, at least, would spare Glororum funds that were much needed elsewhere. Margaret would bring with her one handmaid, as had Herleve; women need the comfort of an old confidant in new and trying situations.

Randall and I rode home well satisfied. The wedding was set for the last day of August, 1202, in Edinburgh. That would scarce give me time to see to their apartments, and gifts for Margaret and her family. So busy were we on the way home, conning our plans, that I had not thought how to graciously tell Herleve that the wedding of her son was soon to be a *fait accompli*. It would have been better by far had I left the telling to Randall, but I entered Old Hall with a head full of plans for refurbishing the second floor of the tower, my parents' old rooms. Near at once, I encountered Herleve, and gave her the news of the wedding, expecting her to be cheered at Randall's good fortune.

Instead, the words provoked an outburst, best left untold. The woman was fair unhinged by the news, threatening ruin upon us all. She went to her room and bided, nor did she come down for supper. Randall went to speak with her, but returned, shaking his head. Never had he seen his mother so wrathful. We hoped that with time she might again come to her senses.

Indeed, in the morn, she left Old Hall early, in the teeth of a howling wind, followed by Julian. Riding her favorite palfrey, she stopped a moment at Bamburgh church, where she asked Cedric for his prayers. Leaving the poor man puzzled, for never had there been great love between them, Herleve then rode up the towering rock of Bamburgh.

Julian recounts what came next. "Aye, with her hawk 'pon her wrist, still hooded, and her hound at her side, the mistress rode straight over the cliff of Bamburgh. I rode furiously to catch her, for her motive had not been plain to me at first. When I saw there was no hope, I called out the castle guard, and we found her body, and that of her horse and hawk, broken in the sea at the foot of the cliffs. Only the dog refused the leap, whimpering and crying."

Why Herleve had taken her life in such a fashion only became plain later. Julian recalled that she had said something about pulling the tinder from beneath the spark. Boots gave me the clue. "Is not your mourning for at least a year? Can Randall then be married?" she asked innocently when I brought her the news. More fool I, I should have suspected. But such a dire bid for so little gain!

Edwin tried to gently bring comfort. "Your lady wife was sore afflicted. 'Twas not the deed of a rational woman. The Church will not consider her death suicide, for her mind kenned not the consequence of her action. Nor are you in any way to blame, or Julian. We must bury her and pray that Our Lord will heal her mind in Heaven."

Cedric was not as sanguine. "She ever manipulated everything to her will, seeking pity where she deserved scorn, and only accepting God where it suited her purposes. Her dementia served to heap coals of fire upon the heads of all about her, and as such, she kept the flames well fanned. 'Tis a fine line she walked, between unknowing and knowing only too well. Her last act was one of defiance, of her family, of custom, and of the law of God. Bury her not at Bamburgh, else she desecrate the holy grounds of the new church."

But I had already made up my mind to bury Herleve at Ellingham, at the little church of St. Maurice that her grandfather had built. Since the estate had broken up, there was no longer a priest in residence. So, with Edwin presiding, we laid my wife to rest in Ellingham churchyard, though in ground that had never been consecrated for burials. Thus Annie's old prediction was at last fulfilled: that "with a bird she will fly away young, and unsainted she will lie." Herleve was not yet forty.

I myself rode back to Edinburgh with the news, only to find that King William had moved his court to Glasgow. It was raining when at last Raynaud and I caught up with Duncan, and my mood was foul. I determined not to let Herleve have the last say; she had caused me grief enough. While a suitable period of mourning was only seemly, the wedding would not be put off for a year. Duncan reluctantly agreed; the wedding would be delayed only till the end of October, before winter shut down the roads. It would be a small party, for few of us wished to travel as far as Glasgow that late in the year. That suited Duncan, as it lessened the expense.

Thus it was that Randall and his bride moved into their new apartment on the second floor of Glororum tower just before the season of Advent, in 1202. Though only forty-three, I began to feel like a patriarch, and I understood my mother's emotions when first I was wed, and she stepped aside to allow a new mistress into the Hall. I prayed that I would be as wise as she in dealing with my new family.

Boots only laughed at me. "You are younger than your son, in many ways. I will never let you grow old! Come, I will show you..." And once again, sheltered from winter's storm and the problems of Old Hall, we seethed with love beneath the snug rafters of the stable. Christ (I could not help but think) brought love into the world in a stable, and thus were we blessed.

Tippie was the only one of us who truly missed her mother. The lady's peculiarities were all the lass had ever known, and so the peace that settled over Old Hall with Herleve's passing seemed unwieldy to the child. She took to following me everywhere, and I had her by my side or before me on the saddle through much of the day. Boots was miffed, for it took time from her, but the child's well-being was uppermost in my mind. At last, after Margaret had settled in, she took the girl beneath her wing, and the two of them found comfort in one another.

Once again, Glororum held the happy sounds of women at work, women singing. Margaret's maid, Elsie, was an outspoken red-haired Scots lass, who carried her mistress's orders to the servants with a great deal more vehemence than Margaret herself would. But the Hall became clean, and a new cook was appointed to help old Eli, so the meals improved. Still we dined on brown bread and pease seasoned with meat, as did our villeins, but now more delicacies appeared—pastries and salats and mawmoney for feast days. Tippie was ever my greatest care, and she still followed me like a puppy as often as allowed. But she had her own maid, Nicolette's daughter, Elaine. Elaine was now eighteen and unmarried, nor was she like to be soon; she had her mother's features and her haughty air. Nicolette herself, after so many years of coping with the demands of Herleve and Old Hall, I wished to put out to pasture, but that would have insulted the old dear dreadfully. Instead, I commissioned her as dowager draper, in charge of all linens and clothing, of embroideries and hangings. 'Twas light work, for she had only to oversee the maids; and the linen presses, unlike her former mistress, were not likely to curse at her and soil themselves.

Elaine began teaching Tippie the arts of sewing and woman-craft, for she had her mother's knack with the needle. Yet my daughter was restless; her mind sought for more. At last, I consulted with Edwin. His advice was to send the girl to a nunnery for schooling. I would not hold still for that, remembering the foolishness that had been instilled into her mother. Edwin reminded me not all religious houses were the same; still, I did not want my little daughter sent from home. In the end, Edwin agreed to teach her with his pages, so that at the least she might learn of manners and her Latin letters.

By 1205, the household was well settled into its new customs. The nave of Bamburgh church was nigh completed, save for the tower, and the crypt was in place. The transepts were complete, even to glass, and the chancel walls near risen. Under Hubert Walter, England was retaining stability and prosperity. Then, of a sudden, that great Chancellor was called home by the dark Traveler. King John immediately moved to take all the power of the kingdom unto himself. To that end, he demanded the monks at Canterbury elect the toadying Bishop of Norwich as Archbishop in Hubert's place. John would then have both civil and ecclesiastical authority in his pocket, and all the money of the kingdom. The monks did as they were ordered, but immediately appealed to Rome. King and pope thenceforth began to quarrel, and all of England entered into turmoil and uncertainty. Philip of France began eyeing the English coasts, as did numerous marauders.

'Twas in March of 1206 that Bamburgh had its little excitement. A cold damp morning began to break on St. Patrick's day, the anniversary of the death of Baby John. Restless, I had awakened early, and as was my wont, was sitting before the embers of the kitchen fire. A horse clattered into the courtyard, and I hastened to see what errand brought such an early visitor.

One of the lads from the castle threw himself from his steed. "Sire," he reported, "Our watch has reported three strange ships, slipping between Bamburgh and the Farne Islands, heading south. Had it not been for a chance rift in the fog, David would ne'er have seen them. They look to be warships, perhaps Danes. They are standing very near the coast, as if looking for an unprotected place to come ashore."

Instantly, I knew Bedehal's cove was the best place for marauders to land. 'Twas sheltered, and the reivers could pull their boats ashore and plunder any of the settlements to the south—Swinhoe, Tucgahal (Tughall), Preston. All the little settlements would be ravished, perhaps as far as Ellingham on the west, and Dunstan hill to the south. Such raiders spared not the lives of our villeins, nor of their women and children. They would spread out and move quickly in the misty morning, ere folk were up and aware. I saw then that the beacon fire had been lit upon the ramparts of Bamburgh castle, warning our folk to the south.

"We need the knights and men-at-arms to assemble at once. Those cutthroats hope to prey on scattered, unarmed folk; any show of force and they will run. Tell Gib to leave the castle with but a few watchers; then do you men-at-arms march south immediately. Many may not have seen the beacon; assemble the people in Ebba's church on the point at Bedehal."

St. Ebba had been the sister of St. Oswald; like him, she was venerated as an angel of good works by the country people. Her old church was set upon Bede's point, well north of the cove, and the church was easily defended, sitting as it did with the sea on three sides. "Get the women and children inside, and call the fyrd; set every villain able to bear staff or bill before the church door. As soon as that be done, keep ye concealed till the raiders have left their boats. Likely, there will be few guards. Dispatch them, and burn the boats. Then move forward; we will try to catch these vikings in the jaws of our trap so that none return home to tell tales." We knew, of course, that this was no Viking invasion, but our lore had been filled for years with stories of such men; 'twas natural to call them by the old word.

I had Raynaud already beside me; I told him to arm our men-at-arms and squires, and to roust Randall. I then sent a messenger to the vill; the women and children were to get to Bamburgh castle, and the fyrd to move up to Glororum. Those slow, rough men could not move quickly enough to assist us at Bedehal, but they could protect the stock at home farm should stragglers from the boats wend this far north.

Yet our small contingent could not face down the marauders alone. Three sleek ships could hold sixty to eighty fighting men, armed with sword and lance and bill. Time was on our side still, but barely. If the raiders penetrated too far inland, our forces would have to scatter too thinly to be effective. We needs must attack them quickly, ere they got to Chathill or the unprotected friars at Brunton. I ran for the stable as hard as I could pelt, and called to Boots. I told her quickly of the danger. "Get ye to William of Lucker as soon as ere you can; have him roust every knight he can find and meet us at Fleetham. We are marching now, and will be sore beset in an hour's time. Then ride as hard as ever you are able; get to Blaise at Ellingham and send him to rouse the priests at Preston and Brunton, then march north. Every vill you pass, call up the fyrd and tell them to seek sanctuary for their womenfolk. Once you get to Ellingham, go to St. Maurice's and stay till I come for you. You will be in no danger yet, riding west, but for God's sake, hurry. Can you remember all that?"

"Aye;" and the lass said it all back perfectly. Then she added "I am taking Hellfire. He is the fastest horse in all Northumberland." She knew I had not time to quarrel with her; if anyone could handle that horse, it was my Boots. I kissed her gently, and ran to arm.

For all our haste, we were near too late. The raiders too had spotted the warning fire atop Bamburgh's ramparts. They put to shore at Sutthernland (Sunderland), which once marked the southern boundary of Glororum's virgates. It now embraced a handful of fisherman's huts and a few poor freeman farmers. Thus my rough plans changed in a flash. On our way south, we spotted the quick flare of burning cots, and knew the marauders had already landed, much farther north than I had anticipated.

*Bay Near North Sunderland
Where the Marauders Came Ashore*

As soon as their long boats were pulled up on the shingle, those warriors stormed the Sutthernland vill. Many of the villeins had already left, those with quick wit who were able to drop everything and run. But not all were so fortunate. One young family, burdened with children—twin toddlers and a babe at breast—moved too slowly. The vikings hacked the father to death, put the babes to the sword, and raped the mother ere leaving her for dead. Another band was occupied with a fierce old man who managed to kill one of the raiders before he and his crone were slaughtered. A third band, heading south after the fleeing peasants, managed to capture poor half-wit Tom. The lad had paused once too often to look back at the flames of his home. His tormentors stopped to mangle their innocent prize, hacking poor Tom apart in little pieces ere at last granting him the mercy of death. But the martyrdom of our blessed people served to slow the baneful horde; the rest of the vill managed to reach sanctuary in St. Ebba's at Bedehal. As the two vills came together, the men of their fyrds stood armed and angry at the church door.

The raiders pulled back and spoke together, unsure whether to pursue the slaughter and rob the church, or turn aside to look for easier plunder. At last, they decided to move inland, put off as much perhaps by the impoverished aspect of the old church as by the grim men a-waiting.

The miserable houses at Sutthernland were plundered and alight. What livestock as could be driven off was being loaded into the boats when the soldiers of Bamburgh charged down from the north. The marauders at once united their two northern bands to protect the boats. 'Twas a grievous battle, for the men-at-arms numbered only eighteen, with four horse; whilst the raiders, drawn up in a circle, were near forty. Murderously, the viking arc advanced, hacking at the horses to dismount our yeomen. Two beasts were killed, and four of the castle soldiers. Sword and bill flashed and clanged in desperate close combat.

We had just passed Elle's ford (Elford) when we heard the battle commence. Spurring, we raced the last mile to succor our sore-beset men-at-arms. Strangely, my mind was filled only with memories of how David and Duncan, Bors and I had won the tourney in Edinburgh so many long years ago. I wished with all my heart I had those worthies beside me again! Raynaud, while battle-tested, had never fought at my side, whilst Randall was a weak reed at best. Julian, due to his age, I had left in charge of the fyrd at Glororum, but we had three sturdy men-at-arms and four well-trained yeoman squires. As young men ever are, the lads were eager for blood-letting. They would have their fill soon enow.

The solid viking advance was cutting down the slowly retreating castle guard. The fighting was desperate. Quickly, I saw that the disciplined arc of the marauders had moved north, away from their boats. "Circle south," I waved to my poor small army, "and get between the vikings and their boats. That will turn them in our direction!" It was a desperate move, but the men of the castle were in dire straits.

Instantly, the reivers turned their advancing arc into a wedge with the wide end open to the sea. They still outnumbered us, but the castle yeomen were much heartened by our appearance. The battle stopped moving northward. We knights of the south were now hard pressed, outnumbered two to one. But our advantage lay in our mounts. "Get in quickly, kill, and get out," I shouted. "Run and wheel; don't let them touch the horses!" Thus we harried the southern flank of the wedge, evening the odds. My long lance tasted blood again; not once, but twice.

The viking band soon realized that they could not make their ships. They also knew that we were too few to hold 'gainst them for long. Slowly, they retreated to a strong point upon the cragside; warily our forces eyed one another. Then their horns sounded, loud in the misty morning air. Soon came an answer from the south; then another, even closer. If their south-marching band returned to close upon our flanks, we were finished; we had not enough strength to hold in the jaws of the marauders' combined force. Yet I was loathe to withdraw and let them take ship, perhaps to return to plunder once again. Few realized how the penury of the English kings had so decimated the noble stronghold of Bamburgh. If these raiders escaped, the easy plunder of our coast would soon be upon every lip.

Desperate, I turned to Raynaud. "If we make a diversion, think you that you can find a burning brand in the cots so we can set their ships afire?"

The canny young knight thought quickly. "Aye. But 'twill make them bold. I think we can not hold them if they break from their ground upon the crag. And their reinforcements are nigh. I am as unafraid of death as the next man, but I wish it not to be in vain."

"What you say has merit. But we are still between them and the ships. Let us form our ranks together; perhaps we may yet hold them awhile. William of Lucker and Blaise from Ellingham should be riding to our succor even now. But while we are a-forming, go ye and steal us some fire."

Thus my young knight rode off to bring fire, no easy task with a war-horse already excited by the smell of blood. But

Raynaud's big grey had been trained by old Peter and by Boots; he would hold. I put Gib and his men then behind a shield wall between the raiders and their boats. Inland, on their flank, I put our mounted yeomen, where they would have room to maneuver. If the men entrenched upon the crag broke downhill toward the ships, we could then sweep in behind them. If the vikings marching up from the south tried to outflank our force, we could swing our horse to quickly engage them. If both moved 'pon us at once, well, God help us! We were a scant twenty; more than thirty yet faced us, and I had no ken of the number to the south, but judged it could be as much as another forty. I liked not the odds.

Raynaud came forth with two burning brands; I set James, Julian's son, to ride quickly to the boats to fire them. We must smoke the rats from their hole ere those reinforcements arrived. Seeing flames licking upon their vessels, the raiders howled and broke from cover to attack the infantry upon the beach. Our horse then rushed toward them, lancing at men as if they were wild swine of the forest. Still, the discipline of the vikings was remarkable. Holding fast, they fought foot by foot back up the hill to their fastness. Trumpeting once more, they were calling their reinforcements. An answering trump sounded near; a scant half-mile.

I rode to encourage Gib and his men upon the beach. Grim-face, they stood ready. I then rode before our mounted fighters, telling them to hold steady and not to attack until the order was given. "'Tis the hardest part, waiting for the battle to be joined. But if any break too soon, he will be dead and our line broken. Hold fast!" And I soothed the horses with a word and a pat as I passed; checked cinches and the set of lances.

We heard the eager clash of their arms, the roar of fury within their throats. They were nigh upon us, and from the corner of my eye, I saw the forces upon the hill standing at ready, waiting for the battle to be joined ere racing down to enfold us between their numbers. Suddenly, I heard it: hooves racing, the peculiar rushing sounds that mounted knights make when a-charge. By my side, Randall laughed a dry choking laugh; he had heard it too.

"For God and St. Oswald," I cried, "the day is ours!" The raiders marching from the south turned in a desperate attempt to stave off the vengeance that drove upon their rear. Headlong, the vikings upon the hill charged forward in a flying wedge; they managed to break through the shield wall even as we rode upon their flank. Two of the ships were merrily ablaze; the third was sputtering and not yet fully afire. Near twenty of the raiders managed to reach that last ship; with unholy effort, they pushed it into the waves with their blood staining the water 'round about. Over a dozen managed to escape, manning the oars whilst others attempted to put out the fire. The corpses of two vikings washed gently upon the shingle, but behind the shield wall, Gib had lost three more men. Of a sudden, all was quiet, save for the blowing of the horses and the groans of the wounded. Raynaud and I rode forward to greet our saviours; we touched hands to helm in salute to William and Blaise and the men who had followed them into battle. Then we four turned to survey the devastation.

Of the English forces, Gib had taken the greatest losses. Ten of his force of twenty-two had breathed their last. Four more had wounds which with God's blessing might heal cleanly. William of Lucker had lost a young squire; three more of those who had ridden up from the south were wounded. Miraculously, though we had a man-at-arms and a squire wounded, Glororum had suffered no loss. Removing my helm and bowing my head in thanksgiving, I felt Stephen very near. Ah, he would not be deprived of this fight! With his intercession, we had come victorious.

The marauders were a different story. Their bodies lay upon our shores from the crag to Sutthernland, full forty dead and dying. Eighteen more sat wounded, quiet, heads upon their knees. If not ransomed, they would surely hang. The following day we would bury the marauder dead in the offal pit of the fish camp at Sutthernland. Those still living were encamped under guard in the ruins of the vill. Later, Edwin came to shrive such as were Christians, and give blessing to all those who lost their lives in such a desperate raid upon foreign shores. Questioning those who remained elicited the information that they were Danes. As a clan, their ways had always been marauding. In most places, their quick strikes left them with plunder a-plenty to share; rich monasteries and abby lands were picked clean ere the monks could say a Paternoster. The vikings had indeed been headed for the priest's mill at Brunton and farm at Preston, when they spotted the castle beacon. Acting quickly, they hoped to make a raid and depart ere the marcher network could be called up. For those miserable men, the slaughter of poor villeins was no different a day's work than butchering swine.

The fight had begun about an hour after dawn and progressed throughout the morning. Several more hours we spent lining up the dead and making arrangements for the wounded and prisoners. Then toll must be taken of the vill, for at that time we had as yet no idea of the losses to our peasant folk. 'Twas late afternoon when we wearily turned toward Glororum; I for one was famished.

Not until Adam came forth to take my horse at the stable gate did I remember Boots. Though the sky was beginning to darken, I could not leave her alone at Ellingham. I called loudly and a page came haring forth from the Hall; I sent him flying for bread and a jug of ale. I told Adam to quickly saddle a fresh horse, whilst I drew water from the horse trough to rinse the blood and grime from face and hands. I was already in the saddle when the page returned with such victuals as he had been able to find.

'Twas full dark when I reined in outside the church of St. Maurice. Venus stood as the evening star 'neath a pale westering moon. My heart was in my throat when I entered the church, for nowhere about had I seen Hellfire tethered. What if aught had happened to Boots? How could I live with myself, knowing I had sent her into mishap?

I needn't have worried. Hellfire himself was in the church, for the lass had no sense of desecration, only the very practical desire to keep her wild horse fast when she had come off without so much as a tether. Our churches had stone floors and no furnishings save at the altar; St. Maurice made a very fine stable. Fortunately, Adam had put a tether upon my saddle, so my fleabite roan spent the night in the churchyard. 'Twould not do to have two stallions quarreling in church. As soon as all was secure, I fell to the floor in a heap beside Boots.

"I am sorry to say I forgot you till I returned to Glororum, else I would have come for you sooner. You did a yeoman's work today; had William and Blaise been ten minutes later, I should not be here now. Praise God, we won the day."

Startled, the girl reached out and held me, armour and all. "Had you not returned, I would have bided here till we met in Heaven," she said simply. "But you have brought bread and ale, let us sup whilst we talk." Thus we did, while I told her of the battle, and of the strong feeling I had of Stephen's presence. Yet the harder part had been hers, waiting alone in the church, not knowing how the fight would go. She must examine me all over for signs of wounds, and though the armour was some dented and my legs bruised from glancing blows, the body was whole. Thankfully, she laid her down next to me, and in God's healing rest we spent the night.

Chapter 24

Tippie

The battle at Sutthernland had consequences beyond what we could imagine at the time. As soon as they were able to march, we herded the prisoners to the King's dungeon at Newcastle. Despite Edwin's care, two more marauders died of fevered wounds and the hardships of the road. The sheriff met us at the castle to take charge of the prisoners; John, he was sure, would want them ransomed. If Richard had squeezed the English cow for pence, John was extracting blood as well.

So it was at Bamburgh also. In 1204, King John had sent a writ notifying the Bishop of Durham, under whose authority Bamburgh had traditionally resided, that Bishop John of Norwich had been granted the revenues from Bamburgh church. By precedence, that had been granted by King Henry to Nostell, to keep a priest in residence. If Nostell wished one of their monks to bide at Bamburgh and receive enough income for his living, they could very well pay off Norwich first.

Upon the same day, in another writ to Durham, John sold off the church again, advising the bishop that perpetual vicarage had been granted to Peter des Roches, for the immense sum of forty marks a year. (You would understand that as near $50,000 dollars today.) From only one place could that remittance be exacted: the farms and tithes that had hitherto supported Bamburgh church. As Richard's appointed vicar, or chancellor of the monies for the church, I was now superseded.

Bishop Philip was still in Poitou and Poitou had fallen to the French. All of John's lands upon the continent were in the hands of King Philip, save for a few scattered islands. A clerk from France had been the bishop's official legate in Durham, but he had no real power. So it was that responsibility for enforcing these nefarious schemes hatched by John fell largely upon the broad shoulders of Prior Bertram, the independent head of the English priory and school at Durham. In 1205 Edwin and I had received summons from Bertram. It boded no good; Annie shook her head and said she saw a dark cloud over Bamburgh church.

When we arrived, a young prebendarite (scholar) of Durham college showed us into the antechamber of Bertram's apartment. The simple elegance we saw there is still 'pressed upon my mind. The walls were sumptuously paneled in polished oak, but the furnishings were simple; a *prie-dieux* of golden oak with crimson cushion before a plain crucifix, and a dark trestle table set before one of the new sidewall fireplaces. Three chairs, also with crimson cushions, and a stool completed the furnishings. To the west, the tower window looked toward the river meadows; unglazed, 'twas shut against the wind by a finely carved shutter. The richness and simplicity of the chamber was perfectly balanced.

When the prior arrived, he set us down with a glass of wine ere he broke the news. I can still see the concern upon his troubled face, how his tonsured head seemed to bristle roundabout with wisps of reddish hair as if all a-stir. "Sir John, 'tis my misfortune to have to tell you that King John does not confirm you in Richard's grant of vicarage at Bamburgh. It was uncommon enough to grant it to a layman; had it not been for your vow and vision, you should not have held it from Richard. Yet your stewardship of the church lands has been above reproach. I ken far more than you wist (know). Of the few marks that come to you for your service to the church, you give tithe for the building, though none is required. Yet King John looks not upon the good of the land, but upon his pocket. He thinks to raise an army of mercenaries to retake his old Norman possessions. We English are sick of fighting French wars and sick of being taxed for them. But John feels the sting of his failures." 'Twas near treason Bertram spoke, but men then oft said what was upon their minds, and devil take the hindmost. Political statement was not equated with blasphemy; the state had not yet become our church.

"Despite the honesty of your vicarage, God now sees fit to relieve you of your vow." Bertram then explained John's intrigues; 'twas a legal tangle. The king was selling privileges everywhere; Richard's wholesale sale of offices prior to the Crusade began to look like child's play. John was also using every subtle twist of law and custom to garner more privileges to sell, whilst systematically robbing the English church of every shilling he could extract. His henchmen were the Bishop of Norwich and the arrogant Peter des Roches of Winchester, a Frenchman, a bishop who would continue to flatter the new young king Henry III even after John was gone. Peter's nefarious schemes brought enormous wealth and power into his crafty hands. Enough was paid to the pope for Innocent to look the other way and make des Roches his representative in England; and enough morsels were repaid the Crown to tempt our luxury-loving kings into settling that fox of a bishop as watcher over the English henyard.

King John in particular was self-indulgent to the point of scandal; much gossip came from court as to his appetites. One such was his hanging of the queen's suspected lover over her bed. Though the lady was of the inclination, no one knew when she might have had an opportunity. John lay a-bed with his Isabella far more than any ordinary man might, rising only to stuff himself gluttonously on dainties ere returning to his play. 'Twas such behaviour as killed him at last.

Bertram went on. "Edwin, since Durham has no hold on Bamburgh, 'twill be up to Norwich to appoint a priest. If John Forster so wishes, he may retain you as personal chaplain. I offer you the option to return to the community here. But I must also tell you that King John is refusing to appoint a new bishop for Durham. I have just been appointed vicar capitular, a mere figurehead to channel all the great revenues of Durham to the Crown. Whatever building was left unfinished when Bishop Hugh died remains incomplete, just as at Bamburgh." Bertram was sorrowful, and as frustrated as I. Edwin refused to leave Bamburgh, however, for he knew our need there as few did. The prior then reassured me that the deed to Bamburgh Hall would stand, though des Roches would require ruinous rents each year.

Despite the sovereignty of the King over all, as God's chosen representative holding the law and order of the kingdom within his hands, I could cheerfully have lopped off John's head as his father's knights had done for Beckett. But I bided my peace. Bertram, his big ruddy face staring at me earnestly, added; "You are disappointed. But as a true knight of Christ, surely you realize that the will of Heaven flows through all our lives. Be unattached to outcomes. Patience and perseverance and humility allow God's plan to work, not through one man, but through many. Pride is the trap of the world; what we achieve is not because of our own efforts, but because the Holy Spirit chooses to work through us for a time."

What Bertram said had merit. 'Twould have to be left in the lap of God. In our time, the king could manipulate the law, and little recourse was there for his subjects. Politics there certainly was, then as now; toadying and clever men, spending their lives on the knife-edge of royal favour, currying wealth and power from the throne. There will always be certain men who enjoy the risk of the game, just as outlaws enjoy the risk of their depredations. Such men were John of Norwich and Peter des Roches of Winchester; of the two, Peter was by far the greatest villain, both in my days and my son's.

The real winner in the quarrels over appointment was King John. Four of us sat at Bamburgh, two concerned for the church, and two sacking its revenues for the crown. Nostell and the Forsters fumed under the scraping Norwich and Winchester, whilst King John's clever intrigues filched money from all our pockets. There was a ditty the workmen sang that told it all: "Four little goats standing in a row, dressed all in silk with nowhere to go. Two did bleat and two did bow, and Bamburgh church came tumbling down." I hated to hear it; being King John's bleating goat suited me not.

The church did not fall down after all; new appointments were made after 1215 and repairs and rebuilding resumed. The chancel, so grandly planned, would be completed after our rebellion, though the tower waited till even my days were finished. Still, by Alfric and Manfred's art, I had seen Sts. Aidan's and Oswald's church well and truly begun, much as it is to this day.

The Forster Private Entrance into the Chancel, St. Aidan's.

King Richard had squeezed England for his wars, but
Glororum had benefited from the Crusade. There was always a nobility about Richard that John entirely lacked, but
John had learned the art of extracting money from the
kingdom very well. The next pinch we were to feel was from
his institution of custom duties. We had been making some
money from the wool trade with Flanders; now John began
wiping out all those profits. I was coming to my wit's end,
for our lands needed to be maintained, and our people kept
from poverty. To add to my woes, I had a beautiful and
brilliant daughter that soon needs must be betrothed.

Betwixt Robin and Raynaud, our fortunes which had
looked so bleak began to shift a little. Raynaud had been in
charge of the booty left by the marauders, stripping the dead
and searching the living. While those desperate men had few
possessions, still there was enough armour to sell and bring
a few shillings. The Crown, of course, collected its fifteen
per cent, but not all that was found trickled into the sheriff's
inventory. There were some silver coins and one particularly
fine bejeweled helm that managed to escape his accounting.

The fruit of the spoils was then divided into four parts:
one for Gib and his men at the castle, one to William of
Lucker and his men; one to Blaise and the men of Ellingham,
and one to us at Glororum. 'Twas meager enough pay for
such a day's work, but Robin allowed as how he could make
it better. "Uncle, let me take that helm to Flanders. With
Ben-Ami's help, I am sure we can turn a profit. If I sail from
Budle 'pon one of our fishing smacks, I can also take a load
of wool untaxed. I know where to sell, the buyer will keep
a tight mouth in his head. Ben-Ami can keep me 'prized of
goods that we might smuggle back in. The Jews should have
contacts here, also."

Raynaud agreed. His elder brother was Robert de Ros of
Yorkshire, near Beverly, one of the great barons of the north.
My young knight would have no trouble getting imported
goods as far as York. So the two concocted a network that
began to do an ever more profitable business as John's grasp

grew tighter and tighter upon the merchants and chartered towns. Smuggling became a profitable protest 'gainst unjust laws. Some of the greatest families in England and Ireland later based their wealth and might upon such clandestine conveyance.

Glororum's benefit was more indirect, but at least the rents and bribes and dues were kept paid. If only we had more land! Raynaud was preparing to ride home for his Christmas leave in 1206 when I bemoaned such to him. He gave me a wink and a jaunty salute. "I shall take care of it, Sire," he said, but I gave his words no further thought.

'Twas early in 1207 when I rode south with him again. He had mentioned our need to his brother, head of the Ros clan, as well as other plans I had no ken of then. Robert de Ros had an answer. His friend and ally, Peter de Brus, lord of Danby and Skelton, was scrambling to garner money—big money—to buy a privilege from the Crown. The wapentake, or county court of Langburgh at Cleveland, was for sale for the enormous sum of 400 marks. If a man were powerful enough to raise that much money, the revenues would provide not only riches, but influence. But even a man like Peter was hard put to find the geld. What he did have was land, with a fair amount only newly assarted, or brought into cultivation. Some of his holdings were scattered far from his seat of power at Skelton; it would behoove a prudent man to turn them to better use.

Peter de Brus also had larger ideas. With men like Robert fitz Walter and Robert de Ros and Eustace de Vesci, murmurings 'gainst John were beginning to emerge from secret corners. The barons of the north country were nigh surfeit with John's foolishness. The earls would need every knight they could get if matters came to a head. After much polite talk and subtle prodding to see where my loyalties lay, Peter at last agreed to sell me land near Derby, just south of Ashbourne. The price for forty virgates, mostly plowland, was eighty marks plus two palfreys, with yearly rent of five pounds and an oath of fealty. I was pleased with the bargain.

I later found that Peter was pleased also, for most of Derby was held by his enemy, William de Ferrers, a staunch supporter of the king.

Thus it was that in September of 1207 I was seized of the land later called Roston. The oath of the wapentake followed its own peculiar ancient custom. Rather than kneel and place my hands between the earl's as sign of service (as was wont among Normans), I strode forth and touched de Brus' sword, saying, "I am your man and will defend you by might of arms." Wapentake, indeed, meant "weapon taking." There was much pride in the ceremony, and 'twas only the northlands that held with the ancient custom.

Peter then handed me a square of turf cut from my new lands, saying, "With this turf I seize you of your land, in return for knight service and for rent of five pounds a year." The steward of Peter's estates made proper entries upon the rolls, and thus ended weary months of negotiation. My daughter would have dower land for her marriage, and Glororum could begin turning some of its worn-out plow-land back to pasture. But greater than all these, with the purchase of the farm, my feet were turned irrevocably toward Runnymeade. I had sold my sword to de Brus.

Such was beyond my ken at the time. I had only a weary sense of a deed well done when I alighted once again in Glororum courtyard. Tippie came running, throwing herself at me with squeals of delight. I had been months a-haggle, and little I'd seen of my daughter in the while. Though an old man nearing fifty, I was still hearty; I picked up the lass and swung her about as if she had been three 'stead of coming thirteen. "Heigh, Tippie!" My voice raised in rejoicing carried across centuries; I remember the instant as if 'twere yesterday. "I have bought us a farm in the south!"

"Ah, clever Pa," she laughed, "when may I see it? Come and let me fetch you some fresh cider; you must tell us all about it!" Her excitement kindled from my own, and she ran to fetch Margaret and her brother. Soon Old Hall was full of eager faces, asking questions and jesting how Dame

Fortune had at last dropped her veil and let us perceive her face. What none could know was how much I owed the Jews, for I had had to borrow heavily.

Boots was somber; she had bided at the stable as always till I could make time for her. "You have been so much away, m'lord; it has been lonely. And your family must come first. But my heart has been nigh broken with the waiting for you." What she said was true, but I knew no remedy. She never called me m'lord unless she was miffed. There was no great love lost betwixt my daughter and Boots. Still, a man needs do what he must. I spent extra time at the stable then, with her and the horses; they were coming along well. I had a great bay destrier with black points, built much like my favorite Black Stone; we worked him in the tiltyard regularly. As a match, I would set him 'gainst the blue fleabite roan, my second warhorse. Boots or Adam would weight both horses equally and we would set them in mock battle, seeing that they coursed straight and swerved cleanly. There was always young stock to be trained, also—destriers and hacks and palfreys. 'Twas work that kept me limber and youthful, much as did Boots' loving ministrations.

Cedric died in December of 1207; he simply took to his bed and called for Edwin to come shrive him, which he did, quietly. Like many an ancient holy man, Cedric then closed his eyes whilst his soul drifted from the cooling body. 'Twas wondrous to behold. A man might envy such a death for himself. Tippie, however, was upset; she was fond of the old priest. He had taught her to play chess, his one worldly vice.

My daughter was much like Herleve might have been, had she been well; still, she was her father's girl through and through. We rode and hawked and played at draughts. She came to my sitting room to read the Book of Hours; 'twas as much a comfort to her as to me. Later, I was to buy her another book, a small and precious book of Psalms. She took the problems of the vill to heart, not as one of equal humanity with the cottagers, as I was wont, but with a certain air of graceful proprietorship. She was truly a lady born.

Randall and Margaret had finally managed to produce a living child in 1206, a girl. There was some quarrel over the babe's name, but Margaret put her foot down. Though 'twas the custom to name children after their grandparents, only Randall thought we should saddle the poor child with Herleve's name. Annie herself went to Margaret, and gave prediction for the girl. "In the grey land she shall wed, and kings will rise from her bed." Truly, she did wed into the clan of the Stewarts. Margaret was content with this, knowing that royal blood flowed in her own veins, no matter how diluted. They decided between them that Herleve was a most unfortunate choice, and harbinger of ill. Instead, Margaret picked Mary, though she had never known my mother. Annie had at last paid my mother the greatest of compliments by lauding her accomplishments with herbs and simples. She made the new mother understand the woman-wisdom that filled the babe's great-grandmother would be inherent in the child if she but bore her name.

Tippie adored her little niece, but child-care chores were not her portion. Instead, as my granddaughter grew, Tippie became a mentor and teacher, so that Mary would carry not only my mother's name and wisdom, but also the certain air of nobility that she learned from Herleve's daughter.

There were times when I considered sending Tippie away to be schooled, but always I brought up short. Margaret had taught her the ways of court, and Elaine had taught her the fine arts of the needle. From Annie, she had learned of healing arts, and the proper address of the village people. From the priests, Tippie had learned to read and write and do simple sums, as well as her prayers. Robin had taught her to sing. There was no lack that could be benefited by sending the girl from home. Yet soon enough I would have to provide a husband for her, for she was not suited to a nunnery. I dreaded the thought; such a comfort she was to me in my old age.

Matters came to a head in 1208, in a way I might have foreseen had I not been so blind. 'Twas in September, and I was riding to Skelton with Raynaud at my back; 'twas time to renew my homage to Peter de Brus and to pay the rents due on the farm below Ashbourne. Hard scraping it had been to acquire the coin for payment, and the Jews too were calling for an interest payment on the loan. Worry had begun to turn my hair silver. But Raynaud seemed in a jaunty mood, and rode quite carelessly. I felt it behooved us to exercise more care, as bandits had increasingly taken to the roads due to John's loving ministrations. But my growls for caution went unheeded.

At long last, my knight companion turned and gazed at me thoughtfully. "Sir John, if you were but to say the word, I might take away many of your worries."

"How say you, man, that you might accomplish this? For already you ride most of the marches, and run hither and thither across the country 'pon my errands." I had grown near fond of the young man, and his brashness was wearing down beneath the weight of his duties. Nor had I to admonish him about the lasses for nigh five years, though he still charmed every woman upon the estate.

"I have but served as honest knight to a noble man." The thought wandered through my pate that flattery oft preceded an uncertain demand. But I said naught, and at length, Raynaud continued. "The last fourteen years have passed as quickly as a gale from the sea. 'Twas fourteen years that Jacob laboured for his beloved Rachel. Yet she was not as fair as Agnes, your daughter, whom I have watched bloom from a laughing child into a such a woman as might break the heart of kings. John, I wish to wed Tippie; I am willing to allow my brother to broker the marriage. But I can tell you myself that 'twould be of great advantage to you." Seeing the stunned look upon my face, he added gently; "No man could care for her more than I. And I believe that she cares for me, too."

Ah, how blind I had been! Of course. Beneath the ever-courtly manner he held for all women, Raynaud had always treated Tippie with something greater: an adoration. 'Twas so kin to my own feelings that I had near regarded him as something of a surrogate father for her. But suddenly, I recalled the day in Bamburgh churchyard when we buried Margaret, and he had taken the girl home before him on his horse. I had known even then that this day would come about, but chose to ignore it. My beautiful daughter, to be married to a man nigh old enough to be her father! And one born on the wrong side of the blanket, to boot, though his father had been rich and powerful, and Raynaud shared in his family's name. Could my heart bear such?

"Man, you are thirty-six, the lass is not yet fourteen. What is this you are asking of me?"

Raynaud smiled at me calmly. "I think that age makes no great difference where love binds fast. Would ye rather see her broken upon the rod of some poor young knight who cared only for her property? Her dowry needs must be small; what kind of son-in-law do ye think it will purchase? King John has heiresses for barter to knights able to pay. Agnes is a lady fit to wed a great baron, one of the Crown tenants who sit in power 'neath the king. And though I am a younger son, my family has resource and revenues that I may command."

"What you say is true. But my first thought is not for revenues or dower, but for the happiness of the maid."

"I have been her own true knight for many years; no other woman under the sun could tempt me away. But I feel that you speak now from a sense of your own loss; with such a daughter, a man could not help but wish to delay her marriage. Yet face it you must, for her woman's instinct will soon rouse her toward a husband."

Of course, he was right. Where might I find a more caring son-in-law, or one who would bide as one of us? But many obstacles set in our path. "Raynaud, I cannot give you a ready answer now; my heart is too full. But I will listen to your brother's offer. At any rate, wait we must. A wedding in church now is beyond the power of any man in the land."

King John's quarrels over appointment of a new archbishop at Canterbury to replace our old friend Hubert

Walter had led to Pope Innocent placing all of England under an interdict. When the monks of Canterbury had elected one of their number, and John had refused to confirm him, ordering them instead to elect John of Norwich, this they had done, but they had immediately appealed to the pope. Innocent then appointed a third man, Stephen Langton. Stephen was an Englishman, though he had studied in Paris. John refused to allow him to set foot in England, not because Langton was offensive, but simply because John's royal will had been balked and he was sulking. 'Twas also because the king had undoubtedly made plans with Norwich to gut the riches of Canterbury. Thus matters seesawed between king and pope for many months; at last, Innocent slapped his interdict upon our land. The churches were closed; no person might find comfort in the sacraments. There were no rites for our dead, no baptisms and no marriages. Of course, John retaliated by seizing the assets of all the churches, because, he said, they refused to perform their accustomed services.

Raynaud was not put off. "If wait we must, then wait we will. But I must take word of your decision to my brother Robert at Christmas." 'Twas a reasonable demand, and I gave him my pledge that he soon would have an answer. Marriages may be brokered by men, but 'tis the women who suffer through them. I could not do less than ask my daughter of her wishes in the matter.

To my surprise, Tippie seemed to already have her mind made up. "I wondered when he would ask. Had you asked me to marry another man, I would have refused. Next to my father"—she smiled coquettishly, lighting every dimple upon her face—"I love Raynaud the best. So it has always been, and I have been afire that he might wed another. But my heart has always known that his regard lay with me alone. Yet you must not let him guess at my eagerness. Put him off with fair words, father!"

"That has already been done, lass. Now we must think of what conditions we will settle upon. Your future means much to me; I am an old man and will not always be here to succor you. You know that the farm near Ashbourne will be your marriage portion?"

"Aye. But Raynaud must promise to allow me to ride home as often as I wish. I will not be stuck away in some country vill, far from kin. Besides, Randall needs my wisdom. I must keep an eye upon the affairs of Glororum."

I near choked, but the amusement stayed in my throat. How like my daughter to take on the airs of a queen, even at her tender age. But she had the truth of it; Randall oft needed her sharp criticism to stay his hand from some foolish endeavor. "I am proud that you think so much of the efforts of your fathers, that you wish to preserve the work of our hands. I agree that 'tis a valid concession. But even more, the deeds to New Farm needs must be made in your name. Look what happened to your Aunt Maud!" And I told her how mother had taken care to see that the property at Hutton was placed in my sister's name, and how providential that had been. 'Twas not said between us, but Raynaud's age made it near certain that he would precede my daughter in death.

"Yes, father, that must be arranged. And you must also tell my husband the secrets of not begetting children, year after year. I will not be a brood sow for any man!" I blushed, but she merely stared at me intently and went on. "I am glad that you find comfort with Ellen, but we think it wise that no children have come from that union." So my peccadillos were common grist for household gossip! Only Tippie could have told me with such poise.

I turned again to the dower arrangements, for speaking of money is ever more comfortable than dredging up the intimacies of the heart. Yet after all was eventually settled, I did give Raynaud that which my daughter sought. The couple eventually had two sons, John and Maurice, and a daughter, Maud. There were no more bairns to break Tippie's health and destroy her spirit, as happened so often with the wives of country knights.

At Christmastide of 1208, Raynaud took our requests to his eldest brother, Robert. As part of the marriage settlement, de Ros agreed to pay off the debts upon the land, upon the condition that the vill be named Roston, after the family. 'Twas easily settled upon. However, we all agreed that if the interdict lasted over two years, the marriage would take place at common law, just as was happening all over the kingdom. 'Tis never wise to let the iron cool too much ere striking. Thus the couple went to live at Roston in the spring of 1210, with only Edwin's quiet blessing to consecrate their marriage. 'Twould be 1213 ere the interdict was lifted from off the land; the couple was married then in the Galilee chapel at Durham, by Bertram himself.

A walloping burden was taken from my back when Tippie became betrothed to Raynaud, but others would soon come to replace it. Meantime, the settling of the new vill, the ploughing of the newly assarted land, and the building of a new hall-and-chamber manor house took every effort I could give for two long years. Boots took to riding south with me, for I greatly needed her solace. I had never worked so hard in all my days born.

Yet good thereby came, as folk grew accustomed to Boots riding at my back. Days were coming when I would sore need her company, need even more her care and her unquestioning loyalty.

Chapter 25

The Rebels

Spring of 1208 smiled and teased like a maiden at court, nor was she less fair. A gown of fairest green she wore, brilliant and shimmering, with no blush of drought or of snow or any other blight. Her skies fell down her back in deepest blue, and a tiara of woolly clouds crowned her sunrises with rosy peaches set in burnished gold. A girdle of yellow daffodils she wore—they drifted everywhere—and the scent of violet and apple blossoms followed her days. 'Twas no wonder that love walked with Spring that year.

Young Henry, smitten by the charms of Spring, saw her reflected in the bonny eyes of Jane of the Waterford. No less bonny were her father William's lands at the Ford and at Etal. Henry the Grey left no grass crushed 'neath his destrier's hooves as he rode south to arrange the betrothal. He was an old man of eighty-five, but his wit was clear, his body thin but straight as a lance. Already Henry Grey had made a will 'gainst his death, which left Colin's Wood to young Henry. He desired that Henry be known as his son, to replace those he had lost; one to the church, and one to God.

It bid fair that Jane would at the least inherit Waterford, for only her and her sister Mary were left of five children. Jane was the elder, nigh as old as our Henry himself, who had just turned 22 in February. But William the father would not marry his daughters off to just anyone. The lasses must needs have husbands to care for the land as William himself had cared for it. Henry Grey persuaded the old baron to loosen his grasp and let his eldest daughter marry our Henry ere covetous Time wore the bloom from her face and faded her hopeful smile.

Thus it was that in May of 1209 we attended at their common-law vows; though the interdict still held, a most joyous occasion it was. The bride, like my Tippie, had her wits about her, and she was as beautiful a lass as any man might wish. Slender of figure, brown of hair and blue of eye, Jane could ride and hawk and hunt, then, not the least fatigued, return home to set her house in order. Annie, of course, did not attend the wedding, but she "saw" the newlyweds. "'Tis well for Henry," she said, "for in that maid is his fortune." And so it proved, for in addition to his own innate canny charm, Henry had an ally for life. Some couples seem to spin God's blessings out of the air when they come together; Henry and Jane were such.

Also in June of '08—for Spring was not yet through with our hearts—Margaret, Robin, Tippie, and Baby Mary rode with me to Berwick. King William was sitting at the old castle there for the summer, and Margaret wished to take the baby for her grandparent's blessing. Robin and I longed to visit once again with Kenneth and Eadra; Robin did not oft get to visit his father, so busy was he with the affairs at Bamburgh. And Tippie, well, Tippie yearned to see what the women of the court were wearing, and what they were gossiping about. She was still at the age when golden threads blinded her to the stink of politics that arose from the armpits of the court.

When I returned to the castle after three days with Kenneth, Duncan cornered me with a somber look. My heart fell, for dickering with Duncan oft took the wind out of a man. Yet what transpired proved to be a blessing, not for my days, which were rapidly fading, but for my son's. Aethelfritha had presented Duncan with a late-life son in 1199; they had called him David. The lad was healthy

enough, but as a page in the court of William, the boy
showed little promise. Like King William's dead brother,
Malcolm the Maiden, young David had a pious streak, and
a thirst for learning beyond the arts of war. He took to Latin
like a reborn priest, and to ciphers and logic; but at target
shooting, he was lucky if not wounded by his own arrow. In
short, he was an embarrassment to his father.

Aethelfritha wrung her hands and told Margaret that she
knew not what to do, for the lad was being nigh ruined in
his raising at court. Then Margaret—good common-sense
Margaret—offered the haven of Glororum for her young
brother. Edwin, she said, could teach him, and Raynaud
would have the patience to set him aright in his training. We
had far fewer lads at the farm now; three pages and two
young squires, and sorely needed new blood. Thus after they
had decided among themselves, Duncan came to ask the
boon of me. I could only think of my own sons, how my
sister Maud had saved my William from ruin when he was
in so much difficulty, and how Henry had fallen into such
fortune at Cornhill. There was only one answer I could
make. David gathered his few possessions and rode home
with us. There are bonds that form between people, tran-
scending the wrappings of time and circumstance. Such
happened between Robin and young David. Robin told me
later that looking at the lad on the journey home minded
him of the same journey he had made at his own father's
back so many years ago. And David, with the child's inborn
instinct for true friendship, turned immediately to Robin as
his benefactor. 'Twas sealed ere we reached the Spindlestone
and home.

David, though now ten, became to Robin the son he had
been denied. Indeed, Robin insisted upon taking the lad to
visit Mary Rose, 'pon his yearly visit after Michaelmas, when
the affairs of the vill and demesne were fairly settled. Maud
was to tell me some years later that David was a comfort to
them both, and I marvelled again at how we find our own
true loves despite the wanderings of blind Fortuna.

'Twas after Michaelmas, too, in 1209, that good Henry the Grey died peacefully of old age at Colin's Wood. He was eighty-six. He had accomplished the last of his life's work when Henry and Jane were wed, and the stewardship of the land he had so cared for was in firm hands. I bethought that God had blessed him as Henry had blessed many another; I could only wish my life to be so well spent.

Young Henry's good fortune must have set Randolph's head abuzz. My eldest son had spent much time at Alnwick, and the politics of power and wealth had not been lost upon him. Eustace de Vesci was as grasping and parsimonious as his father had been before him. Yet by petition to the king's court, he had carefully added to his lands and rents. Not so cautious was many another great lord. In constant litigation, fortunes were gambled on purchase of offices, rights of wardship over the estates of minors, and speculation on property rights. The Forsters could afford none of this, but Randall had one knight to play in the game of riches; his widower father. Widows and their crown lands were for sale by the king; luckily, they or their families could often outbid the greedy suitors. It mattered not to John, as long as his purse was filled. Often, it mattered mightily to the lady.

Early in the year of 1210, all unbeknownst to me, Randall went to the sheriff of Yorkshire to solicit the hand of Nichola, widow of Walter de Fors, on my behalf. The de Forses were a prominent and wealthy family; though Walter had been but a younger son, his estate was a juicy plum. The lady herself was cautious. She would not be bargained for ere she had ridden north to meet the prospective husband and view his ancestral lands.

The lady and her retinue came to visit on a soft day in early summer. The sky was warm and blue, the clouds close, and there was but little wind. I had been working the horses with Boots, and we had stopped awhile to find love among the blankets. Scarce was I dressed than a page came running to tell me that we had company. Grumpily, I walked up to

Old Hall, wondering why my son could not handle such routine affairs himself. Margaret, large in pregnancy, stood with a look of distress as Randall introduced the widow. Nichola wrinkled her nose, for I smelled of horse and sweat and god knows what else. My nose also twitched, for I scented a rat, Randall by name.

Quite courteously, I proffered the lady a tour of our lands. Randall was beside himself at my appearance, for I would not change from my greasy work jerkin; yet he rode along. The tour was necessarily short for the widow rode unwillingly, much like an outraged sow dragging along 'pon the end of a rope, especially when we stopped at our great barn. In the still, damp air, the tannery and slaughterhouse were at their most noisome. After, the party immediately went to Old Hall for nooning. I had the lads take the horses to the stable whilst we dined on pease and onions and brown bread. Such peasant fare but convinced the lady that country knights, like old boars, only grow ranker with age.

Nichola and her men-at-arms and her lady's maid departed that same afternoon. They would not, she said, trouble us for accommodations for the night. Randall, I told her, would be very happy to accompany them as far as Chatta's, where she might find lodging ere proceeding homeward in the morning. He gave me a furious look, knowing he would have to bide with her squealing the livelong way.

My canny Boots, with a most innocent air, brought up the lady's horse herself. I could not look upon her, or my face would have betrayed me; I knew her mind as well as my own. Near ashamed am I to say it, but between Nichola's saddle blanket and her palfrey's tender back, Boots had inserted a cockleburr. There promptly ensued a great haste of parting, when the widow deposited her ample arse upon the saddle. Randall could in nowise keep up.

To say my eldest son was incensed would be to make too little of the matter. Yet I rebuked him but mildly. "If ye think I need a wife, ye should have asked me. But I tell ye now, one wife in a lifetime more than suffices for this old knight. If ye wish another, make leave to marry her yourself."

"But 'twould have been simple, were you not such a stubborn old fool! I had the sheriff on my side"—Randall was obviously out some money—"and her lands were wide and fair."

"Under tenancy to what great lord?" I asked. "Marrying money is the most arduous way in the world to earn it. We owe knight service for our Crown lands, and rents and service to Durham and to Peter de Brus. We can owe no more debts." I was as penurious as Eustace on that count.

"But you ride the march for the king still, and Raynaud pays the service for Roston. We have always made the yearly rent for the southern fields and forest to Durham, nor have they disseized us of any holdings, though John now collects the rents through his chancellor." Bishop Philip had died in 1208; no more pretence was made of allowing the Church any say over the palatinate of Durham; all monies were funneled directly into John's purse.

"And do you yourself now do so little that it makes you wish to take on more service to pay for the lands of a carping fat widow? I am an old man. I will not undertake to bite off more than can be chewed. The way to wealth for a country knight is but to work your own land cannily, play politics gently, and pray for felicitous weather." Still, 'twas many days ere my eldest son spoke to me again.

In 1210, Randall and Margaret produced another girl child. They called her Eleanor, after the Old Queen, but our little queen was taken home by the angels ere she was three, of the great coughing sickness. Many were the children of the vill that were afflicted that year, though few of the others died. Perhaps, I thought, 'tis true; that the sins of the father lie upon the sons...and daughters. Eleanor was Randall's favorite.

Two autumns before Eleanor took ill, I spent much time at the side of Peter de Brus and Robert de Ros. The two men differed like sod and stone; yet together they built a fortress for our hopes. Peter, like myself, had been on Crusade; he was tough and battle-hardened, a powerful man though easily trusted, for his word was his honour. Also like myself, he was not overly tall, though none of us were as small as that fierce old man, Mowbray, who stood no taller than a dwarf. Robert too was honourable in his allegiances, but exceeding canny in his ventures. He was tall, ruddy of face, and bluff of manner. Yet when dealing with Robert, one was wont to count his fingers, ere one or more might have disappeared in his hearty clasp of friendship.

By 1211, the winds of rebellion began blowing everywhere across the northland. No spark had as yet been lit to scorch the country with the wildfire of war. But the free men of the north were murmuring, and we were all of us tied by blood or marriage or land, the earls and churchmen and knights of Northumberland and Yorkshire and Durham. We would not be toadies to an English king, for had we not once held the heart and soul of the kingdom?

Peter had made me privy to the plans of the great earls, fitz Walter, de Vesci, de Percy, Mowbray, and many others. Robert yet urged us to caution. 'Twas not that the kingdom was quite in bankruptcy due to John's foolishness, but that the great Crown tenants hoped to avert such a calamity. They saw it coming, and not far off. Even some of the earls from Lincolnshire south had begun to murmur in their sleeves, and many powerful churchmen with them, though few openly acknowledged it. Across all the land, the customary rights of manors and of churches were being violated. Our forest rights were being harshly curtailed by the king's foresters, who had the power of life and death over anyone caught inside John's woods. Only the very rich could afford the privileges that John was selling, and they were feared that tomorrow both money and privilege would be gone. The stakes of rebellion began to go higher.

'Twas a nigh intolerable situation for those of us who sat in rank 'neath the great earls of the realm, the mesne lords, those in the middle. Though we erst held our land from the king, our fealty was to those lords above us in rank and power. When rebellion severed their fealty to the Crown, we needs must go along, willy-nilly. Not that I had any use for King John, but the thought disturbed my sleep that if our rebellion failed, we mesne barons would pay dearly. I could only ask protection from God in the righteousness of our cause; indeed, He was to hear me.

I had ridden to pay Peter my yearly homage in that fall of 1211, when he showed me a thing most strange and curious. As we sat with Robert de Ros at a table in Peter's solar, a large sunny room on the third floor with several windows of Italian glass, sipping fall's bounty of fresh cider, a clerk brought in a scroll. Opening it, Peter traced with his fingers the odd lines that covered the parchment. 'Twas what he called a chart, a sort of picture drawn of all England, as if looking down upon it from Heaven itself. At first, I could make no sense of it; then when Peter traced the coastline at Budle bay and the rock of Bamburgh, sudden understanding lit in my noggin. "Aye," I said, excited, "there is Alnwick, and there, Robert's castle at Wark, near to Henry's Colin's Wood. There is the castle at Berwick..." And so I went from mark to mark upon that parchment, recognizing many of the places where I had often ridden. All were in their proper places with the sun's alignment, and with the north star. 'Twas a very great marvel.

Peter's clerk then read off the names of castles and of castellans, northland earls and lords both great and small. All were secretly united, whispering of rebellion. But some of the strongest castles still belonged to King John, and they were set 'gainst us. Seeing those documents made some of my caution depart, for the king's castles were few in number and his army largely made up of hired lances from Flanders.

Yet there were strong earls who would remain in the king's camp—de Ferrers of Derby and Ranulf of Chester. Robert held to his caution, nor would he join the plot with de Vesci and fitz Walter to murder the king ere the year was out. Little as I loved John, that same caution held me. As it turned out, the betrayers were themselves betrayed. Eustace fled to Scotland; his wife, like Robert's, was a natural daughter of William the Lion, and her lands were but a day's ride from Alnwick. Fitz Walter sought shelter with relatives in France. A few barons lost their freedom; some lost land and rents to John. Some needs must send their children to court as hostages as well. The great Crown tenants and richer barons could afford to pay the cost and wait a little longer. The time for rebellion was not yet ripe.

In 1213, John levied a ruinous scutage, a tax to pay his foreign troops. He was still smarting from his losses upon the continent, and vowed to retake his former possessions. John Softsword would never be the man to do so, though he was making alliances with Germany and Flanders. We men of the north were weary with the drain of men and money to the ever-quarreling lands of France. We remembered well when our fealty had been to William the Lion of Scotland, and our land prospered and was at peace. But John listened to no one. "I am King," he fumed, "and I WILL rule!"

Yet clever he was, our king. In 1213, he went crawling to the pope, making amends. Stephen Langton, Innocent's choice for Archbishop of Canterbury, was at last allowed to enter the country and take his robes. England was released from interdict, and there was great rejoicing in the land when once more the church bells rang and sang and clanged.

In our deadly chess game, we now had a bishop 'pon our side, and a very doughty churchman he was. First off, he met with us on August 25, 1213, in St. Paul's Church. There he read aloud the coronation charter of Henry I, with its ancient guarantee of rights, according to the customs long held in the land. These, he asserted, were the basis for legal claims in dealing with John. Exile had done nothing to endear the king to him, but Stephen was not vindictive nor did he wish the king bodily harm. Our archbishop truly had the welfare of the kingdom at heart, and wished to redress our grievances by legal precedents.

The year 1213 brought us many another blessing. Edwin said 'twas because God was pleased that once again our churches would be alight with the candles of our lives. On April 13, a son was born to Margaret and Randall, my first grandson. The night was fair, and like the old priest Duns upon the night of my own birth, I stood watch 'neath the stars. In them, were hung the portents for the lad's life. Just before the third hour after midnight, they brought me the news that the babe was wailing and strong; Margaret named him Alfred, for the glory of her ancestry.

And I saw that night, much of his Fate. Saturn was in Leo, the sign of kings, sitting 'pon my left hand in the northwest. In the service of a king, when his hour seemed darkest and his strength ebbing, Alfred would rise to his succor. As our new knight was born, Jupiter rose over the eastern horizon, followed closely by the moon, then by Mars. Though his fortunes might ebb and wane, Dame Fortuna would remain ever with my small grandson, and his strong sword would be gain to him of both honour and riches. These things I wrote upon a parchment, and gave them to his mother for safekeeping.

Then, because I am growing forgetful, I will tell you now that the lad was both tall and strong for his age, and followed me ever, for the rest of my life. He was in temperament like my William, but I was better able to oversee his training. Indeed, when he was but four, I began his practice with an oaken sword and a wattle shield, much as my own training had begun. I would not have him a bully, as was Baldwin, but he would be a page to be reckoned with when we sent him to de Ros at age seven. That was the year I departed this earth, but of this I do know: Alfred stood beside young Prince Edward, and became one of his most trusted advisors during his ascent to the throne. And Alfred was ever a warrior to be reckoned with.

With the lifting of the interdict, many marriages were celebrated in spring of 1214, among them that of my nephew, Henry Essh, Maud's remaining son, to a daughter of Ruald fitz Alan of Richmond. Indeed, Ruald was elder brother of the knight Alan who had accompanied Stephen to the Holy Land. Richmond was a wealthy estate, though Ruald ha' had to bring suit to restore it to his family. Helewise brought to Hutton a rich dower that enabled Henry's manor to prosper throughout all of his short life. After William returned from the Holy Land, he stood beside Henry as steward, and 'twas by William's strength that the estate was sustained in the lean years after Hutton Henry was killed in the rebellion. 'Twas with the greatest sorrow we saw that young valleti struck down; our only consolation was in the new son he left. Helewise named the boy Henry after his father, and it was he who at last built a church and rebuilt the vill at Hutton Henry, so named after his father. Young Henry Essh, like Henry Grey, lived into his eighties and maintained his land and family with honest propriety.

The year 1214 was a robber gatekeeper, taking toll of our lives and fortunes. All was lost in France for John Softsword. Though John had had some success in Poitou, his vassals refused to fight 'gainst Philip Augustus, claiming the French king as their overlord. John could only gnaw at his mustache in frustration. Then John's carefully wooed allies were roundly defeated at Bouvines. Thus were all the old continental fiefs lost for good, in a battle where John was not even in attendance. The wealth of the kingdom had gone toward their endowments and to pay John's mercenary troops, for but few English would serve. Our lives and lands had been spent like water for naught.

Peter de Brus told me in September that all the realm was coming together behind the leadership of the northern barons. We ha' had enough of John and his hollow pomp, his greed and lechery, his dishonourable and treacherous ways. There began a great silent movement of men back and forth across the land, sealing alliances and readying for war.

I was eager to serve, but God held my hand awhile yet. In October, a plague sailed into Berwick 'pon a ship from Venice. Many were the townsfolk that were stricken, and the grip of Satan was so strong that most of them died. My beloved uncle Sir Kenneth came ill nigh at once; as he was breathing his last, Eadra too fell ill, only to die a day later. Robin and I rode forth with the greatest sorrow to see to their affairs; the town had buried them already. Full a third of the burghers hied to the churchyard sods ere the plague was over. We feared the pestilence would spread across the land, but a time of great cold came sweeping down from the north, adding to our hardship. When it moderated, the back of the pestilence was broken.

Christmas of 1214 was a sad and uncertain affair, both for the realm and the family. Robin was his father's only heir, but to obtain justice in John's courts required more money than a country steward could scrape from off his shoes. The mill and tannery were subject to ruinous death heriot, and the Crown insisted 'pon yearly rent to boot. Robin shook his head. "The owning of that property would rend me of wit and purse. My father is no longer there, nor was his heart ever in that machinery, as 'twas in leveling a lance or raising a song. I must sell." And so he did, though it took some months of dickering. Robert de Ros, then in the flush of power, at last gave him near what 'twas worth.

Robin had already made me privy as to what he would do with the geld, nor could I find quarrel with his plans. "Uncle," he said, "I wish to build a house in Durham town. We are growing old, the two of us. Soon I hope to make a home nearer Mary Rose, a home that David in his turn may inherit after me. I will serve you for three years yet, then I wish to be left to my own devises. If—God forbid—aught should happen to you, I will not serve Randall. My life is now too short to deal with his aggravation. 'Twould be best if you found a patient knight to administer for him ere I leave."

"My dearest Robin, I understand your request, though my heart is heavy at the thought of your leaving. You have more than earned the respite, for Glororum nor Bamburgh would have prospered without the labour of your head and hands. I will surely assist you in the building of your new house, and we shall undertake between us to find a steward for Glororum." My mind traveled back to Malta, and to France. "We have been through so much together; 'tis more like we are brothers than cousins. I can never repay you for my life; I can only pray that the love of Christ ever enfolds you and brings you sound unto Heaven."

Robin bowed his head. "Amen," he murmured quietly.

Chapter 26

Runnymeade

The death of Sir Kenneth and his jolly wife, Eadra, in the autumn of 1214, began gloomy times for us all. Trouble seized Glororum by the throat nor would it leave off till we were near spent. Indeed, through the next three years—though deemed momentous by later history—my memories falter, threading a maze of disquiet. I was coming nigh to fifty-six, an aging man who could better recollect the days of youth than the marchers we entertained last week. Yet in the turmoil of our rebellion, which often left this weary knight bedazed, certain scenes remain as clear and bright as if the same sun were shining upon them still.

Among such was the arrival at Chatta's of Peter de Brus, upon the feast of St. Bernard of Clairvaux, in August of 1214. He came riding quietly, with but two men at his back, and he sent Chatta's son, Simon, after me as hard as he could pelt. I was at mass, but left as soon as I beheld the herald at the door. Something momentous had happened. Peter was refreshing himself with bread and ale in Chatta's upper room when I arrived. I see him yet, a stocky man with dark hair grey at the temples, his armour hidden 'neath a padded surcoat of yellow silk. Peter had a great fondness for yellow. "John has sent secret messengers to close all the castles he fortified in 1212. Philip of Oldcotes will be moving more men and material north, and Bamburgh and Norham will shut their gates, as has Newcastle. John himself is on his way home; all is lost in France. At Bouvines. The allies were soundly trounced, though John himself was absent. He kens too well that England will soon be alight."

"Then we gambled well when we refused both service and scutage for France. Yet that was within our rights, as Northumbrians, for our service has ever been limited to cornage, the patrol of the border."

"Aye, but John is clever enough to know that other barons, even those nigh London itself, will now refuse the scutage. Rather than reduce his mercenary troops, he has ordered them on to England; 'tis plain he sees war."

"Had he but meant his promises when we met at Wallingford last November! That charter which he gave to restore our ancient custom and liberty, he revoked within a week." I was bitter; we had been sanguine that reason had won the day. With John, that was ever too much to hope.

"Aye. Our bonny John seems never to learn." Peter was sarcastic. "Had he the fortitude to hold to bold effort, 'stead of circumventing all the while, expending his Plantagenet energy on sly schemes, then he might have won the day in many a circumstance. He shall never change, so long as he lives. Remember the prophecies of Peter of Wakefield?"

We were both silent, remembering the days of May of but a year ago. John had called up all the barons with their knights to Kent, to meet a French invasion fleet that bid fair to land. Raynaud and I and two squires rode with de Brus; and upon those fields of southern England, the rebellion that had fired the north spread to the barons of all England. Much talk there was of the prophecies of a half-mad monk, Peter of Wakefield, who foretold the king's doom. John's new navy repelled the French fleet, but the whispers that began in Kent were unsinkable. The prophecies of Peter of Wakefield began to be self-fulfilling with their retelling.

"What of de Vesci?" I asked. "I mind how angry John was when the Vatican made him grant Eustace and Robert fitz Walter safe-conduct home last year. They held the ear of the pope's envoy, pouring into it how their rebellion of 1212 was only because of the interdict, and John's excommunication." It made us smile, for those worthies had turned John's weapons to their own use.

"Aye," Peter laughed. "It served their purpose. But John evened the field. He complained to *his* papal envoy, and Innocent sent a special letter to Eustace to tell him to stop troubling our poor king."

"And did not John then order the destruction of Alnwick, 'pon the very day he issued the safe-conduct?"

"Ah, but that was in part revenge for another matter entirely. Had ye heard the story of John and Eustace's wife?" When I shook my head, Peter chuckled and went on. "Ye ken well the lechery of John, how if a lady takes his eye, he will move heaven and earth to have her. 'Tis all the sweeter if he can humiliate her husband by so doing. Thus it happened with Lady de Vesci. But being of clever wit, she appointed that she would only come to John's bed under cover of night. Then she set a squire to discover a whore for her, and she sent that worthy woman to John's bed on her behalf, charging her to let no one see her face. Well, John was little interested in her face. But next day, when he was taunting de Vesci of his conquest, Eustace rose in the company and told John how he had been made a fool of. Then he fled, as he had sent his wife on before. But John bided his time. He sent a message with the firing of the castle, saying how hot his love had burnt."

"Ah, well; that sounds like John. But it minds me that danger walks ever with his presence. What are we to do next?"

"I am on my way to Alexander of Scotland. That young man may yet hold our fortunes in his hands." Alexander, but sixteen years old, had just succeeded his father, William the Lion, to the throne of Scotland, a reign that had lasted through most of my own days. It grieved me to see my old friend King William pass on. Peter continued. "John has boasted that he will hunt the red fox cub from his den. As ye ken, England has no right to fealty from the Scots, though

John would like to make it so, as did his father before him. But there is more of the fox to Alexander than his hair; John needs look to his own lair."

"I, too, have relatives at Scotland's court. Is there aught I may do?"

"Nay, John. I have but come to warn you. There is a time when I will call you to our side. Your present situation is precarious enough, for you hold land at Bamburgh of the king. Nor is your income enough to gamble away your patrimony without just cause. Bide ye, and pass fair words to Philip of Oldcote when he stops with you. Men's loyalties will now run to and fro, like bees to summer flowers, gathering honey where they may. We are old soldiers, you and I, and loyalty sits upon our saddles. But 'tis not so with other men. Bide your peace, and let no man know which way your lance will fall."

'Twas good advice, and I kept to it. But there was much dickering, back and forth, with bribes and threats to keep the stronger vassals tied to the Crown. Robert de Ros let none see his rebellion till the fateful week of Runnymeade. In the nonce, John made him a rich man, granting him the castle of Carlisle and many another benefice, to hold Robert to his side. Robert owned several castles, some hard by the few known to be left to the king, and the Crown was headlong to constrain him. To Robert, 'twas naught but good business.

In March of 1215, when the grass was all a-greening, Peter sent word that we were to "gather at Stamford for Easter Mass." I had settled the affairs at home as best I might. With the land in such turmoil, I asked Tippie to stay with us at Old Hall, even after Christmas. She held my second grandson, John, upon her lap as I beseeched her, and she conceded to that wisdom on his behalf. Scotland, after all, was but a few hours away. Whereas Albert was of stern stuff, swaggering and playing at swords, John was a laughing babe. With his soft flat brown hair and Tippie's eyes, John at two still held the ability to climb upon my lap and twine his fingers 'round my heart. If aught befell the lad, part of my heart would be forever stilled.

Raynaud returned to Roston as soon as word came, to leave instructions for spring plowing with his reeve. I would meet him there on the way to Stamford. Randall had instructions to take the family away to Scotland upon the slightest hint of approaching war; he needs must keep men with ears open at Bamburgh and at Chatta's. He was solemn in his duty, for his was the hardest part. 'Twould be of no consequence should I be caught 'pon the wrong side of rebellion; he had yet our land and blood to maintain. "Make no move toward either side till this war be settled," I cautioned, "then offer fealty as needed. Our fathers gave life to this land, and are buried here. 'Tis our trust for yon children"—I nodded toward Alfred at play, with John toddling eagerly behind him, like some small squire.

'Twas a gamble we took, but men whose souls are part of a common land know a kinship with one another that lies beyond words. We knights and barons of the north country—Northumbria, Durham, and York—were entwined not just in marriages and alliances, but in the land which gave its life to our common heritage. I went to Edwin to be shriven ere Easter brought its war and woes, and he said it better. "John, you have a soul that ever seeks the star of personal liberty in the heaven of social justice. Always you will rebel 'gainst tyranny; always you will love this earth of which you are such a part. Go with God, and know our prayers go with you."

Annie, too, prophesied for me, though she was now bent and old beyond the years of most women. Without knowing the words that Edwin had spoken to me, she said a passing strange thing. "Ye have marched for justice before. Ye will woo death for it again, for it runs as the blood of your soul. Not in this lifetime, for ye'll come home with no hair harmed; but in lives untold and countries unknown. In the blessings of sun and moon, wind and rain, may God preserve ye." She rocked a little from side to side, and softly crooned:

"To the south all armed ye'll wend, in hopes the Kingdom soon will mend. The folk will rise and the folk will utter, words the King can only mutter. The words once said will ever stay, but Death will take him soon away." She opened her eyes then, and gave me a wink. "I shall not be here when ye return; I go to dry my mother's tears. Keep my memory alive, and I'll greet ye again in a few short years."

So whilst the prospect of war daunted me but little, the realization of the love I bore to all the folk of Hall and vill near overwhelmed me. For the first time in my life, the spectre of mortality stalked my thoughts. Yet in our love, and in the deeds we do for God, I thought—these and our children and the land wherein we lay our bones—this is our immortality. And I was content.

Not so my Boots. "Ye may speak of justice and of love, John, but ye have left me no reckoning. Without you, I have naught, not life nor heart nor place upon the earth. Take me with you. I shall arm you and keep you warm at night. Take whatever soldiers ye wish, but take me also to keep your tent and horses." I could not argue, for I knew she was right; nor did I wish to be separated from her in the vicissitudes of lingering war. In the last few years, she had become my strong legs and arms, my willing aide in every enterprise. I could not do without her.

So we rode to Stamford, with Raynaud and our two squires, Richard and Gilbert. There we listened to Stephen Langton, as he exhorted us to moderation in our demands upon the king, even as he blessed us. He had been dickering with John in our cause since January, as had Robert de Ros and many others; even William, the old Marshal, made mild words on our behalf. Yet John trusted no one, nor would he listen to reasonable argument.

On May 17, the king had removed his haughty person and his court to Windsor. The knights had had enough of endless words, of negotiation and argument. 'Twas only the rich that were getting richer; justice was no closer than before. Filled with fury, the common knights trampled at the gates of London town. If all else failed, we would open its docks to the French; Prince Louis would become our king. Yet miracles live within the hearts of men. The merchants and clerks and artisans of London espoused our cause; our squires and hostlers and servants had made their way among them and made known our grievances in the course of normal trade. The people of London town found our wrongs matched those John had placed upon their backs. They opened their formidable gates, and made cause with us. There was dancing in the streets that night!

Many then were the favored tenants who abandoned the Crown. Robert de Ros, William de Aumale, William de Fors were among those great barons who at last turned their faces from the king. A new charter of demands was drawn, and a committee of Twenty-Five chosen to enforce the charter upon John. These latecomers constituted no small part. Peter de Brus shunned the Twenty-Five, as did Robert Grelley. "I do not wish to spend the rest of my life shackled to the king," Peter said. "I will fight for our rights, but I will not sit in justice upon John for the rest of our days."

The charter the earls had drawn was given to Stephen Langton, our new Archbishop, for approval. "If ye wish consideration, Sirs, then ye must hold to moderation. Let me rewrite your charter, holding to your demands, but couching them in such a way that John will be less likely to resist." So all agreed, but constrained him to hold to the year of 1189 as being the dividing line between good and evil custom upon the land. In the end, many barons felt that Langton had not held to their charges. John, on the other hand, complained that the charter took his kingdom from him, though he knew not who its final author was.

In June, the king rode out from Windsor to meet with us upon the field of Runnymeade. Most of the knights, like Raynaud and myself, were camped upon the moor outside of Staines, where the great barons sat. Boots and I held one small tent in a field corner, not likely to be much noticed. 'Twas for that reason I had carried a poor brown tent, rather than one more fit. Raynaud pitched next to us, a large golden tent with red upon the scallops over the door. He and the two squires were spoiling for a fight, whereas I was cautious on Boots' account. There were a great many ruffians about, for every peddler and mountebank from London had come out to watch King John receive his comeuppance.

I sit to tell you now that 'twas the Crusade all over again for me. The weather was exceeding hot, with drouth. Dust rose in choking clouds from 'neath the horses' hooves; the fields had turned brown from the passing of so many. The young knights had styled us as the Army of God and Holy Church, and 'twas indeed a crusade for them. For me, 'twas naught but hardship, and I recalled too well the road from Acre, where so many had died 'neath the blazing Eastern sun.

A tent was pitched for the king in the midst of the field of Runnymeade, to keep him from the sun. A great gay affair it was, with broad stripes of red and white. Boots was to remember it vividly, across many centuries. Had it not been for her, bringing me water from time to time, I know not how I would have endured. The sun glared off our armour as it had in the Holy land, and the air was stifling. None dared break ranks, as we stood 'pon our horses the livelong day, well into afternoon. Each great baron had a coterie of men 'round him, and we stood with de Brus. All formed a semi-circle before John's tent, a tower wall of men and mounts, bristling at all points with lance and sword. Knights of Percy and Mowbray and Lacy; of Vesci and Brus and Montbegon; northern barons all, stood firm at the center of the circle. We were prepared to die for what we believed in.

Behind and beside the king's tent stood mounted a few groups of those barons still loyal to the Crown, among them Ferrers of Derby, Peter Oldcotes, William Briwerre, and the hired knights of the churchmen. Between each clump of armed men, the folk of London did run and roil. The din was harrowing. I know not how the men seated in the tent made sense of one another, save that the king's guard would oft emerge and drive away the closest of the mob. By John's side were Langton and William Marshall, and the Justiciar, Hubert de Burgh. Hubert had strengthened the five great castles of the south coast, and though Prince Louis had at last landed, none of them could he take, so well were they fortified.

The noble churchmen of the reign were also there—the bishops of Dublin and Winchester and Norwich, and Simon, the Abbot of Reading. There was Pandulph, the papal legate; and Brother Aymeric, head of the Templars. Aymer was there also; he had been made Archdeacon of Durham, to channel its geld into John's bottomless pocket. For four days, from June 15 to the 19th, the Committee of Twenty-Five advanced to place their arguments and grievances before the king, whilst his advisors whispered among themselves. At last, seeing he could back no further, John set his seal to the Charter of Liberties. It returned us to ancient custom and provided that no man be disseized of his land without due process of law, and no woman be married contrary to her will. Many other customs the Great Charter reaffirmed, and the Twenty-Five were set over the king to distrain him should he act 'gainst its provisions.

Of course, it set the country afire. The Council began to rule by appointing themselves as sheriffs in every county. John countermanded and appointed his own sheriffs. The Twenty-five brought suit under provisions of the Charter to regain both land and castles. Yet other men refused the terms of the Charter, calling them milksop, and began lawless raids upon their fellow countrymen. In the north, we heard, Crown property was being harried, forests destroyed, and game killed. 'Twas plain that we need ride north as quickly as possible to give succor to Randall, ere Glororum itself be stripped of both game and wood.

After the heat of Runnymeade, the hard press toward home was near my undoing. A knight learns to sleep in his saddle when young, but finds no refreshment in it when his head is grey and his bones brittle. We stopped but briefly at Roston, and I slept in a bed for the first time in a month, nor did they wake me for the best part of a day. Had it not been for that, I should have gone home 'pon a litter.

Praise God, all was well when we reached Old Hall; the great bulk of Bamburgh castle standing nigh had thrown protecting arms about the manors that stood in its shadow. Randall was eager to hear our tale, and we repeated it oft at supper. Many times neighbors or travelers came to hear the story from the mouths of those who had stood to watch—how King John had sealed the rights of custom for common knights as well as the great Crown tenants.

Less than a month went by ere John repudiated the Great Charter. We soon heard how the king was calling in all the treasure he might, both from royal castles and from the Church, to pay his mercenary troops. 'Twas rumoured that fickle London was ready to turn again to the Crown. Clouds of war began to loom.

Even though the riches of the country were now in the hands of the Twenty-Five, still they refused the promised fealty to John. Stephen Langton had been interceding with Innocent on their behalf, for John had cried out to the Pope as his liege lord. Innocent later annulled the Charter and excommunicated those who had stood with the Army of God. 'Twas all the same to me; we did what we had to do at the time. But like Langton, most of us began to feel that the truth lay somewhere between the factions. John did not deserve allegiance, but the plundering Twenty-Five could no longer summon our respect. Many barons, men such as de Fors and de Ros and de Lacy, changed direction like hares dancing in the moonlight. Their pipers twain were expedience and greed, playing dirges that stole all the joy from the dance. The realm was on the verge of anarchy such as we had not seen since the days of King Stephen.

Fate, however, hedges about the path that some of us must walk, willy-nilly. The first week of July, Duncan rode into Glororum with his two stalwart sons, William and Malcolm, at his back. Though Margaret greeted her father and brothers with joy, 'twas short-lived, for they brought news that her mother Aethelfritha, had died at Edinburgh ten days before. 'Twas no great surprise, for Annie had died, as she had so predicted, on June 15, the day we met first John at Runnymeade. Nicolette was the next to go, slipping away from her life of pain on St. Alban's day, June 22. We were but awaiting word of the third death, for as you know, the Dark Traveler oft reaps the ripened corn three at a time.

Duncan had other news, also. Eustace de Vesci was at Alnwick, reinforcing the castle and preparing for John's counterattack. He was sure the king would not so easily hold still to the forfeit of his kingdom. De Vesci was at least as clever as the youngest of Henry's sons. John had made his way through the turbulence of the times largely by his wit, for he was neither soldier nor popular with the people. Shrewd Eustace proposed to counter John's legal maneuvers by ceding to Alexander, King of Scotland, the border shires of Northumberland and Cumberland and Westmorland. The Committee of Twenty-Five stood ready to acknowledge Alexander's overlordship of these lands which English Henry had wrested from Scotland—contrary to his given word—so many years ago. In turn, Scotland's wealth would enrich the baron's war chest, and our local knights and yeomen would answer the call to Scotland's banner.

Duncan, as Alexander's faithful steward, was on his way first to Eustace, then to meet with the English at Oxford. But as ever, my dour Scot friend was canny. "Take ye not too much on trust, John. Never a mousie had a hole 'thout a back door. Men's minds ever shift, they run not true as does an arrow. And King John may yet turn north; he has the wealth of the church, his mercenary troops from Poitevin, and the blessing of the Pope. Nay, ye have not heard the last of this rebellion, though Alexander should come tomorrow."

The king of Scots marched to besiege John's castle of Norham on the Tweed, in October of 1215. 'Twas where Boots and I had made our stealthy crossings into Scotland so many years before. De Vesci rode triumphantly north to present Alexander with the ancient sceptre of Northumberland; thereupon many were the Northumbrian knights who rallied to give Alexander fealty. I was among them, though I had come late to the battle. Boots grumbled as she armed me, berating me for an old fool. But a knight must ride when honour sounds the call. The throne of Scotland held my hopes for peace upon the land.

Yet Duncan had spoken wisely. At Christmastide we heard that John was marching north at full speed. King Alexander cautiously fell back into Scotland, for John's energies were never such as to sustain a charge. We were gambling that tomorrow the king would be gone and all would change 'round again.

I had ridden home for Christmas, as there was little use for me upon the siege. Raynaud it was who brought us news of John's march; he had near killed his destrier pelting back from Roston, where he had ridden to see to the farm. Immediately Glororum held its own Table Round. There was Randall and Margaret, as well as Tippie and Raynaud. There was Edwin's wise pate with its tonsured fringe of grey. There was my dear cousin Robin, also grey, with David by his side. His house in Durham was still a-building; the rebellion had slowed his plans. With us too were the two new knights of the household, Carl Carlson and Gilbert Thorson, a sturdy English lad who was son of a sergeant at Bamburgh, his mother, a woman of the vil. Gilbert's great strength and sound wit had made him Robin's sergeant, just as Carl had become first sergeant at Glororum by merit of his faithful service. So often, Carl minded me of his father before him, and my thoughts would stray again to the Holy Land.

I had for long been casting about for ways to renew our manor guards. With Aymer, the king's agent, as Archdeacon of Durham, it did not behoove us to petition there for knights; they would be expensive and of uncertain fealty. When Duncan came, I saw the solution to our problems. We could well enough knight our own men, for 'twas wartime and Duncan was agent of the king. New battle-tried sergeants would soon be easy enough to come by, to replace those we elevated to knighthood. Thus Duncan amiably held an adubment for our two sergeants; in return, a pretty palfrey rambled away with him when he once again took to the road.

By December, Rochester had fallen to the king, and the sheriff's son, William of Lancaster, was taken hostage. One by one, as John moved north the castles tumbled like dominos—Belvoir and Donington ere the year was out. Robert de Ros' great castle of Helmsley stood, but Peter de Brus' Skelton later fell to the Crown. Peter had left it lightly garrisoned and brought his troops north to aid the Scots. With word of John's advance, Peter moved back across the border with his brother-in-law, Alexander. I proposed to join him there for the nonce.

Tippie was practical. "Father, you are of an age when your campaigns should be behind you. Can you not simply stay here and give John fealty when he comes?"

I shook my head. "He would require hostages. Which of you would I care to see imprisoned in his court? Not one." I answered my own question. "Then there are the fines he has been leveling 'gainst any rebel that reverses. 'Twould ruin us for years. William de Albini's ransom after Rochester was said to be 6,000 marks, and fitz Reinfrey's 12,000."

There was much silence whilst all digested those sums, till Margaret timidly asked, "Perhaps he would not know you were a rebel?"

"Ah, well enow he knows me, and my shield, which stood facing him four days in June. John is no man's fool. Besides, the clerk at his elbow made note of every man standing 'gainst the Crown, and no doubt their property as well."

Raynaud started. "I did not see that. Then I, too, am marked as a rebel."

"Aye, I fear it so. But would ye have otherwise? Nor I. Our quandary now is to leave our Crown property here at Glororum unforfeit. Roston we hold as tenants of de Brus; 'twill be forfeit anyway, for we rode in the entourage of de Brus. Ye may well go to Scotland and ride with Peter again,

Raynaud, but Tippie and John needs must go also. They may bide at court awhile; Tippie has friends to grant her shelter if Duncan cannot."

Randall had been listening restlessly. "I ken, Father, that you are not intending to bide with the rebel army. What are you going to do, if not stay here?"

"I am afraid, my son, that all will devolve 'pon your shoulders again. I cannot ride with the rebels, though I shall go awhile and pay my respects to Peter. But as long as I am alive, Glororum will be counted as my property, and thus be forfeit with rebellion. Nor can I stay here. King John has no objection to hooking small fish, if 'twill suit his plans. Never mind if our patrimony be lost; he would sell us into slavery if it so suited him. The only other way outside death that ye may speak as master of Glororum and Bamburgh, is if I become outlaw."

The idea near broke up our war council. All clamored at once, till I held up my hand and began to speak again. "I ken deep in my heart that what Annie said will come to pass; John has not many seasons left to live. We pray God that then reasonable men may govern England. I misdoubt that Alexander will long hold Northumberland; the rents and castles are too valuable for England to let them slip away. In the course of war, many a man is outlawed and redeemed after. Though John may set a price upon my head, 'tis not likely that any will come to seek me out in the turmoil of rebellion. No man now knows who goes with the King, or who against him; nor do wives know where their husbands ride."

Randall protested. "But Father, how do we accomplish all this?"

"Ye have dealt with Philip of Oldcotes when he rode to Bamburgh Castle to strengthen the garrison. Did he question your loyalty to the Crown?"

"Aye, he did; but with our provisioning of him, he became convinced that we were not in rebellion."

"Good. Then he will witness for your good faith before John. All that needs be done is issue a proclamation of enjoinder 'gainst me with the sheriff. Edwin, ye may see to the legalities of that."

Raynaud was following the proceedings with his usual quick mind. "No, John. Issue no proclamations yet. If the Crown forces the issue, perhaps it may come to that. But as yet, we do not even know who John's sheriff will be; Robert de Ros holds the position now as one of the Committee. If Philip of Oldcotes thinks Randall loyal, there will be little need to play such an elaborate charade. A little geld may do; 'tis amazing what a gullet can swallow with a little grease. And an innocent air," Raynaud ended, suiting his look to the words, reminding us all of the mischief he was wont to play when young. I could not help but laugh.

"I believe you to be right; ye are not a Ros for naught. But still, I must disappear for awhile, and bide not too long in the company of our fine rebel barons. They change sides oftener than ye change your shirt."

Thus our plans were hatched, with all gambled 'pon John's early demise. Randall and brave Margaret stayed at Glororum to face the king when he rode to Bamburgh on the 12th day of January, 1216. Unable to take Alnwick Castle the day before, he had fired its vill. Glororum suffered no harm save loss of most of our winter provisions—or at least the ones that had not been hid. John went from Bamburgh to Berwick on the 14th, securing its castle. From thence, his impetus carried him as far as Dunbar in Scotland, but he met none who would stand and fight; nor did it seem he was looking for battle. Alexander stood at Edinburgh, ready, and none doubted that if John were foolhardy enough to advance 'gainst him, our troubles would be over. Like a great gaunt rook, John was merely flapping his wings and making noise. On the 24th, he campaigned back south again, unwilling to tease the "red fox cub" too far.

And I became an outlaw—homeless—with Boots by my side, and Richard for squire. Into cold, grey Scotland we ran, in cold, grey January. Boots has never warmed since.

Chapter 27

Going Home

We spent a week in the warmth of Alexander's court ere taking to our wandering road. I beseeched Richard to stay with Raynaud and Gilbert but he would not, though the prospect of war must have been more inviting than worrying along behind a tired old knight. Richard was but fifteen, third son to James, Will'son of Ellingham. James' small freehold was too poor for the children he had; two sons stayed home, one went to the church, and Richard came to us. An adequate soldier he proved, but his greatest trait was loyalty. England's progress was ever on the backs of sturdy yeomen such as Richard.

We took few appointments and only a little silver toward the horses' provisioning. I had become a knight errant at age fifty-seven, and understood too well why only young men went to seek their fortune—men unburdened still by aches and pains and by other mouths to feed. We begged lodging at abbeys and monasteries, but few monasteries held with keeping a woman, so often we moved on to take shelter with poor thanes or solitary hermits. God knows those accommodations were poor! Often we were hungry, near always cold and full of chilblains. Even the horses began to look meagre. Always we offered knight service, and often accompanied canons or monks 'pon their journeys. Richard was no stranger to penury, and though he was ever short of speech, he had a thousand ploys to keep us provisioned. The young are oft more resourceful than their elders; we grow too firm in our caste-bound ways. Boots and I grew fond of the slender lad, with his unkempt shock of corn-coloured hair.

More than service, the folk of Scotland were eager for news of the rebellion. In the talk of war, oft the tales went back to the Crusade, for by that time not many of the old soldiers were left. People wished to hear of the Holy land from the lips of one who had been there. For many years I had been reluctant to delve into that ugly plot, yet now I found myself doing so, in the eagerness of the listeners. Their deference hunted out my own respect. I was able to face the sorrows of that war headlong, and by so doing was absolved of its festering.

Another gift that hard winter brought was the art of healing reflection. 'Twas not learned easily, but through misery, in the attempts to arise of a morning when bones were knotted from cold, and eyes mattered shut from the smoky peat fires. Old Henry was the first who came to mind when I awoke, only to find the cursed bones gnarled with pain. I remembered then the man-at-arms who first took me to Alnwick, saw again the poor bent body, heard the lash of tongue, smelled the sour breath of stale ale. Henry's anger seemed to mock me. I remembered, too, Stephen in his dying, how his mind seemed far from his body, in a place of great peace, so that even in pain, his temper was sweet and his blessing to be sought. And I recalled what our old knight, Sir Giles, had made plain to me regarding pain, and the healing arts that Edwin used. So once again I learned from those who had touched my life, and each morning ere rising, would send God's healing unto my body by accepting His will with love and serenity. His Son had suffered far more for me. Boots, too, if she saw my pain, would try to warm me, soothing away the knots with the touch of her hands.

By March, we began to hear rumours that John was laired in the south, and sending negotiators to the great northern barons to entreat their fealty. Full weary we all were, and decided to wend our way homeward. Stopping at Edinburgh, we found it true; Peter and Eustace and Robert de Ros had been offered safe-conduct to meet with the king. Indeed, they rode to Dover and treated with John in April. Desperate, John now said he preferred faithful service to geld; he would forgive their fines and rebellion if they would but return to his side.

'Twas all to naught, for in two weeks, Prince Louis was at Dover, and Alexander marching south to meet him. London once again opened its gates to the French Prince. Carlisle fell to the Scots in August, then Alexander and the barons laid siege to Barnard Castle, 'pon the Tees. There the rebellion lost perhaps its greatest leader, for Eustace de Vesci was felled by a crossbow bolt in the encounter, much as had been Richard the King.

John was greatly heartened, and spurred north to strengthen Newark and Lincoln. Alexander halted his advance south and turned quickly about. Rumour told of a great force behind John, and the Scots' king had no secure place of battle.

But fickle Fate turned the glass on John at last; his time ran out. In October, they said, he had urged his baggage train to cross the Wash in the teeth of a powerful incoming tide. Mayhap the cortege might have squeaked through, save that the Wash was treacherous with quicksand. John lost the Crown treasures that day, silver and gold and jewels, ancient holy relics; all, all were sucked into the bottomless sands. Men and horses screamed piteously and cried to God, but there was no succor for them. The suffocating mud slowly stopped both breath and life. No man could think upon it without illness clutching at his bowels.

So 'twas with John also. Dire sick he became; the unshriven souls of his tormented servants called to him from Hell. The royal entourage stopped then at Newark, where John turned in his extremity to a surfeit of cider and fresh peaches, rather than to sackcloth and ashes. 'Twas on the feast of St. Luke, October 18, that John's soul departed this earth. The divine physician had called him to the side of Christ for his healing.

By May, we had felt safe enough to ride back to Old Hall, and devil take the hindmost. So glad was I to be home that King John might have hung me, all uncaring. 'Twas one of the few times I ever saw Boots weep. Ah, blessed Northumberland! With raspberries fresh from the vine and clotted cream, roast suckling pig and tender mawmoney; with the fruits of that glorious land, we were surfeit.

Glororum had been spared, though full wrathful King John had been that I had 'scaped his retribution. Legally, the Crown could do nothing, for Randall had been the very soul of loyalty. Now, that was all behind us, and 'twas well that it was so. The lung affliction came upon me, and I kept to my bed for nigh a month ere God at last spared me. For near three months longer, I had not the strength of a mewling babe. 'Twas then the gift of reflection served me well, for there was little service I might do at Old Hall. Each day began beside the kitchen fire, where at last I brought a pallet of skins, that I might keep the fire through the watches of the night, when sleep fled away with old memories hard upon its heels.

Just before sunup I would rise, and after dipping a cup of broth from the cauldron, settle into the corner next the door. There I would gaze at the flames and pray to God for all our souls. Then in the greatest reverie, I would feel healing flow back into my chest and limbs. At times, wondrous visions passed before my eyes, though I sat far from sleep and wandered not in dreams. 'Twas but some little time ere the most peculiar feeling crept over me, that some great adventure awaited there in the silence of morning. Yet even as I awaited, it seemed to lurk ever farther away, as if repelled by my very eagerness to espy its face.

At last, upon a cold November morn, after the harvest was in the barn and the manor accounts had all been read, the vision bestowed itself upon me. I had set out merely to relax, for I had returned to my usual work, but found I needed this quiet time to ease both mind and body ere dealing with the travails of the day. The broth had near gone cold, in the struggle to clear my wit of various worries and speculations. At last, I felt eased, with the mind able to seek refuge once again in the little chapel of St. Oswald. As I began to settle my vision comfortably into that place, hallowed by imagination, the scene began to shift and change, carrying me far beyond any ordinary reflection.

A child arose, whose beauty was beyond that of earth, and approached me from the left. She was fair, with curly flaxen hair, and eyes of brightness; to cover her she wore but a simple shift of white linen. She reached a pudgy hand toward me, as if imploring succor. My heart was moved with love and anxiety for this light-child. I accepted her small, warm hand.

She led me then to the altar of the chapel, which according to our oldest customs, stood one step up just inside the chancel arch. Here the priest would face the people with the Holy Sacrifice. There upon that sacred altar, the fair child pointed to a silver helm, and made me to know 'twas mine if I so wished. Approaching, I saw letters engraved across the brow. "Accept the Helm, Accept the Quest," they read. I bethought me upon that awhile, whilst the light-child stood patiently. At long last, I reached forth my hand and placed the helm upon my head. It fit perfectly, as if made for me alone. And, wonder of wonders, the voice of the child now came plain into my head, as she took my hand once more and murmured, "Come with me."

Behind the altar we went, and I was wondering greatly from whence we would emerge to begin our quest. The fair child then pointed to a stone in the chancel floor, wherein was imbedded a large iron ring. "Lift the stone," she seemed to say, which I struggled long to do. The weight of ages perchance had sealed shut that stone, for though I toiled with all my might, still it defied me. Yet each time I despaired, light from the little child touched me, and I found my strength renewed. Thus it was, inch by groaning inch, the great stone yielded, and in the blackness beneath, I could dimly make out a narrow stair.

Courage stopped short of that gaping maw, till goaded by the sword of whole-hearted Trust, I descended after the angelic child. I could not have made my way into that dark and fearsome place, except that the child went before; and with her presence the passageway lighted enough to make our footsteps plain.

The forbidding passage proved short, and soon we emerged into a green and summer-flowered meadow, bordered by a wood. We set off through the grass, and weary trudging it was. I had just bethought me that knights are most unsuited to go venturing on foot, when the light-child reassured me. "We shall soon find a steed." And, lo! as we entered the dappled shade of the wood, a dwarf approached. He was stout, though misshapen, and passing ugly.

"Mount upon the dwarf," my companion said, "and he will take us where we must go." I protested then, for never would I go one step upon the back of another man, no matter how evil-appearing he might be.

"Nevertheless," the child said mildly, "only in this fashion may we progress in this world." So reluctantly, I straddled the dwarf's shoulders. Instantly, he became a beautiful steed, shining both black and white; in the way a glossy raven appears purest white when flying in the light. A gentle touch told me that the child had mounted behind me, and that same touch propelled us forward. How that horse flew! Until land seemed to no longer stand beneath his flashing hooves, and we were sailing through the air itself. "This must be the magical steed of long-gone days," I mused to my companion, "perhaps the flying horse which emerged from the mists to carry great Alexander to victory?"

"This is the wraith-horse of Bellerophon, which was first named as Pegasus by the young god of light himself," I heard the child reply. I marveled greatly, but could not help but wish that we might set our mares with this stalwart steed.

Behind me, I heard childish laughter peal at that ordinary thought, and I needs must laugh also, at the commonness of my distraction.

In nowise could I see where we traveled, for the sun in my eyes blinded me to all else. Suddenly, a great dark cloud loomed before us, and Bellerophon's steed rushed toward it. Upon that cloud-land lay a shadowy wood, and our mount touched down at its edge. Before us stood a massive castle whose stones ran mossy black with age.

Riding toward those grim walls, I espied a woman dressed in white with a blue kirtle, all bowed down in the grass as if weeping. As we approached, she raised her face, and her comeliness made my heart grow faint. "Oh, Fair Knight, succor; succor I pray!" she called unto me. I reined toward her with right good will, for her beauty and her plight touched me to the soul.

But the child, all alarmed, cried out, "Halt, oh halt, great Pegasus!" Look ye again, Sir Knight, at yon lady!" I did as she commanded, and saw that from the copious tears the lady shed, a great river took its flow; and circling the castle, became its moat.

"Many worthy knights have drowned in that maiden's never-ending tears," my companion said sadly. "You must harden your heart, or deny your quest." Indeed, I could see poor, drowned faces turned heavenward beneath their crystal flow, and knew the truth of the child's plea. Yet it was but reluctantly that I turned Bellerophon's steed away from the maiden, for my heart lay sore in my breast at her travail.

We soon stood before the closed gate of the grim castle, and I wondered how we might gain admittance. "Blow your horn," advised the child. To my amazement, I found my own horn, the ancient horn of our family, again at hand. Raising it to my lips, I blew a mighty blast. All was quiet. I waited, then once again raised a note that might have tumbled the very towers of Jericho. With much rattling and clashing, the drawbridge began to lower.

I would have ridden in, but the child's hand upon my arm stayed me. "None may go into that dark fortress, save they go alone," she told me. "I will await here with Pegasus. Inside, you will find the gateway guarded by a savage bear. Whatever you do, do not raise your sword and attempt to take the castle by storm. Should you succeed in slaying the bear, you will find yourself in his place, groaning beneath all his wounds. Instead, you must ask admission courteously."

The light-child paused, to make sure I understood. When I nodded, she went on. "The fierce bear will not allow you to pass until you answer his questions. 'Who is Queen in this castle?' he will demand; and you must answer, 'Queen Grace.' Then he will ask you a harder question. 'What are the names of her daughters?' and you must answer, 'Faith, Hope and Charity.' Then he will rumble most fearsomely, 'Are you prepared to meet the King?' Do not let your heart falter, but bravely answer, 'Yes.' It is for this we have come."

Thus did it all happen, though I must admit, I was not prepared to see the size and strength of that huge brute. Even now, my heart stops in my mouth as I remember the guardian. Yet there was nothing of madness in him, only an air of serene but implacable justice.

After I had answered his questions, the great bear led me to the right, into an antechamber wherein a fire burned brightly. As I stood waiting, with my back to the flames, I heard voices emerging therefrom, groans and curses and cries. Unsettled, I turned to gaze upon the fire; it snapped and burned serenely enough, as any ordinary fire. Once again I turned my back to the flames, and the sounds of struggle surrounded me. The very hair stood up upon my neck, for I had heard such awful sounds before, in battle. I seemed to wait a century in that turmoil, though surely but a few moments had passed ere three youths emerged from the flames to stand beside me, two 'pon my right, and one upon the left. Startled, I wondered who they might be, and as if in answer, I heard their replies within the magical helm.

"We are the youths of the fiery furnace; we are the Sons of Faith." Indeed, as I looked, they still seemed to glow white-hot, as if from the very heart of the embers.

The first youth then touched my eyes with glowing fingers and said, "Truth be visible unto you!" The second touched my ears and said in ringing tones (as if a brass bell held his voice), "May your ears discern Truth!" The third brother upon my left then touched my lips with burning fingers, and in their searing heat, I heard him say, "May Truth cleanse the words of your mouth!"

They then led me forth, and I felt humble beyond humility. In the next room stood two more youths, each beside a door. One was fair to look upon, golden and shining, with a gentle smile upon his face. He stood next a white door upon the right. To the left was a similar door, but made of mother-of-pearl, grey with subtle dancing hues. Next it stood a dark youth with an enticing smile. He was robed in grey, with a single scarlet rose, red as blood, in his hand. I saw then that the first youth held a wreath, cleverly woven with tiny white Alpine flowers.

"Are you prepared to meet the King?" the youths of the fiery furnace asked again. When I nodded assent, they said, "Then you needs must choose a door." Perplexed, I stood, for though my heart inclined me toward the fair youth upon the right, I remembered the weeping maiden and knew that in the lands of enchantment all was not as it seemed. I turned to the seductive young man in grey, and with the blood-red rose he beckoned me. But my heart would not be gainsaid. I turned and walked firmly toward the fair youth upon the right.

With penetrating eyes, blue as glaciers, he welcomed me. "You have chosen wisely. We are the sons of Hope, and I am Promise. Had you accepted the red rose of my twin, Despair, you would have entered through his door into the dark sea of Oblivion. At the bottom of that mighty ocean, another life awaits, a life of doubt and trial. From that endless sea of forgetfulness, you would once again struggle to free yourself." Then for the third time, he asked, "Are you ready to meet the King?" I was filled with dread beyond dread, so that my very knees turned to water. But I answered quietly, "Yes, I am."

At which reply, Promise smiled sweetly and laid the white wreath upon my helm. At once, my head felt cold as ice. "Do not fear," he said as he opened the white door, "but enter thou here." At once, I stepped across the threshold of a long room draped in shimmering white and gold, with threads of blue and scarlet skipping through their folds. A maiden glided silently to my side as guide, for the sons of Faith remained behind with the keepers of the portals, the sons of Hope.

The maiden smiled, and the radiance from her countenance lit the entire room. She, too, was dressed in white, as if some ancient Roman matron, and her arms and neck and daintily sandaled feet shone like beaten gold beneath her gown. "I am the daughter of Love," she said simply. "I have come to take you to the King." And she led me to the far end of the great hall.

There upon a carved and crowned golden throne sat a king. I understood instantly that this was King Pellas, the Dark King, from his raven-black hair and beard, his milk white skin, and his piercing eyes like ice. Before him I trembled and fell to my knees, and would have swooned, save for the maiden's hand upon my shoulder.

Upon his breast Pellas wore a purple tabard, embroidered in gold with a most amazing fish. It writhed and turned and swam upon the velvet above Pellas' heart. By this, I understood that he was also called the Fisher King, the great fisher of men. Thus I knew he carried wounds most grievous, and across his side, I saw the spreading crimson of his blood. Great was the pity I felt then, and raised my hands to Pellas, my only supplication being for the healing of his suffering. And the daughter of Love stood fast beside me, and from her touch ran a river of healing that flowed through me and off my outstretched fingers toward King Pellas. He said not a word, but merely nodded, and I felt a great heat creep upon us from behind. Had it not been for the icy wreath upon my brow, I would have surely perished.

Then gazing toward King Pellas' right, I saw what many men have dreamed of, but few have seen. A huge angel stood there, with bloody spear in his left hand, the spear that eternally drips with Pellas' blood. In his right hand, the holy angel held a silver cup in which he caught the sacred blood, and I knew it was Sangreal itself, the Holy Grail. Upon that silver chalice were chased images of men and women and beasts, images that moved and circled 'round the awesome cup, and were never quite the same.

In the terrible heat, I cried out, and thinking to wipe the sweat that began to dim my sight, put hand to brow. It came away covered with blood. Love's daughter then took a white quill, and wiping it across my fiery brow, quickly drew away the blood. She placed that bloody feather across Sangreal, and the blood ran in, mingling with that of Pellas. The feather once again became white as snow. Gasping with fear, I burned to see across the golden rim into that awful cup.

Gently, the daughter of Love led me toward Sangreal. "My name is Immortality," she said. "Only those who feel the pure touch of my hand dare look inside the Sangreal. Look now!" For one blinding moment, I dared peer inside. The Grail was empty, its golden interior spiraling down and down, toward a gateway filled with light.

And with Immortality's touch still gentle upon my shoulders, I tumbled into the coolness within that Holy Cup, and across the empty portal into light. Angel wings seemed to surround me and soften the fall, as I awoke with a thump upon the stones before the altar in the chapel of St. Oswald. From thence, I sat up, dazed and weak as a man new-returned from death, and found myself slumped in my corner of the kitchen at Old Hall.

All through my illness, news of the war had swirled 'round us like autumn leaves; with each traveler north came word of its confusion. All were disheartened by the wasting of land and resource. Though we had attempted to set law and custom above the king, I began to think the Great Charter not worth the effort. Perhaps it would always be as John had protested, that the law is in the king's mouth alone. Yet I could not truly believe that. Life should not be dictated by what is politic, for the state is not yet God.

Upon King John's death, proclamation was read in church that his son, Henry the III, was to be crowned king. William Marshall was chosen as regent; he had faithfully served three kings ere young Henry. William cried out that he deserved to rest upon his fair lands of Pembroke, that he was too old to be shepherding a new king, particularly a lad only nine years old. But across all the kingdom the hue and cry went up that only the old Marshall could save the Crown for England. So it proved. Canny William Marshall reissued our Charter in November, and many were the men who turned to the young king's side. William later granted that our estates be held as they had been before the war; all John's legal wrangling had gone for naught. Prince Louis found himself in a foreign land, a land that was drawing upon itself once more.

Rebellion is like a huge mill wheel; it does not stop all at once, but goes thumping along, slowing all the while. Thus it was in May of 1217 that the rebel barons of the north marched together once again to take the castle at Lincoln. They had tried to overwhelm it in 1216, and the castellan, Nicolaa de la Haye, bought a truce. These knights had little respect for the widow Nicolaa, though she was of far sterner stuff than her husband had been. Now they thought to show their mastery 'gainst the poor lad who had inherited the crown by seizing Lincoln, held only by this weak woman. 'Twas a grave error.

I had ridden to Roston, Boots at my side, for Easter. There was a new son born to Raynaud and Tippie and they named him Maurice, for the churchyard where poor Herleve lay buried. 'Twas uncanny; the lad had Herleve's russet colouring exactly. Yet he would grow to have the de Ros gift of enterprise. He began by horse trading whilst still a squire, and later became one of the largest livestock brokers in all the north country. But in 1217, he was merely a remarkably lusty babe, suckling his mother's milk.

Our domestic bliss was interrupted by two messengers from Robert de Ros. William, Robert's son, was on the march to Lincoln. Robert was calling in debts of fealty to aid him in battle, and his younger brother Raynaud headed the list.

Ray hemmed and hawed and bargained, but 'twas to no avail. The rebels needed every available knight at Lincoln. Yet in the end, his negotiations proved fruitful, for they delayed departure 'pon that most futile venture. At last, Raynaud sent his brother's heralds home with a promise to ride forth in William's cause.

What tie there lies between men's minds, none will ever ken for certain. I know not if Raynaud first had the thought, or myself, but be assured that he spoke not aloud of it. 'Twas up to me to say the words he was only thinking. "Ray, 'tis not meet that you should ride to Lincoln on such a fool's errand. Thy sons need their father. Let me take up shield on your behalf; if aught befalls, none will miss one worn old knight." His very look told me that the words would ha' been his, had he not such respect. So we argued some, but in the end, 'twas settled.

Boots was furious. She had rebuked me oft enough before, though with but a word or two. Now her fears soured into scorching anger. Nor would I take her along; her presence would have told all that the old fool John rode in his son-in-law's place. Richard would ride at my back, and Raynaud's shield and horse would serve me. I had ridden south, as was my custom, in but a hauberk of light chain and an old-fashioned helm, for such gave greater freedom in traveling. Now I must wear Raynaud's greaves and cuisses, and take his great helm. My last memory ere leaving was of Boots strapping on the too-small armour, and crying that I was a simpleton beyond all measure. Besides, she said, I was grown fat and lazy, and would ne'er survive a battle. Her fears were my own, but a knight's duty is ever to the highest cause. Bloody knights, she said, with no sense, only pride. Her words echoed still, when we met again some seven hundred years later.

My heart was not in that campaign, for it had been called to service by greed. Slowly forth we rode, and I welcomed the respite granted when Raynaud's destrier pulled up lame at Alfreton. I took refuge with the canons of the village church, and sent Richard back to Roston for another horse. Had I been a younger man, I would ha' fumed over the delay, perhaps even bought another horse. Now I was certain in my heart that God's grace had been sent to save me despite myself.

So it proved. We arrived at Lincoln late on a Saturday afternoon, and the scorched and empty fields told me I was too late. Richard and I took refuge in an empty croft till nightfall. Not a piece of bread nor a bite of pease had been left, so 'twas both wary and hungry we were when at last we rode up to Lincoln's walls. "The main gate is shut and likely well guarded," I told Richard. "Do you carefully circle the wall and find if a postern has been left open."

Postern gates, admitting but one rider, were used to send messengers or servants to and from the castle. Often in peacetime, or in the aftermath of battle, they were left unguarded, so that a single person might slip unnoticed into the castle precincts. My hunch proved correct. The unguarded postern was too small to admit a horse with rider, so we tied our steeds and went afoot into that dark and silent town. In the castle, lights were ablaze. I had a great foreboding, not assuaged by the flapping of open doors into empty hovels. The wind rustled about our ears, and the stench of blood and manure filled the air. A great grim owl soared sullenly by, as if carrying away the souls of the damned. 'Twas an omen for me. "Richard, disarm ye and leave helm and sword here. 'Tis obvious the battle is over, and we must know the outcome. Great lump that I am, I could ne'er get close enough to converse without raising the guard. Sidle up toward yon courtyard; ye are quick-witted enough to over-hear what has taken place."

Of all the places I ha' been, in whatever life, the eeriest by far was biding in the doorway of that abandoned hovel at Lincoln on the eve after the great battle. The small moon was setting, not far behind the sun. She was in Leo, the sign of the king. It boded not well. Through the night came the chink of armour; the sounds of footsteps and quiet voices, curses and prayers and snatches of song. 'Twas the whole of the age held in a moment.

It seemed an eternity till Richard was back by my side, slipping on the greasy stones of the street. "We must be off! The guards have had their ale and rested after the battle; the patrols are forming now. They are on their way to close the postern." He needed not to tell me that if we were locked inside, 'twould not be well with us. Silently, we retraced our steps. Passing out through the postern, we dared not mount and ride till the moon had slipped away and the guard had shuffled past 'pon the wall. Once again we bided, in the small copse where the horses were hidden. So well trained were they, that not a sound betrayed us, though there was one bad moment when the guard on the wall stopped and peered into the darkness where we lay hiding. Satisfied that all was quiet, he moved on. We took to our heels then, nor did we stop till Skellingthorpe.

On the way, Richard told me what little he had been able to overhear as the guard prepared to secure the castle for the night. Nicolaa, they said, had turned the tables on the rebels full fair. William de Ros was taken hostage, and Mowbray, and the Gant brothers, as well as many others. On all of them was surrender enforced. Their defeat was sealed in the blood of the honest soldiers who had followed them to Lincoln, nor would ransoms come easily to the mesne knights who were taken. Silently I praised God who had so watched over our lives.

Much scurrilous talk there was later of the Fair at Lincoln, for the common folk were in many ways joyed to see the great barons brought down. As one who stood afeared in the night and smelled the suffering, I tell you 'twas no Fair. But from that time on, the back of the rebellion was broken. William Marshall did what he could to heal the great raw wounds that had been laid upon the land. In November, he sealed once again the Great Charter of Liberties, and the Forest Charter as well. Our lands were returned. The king's agents entered the names of all who renounced their rebellion upon the close rolls, though there were many in Northumbria not so entered. Even then, the Crown respected Northumberland as having custom unto itself, nor were there many among us who wished aught but peace.

Boots was joyed to see me again, and all of a piece. Raynaud shook his head at our story; Providence had so obviously ridden at our side. He was well content, for his debt to Robert was fulfilled, and we had come unscathed. His story to his brother was that he had ridden late, and only by great cunning had he escaped being taken for ransom. Since Robert would ha' been liable for his brother's redemption, he was not apt to enquire too closely.

Richard never forgot our skirmish; 'twas a tale he would live to tell his grandchildren. Folk did not go easily into the night in our day, but stayed laired within doors after evenfall. The soldier on patrol stayed close behind his parapet, and even outlaws sought out a cave or hay mound to shelter in. I suppose my errands on behalf of the Little People had accustomed me to the night, though always I trod softly and watched cautiously. After our return from Lincoln, I began to be up often at night, to answer Nature's call. Once more I moved into the undercroft, so as to be near the postern door at Old Hall. Each afternoon I would climb the stairs to the solar and read from the Book of Hours, or watch the clouds cross the western hills. Oft I would doze there awhile, and by these things I knew I had truly come to be an old man at last.

Boots, too; no matter how she cajoled or teased or threatened, things between us were not as they had been before. Yet our esteem and understanding of one another seemed to grow out of infirmity. Through the morning, we would sit in the sun and watch Adam and Jack work the horses, or we would bide in the stable out of the rain, cleaning harness and discussing the many turns our lives had taken.

I nearly always took a turn of the farm, fair weather or foul, and once a fortnight, I rode to Chatta's to sip ale and gossip and stay the night. 'Twas in August of 1218 that the grim Traveler visited the inn whilst I was biding there. Simon came to rouse me from bed, saying his father had gotten up but fallen, and was even then gasping his final breaths. I held my old friend's head 'gainst my breast as he sighed his last. The overwhelming sorrow Chatta's death brought was eased by the gratitude I felt at having been with him at passing. 'Twas an honour granted by God to be by his side; he was ever a man of pleasance and wit.

Through 1219, I rode at times to visit Simon, but 'twas never the same. Still, I rode 'round the farm, for no man can own the land save that the land own him. In the end, there came a benign sense of isolation from the affairs of other men, an insulation that was a comfort. Though Randall or Tippie's family might visit with me, or Henry come with his wife and children, I was more content when they left. Even Boots often took more energy from me than my heart was wiling to give. Only when Robin came to visit, or my son William, would we sit comfortably in silent communion. They came not often and that was as well.

But the stars of the night sky—I was up and out so often—became real friends, and I was thankful for the lore of them I had learned from my mother. Often I would think of her, as I sat by the embers of the kitchen fire, early before the sun was up. I would dip a cup of broth from the kettle over the fire, and bide in my corner. Newly awake, reverie soothed away the aches of body and heart. I never saw my mother, though at times it seemed she was near. Twice, I saw Annie from the corner of my eye; she had come to keep me company. When grave concerns overtook me, there in the silence of morning prayers, several times Our Lord appeared, and always He came to comfort. There are those who will say that I slept, there by the fire, but I tell you, 'twas not so. The spirit of Christ may appear to every man, and still be not diminished.

But my greatest comfort was one of God's most maligned creatures, a lizard. When first I saw him—plain as I am speaking to you, though airier—I thought 'twas a dragon, and started for the knife in my belt. "Nay," the creature said, "I have come to succor you. You have many a quest yet to fulfill, but these will be journeys of the spirit. Look!" And there stood my old steed, Black Stone, waiting for my touch upon saddle and reins. I saw then that the lizard that had brought him was himself armed, with mailed byrnie, and an old-fashioned square-top helm.

"Ye must pardon my ill manners," I said laughing, "but never have I glimpsed a creature as odd-looking as a six-foot blue lizard in a square-top helm, walking 'pon his hind legs (much like a crab, at that) with his tail streaming behind. By what name are ye called?"

He shrugged. "You may call me Blue. You will anyway." How well he knew my naming habits! Thus it was that every adventure we took began the same way: with a light heart. Boots was the only soul I dared tell of our adventures, nor did she think I had gone daft with age, but learned along with me of a world not our own.

"John, you are not like other men; I told you that long years ago. You were born sensitive to things other folk cannot see. Now that you have time to sit and muse, and the cares of Glororum have left your shoulders, you are finding a place in yourself where common folk never go. Our Lord loves you very much, and so do I." So was I comforted, for I realized from all these things that in the life of the Spirit, we are never alone.

Christmas of 1220 came, and I saw that a fatted ox was laid upon the Yule fire, and provision made for every family of the vill. But my heart was tight, for fever often walked with me, nor could I force the growing waters from my body. I tried what herbs I knew, and some relief came. After Christmas Mass, I knew I would soon be confined to bed. I sought out Boots, and told her I was ill, that no matter what happened, I would remain to watch over her. Tippie, too, I told, and made her promise to see that Boots was never turned out, so long as she should live. 'Twas not long till they laid me upon the bed in my old room, where so many years ago I had begun married life with Herleve.

I tossed with fever for three days, babbling with the irrational words of an old soldier dying of the man-fever. When no water will pass from the body, it burns like a living foretaste of Hell. Yet part of me always saw the family taking turns beside the bed. 'Twas near the last day of the year, and I ken it well yet. A man's dying stays with him, life after life; that moment when time is held firm, like an insect in amber. In the dark I saw Randolph standing at attention beside the head of my bed, his face like a mask, waiting for the dark Traveler to come and take me. With sudden clarity I felt his embarrassment, sad mortification at the travesty of humanity his own father had become.

Suddenly then I saw before me—my beloved Alyse. So many years it had been! Yet she was as fresh and young as the day I first saw her, her golden hair fallen across the sapphire blue of her dress. The green and gold of meadow stood behind her, and her milk-white steed quietly blew at her shoulder. "Ah, you have come," I said, sitting up quickly. "I promise you Alyce, I shall live with you once more. By the wounds of Christ, I shall care for you; though it be a hundred years or seven times a hundred..." Then all strength slipped from my worthless body and Alyse reached to raise me by the hand.

Riding Away

Clip-clop, clip-clop, clip-clop, riding away,
Dreary of heart as this damned' French day
From matins to lauds, then naught left to say,
So we're clip-clop, clip-clop, riding away.

Home—home we turn to Northumbrian hills,
Where the heritage waits; each stone and rill
A friend, passed by my father in holy trust,
To hold for my sons, like a hawk well jessed.

Without the master the fires dwindle out,
Churls and plowmen drink and the swine make rout
Of gardens. And the wife I left, I trow,
Does the devil's work. Her nature I know.

Such is the lot to be wedded for blood
And land and the sons a knight must brood
To keep our land from creeping ruin,
That folk might sup in the peaceful even.

O, how far back from Jerusalem come,
For the peace of our hills and the fires of home!
Yet I ride like a man broken at rack
And fain would turn 'round on this dismal track,
Where, crying in the rain, love lies parted,
'Pon the end of the road that sorrow started.

Damme! The stinking drizzle wrecks ruin
On road and armor and courage unscrew'n.
But out of fair meadows now left behind,
Alyse rides forth once again in my mind,
Whence first I beheld in the summer last,
She and her ladies at sport on the grass.

Gold was her hair from its cap fallen down,
Spilling like sun on the blue of her gown.
Riding like Hell with its fury long pent,
Alyse stormed 'pon me like an angel sent.

Sick as death beneath a tree we waited,
Rob and I. My breath so slow and 'bated
That scarce could he uphold me. Then she came,
Splashing the ford, with succor in God's name.

Near a year I stayed, from the Holy Land,
With blight-cursed' bowel and shaking hand
And Alyse my nurse. The man whose name she bore
From France had marched, with Phillip, to war.

'Twas in fall's garden filled with sweet perfume
That first we loved, hot blood ceding no room
To regret, for no man should sow and grieve.
We knew love lasts not long, and knights must leave.

We dallied still, tender moods unsated
Till love held fast what desire had created.
Then—O, word that restored to us our sense—
Her husband lay at Fleur, just three days hence!

For my son I promised patrimony;
And though it be some after century,
This I swear, by ground I trod most holy,
Alyse, we shall live to share life truly.

There was nothing left. Nothing left to say
Besides "I love you", on that dreary day
Of bootless tears and sodden hearts gone grey
As the sad French road that leads me away.

Clip-clop, clip-clop, clip-clop, riding away,
Dreary of heart as that damned' French day
From matins to lauds, then naught left to say,
So we're clip-clop, clip-clop, riding away.

Vows should not be given life so heart-proud
That from graves long buried they cast the shroud
Of kind forgetting, and recall that road
Whose riding I'd leave, if only I could.

Clip-clop, clip-clop, clip-clop, riding away,
Dreary of heart from that damned' French day
Matins and lauds gone, and naught left to say
Clip-clop, clip-clop, but still riding away.

Epilogue
Northumberland Awakening

John Forster died on December 30, 1220, close upon 2:30 AM. As had been foretold so long before, Orion's great body was falling headfirst from the sky onto the western horizon. The moon was dark, and the warrior Mars was carried in the arms of the Sun.

I do not know what adventures John's soul first went through, but after three days, Boots' grief drew him back to her side. Tippie had brought Allie the news, as usual, most tardily and ungently. The girl could neither eat nor sleep; she was near senseless with sorrow and there was no one to care. Except John, and try as he might, he could not make Boots see, could not make her hear that all was well, that he would be beside her and take care of her, just as he had promised. Her very anguish set a barrier of dumbness between them that love could no longer surmount.

It wasn't a week before the girl broke. Unkempt, mute in her suffering, Boots bridled Hellfire. Away they raced, as if to leave grief behind. Through field and moor and upon the sea cliffs, she taunted at Death as if he were a huckster, buying and selling. The villeins of Sutthernland—now Sea Houses—found her, neck broken, beside the wreck of her tall red horse. They dispatched Hellfire quickly, with fear and a broad axe, for every man in the countryside was terrified of the Devil horse. Boots was not so lucky. Four more days she lingered in anguish, till at last her eyes were opened and she saw John beside her. He held out his hand then, as Alyce had done for him.

Tippie saw that Boots was buried in hallowed ground, in Bamburgh churchyard. Though far from John's side, she was placed where her spirit might gaze toward his. The hands that had so often comforted him could not reach where he lay, but her heart was at peace, for she could see him at last, understand that he was with her until the end of the world.

In a far country, more than seven hundred years later, those who once loved so easily still tread unsettled lives together. Yet Northumberland was never quite lost to John's soul. He was too keenly aware that somewhere lay a green and pleasant land, a land that called him home. Sturdy, common-sense Boots at last felt it also. Excited, one lunch hour, my practical ex-Marine friend drew a picture for me. It was a plan of the stable where Boots had bided for so many years. "It's long, and in three parts," he said, "stone and timber, big timbers. Roomy box stall at one end, individual stalls at the other. Tack room in the middle, with a loft for spare blankets and such above it. That's where I slept, where we made love." He spoke today's words but saw yesterday's picture. It was a picture I had no ken of, for my every vision of the stable was from the outside, with its white-washed walls and paddock sloping down to a small mere or pond. Outside its gate, I knew, grew an apple tree. Boots loves apples.

He agreed with me that the Forster home was no castle, rather a large stone house. I saw it often, as if looking back while riding away. There was a green field standing at its foot, a place where horses ran and which became a sea of mud in spring. The paddock was close by there, with the road circling near it. Try as I might to see, I felt that the direction the road ran was northwest. In actuality, it carries west. But I remembered riding—so often—the patrol toward Scotland, and toward the haven of a yellow-stone farmhouse inn, newly carved at the edge of the forest.

Many years we tried to piece together what we could sense of our old lives. I had a clear picture of the ford near the inn, and the road where I rescued the waif, Allie. But where that was in all Northumberland, I had only a few clues. According to later entries in the Foster genealogy, the family manor was a place called Etherstone, then Adderstone. And our American ancestor, Reginald, had left from Brunton, England, in the reign of King Charles I, settling in Ipswich, Massachusetts, about 1638. With him had come wife Judith and seven children.

At last, all began to come together in 1993. I discovered a copy of Tomlinson's *Comprehensive Guide to Northumberland* in the local university library. First published in 1888, it told me of Bamburgh and the Forsters, and the old manor of Adderstone. I found our Brunton, a common enough place name. I itched to visit there, and at Alnwick, which I had excitedly recognized in a television documentary. Its familiar face nearly stopped my heart with homesickness.

Then Fate smiled, and a series of minor miracles set me aloft toward England. I was called to attend a seminar in Oxford and was on the point of declining when I thought, "no, you can do this." The necessary money came unexpectedly at the last moment. Excitedly, I made plans to end that trip with a dash to Northumberland.

It was good I went to Oxford first, to get my feet wet, so to speak. We were also shepherded to Bath, which was familiar to me, and to London, which I approached with some innate caution. Then I was on my own, adventuring north. The first night found me in a comfortable little inn at Alnwick. It was there that Sir John appeared—for the last time—in the mirror. He looked old, and tired. I rushed to grab the camera, thinking "I've got you at last!" But the flash in the mirror nearly washed out the old knight's reflection, so his picture simply teased at me, as his image had always done. But my journal that night described him: "There he was, much older than the youth who stared out at me so long ago. Molded by troubles, he set the power of his mortality against them, and it grew. He reminded me of Dr. X, the set aura of authority, the strong visage of an old military man."

At Alnwick, poking my curious nose into the passageway of Dorothy Forster Court, quite by accident I met the owners, historian William Ford and his wife. They had restored the old medieval town house of the Forsters' into an exquisite and comfortable dwelling. Patiently, Dr. Ford explained much of early Northumberland history to me. Brunton, he said, was a hotbed of rebellion against King James. Unspoken lay the thought that quite possibly my ancestor had been deported. Dr. Ford was also able to explain that Etherstone and Adderstone were one and the same place, being local inflections of Eadred's ton, or homestead. There was nothing old left there, he shook his head; the buildings had all been rebuilt in the 1800s.

Nevertheless, Boots and I both had a strong hunch that the old stable had survived the ravages of time. I had to go to Adderstone to find out, wherever that might be. Next day found me in Brunton, at the lovely B & B run by the Robsons. Ken Robson in particular was helpful, rummaging up copies of Forster genealogy and histories of Brunton. With study, I found they evoked more questions than answers. Eadra—no, make that Brenda Robson—made me comfortable and gave me advice about the road to the coast.

Again, the sea shore was ancient in the times of my heart. Satisfied, I walked the sand, feeling old energies trickling back into my body with the wind and tide and the shells that filled my hands. Driving again up the coast road, a song began deep in my throat, a song that came of its own volition. "The white tide creams upon the sand, where once the vikings came to land; the swords did sing and the armour jingled; upon this shore our blood was mingled." Nor did I understand its significance till John sat with me at the computer (as he often did), and told its story.

So many emotions mixed at Bamburgh town that I literally ran about, sniffing the wind and hunting out places I only felt, like an old dog returning home. I dismissed the climb to the castle as a time-waster, but I stood swept with gladness in the small triangular commons that had been the children's meadow. At last, I explored the church, though not nearly so much as I would have liked. It seemed different; indeed, time has been good to St. Aidan's and St. Oswald's memorial. Praise that God would not let folk forget the blood and prayers left here by the saints, true Britons who swept Christian fervor into this fair land under the wings of angelic protection.

Again, my journal: "The church at Bamburgh set me in a kind of time-warp, a crystal space where my body tingled and my feet walked upon air, ungrounded. I trod centuries, not land; I saw people, not buildings, lives memorialized in ancient stones, lives that still persist. I am living proof. Yet I missed seeing the beam against which St. Aidan died, and the Forster crypt, missed the church records. Does it matter, when I carry so much in my heart?"

Driving down the road to Adderstone, I felt apart, still outside the world and yet formed of these very elements. Oh, the stones, the earth, the sea and wind of Northumberland! With John, I was coming home. Unlike him, I did not know where that home was. But he was glad to leave Bamburgh town, for he said as I slipped the car into gear, "From sad Bamburgh let us away." For all its ties, Bamburgh's wind blew sorrows centuries old upon our back.

I passed the Hall at Glororum. "Just so my Hall used to sit," John said. There was a tremendous excitement, which mounted as a ruined farm building appeared next to the roadside. "That is my stable!" The voice was exuberant. I was startled, but still drove on, reason attempting to override welling emotion. "No," I told myself. "This is Glororum. Adderstone, where the book says we lived, is farther down the road. The farther the road took me away, the more the voice inside panicked. "Turn back, oh, turn back!"

He was right. A lady at the farm kindly showed me around the outside of Adderstone Hall, but the land was wrong; even the older cottages of the farm lay amiss. Back I went to Glororum, stopping first at the stable, and it *was* my stable, where I had worked horses and made love and ridden away. I used up the last of my film, and it was exactly as Boots had drawn it. I even found the stump of an old post that not only snubbed the horses, but anchored the ladder to Boots' lair. The outside, too, was as I had remembered, though the apple tree was long gone. Nothing in this life has ever held the satisfaction of walking again in that love-hallowed place.

At last I drove back toward the house and stood in the road beside it, staring. A young lady emerged from the farmhouse across the road and began to load up her car. Seeing me, she left her son for the moment and came over to ask kindly, "May I help you?" she asked kindly, "May I help you?"

"I used to live here long ago," I answered, not caring if I startled her. To her question, when, I replied, "In the 1200s. I'm a Forster, from America." It fazed her not at all. Related to Dorothy Dryden, Glororum's present owner, she told me how they had tried to research the history of the house, which was lost in dim antiquity beyond the 1400s. Her sister then arrived; they were due to clean a caravan (trailer) in the local park, which the Drydens also owned. Instead, they took the time to show me 'round the outside of that Old Hall which my heart knew so well. I drank it in; John pointed out the age-blanketed earthworks that still faced toward the sea when he was a child. The round-ended apse on the east was made with tiny stones, as if carried in on horseback. It had a tiled roof, rather than slate, old tile I only saw now and again on buildings ancient beyond telling. Yet the apse I saw was not actually there, only the stones were marked where it had once joined the old hall.

My footsteps in the stone courtyard tracked between house and ancient kitchen, now a garage. There I had rescued poor Allie from a stone trough filled with dirty cauldrons. That self-same trough now lay buried among the stones at my feet. Awe transcended even elation, but not reason. I knew I must bid these kind women adieu; besides, there was no more film for the camera.

Time was trickling away, and there was the little stone inn yet to be found. John had said that it lay a distance of three leagues, or about nine miles. He was adamant, but I didn't know how his leagues were measured along which road. Wooler stuck in the mind, and there we next set out. An old Northumbrian humpbacked bridge, barely wide enough for the car, diverted my delight awhile. Beside it, old oaks grew in the river meadow, some of the few I saw in a land once known for them. Upon the bridge abutments were the ancient carved stone cones, set upon a narrow neck, that had marked the bridges in my childhood books. So entranced were we, that I returned here with a bite of cold lunch—and film—bought in a pastry shop at Wooler.

The furthest John could have gone was Wooler, though driving through Chatton, just past the hump-back bridge, he grew happy and excited. Wooler proved a nice town, but far too new, John said, as we turned back. Later, I found that the ancient spring for which Wooler was named had been John's actual destination when he left the inn riding west.

We walked in Chatton awhile, and John was content there, though I was not quite sure of the inn itself. I feel it is still there, overlain by the change of centuries, but John and I were both puzzled. We argued a bit, for his feelings were too ebullient for me to pin down, and the memory pictures I had could have fit more than one site. If we'd had time to settle a bit, and to talk longer to the friendly barman at the new inn, I'm sure we would have found Chatta's old homestead. (Indeed, on a return trip in 1997, we did find Chatta's barn still standing near the ancient ford.)

Meanwhile, the river meadow called us back to lunch, and the stable called us back to Glororum. Neither of us felt the slightest tie to Adderstone, though it was from here that brave Dorothy Forster set out, in 1716, to save her inept brother Tom from execution in the Tower of London. Riding a-pillion behind the Adderstone blacksmith, through the snow and ice of a bitter winter, Dorothy somehow managed to obtain a key to Tom's cell. With wiles and bribes, she saw her brother free, that poor country general caught by circumstance upon the wrong side of rebellion, saved by his saucy sister. It was assumed Tom lived out his days in exile in France, while at Bamburgh, a mock funeral was held for him over a coffin filled with sawdust. Remembering my grandmother, I understood the several tales of the gritty Forster women outshining their menfolk.

Back at Glororum, I recalled how the kitchen gardens once lay walled on the south, while orchards trailed down the old slopes to the east. But John was most excited about a smooth level lawn just below the house to the west. "The tiltyard!" he exclaimed, over and over. "The tiltyard!" There the squires were trained and the horses run in mock combat; its north wall had bloodied John's head in his grievous fall. I took a few pictures as able, without doing the Drydens the dishonor of trespassing. I was still ruminating over the remarkable turn of events over a supper of fish and chips beside the sea.

That evening, quiet in my room, John told me that Glororum had indeed been his home, that later the Forster family split, with one branch going to Bamburgh, and one to Adderstone, when the first Thomas married its heiress. The Old Hall by then was much in need of repair, and its lands worn with centuries of use. The family sold it. Later, they would farm at Brunton, fertile acres rolling from beside the ancient mill, where clouds of white gulls and black rooks swept in arcs behind the clambering plow.

Sunday morning was my last day upon the earth of Northumberland. I walked the fields, glided through the dew. I returned to the church at Bamburgh to exchange a booklet I'd bought; some of the pages turned up blank. My timing couldn't have been worse. Or better. The murmur of

Sunday service filled the air; the glorious windows shone with faith in the Sunday sun. At last, voices swelled to Heaven and the very stones seemed to be singing praise. A women crept out, leaving early. "Hurry in," she said, "whilst they're singing. No one will notice." Thus in hymn did Bamburgh bid me goodbye.

But the land was not yet through with my heart. Driving to the A1, I dawdled along an old road, narrow and comfortingly bare. It stretched like an arrow before me, nestled into the land itself, like some ancient Roman track. Autumn was beginning to stalk the stone walls upon either side; gold poured across earth and the brilliant blue overhead blessed it. I seemed to be traveling into light itself, in ecstasy beyond words or tears or joy. God himself was there before me in the morning. Thus His mercy rewards even sinners.

Travel beyond the dimensions of time and death requires only the leap of faith, faith in the whispers from an esoteric world that impinges upon our own when least expected. Yet sometimes reason has a difficult time recognizing the faces and words that impel our dreams. Such was my difficulty. In September of 1993, I woke to a voice saying simply, "I am going to die." As any rational person might, I realized that for far too long I had sluffed off the idea of mortality, made no provisions for dying. I began to sort papers, had a will made. My health is fragile, so I had a thorough checkup. Nothing seemed too amiss. But the insistence was there; it seemed to haunt me, day and night. I prayed for time to finish John's story, and he sat with me through many a weary evening after work, tales and details tumbling out onto the screen.

We grew closer, the old knight and my modern ego. He hadn't spoken so much since I first recognized him, nearly thirty years ago. In the course of a busy life, one tends to ignore the ghosts one lives with; contemporary predicaments are quite enough. But at night, stumbling up from dreaming, when I would leave my basement lair—just as he had done, 773 years before—I would look to the land sloping away to the northeast and see, not mountains, but the sea beyond Bamburgh. Courtyard stones were beneath my feet. Instead of prowling into the house for a cup of coffee, to sit and meditate awhile in the dark, I was slipping into a seat in the corner of the kitchen at Old Hall. With a cup of broth dipped from the cauldron, John stared into the embers of the dying fire and meditated with me. It was during these early mornings, repossessing our Northumberland joy, that we completely embraced the grace that united our souls. Each at last was happy within the other's life.

I knew that I had been born on John's birthday, had always known that, even if the map of his birth heavens limned upon the computer had not confirmed it. I assumed that when his years had been fulfilled, my own would reflect the same fate. It was near Christmas when, pottering about with dates and genealogy, I realized that this was the time—at age 61, not 62—that John died. The message had been from him, and I had taken three months to understand those simple words!

I told no one, not even my friend Boots, but awaited the year's end with great curiosity. What would happen when the life that completely interlaced my own fled away? The answer, curiously, was very little. I grieved awhile, for John no longer sat so close with me. The ready answers I often needed were no longer there. Yet I knew that John would always be an innate part of my genetic heritage, and thus not far away. Indeed, I found when circumstances closed around and his touch was indispensable, I could meditate and find him beside me with the solution. He was harder to contact, and no longer working through my hands, but he stood beside me. He is there still, as I finish this, looking over my shoulder, content.

The postscript will have to be that when I finally told Boots that John had died, he grew very thoughtful. "I haven't told you," he said, "because it sounds so peculiar, but for two weeks, since the end of the year, every morning as I sat drinking my coffee, he was there with me, close enough to touch. Of course, I don't believe in ghosts, but he was so reassuring, so comforting. It was just as if you had come and touched me." He was quiet a moment. "I think I understand death a little better now. Never again will I grieve myself into harm. I know those we love never truly die; in God's time, we meet again."

Glossary of Archaic Words

Adubment. The ceremony of investiture into knighthood.

Amain. With force; hurriedly, at once; suddenly.

Amour. Chivalrous love, an affair of gallantry and intrigue.

Assart. To clear land for cultivation by grubbing out trees, etc.

Bairn. Baby; small child.

Baldric. A belt slung from the shoulder diagonally across the body, to carry sword or hunting horn. Often decorated distinctively within a clan.

Bar sinister. Heraldic device indicating bastardy.

Beadle. An estate or parish officer, usually under a steward, charged with keeping the peace and summoning people to court or to meetings.

Behest. A command.

Beltane. Ancient festival of spring, celebrated variously on May 1 or June 21.

Berewick. An outlying unconnected property supporting a political subdivision or land grant.

Bill or **billhook.** A long-handled heavy knife with a hook, used by the villeins for pruning limbs of trees or men.

Boon. A gift or benefit.

Boon days. Work days given free to a lord by the peasants according to custom, usually with one or two meals provided.

Burn. A creek or stream.

Byre. Cow shed or pen.

Byrnie. A mail shirt worn by northern knights; a hauberk.

Canon. A priest bound by the rules of a specific community, such as the Augustinian canons.

Chancel. The eastern part of a church, often with an apse or rounded end; separated from the nave or main part of the church by an arch (in early churches) or by a screen.

Coif. A cap of chain mail worn under the helmet, usually wrapped and tied at the neck.

Copse. A grove of small trees, often cut and cultivated for withes or firewood.

Corn. Grain; wheat, rye or barley. There was no maize in the Old World prior to the discovery of America.

Cornage. A service peculiar to the Northumbrian border; border patrol owed to the English king in return for rents. From an ancient word meaning to blow a horn (in alarm).

Corn ale. The best and strongest ale, unwatered.

Cot. Cottage, usually of two rooms; alternately, a small bedstead.

Cottars. Poor villeins or smallholders whose only land consisted of a cottage and croft; less than four acres.

Couch. To hold a lance under the arm in position for attack.

Cozen. To beguile.

Cricks. Upright timbers supporting the ridge beam of a roof.

Croft. Land around a cottage; its outbuildings and gardens; a house and yard.

Cuisses. Armor for the thighs.

Curtain wall. Outer defensive wall around a castle's precincts; loosely, any exterior wall of a fortification.

Cymry. The Celts. There were related branches of Celts in Wales, Ireland, and Scotland.

Demesne. Land kept by a lord and not leased out to others; the home farm.

Destrier. A war-horse.

Divers. Diverse; differing or sundry.

Dorter. Dormitory or bedroom.

Eftsoon. In a short time.

Erst. Before, formerly; at one time.

Fain. To be willing or content.

Fey. Psychic, "fairy-like."

Fief. Estate held on condition of military service.

Fleabite roan. A horse with two colors intermingled in small spots.

Fortnight. Two-week period.

Freeman. A small farmer that owned his own land in payment of rent and/or service, and subject to local courts and custom.

Fyrd. The home guard, all the local men capable of bearing arms in cases of emergency.

Garderobes. Privies, usually built into an outer wall of a castle or manor house.

Geld. Money.

Greaves. Armor for the shins.

-hal. Place-name ending meaning "nook of land", with a proper name of possession, such as Bedehal, Tucgahal, etc.

Hauberk. Shirt of chain mail; see byrnie.

Hayward. A villein official appointed to oversee the rotation of pasturage and cropping of hayfields.

Heriot. Death-duty; usually the best beast of a peasant or the war trappings of a knight, used to outfit his successor.

Helm. Helmet, worn over the coif. Varied from a simple steel cap to the all-encompassing "great helms."

Hie. To go in haste.

Hippocras. Flavored ceremonial wine passed at the conclusion of a feast.

Hosen. Long stockings covering the legs up to the waist, held in place by "points," or thongs tied to a belt.

Hospitaler. A knight of the order of St. John, dedicated to the provision of hospitality to pilgrims, and to the care of the sick.

Hostler. Horse trainer or handler; wrangler.

Housecarl. Male house servant, usually a household guard.

Hurdles. A frame or structure woven of withes, used for fences or enclosures.

Infangenthief. An old Anglo-Saxon custom that gave a lord the right to try and execute a thief taken in the act upon manor property.

Jerkin. A short coat or waistcoat, usually of leather.

Justiciar. Principal political and judicial officer of the early English kings.

Ken. To know (*v.*) or knowledge (*n.*).

Kickerknick. Something given "to boot" in an exchange, an extra compensation.

Kirtle. A woman's short sleeveless jacket, overblouse or wide sash.

Lag. To frame with timbers, as in ship-building.

League. An old Celtic mile; about three statute miles.

Mace. An iron-clad war club.

Mail. Armor made of meshed links of iron.

Manor. A lordship, usually a land grant with certain privileges such as holding court for local offenses, and with rights to the villeinage therein.

Merchet. A fine paid to an overlord when a daughter marries.

Mesne lords. Smaller landholders, usually knights, who held their fiefs under the major tenants of the Crown. The lords "in the middle" between the great earls and the peasants.

Miles agrarios. The agrarian military, country knights; mesne lords.

Miscreant. Without a conscience.

Mummer. An actor, usually in a pantomime.

Night-hawking. Poaching game at night.

Nonce. The present, now; "for the nonce."

Palatinate. A province, esp. under the church, invested with royal rights and privileges

Palfrey. A light horse; a lady's horse.

Paternoster. The Our Father prayer.

Pease porridge. Dried pea soup.

Pied. Varicoloured; esp. white and black in patches.

Points. Thongs attached to a leather belt, worn under the shirt, used to hold up the warm woolen hose worn by men and women.

Pleasance. Cheerfulness, pleasantness.

Postern. A small private door or gate.

Prie-dieux. A portable kneeling-bench for prayers.

Prelate. A high-ranking churchman, often wealthy.

Prior. The governor of a priory or monastery, a religious house usually with an attendant school.

Quintain. A post with revolving crosspiece and target, used for lance play.

Reeve. A manor official, usually a villein, who managed the day-to-day affairs of the farm; a straw-boss.

Reiver. A border raider; an outlaw.

Rood. The cross, a crucifix.

Scion. A male heir.

Scutage. Obligation to give shield (military) service; later the payment given in lieu of such service.

Seethe. To simmer.

Seize. Seizin; to take possession of land, often symbolized by handing the new owner a turf cut from the land.

Seneschal. A steward, often in charge of ceremonies and courts.

Shire. An English county.

Shrift. Confession; short shrift being a short time before punishment or death is inflicted.

Sinecure. A political plum; a well-paid job requiring but little work.

Smallholder. A freeman with only a marginal amount of land and normally subject to the local manor court.

Solar. A solarium or sunny room, popular with the wealthy as glass became more widely available.

Sothly. Truly.

Stead. Place; in place of.

Steward. Property manager; ruling agent of a landowner.

Succor. Aid or assistance; usually in grave matters.

Suzerain. A paramount lord; a Crown (chief) tenant.

Tass. A cup.

Thane. An Old English lord, similar to the miles agrarios, owing military service to a king or a paramount lord.

Tilt. To run and thrust with a lance, especially on horseback.

Tiltyard. A level area of turf where horses and men trained at lance practice.

-ton. A farmstead, with a description; such as Brunton, farm by the burn; Hutton, farm on a ridge or hill-spur; Preston, farm of the priests.

Torc. A metal necklace or collar, denoting warrior status among the Celts.

Tourney. A sporting event featuring mock combat; "war games."

Transepts. The two arms, north and south, of a cruciform church.

Travail. Torment.

Trencher. A usually wooden platter or tray used for serving food.

Trod. Usually past tense of tread; to progress by walking.

Troubadour. An itinerant romantic poet and singer; a minstrel.

Trow. Trust.

Undercroft. Vaulted chamber underlying an important area such as a church or hall.

Valetti. A land-holding squire, not yet knighted.

Vassal. One who holds his land by service to another.

Vill. Cluster of villeins' cottages; a small village.

Villein. A feudal peasant belonging to the land, usually unable to move, and liable only for work service rather than rents. Usual farm hold for a villein was between thirty and a hundred acres.

Virgates. An old land measure; about thirty acres.

Warder. A keeper; especially of a castle.

Waste. Land not under cultivation.

Wattle. Woven of branches, as a hurdle; if covered with plaster or mud, then wattle-and-daub.

Weeds. Clothing, dress.

Withe. Tough flexible branches, usually of alder or willow.

Wont. Habit.

Yeoman. A small farmer; a freeholder with status between lord and peasant.

Hampton Roads Publishing Company

. . . for the evolving human spirit

Hampton Roads Publishing Company
publishes books on a variety of subjects including
metaphysics, health, alternative/complementary medicine,
visionary fiction, and other related topics.

For a copy of our latest catalog, call toll-free,
(800) 766-8009, or send your name and address to:

Hampton Roads Publishing Company, Inc.
134 Burgess Lane
Charlottesville, VA 22902